The Journalist in
British Fiction and Film

Also available from Bloomsbury

*A State of Play: British Politics on Screen, Stage and Page, from
Anthony Trollope to The Thick of It*
Stephen Fielding

*British Working-Class Fiction: Narratives of Refusal and
the Struggle Against Work*
Roberto del Valle Alcalá

The Journalist in British Fiction and Film

Guarding the Guardians from 1900 to the Present

Sarah Lonsdale

Bloomsbury Academic
An imprint of Bloomsbury Publishing Plc

BLOOMSBURY
LONDON · OXFORD · NEW YORK · NEW DELHI · SYDNEY

Bloomsbury Academic

An imprint of Bloomsbury Publishing Plc

50 Bedford Square
London
WC1B 3DP
UK

1385 Broadway
New York
NY 10018
USA

www.bloomsbury.com

BLOOMSBURY and the Diana logo are trademarks of Bloomsbury Publishing Plc

First published 2016

© Sarah Lonsdale, 2016

Sarah Lonsdale has asserted her right under the Copyright, Designs and
Patents Act, 1988, to be identified as Author of this work.

British Library Cataloguing-in-Publication Data
A catalogue record for this book is available from the British Library.

ISBN: HB: 978-1-4742-2053-8
PB: 978-1-4742-2054-5
ePDF: 978-1-4742-2056-9
ePub: 978-1-4742-2055-2

Library of Congress Cataloging-in-Publication Data
A catalog record for this book is available from the Library of Congress.

Typeset by Integra Software Services Pvt. Ltd.
Printed and bound in India

For John, Tom and Olivia

Contents

Epigraph

I hear new news every day, and those ordinary rumours of war, plagues, fire, inundations, thefts, murders, massacres, meteors, comets, spectrums, prodigies, apparitions, of towns taken, cities besieged in France, Germany, Turkey, Persia, Poland, etc., daily musters and preparations, and such-like, which these tempestuous times afford, battles fought, so many men slain, monomachies, shipwrecks, piracies, and sea-fights, peace, leagues, stratagems and fresh alarums. A vast confusion of vows, wishes, actions, edicts, petitions, lawsuits, pleas, laws, proclamations, complaints, grievances are daily brought to our ears. New books every day, pamphlets, curantoes, stories, whole catalogues of volumes of all sorts, new paradoxes, opinions, schisms, heresies, controversies in philosophy, religion, etc. Now come tidings of weddings, maskings, mummeries, entertainments, jubilees, embassies, tilts and tournaments, trophies, triumphs, revels, sports, plays: then again as in a new shifted scene, treasons, cheating tricks, robberies, enormous villainies in all kinds, funerals, burials, deaths of princes, new discoveries, expeditions; now comical, then tragical matters. Today we hear of new lords and officers created, tomorrow of some great men deposed, and then again fresh honours conferred; one is let loose, another imprisoned; one purchaseth, another breaketh; he thrives, his neighbour turns bankrupt; now plenty, then again dearth and famines; one runs, another rides, laughs, weeps, etc. Thus I daily hear, and such-like, both private and public news; amidst the gallantry and misery of the world ... I continue as always, left to a solitary life and mine own domestic discontents ...

Robert Burton, *The Anatomy of Melancholy*, 1621

Acknowledgements

This book started life as my PhD thesis for the University of Kent, and I would like to record my eternal debt of gratitude to my supervisor, Professor Jan Montefiore, whose intellectual generosity has been an inspiration. I would also like to thank my examiners, Professor Chris Hopkins and Dr Chandrika Kaul, who offered very helpful advice and encouraged me to find a publisher. Thanks also to Mark Richardson at Bloomsbury Academic for taking up this project and running with it and for answering endless queries with grace and good humour.

All quotations from books in this work fall under the Society of Authors 'Fair Dealing' guidelines, and all works referred to in the book are listed, with publisher and author, in the bibliography. I would specifically like to thank David Higham Associates for permission to quote from a number of Graham Greene's novels. The short extract from *Yellow Dog* by Martin Amis copyright Martin Amis (2003) is used by permission of the Wylie Agency (UK) Limited. The short extract from *My Name Is Legion* by A.N. Wilson is used by permission of Arrow Books, Random House Group. I would also like to thank the National Theatre of Scotland, *London Review of Books*, and Andrew O'Hagan for allowing me to read, and quote from, the script of their dramatic project *Enquirer*.

I would also like to record my thanks to the writers Sir Arnold Wesker (*The Journalists*, 1972), A.N. Wilson (*My Name Is Legion*, 2004), James Meek (*We Are Now Beginning Our Descent*, 2008), Eric Clark (*The Sleeper*, 1979), Philip Norman (*Everyone's Gone to the Moon*, 1995) and Martin Stellman (*Defence of the Realm*, 1985), who granted me interviews offering fascinating insights into their creative processes and their relationship with journalism. I am also particularly grateful to James Currey, son of 1930s journalist Stella Martin Currey for showing me her press cuttings, memoir and her father's journal. Similarly Selina Hastings, daughter of the journalist Margaret Lane, gave me fascinating insights into her mother's life on the *Daily Mail* in the 1930s.

Finally, I would like to thank my parents, who read endless versions of both PhD and book chapters with love and patience.

Introduction:
A Century of Guarding the Guardians

I

On the final page of *Daily Express* reporter Alphonse Courlander's novel *Mightier than the Sword* (1912), protagonist Humphrey Quain dies a triumphant death for the journalist-hero. Plunging into the middle of a French winegrowers' riot in order to cover the story more closely for his paper, he is crushed by the throng. As he takes his last breath, 'an odd, whimsical idea twisted his lips into a smile as he thought: "What a ripping story this will make for *The Day*."' It is a willing martyrdom. Quain's death will literally transform him into the front-page story he so desires. What is of note in the rather bizarre death scene is that Quain dies telling the story not of kings, generals or prime ministers, but of ordinary working men struggling to earn a decent wage. *Mightier than the Sword* is typical of the period 1900–1914, when novels portraying journalists as high-minded, truth-seeking heroes were apparently the vogue among readers, authors and publishers. The novel is no mere Fleet Street adventure story, however. With numerous passages dwelling on the journalist's attempt to describe a rapidly changing world to a newly literate, newly enfranchised readership, the novel is an act of literary defiance. It tells the educated classes that 'lowbrow' readers now matter. Courlander was a young reporter whose aspirations to be a popular novelist were cut short by his death in the First World War. He and many other Edwardian journalist-novelists including Edgar Wallace, P.G. Wodehouse and Philip Gibbs sought, through their fiction, to raise the status of the journalist from the bottom of the literary hierarchy (see Chapter 1). Sandwiched between a generally sceptical body of Victorian fiction about the press and an overwhelmingly, although not exclusively, hostile body of later twentieth-century fiction, this brief period of positive portrayals speaks volumes for the hopes invested in the new popular daily press. Journalists and writers sharing in the liberal optimism of the time hoped the halfpenny papers would educate and enlighten a new public, and bring them news of scientific advances, political decision-making and international conflict. They also invested hope in newspaper journalism's ability to support financially writers of all genres whether they were producing verse, serial stories, news or polemic – and who were often producing multiple genres for myriad outlets. *Mightier than the Sword* is a forgotten novel, and one of dozens of fictions charting the chequered history of journalism in British society over the past more than 100 years. Readers may be familiar with Evelyn Waugh's *Scoop* (1938) but to this and the better-known Graham Greene's *The Quiet American* (1955) and Michael Frayn's *Towards the End of the Morning* (1967), we must add dozens of novels, plays, poems – and later film and television fictions – all watching, monitoring and recording the activities of society's own self-appointed watchdogs.

The important role played by newspaper journalism in the political, cultural and social history of Britain is recognized by scholars. The economic development of the newspaper press, the rise and fall of the 'press baron', and the lives of major editors and journalists have all received academic attention in the past thirty years.[1] Yet how journalists of the past, particularly those outside elite culture, saw their role within the wider field of cultural production, how they contested various class, social, gender and literary barriers, has yet to receive adequate attention. Two recent studies have used fictions, particularly cinematic representations of journalists, to construct a theory of how the image of the journalist in popular culture shapes people's ideas of how the news industry operates.[2] They conclude that the public's opinion of journalists is profoundly influenced by their representation in films and other genres of popular culture. This book attempts something different in that it examines both fictions written *by* former or practising journalists as well as ones *about* journalists over a lengthy time period. Unlike members of other trades and professions, journalists are compulsive storytellers, and many cannot resist chronicling their own lives and aspects of their trade. As one of the latest in a long line of journalists to turn their newspaper experience into fiction, Annalena McAfee (*The Spoiler*, 2011) says: 'I've only ever met one journalist who didn't want to write a book'.[3] Indeed of the 155 'newspaper' fictions discussed in this book, two-thirds (98) have been written by former or practising journalists. By mapping historical fictions onto the history of the press, this book attempts to recreate the inner lives of forgotten journalists, often writing anonymously, as they negotiated the complex social, political and literary landscape they inhabited. How, for example, did pioneer women journalists strike their bargain between writing for the 'gutter press' and economic independence? How did young men who were denied a university education due to lack of funds negotiate the treacherous route from a life of manual labour to desk work, a collar and tie? How did provincial reporters employed by papers engaged in a 1930s 'newspaper war' adapt their style to help raise circulation? How did poets, novelists and playwrights view the impact of the mass press on politics, society and their own cultural productions? This book, through readings of novels, poems, plays, memoirs, journals and contemporary commentary, attempts to answer these questions. Film and television dramas have increasingly become the way in which the image of the journalist is both presented and consumed. In addition, news and entertainment media have begun to converge both in terms of platform (live streaming, channels like YouTube, which mix news and drama, identical adverts seen in cinemas and embedded in news websites) and content (footage of 'smart' bombs apparently clinically destroying targets as if war were a video game, for example). For this reason a few notable recent screen dramas concerning journalism are discussed, where relevant, and the concluding section of this book will examine the way journalism's current existential crisis is treated in all the narrative arts.[4]

II

Fiction, of course, is a work of the imagination, a miraculous alchemy combining experienced reality, fantasy, personal opinions, individual prejudice and the bravely exposed secrets of the human heart. Are fictions from history evidence that something actually happened, or merely evidence of a particular writer's sour and inaccurate prejudice? Fiction, even literary fiction, must, perforce, generalize, stereotype and exaggerate. Of course, no newspaper proprietor would actually have his reporters assassinated to protect his business interests as in *Defence of the Realm* (1985, Chapter 5); as far as I know, no actual reporter has discovered a plot to fake Christ's tomb and thus bring down Christian civilization (*When It Was Dark*, 1903, Chapter 1) and no journalist – on any self-respecting newspaper anyway – has actually interviewed a cat and presented it as fact (*Murder Must Advertise*, 1933, Chapter 3). However, neither was the journalist Christopher Hitchens wrong when he described Evelyn Waugh's intricate fantasy on the life of the foreign press pack, *Scoop*, as 'a novel of pitiless realism; the mirror of satire held up to catch the Caliban of the press corps'.[5] Journalists know there is an inescapable truth at the heart of Waugh's novel: that the country many reporters inhabit, for better or worse, as they attempt to fix and explain a fluctuating and inexplicable universe, is 'Absurdistan'.[6] Similarly, while no journalist would be reckless enough to fabricate an interview with a cat, fabrication of stories within the pages of newspapers and on television has always taken place. Former *Guardian* Woman's Page editor Mary Stott's memoirs, for example, contain fond reminiscences of a colleague on the *Co-operative News* in the 1920s who 'amused us greatly by keeping going for days a totally fictitious story about a well-known violinist's war-time exploits'.[7] Contemporary high-profile examples of fabrication include the *New York Times* journalist Jayson Blair and former *Independent* commentator Johann Hari.[8] The examination of large numbers of fictions produced within the same time frame, if read carefully and critically, can be dredged for the contemporary commentary they construct on the state of journalism at a particular point in time, as well as writers' particular prejudices both for and against 'the old black art we call the daily press'.[9] It will be seen that fictions produced by former or practising journalists tend to foreground the intricacies of their working lives, whereas those produced by writers with no experience of journalism tend to comment on wider issues of the role of journalism in society and whether or not it is fulfilling its ideal 'Fourth Estate' function of holding power to account and informing the electorate.

III

The overwhelming proportion of fictions studied in this book fall into the category known by scholars of literature as 'middlebrow'. The term is used here with caution, and this book aims to be part of a growing body of contemporary scholarship seeking to remove the word's derogatory associations with 'easy, middle-of-the-road' literature, without artistic merit and using 'narrative modes regarded as outdated'.[10] Famously derided by Virginia Woolf in an unpublished letter to the *New Statesman* as a 'bloodless and pernicious pest', the term 'middlebrow' has been taken to mean commercial, mediocre, unchallenging fiction and has been applied to authors as creative, subtle and diverse as Evelyn Waugh and Rebecca West, as well as thousands of other more pedestrian works.[11] As a consequence of the academy ignoring for decades the vast bulk of fiction produced during the twentieth century, we are in danger of overlooking a richly textured contribution to historical and cultural studies. The 1930s literary critic Philip Henderson described a certain type of novel 'as a form of social activity, rather than as an isolated art-form obeying its own laws'.[12] Henderson contended that the writer who engages with social and political issues of the day 'has left something of value for succeeding ages'. It follows that the study of fiction produced by writers who wrote both novels and journalism as a way of supplementing their income may have left some trace of their negotiations with the literary marketplace in their novels for scholars of the press to make use of. The fictions examined here, whether 'lowbrow', 'middlebrow', 'highbrow' or somewhere in between, are products of the economic, cultural and ideological conditions of the period in which they were written and as such shed light on the relationship that writers needing to earn a living had with both their literary and journalistic work. They are a valuable snapshot of writers' dynamic and complex struggles within the ever-changing field of cultural production. They may be more closely associated with the 'marketplace' than poetry or highbrow novels, but that is no reason to ignore such a vibrant, readable collection of fictions. Dismissed as not worthy of further study, they now gather mildew on second-hand booksellers' shelves. But they should be seen as flickering lanterns, able to show us the way down the dark, dusty corridors of history to a time when pioneer Edwardian women journalists used their pens to scratch a path to freedom from patriarchal oppression, or to the immediate post–Second World War era when early investigative journalists used the methods they learned in wartime intelligence to catch and expose crooks and frauds. Many of these novels are well worth another turn in the limelight. Robert Harling's 1950s newspaper thrillers *The Paper Palace* and *The Enormous Shadow* are particularly fine (Chapter 4). Adeline Sergeant and Dolf Wyllarde's novels about Edwardian women journalists, 'third-rate lionesses of the profession ... in tumbled gowns', are poignant and evocative (Chapter 7).[13] Rudyard Kipling's little-known short story 'The Village That Voted the Earth Was Flat' (1914) is a multi-layered exposé of popular newspapers as well as a nostalgic paean to his own, beloved newspaper traineeship (Chapter 1). Philip Norman's fictionalized reminiscence of his days on the *Sunday Times* during its Harry Evans heyday (*Everyone's Gone to the Moon*, 1995, Chapter 6) is touching and humorous and reveals what so many of these fictions do: the journalist's passion for his or her vocation as a writer, no matter his or her position in the hierarchy of words.

IV

'It is so hard to love one's press' wrote author and broadcaster Christopher Sykes in 1955, at a time when sales of national newspapers were reaching their all-time peak. In his essay for the literary journal *Encounter*, Sykes carefully ticks off press failures, from hypocrisy to 'purveying scandal and smut' and 'keeping the public so stupid', before launching into an ardent defence of press freedom, concluding: 'happy the country which has no press-laws'.[14] The scrutiny to which the profession is subjected in works of fiction during the twentieth century – often by writers either permanently or occasionally employed or at least well remunerated by the newspaper industry – provides historical insights into an occupation that is so often criticized yet is also seen as a vital necessity to a healthy and functioning democracy. Writers, both those wishing to distinguish themselves from the taint of mass reading and those intricately involved in the newspaper industry, appear to use their fiction in order to express their struggles within the literary and journalistic fields as well as to critique the press industry.

Part of my scope concerns the changing relationship between the worlds of journalism and literature. Mid-century critics and authors including Q. D. Leavis, Cyril Connolly and J. B. Priestley described this struggle in great detail although scholars have traced the distinction between journalism and literature, or 'the ephemeral and the enduring' further back, to the moment 'literature leaves the court and enters the market-place'.[15] Writing in 1969, literary historian John Gross concluded that the age of the 'man of letters' who wrote for newspapers and monthly reviews and also engaged in writing verse and prose fiction was over: 'Instead of men of letters there are academic experts, mass media pundits, cultural functionaries'.[16]

As Connolly used the word 'struggle' in 1938 and Q. D. Leavis used the word 'clash' in 1934 to describe attempts by writers to assert themselves over what they saw as the debasing influence of newspapers, so cultural philosopher Pierre Bourdieu uses words like 'battlefield', 'weapons' and 'enemy agent' to describe writers engaged in cultural production:

> In the struggle to impose the legitimate definition of art and literature, the most autonomous producers naturally tend to exclude bourgeois writers and artists whom they see as 'enemy agents' ... In other words, the field of cultural production is the site of struggles in which what is at stake is the power to impose the dominant definition of the writer and therefore to delimit the population of those entitled to take part in the struggle to define the writer.[17]

Bourdieu's concept of the field of cultural production suggests that the literary field is a microcosm of society with its own laws and structures, and containing a range of interested actors: writers, publishers, printers, critics and readers who are all engaged in dynamic flux within the field's boundaries. This model, which Bourdieu evolved through the study of the late nineteenth-century French literary scene, is appealing in that rather than relying on textual analysis alone, it places texts within a socio-historical structure and allows the exploration of the conditions from which texts emerge such as the writer's economic, political and cultural standing within the field. Bourdieu's theory offers 'a sophisticated theory of context which obliges us to see writing and reading as *thoroughly social practices*' (emphasis added).[18] As in any society, much of this social activity involves competing for resources, particularly cultural recognition and economic capital. To unearth forgotten novels about journalism by contributors to the newspaper press as this book does is to expose the dynamic relationship between literature and journalism during more than 100 years of the newspaper press. These overlooked fictions reveal the extent to which authors were trying to position themselves within the field of cultural production, asking, through their fiction, 'what kind of writer am I?' and revealing a sophisticated game of cultural 'musical chairs' in action.

The field of cultural production is inhabited by producers ranging from highly autonomous ones such as poets to more commercial ones such as playwrights and journalists. Within the field, agents are engaged in constant struggles with other agents in their search for cultural capital. In his major work on the literary field, *The Rules of Art*, Bourdieu argues, using an analysis of French novelist Gustav Flaubert's *Sentimental Education* that the social structures novelists create in their fiction mirror the structure of the social space in which the authors are situated. At times when competition either for cultural recognition or for financial reward becomes more intense, tensions within writers' fiction, and other forms of discourse become more apparent.[19] Analyses of fictions about journalists reveal that they display remarkable accuracy when mapped against sociological studies of the press. Historical fictions thus provide a rich resource for those interested in the evolution of journalism and the press, a gateway back into the lives of early journalists, particularly during the period before sociological study became an established academic field. For example, in one of the first sociological studies of British journalists, conducted by Jeremy Tunstall in the late 1960s, he interviews 207 national newspaper correspondents about their attitudes to their work. One of his findings is given:

> The gatherers [correspondents] accuse the processors [sub-editors and night editors] of ... being envious of gatherers ... Some newsgatherers claim that most sub-editors live mole lives in the outer suburbs of South-East London, which they leave only during the hours of darkness, and where they share a socially and sexually frustrated existence with a wife whom they met years ago when working on a small provincial newspaper.[20]

Compare this description to the foreign correspondent Thomas Fowler's musing on the life of a newspaper night editor in Graham Greene's 1955 novel *The Quiet American*:

> Every correspondent, it was assumed, had his local girl. The editor would joke to the night editor who would take the envious thought back to his semi-detached villa in Streatham and climb into bed with it beside the faithful wife ... I could see so well the kind of house that has no mercy.[21]

The description is also remarkably similar to the home life of frustrated crossword-page editor John Dyson in Michael Frayn's *Towards the End of the Morning* (1967). In the novel, Dyson and his long-suffering wife Jannie live in 'Spadina Road, S.W. 23' in the hope of being joined by other upwardly mobile young families, 'but the middle classes didn't come to Spadina Road', where, 'if you cut through the back-streets to the Tube, and the District Line was running normally, you could be in Fleet Street in under the hour'.[22] The envy, and social and sexual frustration of the 'processors' identified by Tunstall and his researchers are clearly identifiable in two novels written during the same time frame. Throughout this book it will be seen that when factors influencing the field, such as paper rationing, circulation figures, the cost of labour or raw materials, or the cultural value ascribed to a product change, so the focus of the struggles between agents in the field changes. In the 1920s and 1930s, for example, a period when modernist intellectuals were openly and widely disparaging of all kinds of mass-produced writing – the so-called 'battle of the brows' – virtually every intellectual writer included in their fictions highly focused criticism of the newspaper press. This criticism was challenged with equal vigour by more popular writers closely associated with the newspaper press, in their own fictions (see Chapter 3). During the Second World War and the years immediately afterwards, when newsprint shortages artificially suppressed newspaper circulations, literary writers appear to call a 'ceasefire' and focus on other issues concerning their art (see Chapter 6). By using these fictions as a primary historical source, it is possible to chart the slow, sometimes agonized, divorce between the genres of literature and journalism, from when they shared, uncomfortably, the same bed at the start of the twentieth century to the moment in history when the 'decree absolute' was issued (about 1979). Even today, there are still occasional arguments over the custody of their precocious, scribbling children.

In the early years of the twentieth century, as today, journalism was undergoing profound and transformative change. Advances in communications technology and production and distribution methods, the entrepreneurial genius of a new kind of newspaper proprietor and a steady professionalization of the journalistic workforce trained to produce 'news' rather than literary comment or political argument all combined to challenge traditional assumptions about the relationship between literary producers and their most lucrative market. While many feared, as one doubtful contemporary commentator put it, that journalism was 'in danger of sinking, from a liberal profession to a branch of business', other writers from the newly literate lower middle classes seized the opportunities presented by what journalist and author Arnold Bennett described as 'the most startling phenomenon of the age'.[23] While writers like Alphonse Courlander, who owed his income to his being a reporter on the *Daily Express*, used their fictions to highlight the positive qualities of the new mass press, 'highbrow' authors used their fictions to distance themselves from it. Ford Madox Ford, for example, in his collaborative novel *The Inheritors*, written partly with Joseph Conrad in 1901, describes a popular newspaper journalist as a 'rat': 'The man was one of the rats of the lower journalism, large-boned, rubicund, asthmatic; a mass of flesh.'[24]

In this novel the narrator, Ford's *alter ego*, is also a journalist. However, he is a writer of essays and sketches of political and literary celebrities as Ford was during this time and not a lowly news reporter.[25] Ford is thus positioning himself extremely carefully in the hierarchy both of journalism and, more broadly, the field of cultural production. While in the novel the narrator acknowledges that his journalism is far from the high art of a sculptor, with whom he compares himself unfavourably, it is also a long way above the journalism produced by the unattractive 'rat' of 'lower journalism'. The sentiment expressed by author and freelance journalist Dolf Wyllarde in her forgotten novel about pioneer women writers, *The Pathway of the Pioneer* (1906), has a different nuance:

> The Press is the pulse of the moment, the incarnate vitality of to-day, and those who once experience the thrill of being the tiniest particle in that great living force, find all things else a dead and silent world.[26]

For this writer, and other early women journalists, the freedom gained by earning a few guineas from journalism outweighs any concerns about cultural capital. Bourdieu's concept of the field is thus disrupted when other forces, in this case barriers erected by gender, prove stronger than the struggle for cultural capital. Recent feminist scholarship on Bourdieu has tended to conclude that Bourdieu formulates a male-gendered conception of social structure and that his otherwise groundbreaking work is 'less than rigorous' in its treatment of gender.[27] This book is a contribution to that ongoing debate in its discussion of women journalists (Chapter 7). The field is also disrupted during the late 1930s, when 'the literary world turned *en masse* to the Left' and writers used their fictions to try to influence the political field and to attack fascism and appeasement as well as newspapers supporting appeasement (see Chapter 4).[28]

V

Late twentieth- and early twenty-first-century novels about journalism display none of the confidence that the power of the press has a benign side, as early twentieth-century ones do. Novelists with close links to newspapers such as James Meek and Gordon Burn and those interested in writing about the press, such as Ian McEwan and Iain Banks, present journalists as having lost their way ethically and personally. In these fictions the press does not speak for the people anymore, and this undermining of its democratic *raison d'etre* thus reveals a crisis in the authority of the press as well as the broader malaise of modern times with a collapse of faith in politics, the Church and the banking industry. Even those – and I count myself among them – who love newspapers cannot but agree with the following statement by journalist and commentator Ray Snoddy. Although written in 1992, it is very much relevant today in the evident lack of humility shown by some sections of the press in the wake of the Leveson Report:

> Three characteristics seem to mark the behaviour of British newspapers: an almost pathological reluctance to admit errors and say sorry, a deep sensitivity to criticism and a marked distaste for thinking about what they do … The degree of complacency and defensiveness involved is a small symptom of a much greater malaise – the lack of self-criticism in the newspaper industry.[29]

Today we can see that a failure to think strategically about its place in the new information society in the mid-1990s has led to a catastrophic loss of readership and influence for the newspaper industry. The industry's slow response to the internet led to its greatest existential threat – that of statutory control and, latterly and more dangerously, irrelevance. Tabloids resorted to playing 'catch up' in the only way they knew how – with increasingly sensationalist stories, often acquired through illegal means. Yet while the internet is partly to blame for the decline in newspaper circulation and relevance, critics have traced the 'de-massification' of the press and other elements of public culture back as far as the 1970s.[30] Indeed newspaper sales in Britain reached their peak in 1956 and have been declining ever since (see Chapter 6). The decline of deference, decline in respect for authority, the growth of individualism and the rise of 'consumer culture' that characterizes modern society have also affected the authority of the press. The authoritative voice of the 'Thunderer' has now been replaced with 'a market dominated by countless versions of "*Daily Me*"', leading to the fragmentation of the news environment into millions of competing bytes of often-trivial information.[31] For burned-out hack Cameron Colley in Iain Banks's *Complicity* (1993), the crisis in journalism is expressed through Colley's inability to tell the terrible story of destruction on the Basra Road during the first Gulf War:

> My body shook, my ears rang, my eyes burned, my throat was raw with the acid-bitter stench of the evaporating crude, but it was as though the very ferocity of the experience unmanned me, unmade me and rendered me incapable of telling it… I sat on a low dune for a while, maybe fifty metres away from the devastation on the strip of ripped, bubbled road, and tried to take it all in. The lap-top sat on my knee, screen reflecting the grey, overcast, the cursor winking slowly at the top left edge of the blank display.[32]

Who am I, he asks, to tell such a great and terrible story. What is my authority as a journalist to report on the vast human tragedy, the 'shredded, cindered bodies and bits of bodies' smouldering under an unforgiving sun. His burning eyes and raw throat suggest he is profoundly affected by the disaster and not a detached, impartial observer able coolly to record dreadful events. This questioning of the journalist's authority to tell the story contrasts sharply with the confidence of the journalists of the pre–First World War era who styled themselves as intellectual observer-heroes in the mould of the great Victorian war correspondents such as G. W. Steevens and George Augustus Sala.

For novelist and former *Guardian* foreign correspondent James Meek modern media has created a public that is not prepared to invest time in really understanding global politics. Modern reporting methods have succeeded in dehumanizing the enemy. In his novel *We Are Now Beginning Our Descent* (2008), a bleak account of one reporter's crisis provoked by having to cover the Afghanistan war post 9/11, long lens digital technology reduces humans to 'a few pixels':

> There could have been a black vertical a few pixels high… There could have been a Taliban fighter there, standing up from under his rock, deaf, exultant and choking from the bombs, opening his arms out wide and yelling to America that he was not martyred yet. Kellas couldn't be sure. Maybe it was a gap in the rock.[33]

Whether the pixels represent a human being, or nothing, is immaterial. The truth will be blotted out by US propaganda. What he writes for a low-circulation liberal newspaper on the edge of Europe doesn't matter:

> The fabulous thing was that it wouldn't matter whether he or anyone else in the great onrushing parade was shouting qualifications, or yelling in a different accent that events were occurring in an altogether other way. America's big, loud story would jostle their little stories on together with its own, and his voice would add to the general din.

Meek represents the individual journalist as unable to explain to a world used to easy generalizations about how messy real war is, and Adam Kellas begins a journey of descent into self-loathing and mental breakdown. Meek's novel is only a few years old, yet it will be seen that modern fictions dating all the way back to the 1960s apprehend the oncoming crisis in mainstream journalism's authority long before circulation declines and the internet make the newspaper industry appear dangerously flawed.

As monolithic news organizations cede ownership of the public sphere to 'bloggers', 'citizen journalists', and a more collaborative way of sharing information erodes the closed newspaper system, the role of the journalist is mutating. How do modern writers now portray the tabloid hack and do they sympathize with his plight as an increasingly anachronistic endangered species, a saucy seaside postcard vendor in the age of porn-on-demand? Writers' fascination, however, for this often ill-dressed, irreverent character who nevertheless occasionally still chases political baddies on behalf of 'The People', as Edwardian fictional journalists did a century ago, is today undimmed and the journalist enjoys more positive portrayals on the big and small screen, at least in the United States. Already fictions are contrasting the traditional image of the old-fashioned hack who nevertheless respects the virtues of investigation and footslogging and scrutinizing authority with the internet-literate information 'geek' or celebrity hunter who lacks a certain humanity (e.g. the film *State of Play* (2009) or Annalena McAfee's recent novel *The Spoiler* (2011, see Conclusion)). Modern portrayals of journalists, although often stereotypical, nevertheless demonstrate a profound anxiety over the direction of contemporary journalism. A National Theatre of Scotland production in 2012, *Enquirer*, poses the question: 'Are we seeing the dying days of the newspaper industry?' and archives the opinions of forty-five newspaper journalists meditating on their trade. In the way history has a habit of repeating itself, twenty-first-century newspapers are beginning to carry serial fiction. Newspaper websites use their technology to carry ebooks, as well as news, to readers.[34] In an echo of the *Times* Book Club, launched in 1905 as a way of saving the struggling newspaper with huge discounts on books for subscribers to the paper, the *Sun* newspaper has joined forces with Tesco supermarket's Book Club to offer readers popular fiction for £2.00 a book with a purchase of the *Sun*.[35] As traditional newspapers a century ago were assessing how to meet the challenge of the new popular daily press, today all newspapers are examining new technical and financial models in their fight for survival in the internet age. 'Do we go halfpenny?' has now been replaced by 'Do We put up a paywall?'

VI

The novelist Stephen Crane may have been right when, while writing his novel about a foreign correspondent, *Active Service* (1899), he exasperatedly scribbled on a postcard 'a journalist is no hero for a novel'.[36] Save for perhaps the complex and alienated Thomas Fowler in Graham Greene's *The Quiet American* (1955), the tortured Andrew Menzies in Gordon M. Williams' *The Upper Pleasure Garden* (1970) and some of their other mid-century companions (see Chapter 6), fictional journalists seldom meditate on the great mysteries of the human condition. Journalists' novels do, however, reveal much about the impact the evolution of the journalism industry has had on its foot soldiers and how writers try to influence contemporary political and social debates. Although this book is not primarily a work of textual analysis, I have included in-depth discussions of specific fictions where they shed new light even on a well-studied author, for example, Rudyard Kipling's short story 'The Village That Voted the Earth Was Flat' and Graham Greene's *The Quiet American*. This study is, however, more an analysis of a particular literary theme, that of the ubiquitous, slightly roguish and sometimes untrustworthy character who, nevertheless, with his pencil and notebook gets 'into the heart of life'.[37]

In announcing the publication of his report on the 'Culture, Practices and Ethics' of the British press, Lord Justice Leveson asked, 'Who guards the guardians?' Implicit in that question is the idea that for too long the British press has been operating as an unaccountable yet all-too-powerful force at the heart of the British Establishment. The answer Leveson was looking for was that for the past 100 years and more, Britain's novelists, poets, playwrights and directors have been keeping a close, critical and questioning eye on Britain's journalists, producing millions of words on their culture, practices and ethics. The history of 'newspaper fiction' is a prism through which to view the history of newspapers and journalists themselves. This book also stems from my own delight in the discovery, and reading, of so many long-lost fictions about the 'rough old trade' that I have participated in for twenty-five years. As well as being a literary, historical and cultural study, this volume also hopes to recover for a wider audience than this author in love with old books, a world of swashbuckling loveable rogues and morally compromised individuals. Upon these unreliable shoulders one corner, at least, of our democracy rests.

Notes

1   See for example James Curran and Jean Seaton's *Power without Responsibility*, Alan Lee's *Origins of the Popular Press*, Stephen Koss's *Fleet Street Radical*, Mark Hampton's *Visions of the Press in Britain*, Jean Chalaby's *The Invention of News*, Piers Brendon's *The Life and Death of the Press Barons* and Martin Conboy's *Press and Popular Culture*.

2   See Korte, Barbara, *Represented Reporters* and Ehrlich, Matthew and Salzman, Joe, *Heroes and Scoundrels*. This latter volume predominantly deals with American film and television portrayals. Barbara Korte's work focuses on the image of the war correspondent.

3   'Annalena McAfee: "I see myself as a recovering journalist"' *Guardian*, 10 April 2011 http://www.theguardian.com/books/2011/apr/10/annalena-mcafee-spoiler-ian-mcewan-interview accessed 16 September 2015.

4   For a comprehensive examination of journalists portrayed on film, see McNair, Brian, *Journalists in Film*.

5   Hitchens, Christopher, 'Introduction' to *Scoop*, p. xiii.

6   Ibid., p. ix.

7   Stott, Mary, *Before I Go*, p. 87.

8   http://www.nytimes.com/2003/05/11/us/correcting-the-record-times-reporter-who-resigned-leaves-long-trail-of-deception.html accessed 16 September 2015; http://www.independent.co.uk/voices/commentators/johann-hari/johann-hari-a-personal-apology-2354679.html accessed 16 September 2015.

9   Kipling, Rudyard, 'The Press' in *A Diversity of Creatures*, p. 214.

10   Brown, Erica and Mary Grover (eds), *Middlebrow Literary Cultures*, p. 1.

11   Woolf, Virginia, 'Middlebrow', p. 115.

12   Henderson, Philip, *The Novel Today*, p. 7.

13   Wyllarde, Dolf, *The Pathway*, p. 36.

14   Sykes, Christopher, 'Thoughts on the Press', pp. 92–94.

15 Uglow, Jenny, 'Fielding, Grub Street and Canary Wharf', pp. 1–21; Connolly, Cyril, *Enemies of Promise*; Leavis, Q. D., *Fiction and the Reading Public*; Priestley, J. B., 'Mass Communications'.

16 Gross, John, *The Rise and Fall*, p. i.

17 Bourdieu, Pierre, 'The Field of Cultural Production', p. 100.

18 McDonald, Peter, *British Literary Culture*, p. 20.

19 Bourdieu, Pierre, *The Rules*, pp. 3–40.

20 Tunstall, Jeremy, *Journalists at Work*, p. 32.

21 Greene, Graham, *The Quiet American*, pp. 64–65.

22 Frayn, Michael, *Towards the End*, pp. 21–22.

23 Escott, T. H. S., 'Old and New in the Daily Press', p. 368.

24 Ford, Ford Madox, *The Inheritors*, p. 229.

25 Ford wrote reviews, sketches and essays for a wide variety of publications, from the *Daily Mail* to the *Outlook* (see Max Saunders and Richard Stang (eds) Ford Madox Ford: *Critical Essays*, p. x).

26 Wyllarde, Dolf, *The Pathway*, p. 35.

27 McCall, Leslie, 'Does Gender Fit?', p. 840.

28 Gallagher, Donat, 'Introduction' to *The Essays, Articles and Reviews of Evelyn Waugh*, p. 10.

29 Snoddy, Ray, *The Good, The Bad*, p. 168.

30 For example see Maisel, Richard, 'The Decline of Mass Media'.

31 Sunstein, Cass, *Republic.com*, p. 192.

32 Banks, Iain, *Complicity*, pp. 291–292.

33 Meek, James, *We Are Now Beginning*, p. 9.

34 http://www.niemanlab.org/2013/07/in-minneapolis-a-newspaper-goes-for-serial-fiction-and-an-ebook/ accessed 25 September 2015.

35 Feather, John, *A History of British Publishing*, p. 153.

36 Good, Howaard, *Acquainted with the Night*, p. 3.

37 Gibbs, Philip, *The Street of Adventure*, p. 96.

Edwardian Journalist-Heroes at the Birth of the Popular Press

Journalists working for the new mass daily press saw themselves as educators to the people, informing and enlightening a newly enfranchised, newly literate public. They also saw themselves as taking on a cultural elite battling hard to retain its privileges. Journalists writing novels about their profession 1900–1914 take pride in revealing the inner workings of 'The Street of Adventure', the engine room, as they saw it of social change. While contemporary scholars today see this period as a time when the journalistic field mutated from its educative, political role to one based on economic profit for its proprietors, it is clear that the lowliest agents in the field – the reporters and freelance writers – still cherished idealistic notions about what a mass press could deliver to the public.

About halfway through Guy Thorne's 1903 bestseller *When It Was Dark*, the foreign correspondent Harold Spence experiences a moment of self-doubt before embarking on his task of saving the Christian world from everlasting darkness. A powerful coalition of priests and politicians has sent him to establish the truth behind a plot to fake a 'new' tomb of Jesus, the discovery of which has undermined belief in the Resurrection story. In this godless world, churches are deserted, the stock market is in freefall and Parliament is in chaos: 'The immediate social result has been an appalling increase in crimes of lust and cruelty.' Spence is waiting to question a Greek stone engraver who might provide the evidence he needs. The stakes are high: 'He realised, or tried to realise – that on him might depend the salvation of the world.'[1] Spence is not a man to flinch from a difficult task, however: 'He was full of grim determination to wring the truth from the renegade. In his hip pocket his revolver pressed against his thigh. He was strung up for action.'[2]

Equipped with 'the pads of paper, the stylographic pens with the special ink for hot countries which would not dry up or corrode, his revolvers, riding-breeches, boots and spurs, the Kodak, with spare films and light tight zinc cases', Spence is special correspondent on the *Daily Wire*. The newspaper is more popular than the *Times*, and is the 'second, perhaps the first, most powerful engine of public opinion in the world'.[3] Spence is a man of the world, partial to showgirls and absinthe but author Guy Thorne, a journalist, notorious bon vivant and 'drinker in the grand style' himself, makes it clear that we should not condemn Spence for his failings.[4] Only a man of Spence's courage and skills can eventually wring the truth from the duplicitous Greek. Priests and politicians shrink from the task but the worldly journalist who wields his pen like a sword, ultimately saves the world. The novel was a runaway bestseller which underwent three reprintings in the year of its original publication alone and sold more than half a million copies.[5] Spence is one of several Edwardian and Georgian fictional journalists who display heroic qualities, are committed in their search for the truth, speak up for the voiceless lower classes and see their role in Fourth Estate terms.[6] Unlike Victorian fictional predecessors such as George Gissing's selfishly ambitious Jasper Milvain (*New Grub Street*, 1891) and Anthony Trollope's socially invasive Quintus Slide (*The Prime Minister*, 1876), Harold Spence and his Edwardian contemporaries are presented by their authors as seeking to enlighten and inform a newly literate public.[7] They do not seek power for themselves; rather, they want to provide ordinary people with the knowledge they need to enable them to become good citizens making good decisions about those who seek to lead them. Here is how Guy Thorne describes Ommaney, editor of the *Daily Wire*:

> No one knew his face – no one of the great outside public; his was hardly even a name to be recognised in passing, yet he, and Spence and Folliott Farmer could shake a continent with their words … While Englishmen read their dicta, and unconsciously incorporated them into their own pronouncements, mouthing them in the street, market and forum, these men slept till the busy day was over, and once more with the setting of the sun stole out to their almost furtive and yet tremendous task.[8]

The journalists' stealing out inconspicuously at night, to do their good work while ordinary men sleep, lends them an almost fairy-tale quality, like the 'helpful elves' of folklore. They are wise men, endowing the public spaces of 'the street, market and forum' – note the classical allusion – with knowledge and rational argument. Neither before 1900 nor after about 1915 do we see the 'good' journalist so often represented in British fiction, and it is worth examining the historical and social reasons for such an apparent anomaly in the long line of cheats, spivs and villains who make up a generally unappealing rogues' gallery of fictional journalists in British literature.

Changes in journalism from 1896

The launch of the *Daily Mail* in May 1896 has been seen by many historians as the most important development in the British press since the abolition of stamp duty in 1855.[9] The combination of compulsory elementary schooling, the 1884 Reform Act, which for the first time pushed the number of eligible voters beyond 5,000,000, and Alfred Harmsworth's business genius changed the British newspaper industry, from its 'traditional mission of watchdog and teacher' into an 'information industry'.[10] The style, content, circulation and readership of the morning daily press underwent a revolution in just a few decades so that by the interwar years, morning papers were unrecognizable from those of the late Victorian era, which were 'suitable only for those who could retire to their clubs at four o'clock and spend two or three hours digesting' them.[11] Bolder typefaces, shorter sentences and shorter articles, the condensing of political speeches, greater emphasis on general news and entertainment articles, women's pages and features are all ways in which newspaper content changed, and continued to evolve in the twentieth century.[12] Early twentieth-century commentators could see the importance of this 'new' way of writing and reading newspapers but were divided on whether or not it was a force for good. There was certainly criticism from the intellectual and political elite, leading to Lord Salisbury's famous disparaging remark about the *Daily Mail* being written 'by office boys for office boys'. Historian G. M. Trevelyan mourned in 1901: 'The printing-press itself has been carried over into the enemy's camp. The Philistines have captured the Ark of the Covenant.'[13] Social idealists, however, embraced the educative potential of the new newspapers which, priced at a halfpenny, reached people who had never read a newspaper before. Literary scholar B. Ifor Evans, for example, argued that for a brief period following the launch of the *Daily Mail* there was a chance that a mass press could give England the gift of an 'enquiring and cultured' democracy, if the proprietors had grasped the opportunity.[14] Former *Observer* editor Edward Dicey argued in 1905: 'So long as the new electorate desire a sound and wholesome article for the gratification of their journalistic appetites there can be nothing wrong in the state of our press. Moreover it is pleasing to me to notice that scientific discourses, reports of new inventions and descriptions of novel manufacturing processes find ready access into the columns of our halfpenny press.'[15]

Another Fleet Street veteran representing the Victorian tradition, H. Simonis, argued that the simpler language of the 'new' journalism – calling a fish as a fish and not 'a finny denizen of the deep' – was a positive change, enabling more people to have access to information about their world.[16]

The launch of Alfred Harmsworth's *Daily Mail* started a huge rise in circulation and proliferation of newspapers in Britain. In 1887, for example, the *Telegraph* claimed the largest circulation of any newspaper in the world, at close to 250,000 copies a day. By 1902 the *Daily Mail* was selling 1.2 million copies a day – what Harmsworth himself then felt was the 'limit of circulation'.[17] The new *Mirror* was selling over 300,000 copies a day by 1904, and by 1914 even the *Observer*, which in 1905 had been selling between 2,000 and 4,000 copies a week, had reached the 200,000 mark; by 1918 the total circulation of the national dailies stood at over three million.[18] This was a time of diversity both in the 'London' and the provincial press, with nearly two dozen London morning and evening papers alone. A thriving and growing popular press was fast emerging, yet older established newspapers still enjoyed influence and decent circulation among 'club land' opinion formers. There would shortly be a culling of older papers which failed to stand up to the challenge of the new halfpenny press, but in 1904 readers could choose from a 'staggering array' including the *Westminster Gazette*, the *Morning Post*, the *Times*, the *Daily Telegraph*, *Daily Chronicle*, *Morning Leader*, *St James's Gazette*, the *Globe*, the *Echo*, the *Pall Mall Gazette*, *Evening News*, *Evening Standard*, *Morning Advertiser*, *Daily Mirror*, the *Sun*, *Daily Graphic*, *Daily News* and *Daily Mail*, *Daily Express*, the *Standard* and *Star*.[19]

The halfpenny papers required an enlarged journalistic workforce, equipped with reporting skills, not just 'literary men' or Oxbridge-educated leader writers. These were men of modest means who had left school at fourteen and who had been apprentices in the provincial press. Many would rise to occupy senior positions in the new popular newspapers and enjoy an income and influence they had never expected.[20] Women journalists, often freelancers, found work writing for the new newspaper women's pages a mixed blessing of gender stereotyping and economic freedom. In the 1891 census, 8,269 people described themselves as belonging to the occupation category 'authors, editors, journalists, reporters, shorthand writers'. By 1901 this figure had risen to 10,663, and by 1911, to nearly 14,000.[21]

The novels discussed in this chapter are 'children' of the Harmsworth era, their authors often benefiting from the new popular press in the early days of mass circulation. The writers were familiar with the world of journalism, all of them spending time either as newspaper staffers or as freelancers. Guy Thorne had freelanced for *The Saturday Review*, *London Life* and *The Echo* before taking a staff job in the early days of the *Daily Mail*.[22] Philip Gibbs (*The Street of Adventure*, 1909) was appointed literary editor of the *Daily Mail* in 1902 and subsequently worked as a reporter, and then editor on other London papers including *The Daily Express*, *Daily Chronicle* and *The Tribune*.[23] C. E. Montague (*A Hind Let Loose*, 1910) had worked both as reporter and as assistant editor on the *Manchester Guardian* since 1890; Alphonse Courlander (*Mightier than the Sword*, 1912) was a reporter on the *Daily Express*,[24] Rudyard Kipling ('The Village That Voted the Earth Was Flat', 1913/14) worked as a journalist in India from the age of sixteen to twenty-three;[25] Adeline Sergeant (*The Work of Oliver Byrd*, 1902) was a lifelong contributor to the *People's Friend*; Edgar Wallace (*The Four Just Men*, 1905 and the *Council of Justice*, 1908) was a foreign correspondent and home reporter on the *Daily Mail* from 1898 to 1907;[26] Jerome K. Jerome (*Three Men on the Bummel*, 1900, and *Tommy and Co*, 1904) began his writing career as a freelance journalist, 'penny-a-lining' at reporting from police courts and inquests; he later co-founded the *Idler* and the weekly journal *To-Day* in 1893;[27] P. G. Wodehouse (*Psmith Journalist*, 1909) began his writing career as a freelancer in 1902, contributing fiction and journalism to the *Globe* and several other London and then New York titles before he became fully established as a novelist;[28] Patrick MacGill (*Children of the Dead End*, 1914) was taken on by the *Daily Express* on the strength of a handful of freelance articles.[29] Arthur Conan Doyle, Katherine Cecil Thurston, E. V. Lucas, H. G. Wells, John Keble Bell, Arnold Bennett, Dolf Wyllarde, John Davidson, Ford Madox Ford and G. K. Chesterton, all of whom wrote novels, poems or plays involving journalist characters or long discussions of the press, and who will also be referred to in this chapter, also had close associations with newspapers. While the worlds of journalism and literature had by the turn of the century slowly begun breaking apart, they both still shared common characteristics and personnel. As in the late nineteenth century, 'virtually every writer had some connection with journalism', and vice versa.[30] But changes were taking place, often unnoticed, on a daily basis, creating tensions within the field, particularly for those agents among the lowest social classes who could not rely on private means to subsidize their incomes. This partly explains why such a large group of writers devoted lengthy discourses to promoting journalism as a literary genre deserving cultural capital. Indeed the fierce loyalty many show in their fictions to a genre of writing viewed as degraded by the cultural elite enables us to reconstruct some of the complex social structures of the field of cultural production at the very time of their formation.

That many of these authors worked for the new popular daily papers, particularly the *Daily Mail* and *Daily Express*, is important. They had been given their 'big break' by the new press and shared the early hopes invested in it by some liberal commentators. Employees of the new newspapers enjoyed reasonable pay and took pride in their papers' independence from old-style political patronage.[31] Starting salaries for reporters on popular dailies were £2.00 a week. Freelance rates were generous: in 1904 most national dailies and consumer magazines paid £1 1s per 1,000 words; *Chambers Journal* paid £1 11s per 1,000 words; the *Athenaeum* 15s per 770-word column and the *Spectator* £5 5s per article.[32] This compares with the average wage in 1902 of 18s 3d per week.[33] Productive freelancers could make large sums of money. P. G. Wodehouse, for example, having been sacked from his job at the Hong Kong and Shanghai Bank in 1902, spent the next seven years freelancing on London newspapers and periodicals. They published both his fiction and non-fiction, and he was grateful to the London press for giving him his start as a professional writer. This extract from his memoir reveals how richly diverse and lucrative the early twentieth-century print market was even for jobbing freelancers:

> There were so many morning papers and evening papers and weekly papers and monthly magazines that you were practically sure of landing your whimsical article on 'The Language of Flowers' or your parody of Omar Khayyam somewhere or other after about say thirty five shots ... I left the bank in September and by the end of the year found that I had made £65 6s 7d ... My income rose like a rocketing pheasant. I made £505 1s 7d in 1906 and £527 17s 1d in 1907 ... on November 17, 1907 I ... bought a second hand Darracq car for £450.[34]

The serialization of novels in the *Daily Mail*, *Daily Express* and *Daily Mirror*'s 'feuilleton' sections was another income stream for authors such as Arnold Bennett, H. G. Wells and Katherine Cecil Thurston.

The majority of the novelists studied here were either from lowly backgrounds or the middle and lower middle classes, and few went to university. Edgar Wallace was the typical journalist of the new mass medium: saved from a Greenwich poorhouse by a philanthropic Billingsgate fish porter, Wallace attended a board school in Peckham, where he learned to read and write. He began selling poetry to newspapers by the yard until his despatches from the Boer Wars caught the eye of Thomas Marlowe, editor of the *Daily Mail*.[35] Desire to defend the new popular press against attacks from aristocratic politicians or elitist commentators is a theme that runs through many of the Edwardian novels examined here. In Edgar Wallace's thriller *The Four Just Men* (1905), older 'serious' newspapers such as the *Telegram* can only snipe as the *Daily Megaphone*, modelled on the *Daily Mail*, clinches scoop after scoop on the story of an anarchist plot to kill a leading politician:

> 'It is not so easy to understand', said the *Telegram*, 'why having the miscreants in their hands, certain journalists connected with a sensational halfpenny

contemporary allowed them to go free to work their evil designs ... unfortunately in these days of cheap journalism every story emanating from the sanctum sanctorum of sensation-loving sheets is not to be accepted on its pretensions.'[36]

To the reader, who knows that the editor of the *Megaphone* has risked his life in the drama, the *Telegram* looks foolish and spiteful as well as hopelessly verbose. Moreover, the editor of the *Megaphone* has the presence of mind to ask the anarchists for an exclusive article on them and is rewarded with a scoop: "'Sir," said the masked man – and there was a note of admiration in his voice – "I recognise in you an artist. The article will be delivered tomorrow."'[37]

In the sequel, *The Council of Justice* (1908), Wallace once more attacks the *Daily Mail*'s rivals, portraying the *Megaphone* as a supremely professional outfit that handles a breaking political story with consummate ease and the only paper that can really communicate with the mass of reading public: 'There was no flurry, no rush ... taxi after taxi flew up to the great newspaper office, discharging alert young men who literally leapt into the building... It was the *Megaphone* that shone splendidly amidst its journalistic fellows ... It was the *Megaphone* that fed the fires of public interest.'[38]

Like Alphonse Courlander (see Introduction) and Guy Thorne, Edgar Wallace is, in his fictions, positioning the popular newspaper journalist quite deliberately within a section of the field that other cultural producers would have him barred from. He is culturally important, telling the public of significant political events with his skill and professionalism. He is an artist because he recognizes a shift in public taste. Wallace is also indicating with the phrase 'fed the fires of public interest' that the field itself is undergoing a significant distortion, with a new kind of cultural consumer now asking to be catered for. The novels in this chapter, as an ensemble, thus represent a concerted challenge to elite assumptions about the new mass press and its contributors. The challenge is made on many fronts: on modernity, accessibility, readership, social change and on assertions, as 'highbrow' writers Joseph Conrad and Ford Madox Ford attempted to make, that contributors to the mass press were simply lowly 'rats' and not worthy of the label 'writer' at all.[39]

Modernity and the thrill of new technology

These novels celebrate technology and the excitement of 'the rush and scurry' of Fleet Street.[40] New methods of newspaper production following the introduction of the Linotype machine during the late 1890s allowed for machine setting, which was six times faster than the old hand-setting method, and the rotary printing machine, which increased the speed of production from 6,000 copies an hour to 30,000.[41] Advanced telegraphy systems enabled newspaper editors and foreign correspondents to gather and disseminate news often faster than official government channels. In 1904 during the Russo-Japanese war, the *Times* became the first newspaper in the world to use wireless telegraphy, still in its infancy, from a boat in the Yellow Sea. The correspondent Lionel James recalls in his memoirs his excitement at hearing the 'three-inch spark cracking out its message ... the first war cable of all time, sent by wireless from an area convulsed by naval war'.[42] The *Daily Mail* boasted in its advertisement celebrating the third anniversary of its Continental edition, 1908: 'Thus by means of telegraphy produced simultaneously in London, Manchester and Paris ... it may be obtained in places where, until its coming, no English newspaper was ever seen ... for the first time in the history of newspaper production, to deliver virtually the same newspaper on the same day to a reader in Aberdeen and Marseilles.'[43]

Foreign correspondents on profitable papers were well equipped and took with them baggage trains of supplies that far-outstripped Spence's 'stylographic pens'. In his memoirs of his thirteen-year service as a *Times* foreign correspondent, Lionel James describes first meeting the 'Great War Correspondents ... portrayed as picturesque heroes in magazines' on the Nile in 1898: 'George Steevens, equipped at the expense of the *Daily Mail* with a larder tinned by Fortnum and Mason ... Frank Scudamore, financed by the *Daily News*, with one camel devoted exclusively to laager beer and another carrying an ice-machine.'[44] The correspondents Augustus Sala of the *Telegraph*, Archibald Forbes of the *Daily News* and G. W. Steevens of the *Daily Mail* saw themselves as heroes of the stories they were telling, risking all to bring the world the first news of military engagements. Steevens' famous despatches from the battle of Omdurman in 1898 were one of the greatest scoops in the early days of the *Daily Mail* and helped push sales to nearly one million.[45] The powerfully impressionistic style of Steevens' reports, placing the correspondent – the 'intellectual observer-hero' equipped with all the latest tools of the trade – at the centre of the action helped, promote the image of the journalist as an almost superhuman truth-teller.[46]

Despatches sent to newspapers from the Boer Wars made much of whether they had been sent as letters, telegrams, by runner or heliograph. The *Daily News* dedicated a long feature on 'How the news comes home: Cables from the Cape' on 6 January 1900, emphasizing the 'honour of co-operating with the fourth estate' telegraph companies felt. The interconnectedness of Fleet Street to the rest of the world via technology is celebrated by the poet John Davidson in his 1907 poem 'Fleet Street: A Song':[47]

> Networks of wire overland
> Conduits under the sea,
> Aerial message from strand to strand
> By lightning that travels free,
> Hither haste to hand
> Tidings of destiny:
> These tingling nerves of the world's affairs
> Deliver remorseless, rendering still
> The fall of empires, the price of shares,
> The record of good and ill.[48]

This technology, delivering information widely, has conquered all physical states: sea, land and air, and there is powerful excitement in the 'lightening that travels free', reminiscent of James' 'three inch spark cracking out its message'. In another poem, 'Fleet Street', the world of newspapers' modernity, 'our modern, actual magic, black and white', is celebrated again. 'News' becomes a miraculous synthesis of great elemental forces and human ingenuity:

> Never forget that men have tamed and taught
> The lightening; clad it in a livery known
> As news ...
> Our modern, actual magic, black and white.[49]

Davidson, a late Victorian and Edwardian 'man of letters', contributed to newspapers which still readily took poetry, including the *Glasgow Herald*, *Pall Mall Gazette*, *Daily Chronicle* and the *Daily News*. In a few years, newspapers would exclude poetry and Wodehouse's whimsical 'Turnovers' from their pages in favour of news. But this was the high-water mark of the age of mass reading; these were the days when poets were celebrities, when Rudyard Kipling's pneumonia in 1899 was front-page news across the world and when the scoop of publishing a new poem by a leading poet could boost a paper's sales.[50] Davidson could earn up to 25 guineas selling his poems to the daily press.[51] His sense of the energy and excitement of Fleet Street is noteworthy, as when writers turn against the press about mid-way through the First World War, the poets will lead the charge. But before the First World War, newspapers were still seen as a natural home for poets, both their verse and their ideas. When Davidson picked an argument with the high-Tory literary magazine *Academy*, for example, the row was carried on the front page of the popular evening newspaper the *Star* (*Star*, 1

December 1908). When he went missing, his disappearance was chronicled on a daily basis in the *Daily Mail* ('Missing Poet', 26 March 1909; 'Mystery of John Davidson', 27 March 1909; 'Mystery of Missing Poet', 31 March 1909; 'Missing Poet: £20 reward', 1 April 1909).

In *John Chilcote MP*, Katherine Cecil Thurston's political novel, serialized in the *Daily Mail*, and claimed as 'the most remarkable serial story that has ever been published' (*Daily Mail*, 10 September 1904), Lakeley, the 'vigorous, energetic, shrewd, irrepressible' editor of the *St George's Gazette*, is always first with the news. He beats the foreign secretary with his overseas despatches and sometimes even forgets his manners in his haste to communicate them:

> Lakeley entered the room. His face was brimming with excitement and his eyes flashed. In the first haste of the entry he failed to see that there were ladies in the room, and crossing instantly to Fraide, laid an open telegram before him. 'This is official, sir!' he said. Then he glanced around the table. 'Lady Sarah!' he exclaimed, 'Can you forgive me? But I'd have given a hundred pounds to be the first with this!'[52]

The fine ladies and gentlemen forgive Lakeley's momentary lapse and are thrilled to be the first consumers of his news. C. E. Montague's *A Hind Let Loose* (1910) describes with heavy irony how a new halfpenny paper *The Day* outperforms two older newspapers, with its high-speed telecommunications system: 'the lusts of New York and the homicides of California enriched for the first time the sacred home life of English families at their next morning's breakfast'.[53]

Over just a few decades, Fleet Street had transformed from the shabby back alleys and attic-room editorial offices of 'Grub Street' to an electric-lit industrial complex with new buildings built to house the heavy printing plant and larger editorial staffs required by the large circulation newspapers.[54] The novels portray the excitement of the young journalist entering this world: in *Mightier than the Sword*, Humphrey Quain is overwhelmed by the new *Day* offices 'with its arrogant dome-tower (lit up at nights), its swinging glass doors and braided commissionaires'.[55] When Harold Spence first enters the offices of the *Daily Wire* in *When It Was Dark*, the backdrop is the sound of typewriters clicking, the 'thud of a "column-printer" tape machine' and all the rooms are 'brilliantly lit'.[56] Both Philip Gibbs' *The Street of Adventure* and Alphonse Courlander's *Mightier than the Sword* explain in great detail the processes of subbing and composing: 'Their machines were almost human. They touched the keys as if they were typewriting, and little brass letters slipped down into a line, and then mechanically an iron hand gripped the line, plunged it into a box of molten lead.'[57] When the presses start up each night, it is a hugely powerful event: 'the grey building shivered and trembled, as if in agony, and there came up from its very roots of its being a deep roar, at first irregular, and menacing, but gradually settling down to a steady, rhythmical beat, like the throbbing of thousands of human hearts.'[58]

The machines are 'almost human' and the journalists are part of the machinery, described in fiction at a time when journalism moves away from its political, educative role and becomes an industry. Although these new-style news reporters are small cogs in an industrial process which critics will later describe as the 'commodification of discourse', they do not see it this way.[59] They see themselves as bringing information and literary discourse to a large public and are enjoying the thrill of belonging to 'the world's most famous street'.[60] Edwardian man of letters G. K. Chesterton defends 'mere' journalism in an article published in the *Darlington North Star* in 1902, dismissing intellectual concerns over 'new' journalism as mere snobbery. Chesterton evokes mystical qualities in a paper, describing newspaper offices, with 'great lights burning through darkness into dawn' and 'the roar of the printing wheels weaving the destinies of another day'. Not since the erection of the 'great Christian cathedrals', claims Chesterton, has there been 'the largest work ever published anonymously' as in a newspaper. For Chesterton, journalism is modern-day poetry: 'The great merit of journalism is that it has reasserted finally the poetry of the actual world ... it is no small and no slight thing that the most popular and widely read of all romances is simply the record of the common doings of the common day' (*Darlington North Star*, 3 February 1902). The personal impact, that is, the stress of having to work for a highly competitive industry, will emerge in journalists' fiction of later decades, but for these early agents of the mass press, the excitement of moving into a club previously occupied by only a small elite is enough.

A new kind of journalist: The news reporter

In *The Street of Adventure*, Philip Gibbs chronicles the life of a new breed of professional reporter. Frank Luttrell is employed to write in a bright manner for the thousands of elementary school graduates who had just learned to read:

> He had to write a sketch of a Christmas party given by the Salvation Army in Eagle Street, Drury Lane, where the children of thieves, murderers, out-of-works and unemployables fought tooth and nail for buns, crackers ... A week later he described the Fancy Dress Ball at the Mansion House, where the children of

the well-to-do showed off... Perhaps the strangest work he was called upon to do was take a party of men and women across the Channel and back to test an alleged cure for sea sickness.[61]

Frank Luttrell and his fellow reporters are sent to cover celebrity weddings and low-life court cases and to a village in Somerset where five octogenarians live.[62] Yet the trivia they sometimes have to write is outweighed by their role as social crusaders. Fictional reporters are depicted as courageous and endowed with a strong moral sense. In Philip Gibbs' *The Street of Adventure*, Brandon, the crime reporter, prevents a potential miscarriage of justice through his investigative powers, finding a vital clue that the police have overlooked; Edmund Grattan, the fearless foreign correspondent, has witnessed wars, revolutions and *coups d'état* but finds time to comfort dying soldiers on the 'bloody battlefields of South Africa' as well as championing the causes of Women's Suffrage and the unemployed.[63]

In Courlander's *Mightier than the Sword* journalists die for their vocation. Wratten, the leading 'descriptive writer' on *The Day*, dies of pneumonia after refusing to leave the scene of a mining disaster in case he should miss some extra details. The protagonist Humphrey Quain is crushed to death in a mob of angry French winegrowers. The journalists die in their zeal for telling the stories of the people. Miners and the farm labourers are the protagonists in their newspaper stories. Gibbs, Courlander, Wallace and Thorne, men of modest backgrounds, illuminate in their novels the lives of early professional reporters and the precarious existence of men given the chance to wear a collar and tie thanks to their board school education. James Lansdale Hodson, for example, who would later become editor of the northern edition of the *Daily Mail*, avoided following his brothers and sisters into the Manchester cotton mills because, unlike his older siblings, he had learned to read and write.[64] This new world of opportunity is portrayed in the novelist, poet and journalist Patrick MacGill's fictionalized memoir *Children of the Dead End* (1914). Describing a poor Irish labourer's journey across Ireland and Scotland, the novel achieved critical acclaim for its unstinting description of working-class life. The only escape the hero, young Dermod Flynn, finds is in literature and in the telling of stories. After one blasting disaster which ends in the death of a fellow navvy, Flynn, when his eye chanced on a newspaper 'wrapped around a chunk of mouldy beef', decides to send his account of the tragedy to that paper: 'It was the *Dawn*, a London halfpenny paper. I had never heard of it before.'[65] The real-life MacGill had in fact sent his story to the *Daily Express*, edited by R. D. Blumenfeld. The editor paid Flynn/MacGill two guineas for his story and asked him for more. Flynn/

MacGill admits, however, that his success gave him no pleasure: 'I at first felt as if I was committing a sin against my mates.'[66] He wrote four more articles for the *Dawn*, and then accepted the offer of full-time work. Although Flynn/ MacGill's stint on Fleet Street was short-lived and discomfiting – in his words, 'I had never used a fork when eating ... I wore my first collar when setting out for London. It nearly choked me' – his great chance, to escape the grinding hard work and terrible conditions of navvying, was offered him by the new popular press.[67] That a poor Irish farm boy could be offered a staff job for £2 a week on the strength of a few articles about navvying life once again emphasizes the kind of opportunities Fleet Street offered at that time. This novel and Hodson's later descriptions of journalism after the First World War (see Chapter 2) also portray conflicting tensions experienced by agents arriving from the lower classes into 'an essentially middle class discourse and institution'.[68]

Crusaders for social justice

The political balance of the press changed from being dominated by Liberal supporters from the 1870s until 1900, then being roughly in balance, with Liberals having a slight edge during the first years of the twentieth century, to becoming Conservative-dominated press by the time of the outbreak of the First World War.[69] Gibbs, Courlander and others saw themselves and their profession as being on the side of the forces of progress. While the *Daily Mail* moved steadily towards the right during the first decade of the twentieth century, it also embraced the tradition of campaigning for social justice in a similar vein to its contemporaries, namely the *Daily News*, *Westminster* and *Pall Mall Gazette*.[70] It is useful to compare, for example, *Daily Mail* reporter Charles Hands' coverage of the 1912 National Coal strike with the *Daily Mail*'s famously suppressed 'For King and Country' leader denouncing the unions on the eve of the General Strike in 1926.[71] In Charles Hands' despatches – in prime position on the leader page – he identifies with the miners entirely: 'those of us ... who work in the coalmines were hoisted to the surface eight or ten at a time in a cage and breathing the free air of heaven, if the atmosphere largely comprised of steam, smoke, drizzle and coal dust at the pit head can so be described' (*Daily Mail*, 4 March 1912). Although after attempts at settlement had failed, the *Daily Mail* urged the unions to think again: leaders in the run-up to the strike showed sympathy for the miners that a modern-day reader of the *Daily Mail* would not recognize:

The miners' desire for better wages and more consistent earnings is human and intelligible. The public has strong sympathy with these men who toil under such disagreeable conditions, away from the light of the sun in circumstances of continual danger. (*Daily Mail*, 9 January 1912)

The historian A. J. P. Taylor has argued that much Edwardian working-class dissatisfaction with the social status quo, which eventually led to the widespread pre–First World War strikes and the rise of the Labour Party, was promulgated through the popular press. For the first time working-class readers not in service could observe the lives of the rich and famous and compare their conspicuous consumption with their own straitened circumstances.[72] This idea is pursued by the essayist and biographer (and former reporter for *The Globe* newspaper) E. V. Lucas, in his 1912 novel *London Lavender*. In a discussion about politics the Socialist Spanton is delighted that the 'spectacle of the upper world of wealth', as reflected in the halfpenny papers, must irritate the 'toiler' – a very different take on today's celebrity exposés:

> In the old days when the poor couldn't read, or papers were too expensive such [luxurious aristocratic dinner parties] had a chance of being missed; but today everything is made public and reaches even the poorest, and helps very properly to inflame them. This is one of the principle reasons why nothing is ever going to be the same any more.[73]

In an era characterized by excessive displays of wealth, on the one hand, and increasingly visible poverty, on the other, as revealed in a series of reforming reports through the Edwardian period, the reporter in the new press occupied an interesting social and political position.[74] His exposure of the lives of the wealthy was clearly seen by some as providing a tool for socialism and yet he worked for an increasingly capitalistic industry.

At the same time as popular newspapers were reporting on the antics of the wealthy, old-style 'elite' journalists and newspapers were still producing work which contributed to the traditional idea of the press being an instrument of social reform. C. F. G. Masterman, the Liberal journalist who became literary editor of the *Daily News* (and later MP), published a series of reports on London slum life, first in the periodicals *Commonwealth* and *The Speaker* and then in book form. *From the Abyss* (1902) is a detailed exposé of the conditions of London's poor ('We are many, we are struggling, and we are silent') and still stands as a landmark of Liberal journalism and the belief that in exposing suffering, something can be done to help.[75] The progressive and campaigning character of newspapers and journalists is a major theme of these Edwardian novels. In Adeline Sergeant's *The Work of Oliver Byrd* (1902), for example, the heroine Eleanor Denbigh writes investigative campaigning articles about 'the condition of children in certain London slums; and she had gathered together a mass of facts and details relative to their condition and their heredity which was becoming very useful to the statisticians and philanthropists of her time'.[76] Alphonse Courlander uses his experience of journalism to expose in *Mightier than the Sword* the injustice of poorly maintained coal mines and the impoverished lives of the children living in London's East End. Wratten is the hero of the novel because he dies exposing the consequences of mine-owners putting profit before their workers.

The loveable rogue

Another novel of this period, *Tommy and Co* by Jerome K. Jerome (1904), emphasizes the idea of the 'journalist-as-social-upstart' when the protagonist, Tommy, a street girl, scoops the rest of Fleet Street, getting an interview with a foreign prince by climbing into his moving train carriage.[77] For a moment, the very lowest in society occupies the same enclosed physical space as the very highest, through the medium of journalism. Not only do journalists upset the social status quo in their work but their income enables them to rise up the class ladder. This had been an ongoing process in the late nineteenth century. By the 1880s 'peers who had been accustomed to regard reporters in much the same light as poachers, were happy to dine with them'.[78] In Adeline Sergeant's *The Work of Oliver Byrd* (1902) the upper classes are rather more uneasy of the journalist's ability to rise through the social strata. Here Lord Westover is assessing the newspaper editor Claude Ayrton, a rival for the hand of Eleanor Denbigh: 'I should not say that Mr Ayrton is an adventurer. He has a certain position and a fair income, and he is a rising man. A journalist – with brains and an attractive manner – may aspire to anything nowadays.'[79]

Keble Howard in his novel about Alfred Harmsworth's early career, *Lord London* (1913), presents Hannibal Quain's ability to promote young men of lowly origin over privileged sons of wealthy men as a wholly positive departure. Using the example of Meadowsweet, the heir to a businessman's fortune, and Sandown, who arrived at the *Little Daily* as a boy of fifteen to lick envelopes, Howard describes how Meadowsweet is sacked after failing his trial work placement. Sandown meanwhile is promoted to eventually being given control of five titles and 'a fixed salary of fifteen hundred a year'.[80]

While fear of starvation dogged some early twentieth-century reporters, others, including, as we have seen, P. G. Wodehouse, did well freelancing for a variety of publications.[81] Wodehouse's light-hearted novel *Psmith Journalist* was first serialized in *The Captain* magazine – 'A Magazine for Boys and Old Boys' – in 1909–1910. Although it is set in New York and concerning an American weekly paper *Cosy Moments*, the star, Psmith, is an Englishman looking for fun during his long vacation from Cambridge University. The novel seems to have been inspired partly by Wodehouse's early experiences as a London freelancer, but also by a short trip he made to New York in 1904.[82] Like Wodehouse, Psmith had been destined to work for a merchant bank, but writing a few lines in *Cosy Moments* sets him on another course. Not content with turning out dull stories for a dreary paper, Psmith, with the cooperation of the ambitious temporary editor Billy Windsor, embarks on a new direction:

'We must chronicle the live events of the day, murders, fires and the like in a manner which will make our readers' spines thrill. Above all we must be the guardians of the People's rights. We must be a searchlight, showing up the dark spot in the souls of those who would endeavour in any way to do the PEOPLE in the eye.'[83]

They launch a campaign against the run-down state of New York's privately owned tenement blocks and expose their pitiless owner 'for *Cosy Moments* cannot be muzzled'.[84] The cause is a fashionable one for a journalist wishing to assert his or her honourable credentials. Since the publication of journalist and photographer Jacob Riis' shocking exposé of life in New York tenements in *How the Other Half Lives* (1890), liberal newspapers campaigned hard to end the exploitation of the poor by unscrupulous private property owners. By giving Psmith the cause of the tenement-campaigner, Wodehouse is consciously putting him on the side of good against evil. But Psmith is also a wag and a damn good boxer. With his excellent right hook and fearlessness in the face of dastardly crooks, Psmith is evocative of the real-life adventurers and 'wild-eyed Scotsmen' whom Fleet Street employed in the first years of the twentieth century.[85] Certainly the list of characters Lionel James met in his years as *Times* foreign correspondent in the early twentieth century – including the baritone-singing Wyon, who despite his enormous girth follows partisan fighters across Eastern Europe for his copy, and McKenzie of the *Daily Mail*, who leaps into a tiny boat in a fast-flowing river to convey his 'scoop' to the nearest telegraph office, are stuff to inspire *Boy's Own* magazine. James himself stopped a mail train with smoke bombs in order to board it and locked up a rival reporter, having plied him with champagne, to prevent him stealing his 'scoop'.[86]

The rugby-playing reporter Ed Malone of the *Daily Gazette*, narrator of Arthur Conan Doyle's *The Lost World* (1912) and *The Poison Belt* (1913), is certainly loveable for all his mischievous behaviour. Indeed we admire his courage when facing up to the formidable Professor Challenger. The humorously self-deprecating Malone has forced himself to try to be a hero in order to win the hand of the heartless Gladys, and his magnificent storytelling skills keep the reader breathlessly concerned for the fate of Challenger and Malone and the other adventurers until their safe arrival back in London. In *The Poison Belt*, Malone's recording of his and Challenger's final hours as the last living men on earth as a poisonous 'ether' envelopes it acquires heroic proportions, although he is characteristically modest about his abilities:

> The old instinct of recording came over me. If these men of science could be so true to their life's work to the very end, why should not I, in my humble way, be as constant? No human eye might ever rest upon what I had done... Had I the literary touch [my notes] might have been worthy of the occasion. As it is, they may still serve to bring to other minds the long-drawn emotions and tremors of that awful night.[87]

Despite Malone's modesty, his author entrusts a humble reporter with the task of recording nothing less than the end of history. Challenger's description of Malone as 'half-educated' brings to mind the disparaging description of George Gissing's 'quarter-educated' board school graduates and is a deliberate ploy to remind readers of the importance of accessibility in a writer, something Doyle believed strongly in.[88] Malone is an interesting fictional character as Doyle takes up his adventures again in the late 1920s. It will be seen, however, that a man as honourable and likeable as Malone has no place in interwar newspaper journalism (Chapter 3).

Rudyard Kipling and 'The Village That Voted the Earth Was Flat' (1913/14)

The young Rudyard Kipling, who between 1883 and 1887 represented 'fifty per cent of the editorial staff of the one daily paper of the Punjab', learned very quickly of the inside workings of newspapers.[89] While reports of garden parties, official dinners and government announcements bored him, from the very first weeks on the *Civil and Military Gazette*, Kipling became aware of newspapers' myriad subtexts. The idea that under the surface of church notices, court lists and crop and weather reports there was a whole layer of other information, some half-truths, some propaganda and some secret messages fired the young writer's imagination. An early lesson he learned was the hidden meaning of secret messages published in the 'New Advertisements' section of the classified columns. During the hot season when most British residents moved into the cool hills of Simla, with husbands and wives travelling for days, sometimes weeks apart, the opportunities for adulterous liaisons arranged through the newspaper abounded:

> Darling, your letter safely received, write fully as promised, nothing to fear from my quarter. I will not write to you without your permission, G.B.
>
> Hope you will enjoy your ten days at F – h, from the 22nd with your old pal, do not forget your make up box, after which sing 'Ask nothing more of me'.[90]

Other experiences on the *Civil and Military Gazette* ranged from faking correspondents' letters, to writing glowing reviews of plays he performed in, once describing himself as 'the hero of the evening', to publishing reports and poems under false bylines. These deliberate distortions of reality would present Kipling with the idea of the apparently reliable reporter/storyteller whose unsettling narrative often doesn't quite add up. He used this technique in many of his early *Plain Tales from the Hills*, creating an unsettling experience for his reader.[91] He later employed the image of the newspaper as a many-layered text for misuse by press insiders in 'The Village That Voted the Earth Was Flat'.

The story is about how three disgruntled journalists – Woodhouse, Ollyett and the narrator – with an MP and a music hall impresario, gain revenge on a corrupt magistrate and 'Rad' MP Sir Thomas Ingell, who has abused his power in his local court house. The journalists use their newspapers *The Cake* and *The Bun* as medium for their revenge, circulating increasingly ludicrous stories, both true and fabricated about Ingell's constituency village of Huckley, 'a little pale-yellow market town'.[92] Finally, after a visit from the 'Geo Planarian Society' the village votes unanimously that the Earth is flat. Bat Masquerier, 'a large, flaxen-haired man … with gunmetal-blue eyes' who owns a chain of music halls, uses his access to the mass public to compound and intensify the press stories.[93] When it emerges that the villagers have voted that they believe the Earth is flat, the story takes on a life of its own – 'went viral' as we would say today. 'The Village …', although wholly of its time, also contains surprising and instructive parallels with today's technological and ethical 'crisis' in journalism. Today when 'traditional' news organizations like the BBC make journalistic errors as in the recent Lord McAlpine affair, the error is magnified, indeed rages out of control on social media networks. In 'The Village …' newspaper fabrications are magnified through other forms of contemporary media including the music hall, popular songs and the burgeoning magazine industry.[94] Ultimately, the journalists and Bat lose control of the 'story': 'We've put it over the whole world – the full extent of the geographical globe. We couldn't stop it if we wanted to now ... I'm not in charge any more.'[95]

Narrated by one of the journalists responsible for the shocking and humiliating fate of Ingell, the story is also a sophisticated exercise in 'spin' that today's experts in the modern art of public relations would be proud of.

Kipling was schooled in, and had a nostalgic fondness for, what he calls 'the old Black Art' in the poem 'The Press', which accompanies the short story.[96] He acknowledges the debt of gratitude he owed to his early days as a journalist, both in being given the chance to write fiction and also for the rigorous training writing for newspapers gave him, in his memoir: 'I have told what my early surroundings were, and how richly they furnished me with material. Also how rigorously newspaper spaces limited my canvases ... it was necessary that every word should tell, carry, weigh, taste, and, if need were, smell.'[97]

Here Kipling attributes his famous concision and distinctive robust style to his newspaper apprenticeship. The technique took him 'an impatient while to learn' but, once mastered, allowed him to 'keep abreast of the flood' of all the things he wanted to say and report on even in short genres of writing.[98] Thus as a new writer in London in the 1890s, he found it easier to write short stories for the literary journals of the day, 'with a daily paper under my right elbow' like some kind of talisman.[99] That fondness for his first trade is highlighted in his earlier stories featuring newspapers, such as *The Man Who Would Be King* (1888) and 'A Burgher of the Free State' (1900). In *The Man Who Would Be King*, the journalist-narrator highlights the strange duality of the journalist's existence, hovering indeterminately between palace and gutter: 'Sometimes I wore dress clothes and consorted with Princes and Politicals, drinking from crystal and eating from silver. Sometimes I lay out upon the ground and devoured what I could get, from a plate made of leaves, and drank the running water, and slept under the same rug as my servant.'[100]

Once the 'vagabond' phase is over, the journalist returns to the 'respectable' newspaper office, rigorously working to the timetable of the deadline.[101] In the story one of the rewards of journalism is the regular pattern of crisis and release, both physical and psychological as the deadline is reached and the order to print is given, in contrast to the unfettered anarchy of the native states where most of the story is set:

> I sat there while the type ticked and clicked, and the night-jars hooted at the windows ... as the hands crept up to three o'clock, and machines spun their fly-wheels two or three times to see that all was in order before I said the word that

would set them off, I could have shrieked aloud. Then the roar and the rattle of the wheels shivered the quiet into little bits.[102]

The familiar cycle of crisis and calm is captured with nostalgic fondness in the 1913 poem 'The Press' written alongside 'The Village ...'. In the poem, Kipling presents the striking image of the man who 'Has lit his pipe in the morning calm/That follows the midnight stress', admitting 'He hath sold his heart to the old Black Art/We call the daily Press'.

'The Village ...' is no light nostalgia trip, however. It is one of Kipling's dark revenge fantasies, possibly the darkest of the lot. As in other revenge tales like 'A Friend's Friend' (1888) and 'Steam Tactics' (1904), the avengers are deadly serious. As with the other revenge tales, ridicule is used as a way of righting the wrong and there is certainly delight in the mischievous journalists using the circulation, readership and resources of *The Cake* and *The Bun* newspapers, together with Bat's influence, to heap ridicule upon their quarry and his fiefdom. The fabricated stories begin in a low-key way, provoking indignant letter-writing from Huckley residents, which the journalists give 'good space' to, understanding that all publicity is good publicity.

Other papers start picking up on *The Bun* and *The Cake*'s Huckley stories: the *Spectator* first, then another newspaper, the *Pinnacle*. Other publications including *Punch*, *The Lancet* and the *Times* become involved. The Press Association and Reuters, global news agencies with the latest communications technology at their disposal, are evoked: 'I mean to have it so that when Huckley turns over in its sleep, Reuters and the Press Association jump out of bed to cable.'[103] We are in the first age of mass media where owning a paper or periodical brings access to vast wells of public opinion. Even a 'ponderous architectural weekly' is brought into play to discuss Ingell's contemptuous treatment of the fourteenth-century font he removes from the village church.[104] As the story starts to take on a life of its own, the journalists begin to be slightly afraid. Like the sorcerer's apprentice, they couldn't stop it if they tried. Unlike in *The Man Who Would Be King*, where the order and modernity of the newspaper office represents the civilized world, this modern newspaper office is confused, anarchic and run by men who don't quite understand what it is they are doing. In addition, they are being run by Bat, of whom even the worldly Ollyett is afraid: 'He's the Absolutely Amoral soul. I've never met one yet.'[105] The journalists' amorality and inability or refusal to take responsibility for what they and their papers have done is a disturbing message, which runs counter to most fiction about the press written 1900–1914. Kipling's is virtually a lone voice of warning and it will not be until after the First World War that other writers catch up. Although Kipling's early newspaper training was clearly a source of delight to him, he was also wary of the direction the new commercially driven press was taking. The idea in 'The Village …' that something becomes news simply because the global media says it is, in 1913, is a relatively new idea and is taken up in later fictions (see Chapters 3 and 5).

Huckley is disparaged both in the press reports but also by the narrator in the meta-text of the short story. When the narrator returns to Huckley at the height of the village's notoriety, he is 'disappointed' and finds it 'as mean, as average, as ordinary as the photograph of a room where a murder has been committed'.[106] The village pub and tea shop are making money out of Huckley's notoriety; the sexton's wife is selling post cards of the famous fourteenth-century font, the only piece of heritage in the village, replaced by Ingell with a horrific-sounding 'new one of Bath stone adorned with Limoges enamels'.[107] Huckley, as one might say, is being done up like a kipper. But who is telling us these things about Huckley? Not a detached narrator, nor even a neutral participant who has nothing to gain in describing Huckley in such disparaging terms. We are told these things by one of the agents of revenge, a journalist with shares in *The Bun*. During the story he is rapidly learning his trade, from fabricating events, to creating fantasy correspondents in the letters page, to faking photographs. While reports of Huckley that appear in the newspaper are obvious lies, we must also suspect the meta-text of the narrator's story: 'The Village …' is some kind of 'Dodgy Dossier'.[108] The journalist, with a few well-chosen or ambiguous words, can subtly direct the reader's response to an apparently innocent text. We must be alarmed and afraid, as the narrator keeps telling us he himself is, of this terrifying new force in society, fed by the 'impersonal and searing curiosity' of a new kind of newspaper reader interested in gossip and trivialities rather than serious, political news.[109]

Newspapers, journalists and the craft of fiction

Authors of this early period report in their memoirs mixing the genres of journalism, prose fiction and poetry. For some, like Kipling, journalism helped hone his economical style, and newspapers were the first outlet for his short stories. For others, like Bernard Falk and James Lansdale Hodson (see below), their careers in journalism began with writing fiction for newspapers. When Wodehouse and Jerome K. Jerome were starting out on their literary careers, it seemed perfectly natural for them to mix journalism with fiction. Jerome

K. Jerome, a struggling freelance in the late nineteenth century, records in his memoir he might follow Charles Dickens' career, another journalist-novelist: 'I took up shorthand at this period. Dickens had started his career as a Parliamentary reporter. It seemed to me I could not do better than follow in his footsteps.'[110]

Journalist Russell Stannard, who became news editor of the *Sunday Express* after the First World War, recalls his early days as a reporter on the *Daily Mail* when the fiction editor was an established and powerful member of staff and reporters were encouraged to contribute short stories to the paper.[111] He also recalls other 'men of letters' who seemed happily to divide their time between journalism and fiction, including the popular novelist 'Seamark', who wrote both journalism and fiction for the *Daily Mail* and *Daily Express* in the newspapers' newsrooms.[112]

In another memoir *He Laughed in Fleet Street* (1931) by Bernard Falk, the author, who became editor of the Northcliffe-owned *Sunday Dispatch*, recalls his first job in journalism on the *Urmston and Flixton Telegraph* during the late 1880s. His first piece of copy he had published in the paper was a short story: 'I wrote, and had set up, a short story with a Russian background, entitled "The Woman with the White Hair." Though not so good as Checkoff's (sic) best it pleased the proprietor who agreed to print it.'[113]

As we have seen, writers of fiction were at this time also journalists, and journalists writers of fiction. But the changing demands of a newly professionalising industry were taking their toll on writers' energy and style, as revealed in their fictions. In Gibbs' *The Street of Adventure*, hero Frank Luttrell is a sensitive, educated young man who wants to be a novelist and works as a reporter on Fleet Street until he can earn enough money to support his literary work. Although ultimately Frank rejects fiction in favour of newspaper journalism, in his early days as a reporter he is dismayed at how the subeditors' blue pencil had left his prose just a string of 'jolting sentences and disconnected phrases'.[114]

The idea that journalism is a necessary evil to support the struggling poet or novelist financially is a familiar one, from works written before *The Street of Adventure* to those written in the twenty-first century. Elizabeth Barrett Browning's poem *Aurora Leigh* (1853–1856), written during another period of newspaper proliferation when the abolition of stamp duty brought the price of newspapers down dramatically, is one such literary work to express this dichotomy, contrasting the 'mud' of journalism which she must engage with in order to eat, with her real 'art', poetry.[115] Aurora Leigh finds no redemption in writing to keep alive: 'what you do/For bread will taste of common grain, not grapes'.[116] However, Frank Luttrell appreciates that his journalist training will inevitably aid his fiction work: 'He must get to the heart of life before he could become a man of letters. He must know and see and suffer before he could be a truth-teller.'[117] For Gibbs/Luttrell journalism is not just about earning money to pay for one's 'art': it helps one become a better artist by showing what real life is all about. For Humphrey Quain in *Mightier than the Sword* journalism is an end in itself: he sees no nobler vocation than bringing the news back to his paper, and the prose he writes is not inferior to that of a novelist – maybe indeed journalism is more 'true' than any other kind of writing: 'It did not content him to think that a street lamp was merely a lamp. He would ask himself, almost unconsciously, "What does it look like?" and search for a simile. His thoughts ran in metaphors and symbols.'[118]

In the early years of the twentieth century, newspapers and weekly magazines, continuing the nineteenth-century periodical tradition, carried far more fiction, usually in the form of short stories, serial stories and verse, than they do today. This created opportunities not just for reporters but for fiction writers who gained financially from having a story published in publications such as the *Daily Mail*, *Daily Express* or *T. P.'s Weekly*. Good literary agents would work hard at getting their authors 'boomed' in the popular press to increase sales.[119] Even the *Times* carried a serial story in its weekly edition until the early 1920s including H. G. Wells' *Love and Mr Lewisham* (November 1899 to February 1900) and Arnold Bennett's *Denry the Audacious*, through the Spring of 1910.[120] Although they were glad of the money, however, 'highbrow' writers did not always enjoy seeing their words printed in the popular press. In his autobiography *Return to Yesterday* (1931), Ford Madox Ford recalls an incident when Joseph Conrad tried to throw the art critic Charles Lewis Hind downstairs after Hind congratulated him on having *Nostromo* serialized in the popular *T. P.'s Weekly*:

> Conrad ... despised the journal, and himself more for letting his work appear in it ... This had driven him nearly mad and he had really taken the congratulations of Mr Hind as gloatings over his bitter poverty ... dreadfully harassing poverty alone had driven Conrad, mercilessly, *to that degradation of his art*'. (emphasis added)[121]

Ford and Conrad's co-written novel *The Inheritors* (1901) addresses in fiction the dilemma of the literary man forced, through financial necessity, to have his work published in popular newspapers. In *The Inheritors* the hero, Granger, is very much a struggling 'Victorian man of letters' whose book sales are not enough to survive on. Granger writes sketches of literary and political celebrities for the *Hour*, a weekly paper edited by Fox, 'the Journal-founder', modelled on Alfred Harmsworth.[122] At one point, the contrast between Granger's mercenary journalism and real art is brought to dramatic relief as he sees a sculptor working in a garret opposite him:

> The ink was thick, pale and sticky; the pen spluttered. I wrote furiously, anxious to be done with it. Once I went and leaned over the balcony, trying to hit on a word that would not come ... Through the open window of an opposite garret I could see a sculptor working at a colossal clay model. In his white blouse he seemed big, out of all proportion to the rest of the world.[123]

The insignificance of the narrator's journalism, which tears the 'coarse paper' he is writing on, compared to the almost super-human sculptor creating a work of art renders him ashamed and he experiences a violent attack vertigo.[124] This physical response to a literary dilemma illustrates how acutely writers experienced their struggles for positioning within the field of cultural production. Where their work is published is seen here as every bit as important as what they are writing.

The changing language of newspapers was an outward sign of changes within the field. With increasing emphasis on news came a more stylized, pared-down way of reporting it. We get a taste of reporters adapting to this new style of writing in *Mightier than the Sword* when Humphrey Quain struggles with writing his first news story. His mentor Wratten tells him what to do: 'Don't bother about plans. Start right in with the main facts and put them at the top. Always begin with the facts, and tell the story in the first two paragraphs.'[125]

Similarly Hardcastle, the cub reporter in James Landsale Hodson's *Grey Dawn – Red Night*, is ordered to write 'three hundred words at the outside, first person, with the guts in the first paragraph, not in the last sentence'.[126] In *The Street of Adventure* Frank Luttrell, after a busy day's reporting, is too exhausted to write fiction in the evenings: 'Sometimes when he had an evening alone in his rooms at Staple Inn he sat down before blank sheets of paper with the idea of writing something that would satisfy his desire of artistic expression, but the thought of the day's adventures prevented all concentration of mind.'[127]

We are seeing expressed here – if just hinted at – writers beginning to have difficulty in bridging the worlds of journalism and fiction. However, the field in this period is surprisingly homogenous. Apart from a small section of highly literary writers (such as Henry James and Joseph Conrad – although we have seen that even the latter could not altogether avoid being published in the popular press), novelists also practice journalism in that they contribute sketches, features, short fiction and reviews to the daily and weekly press. The gulf between 'highbrow' writing and newspapers was widening but not unbridgeable. The writers Edmund Gosse and Ford Madox Ford, for example, each edited the *Daily Mail*'s weekly literary supplement during the early 1900s, and Ford filled the pages of the paper with contributions from 'admirable but needy writers'.[128] Journalists are engaged in writing fiction and verse as well as compiling news reports. The roles are virtually interchangeable. In his memoirs, for example, journalist and novelist Keble Howard records: 'I wrote *Love and a Cottage, The God in the Garden* and *Love in June* in the hours between dinner and midnight whilst I was editing *The Sketch* [1899–1904], in addition to writing "Motley Notes", articles for the *Daily Mail*, short stories and any matter that might be wanted in a hurry for *The Sketch*.'[129]

In *The Street of Adventure*, during 'down time' in the newsroom reporters discuss an admirably wide range of 'brows': 'Meredith, the art of Oscar Wilde, the characteristics of Marie Corelli, the latest murder trial'.[130] The popular newspaper newsroom is thus a liberal space within which high- and lowbrow literary culture easily mix. That many of the novels studied here contain lengthy passages regarding the process of writing, both journalism and fiction, suggest journalists in the first few years of the twentieth century were trying to define their position within the field of cultural production, responding to the pressures of being news reporters, yet having grown up with a different expectation and understanding of what 'journalism' was.

Notes

1   Thorne, Guy, *When It Was Dark*, pp. 219 & 326.
2   Ibid., p. 342.
3   Ibid., pp. 163 & 159.
4   Guy Thorne is the pen name of the journalist and author Cyril Ranger Gull. Compton Mackenzie remembers Gull in his memoirs: 'Ranger Gull was a drinker in the grand style. When he went to live in Cornwall he made a habit of concealing bottles of whisky all over the moors so that on country walks he could boast he was never more than a quarter of a mile from refreshment' (Mackenzie, Compton, *My Life and Times*, p. 12).
5   The novel underwent eight further reprints between 1905 and 1909, was the subject of hundreds of sermons and was one of the most talked-about books of its time (Cockburn, Claud, *Bestseller*, pp. 27–50).

6   The idea of the press being the 'Fourth Estate of the realm' appealing to the enlightened forces of public opinion and safeguarding the electorate from corrupt politicians is expressed in the famous *Times* leader of February 1852. Its evolving into a powerful myth, particularly after the launch of the *Daily Mail* and the liberation of newspapers from political interference, is discussed by George Boyce in 'The Fourth Estate'.

7   Trollope, Anthony, *The Prime Minister* (1876). Gissing, George, *New Grub Street* (1891).

8   Thorne, *When It Was Dark*, p. 160.

9   See, for example, Seymour-Ure, Colin, 'Northcliffe's Legacy', pp. 9–23; Bingham, Adrian, *Family Newspapers?* pp. 22–34.

10   Bertrand, Claude-Jean, *The British Press*, p. 17.

11   Political and Economic Planning (PEP), *Report on the British Press*, p. 93.

12   For a thorough examination of the changes in early twentieth-century newspaper content, see, among others, Seymour-Ure, 'Northcliffe's Legacy'; Hampton, Mark, *Visions of the Press in Britain 1850–1950*; Chalaby, Jean, *The Invention of Journalism*.

13   Trevelyan, G. M., 'The White Peril', p. 1047.

14   Evans, B. Ifor, 'The Rise of Modern Journalism', pp. 233–234. Writing in 1930, however, he described it as a 'tragedy' that the press had not grasped its social responsibilities and instead went for commercial success.

15   Dicey, Edward, 'Journalism New and Old', p. 916.

16   Simonis, H., *Street of Ink*, p. 14.

17   Griffiths, Dennis, *Fleet Street*, p. 141.

18   Murdock, Graham and Peter Golding, 'The Structure, Ownership and Control of the Press, 1914–76' p. 130.

19   Koss, Stephen, *The Rise and Fall*, p. 2.

20   See for example memoirs by Fleet Street journalists including Bernard Falk's *He Laughed in Fleet Street* (1931) and Russell Stannard's *With the Dictators of Fleet Street* (1934). Both began their careers in the late nineteenth century in the provinces and rose to become senior executives on the new popular newspapers.

21   Office of National Statistics, Census.

22   Waller, Philip, *Readers Writers, and Reputations*, p. 1011.

23   Gibbs, Philip, *Adventures in Journalism*, pp. 1–8.

24   There is a lengthy reference to Courlander in Gibbs's memoirs (1923 (ii): 145): 'One comrade who has "gone west" as they used to say in time of war, was a brilliant young Jew named Alphonse Courlander ...'

25   See Rudyard Kipling's autobiography *Something of Myself* (1937), especially Chapter Three.

26   See David Glover's introduction to the Oxford Popular Fiction edition of *Four Just Men*, 1995.

27   See Jerome, Jerome K., *My Life and Times*, p. 56,

By luck I came across a chum, one with whom I had gone poaching when a boy. He too had fallen upon evil days and had taken to journalism. He was now a penny-a-liner – or to be exact a three-half-penny a liner. He took me around to police courts and coroners inquests. I soon picked it up. Often I earned as much as ten shillings a week.

28 See *Over Seventy* by P. G. Wodehouse (1957: 28):

There was an evening paper in those days called the *Globe*. It was a hundred and five years old and was printed – so help me – on pink paper … It had been a profitable source of income to me for some time because it ran on its front page what were called Turnovers, thousand-word articles of almost unparalleled dullness which turned over onto the second page. You dug these out of reference books and got a guinea for them.

29 O'Sullivan, Patrick, 'Patrick MacGill', pp. 203–222.

30 Hampton, *Visions of the Press*, p. 7.

31 Taylor, A. J. P., *English History*, p. 187.

32 Low, Frances, *Press Work for Women*, pp. 65–77.

33 'The agricultural labourer and the price of food', *Spectator*, 24 February 1905, p. 8.

34 Wodehouse, *Over Seventy*, p. 28.

35 Wallace, Edgar, *People*, pp. 97–121.

36 Wallace, Edgar, *The Four Just Men*, p. 46.

37 Ibid., p. 45.

38 Wallace, Edgar, *The Council of Justice*, p. 188.

39 See Introduction, p. 1.

40 Gibbs, Philip, *The Street of Adventure*, p. 315.

41 Griffiths, *Fleet Street*, p. 151; Spender, J. A. 'The Press and Public Life', p. 106.

42 James, Lionel, *High Pressure*, p. 252.

43 Advertisement in *The Times*, 22 May 1908: 13.

44 James, *High Pressure*, p. 4.

45 'The Big Battle, First Full Report by Mr G. W. Steevens', *Daily Mail*, 10 September 1898 (The battle took place on September 2).

46 Kaarsholm, Preben, 'Imperialism and New Journalism circa 1900', p. 183.

47 This poem first appeared in the *Pall Mall Magazine*, 40 (July–December 1907).

48 Collected in Sloan, John (ed.), *Selected Poems and Prose of John Davidson*, p. 127.

49 Collected in Davidson, John, *The Poems of John Davidson volume II*, pp. 446–447.

50 See for example Waller, *Readers, Writers and Reputations*; Montefiore, Jan, *Rudyard Kipling*, p. 125.

51 Sloan, *John Davidson*, p. 274.

52 Thurston, Katherine Cecil, *John Chilcote MP*, p. 203.

53 Montague, C. E., *A Hind Let Loose*, pp. 163–164.

54 See the City of London Corporation's *Fleet Street Conservation Area Character Summary* (1996) for a list of late nineteenth and early twentieth-century buildings in and around Fleet Street and associated with the newspaper industry, https://www.cityoflondon.gov.uk/services/environment-and-planning/planning/heritage-and-design/conservation-areas/Documents/Fleet%20Street%20Character%20Summary.pdf and add accessed 22 November 2015.

55 Courlander, Alphonse, *Mightier than the Sword*, p. 47.

56 Thorne, *When It Was Dark*, p. 149.

57 Courlander, *Mightier than the Sword*, p. 85.

58 Ibid., p. 87.

59 See, for example, Chalaby, *Invention of Journalism*, p. 66.

60 Davidson, John, 'Fleet Street' Collected in Davidson, John, *The Poems of John Davidson* volume II, pp. 446–447.

61 Gibbs, *The Street of Adventure*, p. 114.

62 Ibid., p. 154.

63 Ibid., p. 120.

64 Hodson, James Lansdale, *Grey Dawn, Red Night*.

65 MacGill, Patrick, *Children of the Dead End*, pp. 227–228.

66 Ibid., p. 228.

67 Ibid., p. 274.

68 Chalaby, *Invention*, p. 74.

69 Lee, Alan, *Origins of the Popular Press*, pp. 130–160.

70 See for example Koss, Stephen, *Fleet Street Radical* and Chalaby, Jean, 'Northcliffe as Proprietor and Journalist'.

71 Printers at the *Daily Mail* refused to publish the leader which claimed 'A general strike is not an industrial dispute ... It is a movement which can only succeed by destroying the Government and subverting the rights and liberties of the people' (Griffiths, *Fleet Street*, p. 215).

72 Taylor, A. J. P., 'Introduction' to *Edwardian England*, p. 17.

73 Lucas, E. V., *London Lavender*, pp. 66–68.

74 For example L. G. Chiozza Money's Riches and Poverty (1905), Rowntree's Poverty: A Study of Town Life (1901) and Sidney and Beatrice Webb's Minority Report of the Poor Law Commission (1909).

75 Masterman, C. F. G., *From the Abyss*, p. 10.

76 Sergeant, Adeline, *The Work of Oliver Byrd*, p. 224. Adeline Sergeant was a novelist and essayist who worked on the staff of the *People's Friend* magazine 1885–1887 and was a regular contributor until her death in 1904 (Oxford Dictionary of National Biography).

77 Jerome, Jerome K., *Tommy and Co*, p. 25.

78 Brendon, Piers, *The Life and Death of the Press Barons*, p. 85.

79 Sergeant, *The Work of Oliver Byrd*, p. 72.

80 Howard, Keble, *Lord London*, p. 216. Keble Howard is the pen name of John Keble Bell, one-time editor of the *Sketch* and regular contributor to the *Daily Mail* during the Edwardian era (Howard, Keble, *My Motley Life*).

81 See, for example, Philip Gibbs' memoirs *Adventures in Journalism*.

82 Wodehouse, *Over Seventy*, p. 30.

83 Ibid., p. 33.

84 Ibid., p. 58.

85 James, *High Pressure*, p. 254.

86 Ibid., pp. 199–200 & 258.

87 Doyle, Conan, *The Poison Belt*, p. 210.

88 Ibid., p. 212; Doyle, Arthur, *Through the Magic Door*. Although Doyle mainly wrote fiction for a variety of magazines (e.g. *Strand, Cornhill*) as well as newspapers, he spent time as foreign correspondent for the *Westminster Gazette* in Egypt in 1895. He also wrote occasional pieces of journalism, including a write-up of the Marathon in the 1908 Olympics for the *Daily Mail*, of which he was especially proud (Doyle, Arthur Conan, *Memories and Adventures* particularly, pp. 229–235).

89 Kipling, *Something of Myself*, p. 22.

90 Advertisements in the *Civil and Military Gazette*, March 1886, reproduced in Allen, Charles, *Kipling Sahib*, p. 163.

91 For the wide range of falsehoods and secret messages Kipling encountered on the *Civil and Military Gazette*, see Allen, Charles, *Kipling Sahib* particularly, pp. 119–202.

92 Kipling, 'The Village …', p. 163.

93 Ibid., pp. 165 & 167. This description could be attributed to Lord Northcliffe, founder of the mass popular press, who was blonde, blue-eyed and, by 1913, a corpulent figure.

94 In November 2012 a BBC *Newsnight* item incorrectly suggested that the Tory peer Lord McAlpine – without naming him – had sexually abused a young man in a children's home. There then followed a 'Twitter storm' where high-profile 'tweeters' named Lord McAlpine, who successfully sued several of them for libel.

95 Kipling, 'The Village …', p. 207.

96 Kipling, Rudyard, 'The Press', p. 214.

97 Kipling, *Something of Myself*, pp. 109–110.

98 Ibid.

99 Ibid., p. 42.

100 Kipling, Rudyard, *The Man Who Would Be King*, p. 247.

101 Ibid., p. 248.

102 Ibid., p. 250.

103 Kipling, 'The Village …', p. 179.

104 Ibid., p. 194.

105 Ibid., p. 176.

106 Ibid., p. 196.

107 Ibid., p. 194.

108 This is a reference to the dossier compiled by the Blair government to convince the nation we needed to go to war with Iraq in 2003. Its contents have since been found to be unreliable.

109 Kipling, 'The Village ...', p. 191.

110 Jerome, *My Life and Times*, p. 57.

111 Stannard, *With the Dictators of Fleet Street*, pp. 48–49.

112 See also Stannard, *With the Dictators*, p. 48: 'An interesting young man of letters in those days had the name of Shanks. He did not stop very long on the *Mail*, and later won the Hawthornden Prize. I never thought he would like Fleet Street, but he is now one of the brightest spirits on the *Evening Standard*.'

113 Falk, Bernard, *He Laughed in Fleet Street*, p. 22.

114 Gibbs, *The Street of Adventure*, p. 96.

115 The abolition of newspaper stamp duty ('A tax on knowledge') in 1855 had an immediate effect on the numbers of newspapers, and readers. The *Daily Telegraph*, for example, was launched in 1855 at a price of 1d (compared to the *Times*, priced 5d). Griffiths, *Fleet Street*, pp. 92–113.

116 Browning, Elizabeth Barrett, *Aurora Leigh*, p. 125.

117 Gibbs, *The Street of Adventure*, p. 96.

118 Courlander, *Mightier than the Sword*, p. 62.

119 There is a detailed account of the interconnectedness between authors and the popular press, both their need for good reviews and their need for serial stories, in Ford Madox Ford's autobiography *Return to Yesterday*, pp. 182–201.

120 See multiple copies of *The Times*, classified and display advertising pages, 1900–1931.

121 Ford, *Return to Yesterday*, p. 25.

122 Ford, Ford Madox, *Inheritors*, p. 41; McDonald, Peter, *British Literary Culture 1880–1914*, p. 178.

123 Ford, *Inheritors*, p. 121.

124 Ibid., p. 122.

125 Courlander, *Mightier than the Sword*, p. 102.

126 Hodson, *Grey Dawn*, p. 75.

127 Gibbs, *The Street of Adventure*, p. 97.

128 Ford, *Return to Yesterday*, pp. 194–195.

129 Howard, *My Motley Life*, p. 178.

130 Gibbs, *The Street of Adventure*, p. 97.

2

Despatches from the Trenches:
Poets as War Correspondents

War poets react with violent imagery to newspaper coverage of the First World War, their poetry a documentary literature of 'correction' in opposition to the perceived lies, platitudes and lack of dissent against government policy in the press. Writers from a wide range of backgrounds and experiences attack mainstream newspapers for underplaying the horrors of the trenches, now our acknowledged 'national psychic wound'.[1] Other writers attempt to express, in their fictions, how Britain was a country utterly changed by four years of industrial warfare, and the part the press had played in this transformation.

Just a few years after the positive portrayals of the Edwardian period, Siegfried Sassoon's poem 'Fight to a Finish' fantasizes how soldiers returning from the First World War might run the 'Yellow-Pressmen' through with their bayonets:[2]

> The boys came back. Bands played and flags were flying,
> And Yellow-Pressmen thronged the sunlit street
> To cheer the soldiers who'd refrained from dying ...
> Snapping their bayonets to charge the mob,
> Grim Fusiliers broke ranks with glint of steel,
> At last the boys had found a cushy job.
> I heard the Yellow-Pressmen grunt and squeal
> And with my trusty bombers turned and went
> To clear those Junkers out of Parliament.[3]

With violent imagery the poem expresses the hatred that soldiers felt towards journalists, who were seen as having painted an unreal and sanitized account of life in the trenches for the public back home. In linking his dual targets, the 'Yellow-Pressmen' and the 'Junkers' of Parliament as the common enemy, Sassoon is initiating a theme that will be taken up, particularly by writers of the Left in the 1930s: that the role of the press has now become that of defending the agenda of the political elite. The ideas behind the poem foreshadow later ideas of mass media, that its purpose is to 'manufacture consent' among the general public to allow privileged groups to maintain their hold on power.[4] Here, the press in Sassoon's eyes is guilty of manufacturing consent among the British public for the war's prolonged continuation. The phrase 'Fight to a Finish', implying there should be no peace until Germany was crushed, was employed in newspaper headlines, letters, leaders and advertisements throughout the war, particularly in Northcliffe's *Daily Mail* and *Times*, where the phrase occurs more than 100 times from August 1914 to November 1918.[5] Its ironic use in this poem implies there will be no ceasing of hostilities until all the 'Yellow-Pressmen' are dead. Although one of the most prominent critics of the press during the war, Sassoon was by no means the only literary writer to target Fleet Street journalism in his writing during, and immediately after, the conflict. From Ezra Pound's 'flies carrying news' to Max Plowman's accusatory 'the journalistic blather is like a grinning mask on the face of death', writers from a wide range of backgrounds and experiences chose very deliberately to attack mainstream newspapers on a number of fronts: for peddling lies, for dividing a nation and undermining faith in the written word.[6]

Edwardian commentators had expressed unease about the debasing effects of popular journalism 1900–1914 (see Chapter 1), but there was a distinct increase in venom directed at the press by writers, particularly poets, soon after the outbreak of the First World War. The Imagist poet Richard Aldington consistently attacked both the British press and its readers in the *Little Review*, from March 1915. For example: 'newspapers have spoiled our sense of poetry'; 'no man, not even a paid journalist is such a fool to write such stuff in prose'. The hostility continues, on an almost monthly basis. Aldington attacks journalists in prose and in poetic form for expecting to be paid for their work in his poem 'Retort Discourteous': 'They tell/Us we shall never sell/Our works (as if we cared)/We're "highbrow" and long-haired/Because we don't/Cheat and cant'.[7] The idea here that poets tell the truth and are not paid for it, whereas paid journalists 'cheat and cant' is an instance of the major rift between 'literature' and 'journalism' which had imperceptibly been taking place but which during the war and interwar years became increasingly rapid, venomous and vocal. Practitioners of 'art for art's sake' literature – poetry and modernist prose – would adopt a hostile attitude towards journalism and also towards the more worldly and profitable literature of establishment writers, many of whom had very publicly joined the government propaganda machine in September 1914.[8] The enormous and growing resources of the newspaper press, with its 'unexampled circulation', now towered over the 'unpopular weeklies doleful with intellectual tears', according to an analysis by the contemporary novelist and scientist Robert Briffault in the *English Review*. By 1918 the combined circulation of the national daily newspapers was 3.1 million, a hitherto unheard of quantity, with the *Daily Mail* and *Daily Express* selling most.[9] Paper shortages made publishing unprofitable material a difficult prospect. While 'little' literary magazines struggled on through the war, several failed to survive long after the Armistice, including the *Egoist*, *Art and Letters*, *Coterie* and *Wheels*.[10] Royalty payments, publication schedules and the commissioning of imaginative literature were all disrupted, particularly in the first two years of the war.[11] Literature was now 'the only form of printed paper that is becoming uncashable'.[12] The aggressive nature of the poets' attacks on the newspaper press at this time is consistent with Bourdieu's concept of the field of cultural production. When the journalistic field becomes too powerful and starts to distort other fields such as the political and literary fields, then cultural producers, starting with those with least economic capital (i.e. poets), 'more or less frequently' adopt a predictable attitude, which is to 'firmly delimit the field ... to restore the borders threatened by journalistic modes of thought and action'.[13] The time when newspapers and government-sponsored literary propaganda were the dominant media, when low-circulation periodicals were closing and newspaper proprietors were even dictating government policy was clearly a moment for poets to 'restore the borders' of their highbrow endeavours by emphasizing the idea of distinct hierarchies of quality within the field. Like a tribe under siege, they erected a palisade and claimed that everything without was Barbarian. Aldington's 'Retort Discourteous' illustrates this stance: the unpaid poet who tells the truth occupies a rarefied and culturally superior area within the field than the paid and lying journalist.

Over the period of the First World War the subject of journalists and journalism in fiction changes quite dramatically: while the Edwardian novels explain, from an insider's point of view, the struggles and triumphs of the journalist and his trade, now the dominant discourse is from press outsiders adopting a critical stance towards newspapers, journalism and its producers. But the violent imagery is much more than competing agents jockeying for position within a changing field. The imagery is violent because the war was violent and poets were reacting to a virtually total lack of eye-witness reporting of life in the trenches by the news media. Poems addressing war reporting will emphasize the poet's 'I' – illustrating that the poet, unlike the war correspondents who spent much of their time in comfortable chateaux miles from the front line, was actually there, seeing and suffering along with his fellow soldiers.

Other themes emerge during this short period, one being a self-conscious desire first by poets, and then other writers, to break with everything that went before the outbreak of the war. If one, for example, compares Richard Aldington on newspapers spoiling our 'sense of poetry' to the attitude of the prominent turn-of-the-century poet John Davidson (see Chapter 1), the change in attitude is stark. In an essay, 'Pre-Shakespeareanism', Davidson had argued the complete opposite of Aldington: 'the newspaper is one of the most potent factors in moulding the character of contemporary poetry'.[14] Davidson, echoing G. K. Chesterton's idea that news reports constitute 'the poetry of the actual world', states that newspaper articles about grim poverty on the streets of London should be the inspiration of the poet; perhaps his singing of these things will improve the plight of the poor.[15] For Aldington poetry and newspapers belong to two different spheres: 'I am not willing to have a poem read cursorily and quickly as one reads a column of newspaper print ... Mr Yeats is right when he complains that newspapers have spoiled our sense of poetry; we expect poetry to tell us some piece of news, and indeed poetry has no news to tell anyone.'[16]

Aldington is of course very deliberately breaking with his Victorian predecessors, but he is also pointing an accusatory finger at newspapers for undermining readers' ability to admire a poem for its own sake, to work at its meaning, because they have been fed an easy diet of demotic informational prose in bite-size chunks. He is attacking the idea that there has to be some utility in reading. In addition, the political machinations of Max Aitken (later Beaverbrook) and Northcliffe in the period leading up to the deposing of Prime Minister Herbert Asquith (described by Beaverbrook as 'the biggest thing [I] have ever done') led to fears that the democratic process was being controlled by newspaper barons.[17] The appointment of Northcliffe and Beaverbrook to Lloyd George's government only confirmed these fears. Before these themes are discussed in more detail, it is necessary to describe the context from which journalism and literature of the First World War emerged.

Boer War coverage

The previous conflict that war reporters had as template for covering the First World War was the second Boer War (1899–1902). The sieges of Mafeking, Ladysmith and Kimberley were covered with the help and consent of the army, which often provided reporters with telegraphic facilities. Many army officers were commissioned as special correspondents for the newspapers, particularly older and established papers like the *Pall Mall Gazette* and *Daily Telegraph*.[18] Some correspondents, like Edgar Wallace, had been soldiers previously and together the journalists and military correspondents constructed 'a myth of British endurance in appalling circumstances in which the very best characteristics, typical of the British at bay, were demonstrated'.[19] The period 1865–1914 has been described as the 'golden age' of the war correspondent, not least because after Waterloo, no conflict until 1914 threatened the British Isles directly: 'Thrilling accounts of battles, slaughter and bravery could be reported from both sides with no danger of the reader's identifying himself with anyone except the intrepid war correspondent, who, as a result, rapidly became the hero of his own story'.[20] The contemporary writer and journalist H. M. Tomlinson describes how reporting the South African wars was an opportunity for newspaper star writers to hone their prose into something approaching poetry: 'The bright morning-paper stars were rising thickly there [in South Africa], and they sang together of war, in music, with everybody's approval, that was known as prose-poetry'.[21] This, for example, is the *Daily News*' marvellously romantic report of the mass slaughter of Highlanders at Magersfontein on 14 December 1899:

> In a second, in a twinkling of an eye, the searchlights of the Boers fell broad and clear on the doomed Highlanders… The Highlanders reeled from the shock, like trees before the tempest. The best, the bravest fell in that wild hail of lead… Once again the pipes peeled out and 'Lochaber no More' cut through the stillness like a cry of pain, until one could almost hear the widow in her Highland home moaning for the soldier that she would welcome back no more. (*Daily News*, 8 January 1900)

A report of the same event in the *Daily Mail* describes how 'The Highland Brigades marched in quarter columns to their doom, almost falling into the Boer trenches in the dim light of early dawn' (*Daily Mail*, 11 January 1900). Even the sober *Times* described the Boer attack as 'A fusillade that must have emptied the magazine of every Boer Rifle for a space of a quarter of a mile… the most devastating volley that has probably been poured into any body of men' (*Times*, 8 January 1900). This kind of grandiloquent style celebrating magnificent sacrifice is parodied in G. K. Chesterton's novel *The Napoleon of Notting Hill* (1904), about a fantasy war between London Borough 'city states' set in 1984: 'Blood has been running, and is running, in great serpents that curl out into the main thoroughfare and shine in the moon.'[22]

The hyperbolic style developed during the Boer War was initially employed – in a more upbeat way – for the far greater conflict of the First World War. Paul Fussell in *The Great War and Modern Memory* describes how the British

Expeditionary Force's desperate efforts to get to the Belgian sea ports in November 1914, before they were cut off by the German army, were reported using the same journalistic formula as used to describe Edwardian and Georgian adventurers and their 'Race to the Pole'. However, now it was 'The Race to the Sea... Rehabilitated and applied to these new events, the phrase had the advantage of a familiar, sportsmanlike, Explorer Club overtone, suggesting that what was happening was not too distant from playing games, running races and competing in a thoroughly decent way'.[23] The emphasis on 'magnificent sacrifice' appeared justified for the Boer War correspondents who were much closer to the fighting and who suffered alongside the soldiers in the besieged camps and on the field of battle. During the Boer War, Kitchener's tactics had been 'to make the twenty-six correspondents with him run exactly the same risks as his soldiers'.[24] The First World War correspondents were corralled well behind the lines, sometimes miles from the trenches, in the relatively luxurious surroundings of French country houses, with the 'lighted chateaux gleaming white amongst scatheless woods', as described in *Manchester Guardian* journalist C. E. Montague's eloquent expression of post-war regret, *Disenchantment*.[25] Official war artist Major Neville Lytton describes how tightly managed the press were compared to war correspondents in South Africa in his immediate post-war overview, *The Press and the General Staff* (1920):

> In those days [the Boer War correspondent] trotted about on a pony with a pocketful of gold... [but in the First World War] correspondents would be given a lecture on the plan of battle... would go to their rooms, take an early dinner and a few hours' sleep then proceed by motor to some hill-top just behind the battle line... they would all return to their mess by two o'clock.[26]

Boer War correspondent Lionel James, who fought as a soldier in the First World War, also notes this contrast in his memoirs:

> In the days of which I am now writing [Boer War], the business of a Correspondent in the Field enabled him to see for himself at least a panel of the events he had to chronicle. The Great War produced another order of things, and the War correspondent was denied the liberty of movement and the choice of subject-matter that was possible in my time.[27]

Several Boer War correspondents were killed, others badly injured from being close to the fighting. Edgar Wallace records as follows in his memoir: 'From a hill I watched the Battle of Belmont, and later saw E. F. Knight, the *Morning Post* correspondent, with his arm shattered by a bullet'. The *Daily Mail* correspondent Hellawell was captured by the Boers trying to get his despatches out of besieged

Mafeking. G. W. Steevens of the *Daily Mail* and Mitchell of the *Standard* died of 'enteric' (typhoid) at Ladysmith in early 1900.[28] Steevens' death provoked expressions of regret from the army commanders Kitchener and Roberts as well as all the London newspapers, some of them fierce rivals of the *Daily Mail*.

Correspondents in the First World War were accused of covering up tragedy and defeat, whereas reporters covering the Boer War appeared to relish telling the story of magnificent sacrifice. While writers parodied some Boer War correspondence, other journalists employed a 'brisk and vivid realism' which was imitated, rather than derided, by poets of the Boer War.[29] G. W. Steevens' despatches for the *Daily Mail* transcended even Tomlinson's idea of 'prose-poetry'. The impressionistic style – described as 'literature in its truest sense' by his employer Alfred Harmsworth (*Daily Mail*, 22 January 1900) – with which he reports the progress of a gun battle lies right on the interface between journalism and poetry, with its experimental style and form expressing the disorientation of men in war.

> Ting-a-ling-a-ling! buzzed the telephone bell.
>
> The gaunt up-towering mountains, the long, smooth, deadly guns – and the telephone bell.
>
> The mountains and the guns went out, and there floated in that roaring office of the *Daily Mail* instead, and the warm, rustling vestibule of the playhouse on a December night. This is the way we make war now; only for the instant it was half joke and half home-sickness. Where were we?
>
> 'Right-hand Gun Hill fired, sir' came the even voice of the blue jacket. 'At the balloon.'
>
> 'Captain wants to speak to you sir,' came the voice of the sapper from under the tarpaulin.
>
> Whistle and rattle and pop went the shell in the valley below...[30]

The dizzying sequence of sounds – the telephone, the guns, the 'roaring' newspaper office, the theatre crowd and the exchange between soldiers – and sights – the 'up-towering mountains', the guns and the bright blue of the soldier's jacket – are a bold attempt in a popular newspaper to express the profound confusion of being caught up in conflict. Steevens carefully crafted his phrases as well as his persona as the war-weary correspondent: 'more death-piping bullets than ever. The air was a sieve of them'; 'tack-tap, tack-tap, each shot echoed a little muffled from the hills, tack, tack-tap as if the devil was hammering nails'; 'I am sick of it – everybody's sick of it ... nothing to do but endure'. His and other correspondents' Boer War reportage presented precisely the 'forceful challenge' to fictional realism that has been identified in late nineteenth-century and early twentieth-century journalism.[31] Why read fiction if the journalist can report real life just as well, or better?

Newspapers and dissent

The British soldiers sent to fight the Boer War made up Britain's first 'truly literate' army.[32] There certainly was an outpouring of poetry, both from the troops and from those back home, during this conflict, but there was little specifically focused on the press. While troops' papers in the First World War trenches would parody and satirize the war correspondents, in South Africa the correspondents helped edit contributions from soldiers. G. W. Steevens of the *Daily Mail* and W. T. Maud of the *Graphic* edited the *Ladysmith Lyre*, which welcomed contributions in verse and prose from the ordinary soldiers.[33] Back home the newspaper press was split over the rights and wrongs of the Boer War, with the *Morning Leader*, *Pall Mall Gazette* and the *Daily News* taking anti-imperialist stances and the *Daily Chronicle* changing tack to becoming imperialist during proceedings.[34] The *Manchester Guardian* under C. P. Scott was highly critical of British military action.[35] As a result, anti-war poets and writers had wide access to the public, through newspapers, as well as pacifist periodicals. A poem by Herbert Cadett, published in the *Daily Chronicle* on 20 October 1899, for example, reads: 'A lung and a Mauser bullet; pink froth and half-choked cry… A burning throat that each gasping note scrapes raw like a broken shell'. These lines presage the close-up horror of Wilfred Owen's 'froth-corrupted lungs' of a gas victim, discussed below. The vivid depiction of bloody and painful death in the Boer War was published, however, in a widely read daily newspaper, not a small-circulation poetry volume, thus obviating the pressing desire felt among the First World War poets to publish a 'literature of correction', much of it aimed against the press. During the First World War dissent was virtually absent from mainstream papers. Penalties for publications which strayed too far from government policy were heavy. The respected radical journal the *Nation*, for example, was banned from exporting overseas in April 1917 because it was perceived to be in favour of suing for peace.[36] In 1917 the writer S. K. Ratcliffe commented that in contrast to the current state of affairs, in previous conflicts England at war had 'always meant an educated public bitterly divided, with the intellectuals mostly in opposition. Even during the Napoleonic wars, some of the greatest writers of the age were openly admiring of their country's arch-enemy'.[37] Nicholas Hiley argues, however, that the two-week suppression of *The Globe* newspaper in

November 1915 after it reported the imminent resignation of Kitchener was all the evidence editors needed that government censure would be implacable if newspapers strayed beyond the strict limits imposed by the Press Bureau.[38]

There were shortcomings in the Boer War reporting, for the famous 'first casualty' phrase can be applied without exception to every conflict. Correspondents working for imperialist newspapers 'played their part in encouraging jingoism and circulating stories of Boer atrocities'.[39] In his much-admired volume on war correspondence, *The First Casualty*, Phillip Knightley cites two specific examples where newspaper correspondents ignored British failings: the scandalous lack of even basic supplies such as bandages and sheets at the military hospitals – although the MP who exposed this, William Burdett-Coutts, published his findings in the *Times*. The second major issue of the concentration camps for Boer women and children, where thousands died, was brought to light by the Quaker campaigner Emily Hobhouse.[40] But this was not a censored topic: there was at the time much debate and correspondence – with plenty of arguments on both sides – in the pages of the national press throughout 1901 on this issue.

Criticism of the First World War press coverage

The failures of the British Press during the First World War have been well chronicled: 'More deliberate lies were told than in any other period of history … a large share of the blame for this must rest with the British war correspondents.'[41] Devastating post-war demolitions of false 'atrocity stories' published in newspapers – such as the claim that the Germans boiled down their dead to provide lubricating oil, a report initially published in the *Times* – were provided as early as the mid-1920s by Arthur Ponsonby (*Falsehood in Wartime*, 1928), Harold Lasswell (*Propaganda Techniques in the First World War*, 1927) and others. Other stories, all later found to be mendacious propaganda, were printed as fact in the press. Here is just a small selection: 'Baby Bayoneted … an infant callously dragged from its sick mother and thrown from the window to bayonet point' (*Daily Express*, 10 October 1914); 'German Atrocities … One man whom I did not see told an official of the Catholic Society that he had seen with his own eyes German soldiery chop off the arms of a baby which clung to its mother's skirts' (*Times*, 28 August 1914); 'Murdered priests – Germans' appalling record … 27 priests in the Bishopric of Namur killed and 12 missing' (*Telegraph*, 16 December 1914); 'The Germans and their Dead … There is a sickly smell in the air as if glue were being boiled. We are passing the great Corpse Utilisation Establishment' (*Times*, 19 April 1917).

In the first few weeks of the war, British newspaper correspondents struggled to get near the fighting, but without help from the army their job was exceedingly difficult. Within a few weeks, in marked contrast to his attitude during the Boer War, Kitchener had branded war correspondents as outlaws liable to arrest if found anywhere near the Western Front.[42] After May 1915, the five accredited correspondents representing most daily newspapers were allowed to work in France, but the army controlled heavily their access to information and their mobility.[43] War correspondents saw it as their duty to censor their reports, highlighting the good and glossing over the bad. Philip Gibbs, one of the five accredited correspondents, admits in his memoir: 'There was no need of censorship of our dispatches. We were our own censors.'[44] The correspondents, censored by the army and imposing their own censorship, evolved an upbeat, triumphal style of reporting that became notorious. Bombardments were 'terrific', battles were 'glorious'; the Germans ('the Hun') were generally presented as being disorganized, in retreat or having come off worst in any major skirmish. One can only now read reports telling readers: 'we have economised life, not squandered it, on these fields' (*Daily Mail*, 6 December 1917) with a terrible poignancy and also anger.

Were newspapers actively prevented from reporting the truth about the war? Colin Lovelace argues that the tiny handful of prosecutions of editors under the 1914 Defence of the Realm Act suggests that the 'sanctions' against newspapers reporting the war more thoroughly were merely a smokescreen for poor journalistic standards.[45] Perhaps the powerful sanction of a fall in circulation when publishing 'unpatriotic' reports was more important; after the *Daily Mail*'s critical report on the lack of shells at the front on 21 May 1915, the paper lost nearly a quarter of a million sales within a week.[46] In place of 'hard' news, writers, many established and highly respected such as Hilaire Belloc, Arnold Bennett and Arthur Conan Doyle, and journalists, filled the vacuum with upbeat propaganda, in which they concealed the 'sordid reality' of trench warfare.[47] Authors were motivated by both a sense of patriotic duty and the need for money; often writing propaganda was the only way they could now get paid work. Younger writers who served in the trenches 'turned against their elders', having 'lost confidence in the authority of the written word'.[48] Before the War Office made arrangements for the five accredited war correspondents to cover the war from France in spring 1915, many journalists tried, mostly unsuccessfully, to get near the action. Philip Gibbs describes in his memoirs how 'distinguished old-time war correspondents' were kept 'kicking their heels in waiting rooms of Whitehall, week after week, and month after month ... in the absence of firm news ... it must be admitted that the liars had a great time'.[49] H. M. Tomlinson, a reporter and leader writer for the liberal *Daily News*, who tried to cover the war without army help in the early weeks, fictionalized his failed efforts in *All Our Yesterdays* (1930). The novel, published like much war fiction in the late 1920s and early 1930s, traces the initial excitement and gradual disenchantment of a war correspondent who, unable to report the war independently, takes a job as an official correspondent working directly for the War Office, as Tomlinson himself did from late 1914 until 1917. The anonymous narrator describes the fruitless journey he and fellow foreign correspondent Jim Maynard make from Amiens through northern France, sometimes accompanied by soldiers going one way, other times by refugees going another, relying on censored French newspapers and the distant sound of guns as their only guides to where the action was. Unable to report on the actions and treated dismissively by British army officers, they are expelled from the area and retreat to Paris before heading back to London. The fictionalized account is based on Tomlinson's real-life experience, described in his essay 'On Being Out of Date'. The 'palm trees' metaphor partly explains the state of mind of journalists and censors at the time:

> I was soon on the Continent ... The telegraphs and telephones were dead, and at first a war-correspondent was an outlaw ... I saw British infantry, in the early weeks of that war, swinging along towards it, singing 'Tipperary'. The song was not sung in France after the September of that year, though it remained a favourite at home. To this day when I hear that foolish and sentimental air, I know very well why a man has been known to go apart, to think over what might have been, and what is, and to weep in secret ... Perhaps here I had better bear in mind an Arab proverb, reminding us that it is good to know the truth, but better to know it and talk of palm trees.[50]

British newspapers were readily available in France and soldiers on leave or convalescing back in England were also able to see how the war was being reported back home. Another 'War' novel written by a journalist is *Grey Dawn – Red Night* (1929) by James Lansdale Hodson. The heavily autobiographical novel depicts a friendly, enlightened pre-1914 newsroom offering the hero John Hardcastle an escape from cotton mill work that was the fate of his siblings. However, Hardcastle, who joined up in 1914, experiences shame for his profession as a soldier in the trenches: 'Those damned war correspondents – writing about troops going into battle with a football; making a game of it ... Doubtless they had to write cheerfully; victory piled upon victory. He felt a little ashamed of journalism.'[51]

Hardcastle himself has a letter home destroyed because in it he had criticized the loss of 'hundreds upon hundreds' of men for the sake of capturing 'a few yards of wood'. As a journalist, he was embarrassed that while his and other soldiers' truthful accounts were being destroyed, back home, thanks to the press, 'people think war's a joke'.[52]

Soldiers' letters to friends back home reveal the disgust they felt towards newspapers. This one, by the poet Max Plowman – who would between the wars become a prominent pacifist – is dated 13 August 1916:

> I find there's very little to read out here. The newspapers on the war are nauseating ... whether the general censorship is to blame or not I don't know but it's all unreal – the horror and terror and misery are all 'written down' or covered with sham heroics by cheap journalism ... truth has been sunk so deeply down the well now one wonders how long it will take to draw her up again ... and the journalistic blather is like a grinning mask on the face of death.[53]

The young Sir Alan 'Tommy' Lascelles, a minor aristocrat who served as a cavalry officer during the war, in a letter written on 27 September 1916, sympathizes with a friend over the loss of a mutual acquaintance: 'Their [the Grenadier Guards] performances catch one by the throat like some passage in Homer; even these vulgar, lying journalists cannot make them ridiculous, because all their fulsome adjectives fall below the truth.'[54]

Siegfried Sassoon's reaction to the articles he read while convalescing is recorded in his fictionalized *Memoirs of an Infantry Officer* (1930):

> As I opened a daily paper one morning and very deliberately read a dispatch from 'War Correspondents' Headquarters': 'I have sat with some of the lads, fighting battles over again, and discussing battles to be,' wrote some amiable man who had apparently mistaken the war for a football match between England and Germany ... I wondered why it was necessary for the Western Front to be attractively advertised by such intolerable twaddle. What was this camouflage War which was manufactured by the Press to aid the imaginations of people who had never seen the real thing?[55]

Like Lascelles and Plowman, Sassoon feels the enormous sacrifices which he and his comrades have been making have been misrepresented and trivialized by the press. The idea that the slaughter of thousands has been presented to the reading public as some kind of football match breeds results in an outpouring of shocking, violent, vivid poetry as writers who had suffered in the trenches correct what they perceive to be a false impression. The poets' strategy was clear: reviewing Sassoon's poetry in July 1918, Virginia Woolf describes Sassoon's 'terrible pictures which lie behind the colourless phrases of the newspapers'.[56]

As in the Boer War, the First World War provoked a tidal wave of poetry from the fighting men and civilians. Memoirs by men who had served reveal the trenches and the behind-the-lines billets as literary spaces where books, newspapers and journals were read, freely shared and created and where more than 2,000 soldier-poets were creating verse from 'genius to doggerel'.[57] Correspondents and writers were subjected to ridicule in trench newspapers such as *The Wipers Times* and the *BEF Times*.[58] The *Daily Mail*'s William Beach Thomas, for example, was nicknamed 'Teech Bomas' and here his style, describing tank movements, is lampooned in the *BEF Times*: 'How could one fear anything in the belly of a perambulating peripatetic progolodymythorus ... every wag of our creature's tail threw a bomb with deadly precision and the mad, muddled murderers melted.'[59]

As well as daily newspapers, literary journals including the *Times Literary Supplement* and even the pacifist *Cambridge Magazine* were read by troops in France.[60] The poet Edmund Blunden recalls how his commanding officer was 'overjoyed' to read in the *T.L.S.* that one of his men had had a volume of poetry published.[61] In his memoir of the war, he notes ironically how, when called to engage in a skirmish, 'I had to thrust aside my *Cambridge Magazine* with Siegfried Sassoon's splendid War on the War in it' and take up arms. In 1919 T. S. Eliot noted that soldier-poets had either produced 'Romance' or 'Reporting' from the trenches, the 'Romance' giving way to 'Reporting' under the grim weight of evidence.[62] By 1916, Robert Graves was writing of the death and suffering he encountered, repudiating the early war poetry of 1914–1915 which still maintained chivalric notions of fighting and dying for one's country, as exemplified in Rupert Brooke's famous '1914' Sonnets. Graves' poem 'A Dead Boche' (1916) shows he has had enough of idealized images of the war:

> To you who'd read my songs of War
> And only hear of blood and fame ...
> Today I found in Mametz Wood
> A certain cure for lust of blood:
> Where, propped against a shattered trunk,
> In a great mess of things unclean,
> Sat a dead Boche; he scowled and stunk
> With clothes and face a sodden green
> Big bellied, spectacled, crop-haired,
> Dribbling black blood from nose and beard.[63]

The image, unsparing in its detail of stench and decay, is, as signalled in the first line, a correction to earlier poems that had tended to romanticize the conflict. The cure is as much for himself as for the readers. The emphasis on 'Today *I* found' is a signal to readers that what he has to say now is much more important than idealized images of magnificent sacrifice that characterized the early weeks of the war, before the blood started flowing.[64] He is a first-hand eyewitness, a war correspondent without a newspaper. The image of the 'sodden green' rotting soldier, the stench of death and the 'black blood' is like a close-up photograph and is enormously shocking. The soldier has clearly been dead some time, but has been left unburied, 'propped' like a puppet or doll in a ludicrous position. The poem is meant to have a curative effect, to shatter complacent and unreal notions of what the war was like, held by civilians, 'whose vaguely romantic ideas of war had been rendered even more hopelessly false by distorted newspaper accounts'.[65] In this poem the press is not explicitly mentioned, but in others it is, and as early as December 1915, soldier-poets were accusing the press of distorting the truth or whipping the British public into a jingoistic frenzy. Edward Thomas, for example, an established writer by 1914, enlisted in the Artists Rifles in July 1915 and in December of that year, while waiting to sail to France, wrote 'This Is No Case of Petty Right and Wrong', attacking the black-and-white portrayal of the war in the newspapers:

> I hate not Germans, nor grow hot
> With love of Englishmen to please newspapers.[66]

In this poem, he blames the press for stoking bellicose sentiments in the public. The 'one fat patriot' he hates more than the Kaiser is a complacent editor sitting in his office in Fleet Street creating jingoistic images in his 'cauldron' that put the public under a spell, unable to see or hear the truth through the war clamour conjured up by the papers.

Press reports read by the troops would certainly have confirmed the impression that the public back home were told nothing of the soldiers' suffering. The downplaying of the effects of a new kind of chemical warfare in the spring of 1915 – gas – was particularly heinous. Here, for example, is an account of a gas attack during the Battle of Ypres, May 1915, as reported in the *Times*: 'A Match for German Chemicals: The wind however was strong and dissipated the fumes quickly, our troops did not suffer seriously from their noxious effects' (*Times*, 3 May 1915). One report in the *Daily Mail* describes the effects of gas as 'only temporary' (26 April 1915). At other times articles report that Germans

(*Daily Mail*, 24 September 1917) and Italians (*Daily Mail*, 29 October 1917) are killed by gas to which the British appear impervious. There is only a veil of silence over the effects on British troops even when it was reported that 600 shells were 'pitched' into the British trenches. The article is titled 'German Rush Checked' (*Daily Mail*, 1 January 1918) and it only mentions the 'drenching' of British soldiers in gas in passing, with no reference to its effects. The reality was very different. Estimates of total gas casualties (deaths and injuries) during the war range from 560,000 to 1.3 million, with 186,000 men from the British Expeditionary Force either killed or injured.[67] Chlorine gas, used initially, caused more deaths at the front, while Phosgene, used later, caused long-term injuries and death through 'drowning of the lungs' from three hours to several days after exposure.[68] Wilfred Owen's famous account of a gas attack in his poem 'Dulce et Decorum est' (1917), written in response to pro-war propaganda, provides eye-witness testimony, whereas the newspaper accounts rely on censored Press Bureau information:

> Gas! Gas! Quick, boys! – An ecstasy of fumbling,
> Fitting clumsy helmets just in time;
> But someone still was yelling out and stumbling
> And flound'ring like a man in fire or lime …
> Dim, through the misty panes and thick green light,
> As under a green sea, I saw him drowning …
> In all my dreams, before my helpless sight,
> He plunges at me, guttering, choking, drowning.[69]

Owen's own first-hand 'reporting' of the attack is underlined in the poem by his watching the dying man through the 'misty panes' of his gas mask. Again and again the poet underlines his authority to describe the effects of gas: 'I saw him … my sight … and watch … If you could hear.' His description of the soldier's tongue, covered in 'vile incurable sores', suggests that he will not be able to speak of his experience, if he lives. It is therefore the poet-witness' duty to record the event. The documentary attention to detail in this and other poems from the trenches ('Men marched asleep. Many had lost their boots/But limped on, blood-shod') again emphasizes that this is more than poetry. This is reportage. The poets' position as first-hand reporters is contrasted with journalists relying on hearsay in Siegfried Sassoon's poem 'The Effect', wherein he quotes an extract from a newspaper article using the now-suspicious and degraded phrase 'one man told me': 'The effect of our bombardment was terrific. One man told me he had never seen so many dead before.'[70]

A divided nation

Siegfried Sassoon again mocks the inadequacy of the press in his poem 'Editorial Impressions' (1917):

> He seemed so certain 'all was going well,'
> As he discussed the glorious time he'd had
> While visiting the trenches. 'One can tell
> You've gathered big impressions!' grinned the lad
> Who'd been severely wounded in the back
> In some wiped-out impossible Attack ...
> I hope I've caught the feeling of 'the Line'
> And the amazing spirit of the troops
> By Jove, those flying-chaps of ours are fine!
> I watched one daring beggar looping loops
> Soaring and diving like some bird of prey ...
> The soldier sipped his wine
> 'Ah yes but it's the Press that leads the way!'[71]

The unobservant journalist appears more interested in whether he has used the right imagery in his piece ('I hope I've caught the feeling ...') than in the soldier's serious injury. The journalist – who, the poet makes clear, is only 'visiting' – has failed in his duty to report the conditions in the trenches: he concentrates not on the young wounded soldier on the ground, but the antics of the planes in the sky above him, which lend themselves more easily to his upbeat language: 'soaring and diving like some bird of prey'. Judging by the movement of the plane, however, it is clear the pilot is engaged in some life-or-death dogfight of which the journalist is apparently unaware. The journalist is looking up, averting his gaze from where it should be keenly focused. The young soldier has been wounded in the back – not, then, by the Germans in front of him, but by his military masters and, one infers, the press back home.

This idea of the 'Enemy to the Rear' is explored in Paul Fussell's *The Great War and Modern Memory*, where he concludes: 'The visiting of violent and if possible painful death upon the complacent patriotic, uncomprehending, fatuous civilians at home was a favourite fantasy indulged by the troops.'[72] The resentment the soldiers feel for people back home is emphasized in James Lansdale Hodson's novel *Grey Dawn – Red Night*. One day the soldiers at the front read in the newspaper about an explosion in a munitions factory in England, causing many civilian casualties, and instead of being horrified, the soldiers nod approvingly: 'That's the stuff. That'll wake them up.' In gruesome rivalry they then complain about the amount of coverage the factory explosion receives, whereas when their entire battalion is wiped out, 'not a word of it' is printed in the papers.[73] The war correspondent in H. M. Tomlinson's novel *All Our Yesterdays* explores the same theme. Recalling a visit to the trenches, the narrator realizes he and the soldiers are divided by an unbridgeable gulf: 'we now belonged to different spheres... The war was getting old. We had drifted apart'.[74] Soldiers' alienation towards the public back home is explored in Wilfred Owen's poem 'Smile Smile Smile', written towards the end of the war after reading articles in the *Daily Mail* and *Times* relaying empty promises from politicians. His exasperated 'O Siegfried make them stop!' in a letter to Sassoon explaining the impetus for the poem, like Sassoon's 'Fight to a Finish', links politicians and newspapers in some kind of joint enterprise of disinformation:[75]

> Head to limp head the sunk-eyed wounded scanned
> Yesterday's *Mail*: the casualties (typed small)
> And (large) Vast Booty from our latest Haul.
> Also they read of Cheap Homes, not yet planned,
> 'For' said the paper, 'when this war is done
> The men's first instincts will be making homes.
> Meanwhile their foremost need is aerodromes
> It being certain war has but begun ...
> The greatest glory will be theirs who fought,
> Who kept this nation in integrity.'
> Nation? The half-limbed readers did not chafe
> But smiled at one another curiously
> Like secret men who know their secret safe.
> Pictures of these broad smiles appear each week
> And people in whose voice real feeling rings
> Say: How they smile! They're happy now, poor things.[76]

Although the poem lacks the violence of Sassoon's 'Fight to a Finish', it accuses the press not only of distorting the truth about the war but of encouraging its continuation. The feelings of the wounded soldiers are a warning of the social unrest that is to come in the following years, and offer an explanation of why the soldiers will feel so alienated upon their return: 'Nation? The half-limbed readers did not chafe/But smiled at one another curiously.' The 'Nation' may be kept safe from the Germans, but it will be divided in another, potentially more damaging way. Even this is not enough for Owen: the ironic smiles are snapped by the press photographers and published in the papers, stupidly misinterpreted by the readers back home as smiles of happiness at the thought of cheap homes when the war is over. Yet the 'half-limbed' soldiers disdain the hollow government promises, the propagandists of the press and the gullible readers in Britain. Robert Graves in his celebrated memoir *Goodbye to All That* (1929) similarly observes that the war had created a great divide between the combatants and those at home, and that newspapers were responsible: 'England looked strange to us returned soldiers. We could not understand the war-madness that ran wild everywhere, looking for a pseudo-military outlet. The civilians talked a foreign language; and *it was a newspaper language*' (emphasis added).[77]

Non-combatants

The public, of course, was not unaware of what was going on at the front. Many women volunteered as nurses (VADs) and saw for themselves the wounds and the shell shock. The regular, dreaded telegrams from the War Office punctuated daily life. Newspapers became a bizarre parallel universe, but also contradicted themselves. While news pages reported 'terrific' and 'glorious' battles, the features pages offered advice on how to cope with bereavement, cheap ways of dyeing clothes black for funerals and recipes for feeding long-term convalescents.[78] The growing lists of British casualties published daily in the press were increasingly at odds with the upbeat accounts of the war found on adjacent pages. Vera Brittain notes in her famous memoir *Testament of Youth* (1933):

> As usual the Press had given no hint of that tragedy's dimensions, and it was only through the long casualty lists, and the persistent demoralising rumours that owing to a miscalculation in time thousands of our men had been shot down by our own guns, that the world was gradually coming to realise something of what the engagement had been.[79]

This strange disjuncture between upbeat news reports and the inescapable reality that thousands of men were being killed and wounded is explored in a number of wartime novels. Very early on in the war, writers, whose currency is the written word, began to worry about the implications of a daily dose of fantasy in the newspapers. The writer Arnold Bennett, for example, records in his journal having lunch on 9 May 1915 with fellow writers including H. G. Wells where they agree to launch a campaign against 'yellow-pressism'. In the October of that year, he has lunch with an officer who had spent ten months in Ypres: 'He said the newspaper correspondents' descriptions of men eager to go up over the parapet made him laugh. They never were eager ... he had seen a whole company of men extremely pale with apprehension and shaking so they could scarcely load their rifles.'[80] In his wartime novel *Mr Britling Sees It Through* (1916), H. G. Wells vividly portrays the confusion among the civilian population reading of English victories, on the one hand, yet, on the other, being told of an ever-advancing German army: 'the defeated Germans continued to advance'. Britling and his son Hugh spend one Sunday reading the *Observer*, noting with astonishment that the Germans, who according to despatches 'had been mown down in heaps', were closing in on Paris.[81]

Rose Macaulay's novel *Non-Combatants and Others* (1916) vividly describes both confusion and wilful delusion on the home front. In May 1915, Macaulay, who would later become one of the most successful women writers of the interwar years, gave up her fledgling literary career in London and signed up as a VAD. She worked at a large house in Great Shelford, where her parents lived and which had been converted into a convalescent home. There she saw, at first hand, the wounded and traumatized soldiers, less than a year into the war.[82] In *Non-Combatants and Others*, soldiers in the trenches lie in their upbeat letters home; civil servants with 'inside information' withhold information about the manner in which soldiers die; non-combatants smother their feelings as their loved ones depart for France. War correspondents of course distort the reality of life at the front. Communication and lack of it are themes running throughout the novel: the entire nation appears to be engaged in some vast exercise in deception and newspapers are often implicated in the distortions of the truth. Stories about German spies, Zeppelin attacks, atrocities and low enemy morale are regularly discussed by the occupants of 'Violette', a suburban villa representing the middle-class reading public:

> The *Evening Thrill* came in, and Kate opened it, for Mrs Frampton liked to hear tit-bits of news while she worked. 'Stories impossible to doubt,' read Kate in her prim, precise voice, 'reach us continually of atrocities practised by the enemy ...' Kate next read a letter of a private soldier at the front. 'The Boches are all cowards. They can't stand against our boys. They fly like rabbits when we charge with the bayonet. You should hear them squeal like so many pigs. There's not a German private in the army that wants to fight ... It's wonderful how long the war goes on, since all the Germans are like that,' said Kate.[83]

Kate's evidently unironic sentence expresses similar puzzlement to Britling and his son, who cannot make sense of reports of the defeated Germans. When newspapers do, occasionally, report the truth, no one believes them anyway. Mrs Vinney, a visitor to Violette, reveals an advanced cynicism about the newspapers although she has lost the ability to distinguish truth from lies: 'It's not a bit of use being depressed by the news, because no one can ever tell if it's true or not ... Why, they said there weren't any Russians in England, when everyone knew there were crowds.'[84] Another wartime novel featuring journalists which dissects the public's increasing suspicion of the press during hostilities is Stephen McKenna's *Sonia* (1917). The novel, a wonderful period piece and now sadly long-forgotten, traces the fortunes of a group of young graduates from Oxford, from 1898 through to 1915, and although its main theme is the complacency of Britain's public school-educated 'Governing Classes', the press comes in for particular scrutiny. McKenna agrees with contemporary opinion, both in fiction and non-fiction, that while the pre-1914 press was not perfect, it was worlds away from what it became during and after the war. The narrator, George Oakleigh, a Liberal politician, becomes increasingly disillusioned with public life as the war progresses and describes how the press had managed to 'drug the sense of a nation, to render an impassive people neurotic, to debauch the mind of a generation'.[85] Oakleigh sees the press as responsible for the fall of the Liberal government he had served in and its replacement by a coalition which was 'a London journalistic triumph, desired of no man but foisted on the country by large headlines and hard leader writing'.[86] Oakleigh concludes, after surveying British society in the first few months of 1915: 'In May I was to find that politics and journalism had so eaten their way into our being that even the scalpel of war failed to dislodge them. Unborn tomorrow must curb its press or educate itself into independence of it.'[87]

Oakleigh's bitterness reflects McKenna's own feelings; long involved in Liberal politics, McKenna saw the First World War as the burial ground of British Liberalism. His suggestion that a future generation may need to 'curb its press' echoes current debates over press standards and the threat of statutory control. He saw the new aggressive, cynical journalism that the war gave birth to, as complicit in the murder of his political faith, as his memoirs reveal: 'A British political faith has never been so tidily demolished as was British liberalism, with its organisation and its army, at the hands of a Welsh solicitor [Lloyd George], an Irish newspaper proprietor [Northcliffe], a Canadian financier [Beaverbrook] and their satellites, aided by the inexorable logic of events.'[88]

'You can't believe a word you read'

Ezra Pound's ironic comment in an article in the literary journal *The New Age* in October 1919 that 'in recognising that the *Daily Mail* has won the war one should also consider that it would in due time create an order of things in which there would be no art, no literature, no manners, no civilisation' speaks for the way the literary classes were now opening up a front against their new enemy.[89] After four years of lies and propaganda, it was necessary to restore faith in the written word for those who lived by it. One way of doing this was to cast out the lowest agent in the field – 'the paid journalist' – blamed for a drop in standards. The writers' task was an urgent one before cynicism and journalism, as they saw it, rendered their product redundant. Even the unthinking residents of 'Violette' in Rose Macaulay's *Non-Combatants and Others* can't get over the suspicion, when reading the papers, that there is now some kind of *agenda* attached to the information they read, that they are being hoodwinked in a concerted manner: 'Lord Northcliffe says so doesn't he?' a character replies when someone questions why conscription is needed.[90] It was not enough for the war poets to attempt to correct perceptions of life in the trenches. They had to go further: associate the 'carefully taught parrot press' with lies, and associate their more literary output with truth.[91] As C. E. Montague concluded in his contribution to immediate post-war debate, *Disenchantment*: 'So it comes that each of several million ex-soldiers now reads every solemn appeal of a Government, each beautiful speech of a Premier or earnest assurance of a body of employers with that maxim on guard in his mind – "You can't believe a word you read."'[92]

It is not possible, however, to wrap this chapter up so simply and neatly. The field of cultural production is, after all, governed by human agents who as well as seeking cultural and economic capital seek political and moral influence and satisfaction in personal relationships too, which are all changeable and hard-to-pin-down variables. British newspapers have always been a broad, pluralistic and cacophonous body produced by an 'unorganized multitude of persons' according to H. G. Wells in a contemporary commentary, and within their pages, there is room for a wide range of views.[93] Despite newspapers and literature being in the process of separation, there was still in the interwar years much overlap between the two worlds, a source both of conflict and of sympathy, as will be seen in the next chapter. In 1918 also daily newspapers controlled access to an enormous well of public opinion, something any writer who wanted an audience for his or her work could not simply ignore. Just a few months after the Armistice Siegfried Sassoon, one of Fleet Street's harshest wartime critics admitted 'pleasant was it also to be sauntering along Fleet Street' to his new job as literary editor of the popular *Daily Herald*. Although he did not stay in the job long, he wrote his literary notes with deliberate 'cocksure jauntiness' fitting for readers of the socialist newspaper, believing that he was playing his part in bringing literary knowledge to the Labour-voting masses.[94] He paid writers generously, commissioning E. M. Forster, Walter de la Mare and H. M. Tomlinson's 'special' articles at £10.00 each. As part of his job Sassoon had to go cap in hand to book publishers seeking advertisements to make his page economically viable. The increasingly commercialized book publishing industry, however, was now headed by men who 'disliked the *Daily Herald* and its disruptive ideas', and Sassoon was usually sent away empty handed, an illustration how newspapers, commerce, politics and the literary world create between them an uneasy set of fluctuating relationships.[95] While in the literary editor's chair, Sassoon received a volume of 'privately printed' verse about rural Kent from an obscure poet. With the chatter of typewriters and the ringing of the telephone bell in the background, Sassoon opened the book and 'forgot that [he] was in a newspaper office, for the barn was physically evoked, with its cobwebs and dust and sparkling sun', as the poetry of Edmund Blunden effaced the world of journalism around him. The powerful image Sassoon conjures – the scent of cow-cake and straw delighting his nose as he sits in Fleet Street – is yet another example of the interdependence of both worlds. Similarly a year after the war, Rose Macaulay applied for a job on the liberal *Daily News*, and when a breakdown prevented her from taking it, she resorted to freelancing, telling her cousin: 'the whole press having apparently taken into its head at once that I should write articles for it ... I love the *Telegraph* because it asks me to name my own terms and then falls in with them ... Meanwhile I babble for the *Star*, the *Daily Chronicle*, *Everyman* etc'.[96] This access to the reading public and her characterization in popular newspapers as 'Rose Macaulay, the novelist' and 'Rose Macaulay who is a novelist, and single' would play a crucial part in Rose Macaulay's literary and journalistic success although her relationship with newspapers would always be conflicted (see particularly Chapter 7).[97] Writers negotiating this ever-shifting maze would react with an explosion of portrayals of the newspaper world during the interwar years, as will be seen in the next chapter.

Notes

1   Motion, Andrew, 'The Lost Generation', *Guardian*, 5 July 2011.
2   Sassoon, Siegfried, 'Fight to a Finish' first published in *The Cambridge Magazine*, 27 October 1917.
3   Sassoon, Siegfried, 'Fight to a Finish', in *War Poetry*, p. 96.
4   Sassoon's linkage here foreshadows Herman and Chomsky's idea of mass media: that 'the societal purpose of the media is to inculcate and defend the economic, social, and political agenda of privileged groups that dominate the domestic society and the state' (Herman, Edward and Noam Chomsky, *Manufacturing Consent*, p. 298).

5 For example, 'Fight to a Finish – Peril of a Premature Peace', *Daily Mail*, 21 August 1914; 'A Fight to a Finish', headline in a leader 21 September 1914. The phrase is used 39 times in the *Daily Mail* and 66 times in *The Times* between the outbreak of the war and the date of Sassoon's poem.

6 Pound, Ezra, Canto XIV, *Draft of XVI Cantos*, p. 19; Plowman, Max, *Letters*, p. 47.

7 Aldington, Richard, 'A Young American Poet', *Little Review March 1915*, pp. 22–25; 'The Poetry of Paul Fort', *Little Review* April 1915, pp. 8–10; 'The Retort Discourteous', *Little Review*, June–July 1915, p. 4.

8 Fifty-three of the country's leading writers including H. G. Wells, G. K. Chesterton and J. M. Barrie signed a declaration condemning Prussian militarism and promoting the justice of the allied cause. Peter Buitenhuis' *The Great War of Words* is excellent on establishment writers and the propaganda machine.

9 Murdock, Graham and Peter Golding, 'The Structure, Ownership and Control of the Press', p. 127; daily papers were hit by newsprint shortages too, and for long periods during the war, newspapers were only six and sometimes only four pages long.

10 Harding, Jason, *The Criterion*, p. 17.

11 Buitenhuis, Peter, *The Great War of Words*, p. 6.

12 Briffault, Robert, 'The Wail of Grub Street', p. 512.

13 Bourdieu, Pierre, *On Television and Journalism*, p. 75.

14 Davidson, John, 'Pre-Shakespearianism' in *Selected Poems and Prose*, p. 158.

15 Chesterton, G. K., 'A Word for the Mere Journalist' in *Darlington North Star*, 3 February 1902.

16 Aldington, 'A Young American Poet' in *Little Review*, March 1915, pp. 22–25.

17 Taylor, A. J. P., *Beaverbrook*, p. 102.

18 See, for example, the *Daily Mail*'s 4 January 1900 leader 'Working the Press', where the paper complains of favourable treatment by the army to its own military correspondents.

19 Beaumont, Jacqueline, 'The British Press during the South African War', p. 1.

20 Knightley, Phillip, *The First Casualty*, p. 44.

21 Tomlinson, H. M., *All Our Yesterdays*, p. 114.

22 Chesterton, G. K., *The Napoleon of Notting Hill*, p. 204.

23 Fussell, Paul, *The Great War and Modern Memory*, p. 9.

24 Knightley, *First Casualty*, p. 56.

25 Montague, C. E., *Disenchantment*, p. 101.

26 Lyton, Neville, *The Press and the General Staff*, pp. vii–xii.

27 James, Lionel, *High Pressure*, p. 116.

28 Wallace, Edgar, *People*, p. 113; Knightley, *The First Casualty*, p. 74; James, *High Pressure*, p. 142.

29 Wyk Smith, Malvern van, *Drummer Hodge*, p. 152.

30 This despatch is dated 6 December 1899; sourced in Steevens, G. W., *From Cape Town to Ladysmith*, p. 138.

31 Ibid., p. 53, 106 & 124; Keating, Peter, *The Haunted Study*, p. 301.

32 Wyk Smith, *Drummer Hodge*, p.5.

33 James, *High Pressure*, p. 138.

34 Wyk Smith, *Drummer Hodge*, pp. 125–130.

35 Hampton, Mark, *Visions of the Press*, p. 116.

36 Atkin, Jonathan, *A War of Individuals*, p. 84.

37 Quoted in Buitenhuis, *The Great War of Words*, p. 6.

38 Hiley, Nicholas, 'Lord Kitchener Resigns', pp. 28–41.

39 Ibid., p. 75.

40 Ibid., pp. 76–79.

41 Ibid., p. 84.

42 Farrar, Martin, *News from the Front*, p. 13.

43 Although these changed from time to time, the main five were Philip Gibbs (*Daily Chronicle* and *Daily Telegraph*), William Beach Thomas (*Daily Mail* and *Daily Mirror*), Percival Phillips (*Daily Express* and *Morning Post*), Perry Robinson (*Daily News* and *The Times*) and Herbert Russell (Reuters) Farrar (1999: xii).

44 Gibbs, Philip, *Adventures in Journalism*, p. 248.

45 Lovelace, Colin, 'British Press Censorship during the First World War', p. 313.

46 Griffiths, Dennis, *Fleet Street*, p. 186.

47 Buitenhuis, *The Great War of Words*, p. xvii.

48 Ibid., pp. 20, 6, 42 and xviii.

49 Gibbs, *Adventures in Journalism*, p. 233.

50 Tomlinson, H. M., *A Mingled Yarn*, pp. 144–145.

51 Hodson, James Lansdale, *Grey Dawn*, p. 264.

52 Ibid., p. 263.

53 Plowman, *Letters*, p. 47.

54 Lascelles, Alan, *End of an Era*, p. 212.

55 Sassoon, Siegfried, *Memoirs of an Infantry Officer*, pp. 185–186.

56 Woolf, Virginia, 'Two Soldier-Poets' in *Times Literary Supplement*, p. 323.

57 Quoted in Das, Santanu (ed.), *Cambridge Companion to the Poetry of the First World War*, pp. 5–6.

58 Fussell, *The Great War*, p. 87; Farrar, Martin, *News from the Front*, pp. 133–134.

59 Quoted in Farrar, *News from the Front*, p. 134.

60 Blunden, Edmund, *Undertones of War*, pp. 73 & 169.

61 Ibid., p. 73.

62 Eliot, T. S., 'Reflections on Contemporary Poetry' in *Egoist*, p. 39.

63 Graves, Robert, 'A Dead Boche' in *Robert Graves: The Complete Poems*, p. 27.

64 See Enright, D. J., 'The Literature of the First World War', pp. 154–157 for Rupert Brooke and other poets who initially portrayed the war in romantic, patriotic terms.

65 Johnston, John, *English Poetry of the First World War*, p. 77.

66 Thomas, Edward, *Selected Poems*, p. 77.

67 The largest single body of casualties was from the Russians who suffered nearly half a million deaths or injuries from gas.

68 Haber, L. F., *The Poisonous Cloud*, pp. 104 & 239–243.

69 Owen, Wilfred, *The Poems of Wilfred Owen*, p. 117.

70 Sassoon, Siegfried, 'The Effect' in *The War Poems of Siegfried Sassoon*, p. 27.

71 Sassoon, Siegfried, 'Editorial Impressions', in *War Poetry*, p. 89.

72 Fussell, *The Great War*, p. 86.

73 Hodson, *Grey Dawn*, p. 264.

74 Tomlinson, *All Our Yesterdays*, p. 417.

75 Owen, Wilfred, *Selected Letters*, p. 349.

76 Owen, *The Poems of Wilfred Owen*, p. 167.

77 Graves, Robert, *Goodbye to All That*, p. 188.

78 Lonsdale, Sarah, 'Roast Seagull', pp. 1–15.

79 Brittain, Vera, *Testament of Youth*, p. 110. This entry refers to British losses at the battle of Neuve Chapelle, March 1915.

80 Bennett, Arnold, (ed.) and Newman Flower, *Journals Vol II*, pp. 132 & 173.

81 Wells, H. G., *Mr Britling*, p. 142.

82 LeFanu, Sarah, *Rose Macaulay*, p. 107.

83 Macaulay, Rose, *Non-Combatants*, pp. 64–65.

84 Ibid., p. 66. A reference to rumours that swept the country that the Russians were coming to Britain's aid, and had been seen marching south, with snow still on their boots. See Arthur Ponsonby's *Falsehood in Wartime*: 'No obsession was more widespread through the war than the belief in the last months of 1914 that Russian troops were passing through Great Britain to the Western Front' (p. 62).

85 McKenna, Stephen, *Sonia*, p. 244.

86 Ibid., p. 443.

87 Ibid., p. 445.

88 McKenna, Stephen, *While I Remember*, p. 197.

89 Pound, Ezra, 'Pastiche' in *The New Age*, p. 432.

90 Macaulay, *Non-Combatants*, p. 93.

91 'Notes of the Week' *New Age*, p. 385.

92 Montague, *Disenchantment*, p. 103.

93 Wells, H. G., *The Salvaging of Civilisation*, p. 185.

94 Sassoon, Siegfried, *Siegfried's Journey*, pp. 143–145; Thorpe, Michael, *Siegfried Sassoon*, p. 51.

95 Ibid., p. 145.

96 Macaulay, Rose (ed.) and Ferguson Smith, *Dearest Jean*, p. 39.

97 *Daily Mail*, 20 August 1929; *Daily Mail*, 26 October 1929.

'The interview with the cat had been particularly full of appeal': The Interwar 'Battle of the Brows' from Below[1]

The profession and character of the journalist is of enormous interest – verging on an obsession – to writers of the interwar period. I have identified more than sixty novels, short stories, major poems and plays which, during the twenty-year-period 1919–1939, examine either as their main focus or at least a major sub-focus, the business of journalism and the character of the journalist.[2] 'Highbrow' disdain for the lowly reporter and his writing is often mixed up in class snobbishness and Modernist horreur of 'the masses' he represents. Fictions written by 'middlebrow' and 'lowbrow' writers, themselves often, through financial necessity engaged in writing for the press, are illuminating on the evolution of the press during the interwar years, on readers' and writers' relationships with it and the increasing demands it places on its journalists.

Hector Puncheon is a junior reporter on the *Morning Star*, a popular daily newspaper in 1933. Puncheon has been sent to report on a warehouse fire in the city and, 'in a comparatively brief time', has compiled several reports for different editions of his paper, including a detailed article, 'complete with the night-watchmen's and eye-witnesses' stories and a personal interview with the cat' for the main evening edition. Puncheon is pleased with himself:

> not even the most distinguished of the senior men could have turned in a column more full of snap, pep and human interest than his own. The interview with the cat had been particularly full of appeal. The animal was, it seemed, an illustrious rat catcher, with many famous deeds to her credit. Not only that, but she had been first to notice the smell of fire and had, by her anguished and intelligent mewings attracted the attention of night watchman number one.[3]

Dorothy L. Sayers' *Murder Must Advertise* (1933) is one of her popular series of Lord Peter Wimsey novels in which Hector Puncheon plays a minor, if pivotal, role. Puncheon is amiable enough but, although a new newspaper recruit, he completely understands the demands of a newspaper that must sell millions of copies to attract advertising.[4] His personality has been utterly subsumed into meeting the commercial needs of his newspaper. Not only is he adept at fabricating interviews but he speaks in advertising slogans: "'Guinness is good for you – particularly on a chilly morning'"; "'Nutrax for Nerves,' suggested Hector Puncheon'.[5] Living by 'stunts' and sensational stories and talking advertising jargon, Puncheon is more automaton than man, securing the cat's next litter of kittens for readers to apply for as a way of continuing interest in the story.

What are we to make of a successful thriller writer taking time out of her elaborate 'whodunnit' plot to make a dig at the press? Not just any old dig either but a deliberate lassoing together of the advertising industry, of which Sayers was familiar, and the by now enormous newspaper industry, which by the mid-1930s surpassed shipbuilding and chemicals in terms of net output.[6] Sayers' Hector Puncheon is the personification of a growing characteristic of the interwar press, a major source of concern for writers and intellectuals. As early as 1921, H. G. Wells was warning that British newspapers were now utterly changed from their Victorian predecessors. Modern newspapers, he said, were now, 'sheets of advertisements with news and discussions printed on the back'. The proprietors' commercial interests now stood 'between the public and a writer' in a way that would never have happened before 1914, he argued.[7] Another critic of the modern popular press, H. W. Massingham, outspoken former editor of the Liberal *Nation*, had also described modern news-editing as having 'borrowed the methods of advertising'; clever newspaper executives were 'good trade psychologists' who knew how to entice readers into buying a paper with pictures and teasing headlines.[8] In 1931, the Audit Bureau of Circulations was established as a reliable way of measuring newspaper readership to help 'newspapers deliver[ed] readers to advertisers'.[9] By creating Hector Puncheon, Sayers was adding her viewpoint to a lively contemporary debate. She was also following a major literary trend. Quite simply, everybody was doing it. From the top – James Joyce and his 'Windy Scribes' of *Ulysses*, Ezra Pound's 'betrayers of language', W. H. Auden's 'Beethameer bully of Britain' and Virginia Woolf's dissection of inane headlines in *Mrs Dalloway* – through the middle – Evelyn Waugh, Graham Greene, Aldous Huxley, John Middleton Murry, Elizabeth Bowen, John Lehmann, Rose Macaulay, J. B. Priestley, Storm Jameson, Winifred Holtby, A. S. M. Hutchinson, Arnold Bennett, H. G. Wells and many more – right down to the lowbrow – Gilbert Frankau, Noel Langley and Cecil Hunt – it seemed that no writer could pick up a pen between the wars without producing a novel, play or poem about the British newspaper press.[10]

The hostile attitude towards mass culture of interwar canonical writers and intellectuals such as Ezra Pound, F. R. and Q. D. Leavis, Virginia Woolf and T. S. Eliot has been well chronicled.[11] These studies ignore, however, how the many more popular writers engaged with the 'problem' of the press through their fictional output. Interwar 'middlebrow' writers who also wrote for newspapers constructed a critique of the press more nuanced and thoughtful than the conventional 'dumbing down' theme pursued by intellectual critics. The poet Richard Aldington's parody, for example, of readers of the '*Diley Mile*' [*Daily Mail*] may have seemed witty in 1916 but today it just reads like unthinking upper-class snobbery.[12] Those interested in the history of the press would find more of use in the novel of the forgotten journalist and novelist Stella Martin Currey, who wrote for the *Bristol Times and Mirror* 1926–1932 at a time when that traditional provincial newspaper, founded in 1792, was engaged in a fight-to-the-death (which it eventually lost) with the new Northcliffe Press-owned *Bristol Evening World*. Stella Martin Currey's first novel, *Paperchase End* (1934), is dedicated 'to those who have known the comradeship and suffering of a newspaper war'. The novel describes the pressures reporters working for the 'Ravenport' *Courier* are put under to make their newspaper more attractive to readers tempted by the new *Dispatch*, which was printed 'with attractive type and well sprinkled with pictures'. Upbraided by her news editor for turning in a truthful, if dull, article on a local Mothers' Conference, the protagonist Susan Calvin admits that the rival paper's version, titled 'Married Women Tell Their Secrets', although 'wasn't a true description of the conference', was 'much more racy and interesting' than her account. 'What did it matter if her own report was truer, when it was infinitely duller', she asks herself.[13] The novel is an intelligent meditation on the responsible journalist's tightrope walk between giving the public what it wants and fulfilling his or her nebulous and ill-defined role in informing citizens on council affairs, court proceedings and health and scientific advances. It was a tightrope the author herself walked. Stella, the daughter of the children's nonsense writer J. P. Martin, had literary ambitions from an early age.[14] One of her first assignments for the *Evening News* was to write about the Bristol soup kitchen set up after the General Strike began in May 1926. She recalls in her memoir: 'the sight of the women and children queuing for soup and the pervasive air of quiet misery made me feel angry and guilty. My editor wrote: "Re-write more objectively"'. As her paper tried increasingly frantically to compete with the *Evening World*, Stella became the paper's zoo correspondent, writing about, among other articles, Betty the bag-snatching chimpanzee, and fabricating the 'slimming diary' of Judy the overweight elephant.[15]

'A deluge of printed matter pours over the world'[16]

During the interwar years, the combined circulations of daily newspapers rose from 3.1 million in 1918 to 10.6 million in 1939, with the popular *Daily Express*, *Daily Mail*, *Daily Mirror*, *News Chronicle* and *Daily Herald* leading the field.[17] The Sunday newspaper market was even more buoyant, with sales of 14.9 million by 1938, nearly half of which figure was accounted for by just two 'popular' newspapers, the *News of the World* and *The People*, each with a circulation of over three million.[18] By 1936, the British were the largest consumers of newsprint in the world at 59.8 lb per head, higher even than American readers (57 lb).[19] At the same time, the major newspaper groups were also launching weekly and monthly magazines since the successful launch of the Harmsworth-owned *Woman's Weekly* in 1911, which sold 500,000 copies in its first week.[20] By 1938, the combined circulations of the most popular women's weekly magazines (*Woman*, *Woman's Own*, *Home Notes*, *Woman's Weekly*, *Woman's Illustrated*, *Home Chat*, *Woman's Companion* and *Woman's Pictorial*) had reached over 2.3 million.[21] For some the rise in access to reading matter was something to be praised. As the authors of the influential *Report on the British Press* (1938) by the think tank Political and Economic Planning pointed out, for millions of people, theirs was the first generation to read a newspaper at all: 'It is frequently overlooked that many of the readers of such newspapers have only quite recently entered the newspaper-reading class ... For at least one class of readers all four of the great popular dailies therefore represent an improvement in taste and information.'[22]

For others, such as F. R. Leavis, 'the age is illiterate with periodicals', as he claimed in his 'Manifesto' in the first volume of his influential journal *Scrutiny*.[23] Democratization of knowledge versus charges of 'dumbing down' thus formed, 100 years ago, as debates around the internet do today, the kernel of concern over the interwar press.

In addition to rapidly increasing circulations, newspaper ownership was becoming concentrated in the hands of a few powerful groups, the Harmsworth group (*Daily Mail*, *Daily Mirror*, *Evening News*, *Sunday Dispatch*, *Sunday Pictorial*) headed, after the death of Northcliffe in 1922, by his brother Lord Rothermere; the Beaverbrook group (*Daily Express*, *Sunday Express* and *Evening Standard*) and the Berry Group (later Kemsley Group, *Sunday Times*,

Financial Times, Daily Sketch (from 1926) and *Daily Telegraph* (from 1927)).[24] These powerful combines, headed by charismatic and influential proprietors (discussed in Chapter 5), pulled in a glittering array of writers – many of whom were highly critical of the rise of the popular press in their fiction – including Clemence Dane and Edith Sitwell to the *Daily Mirror*; J. B. Priestley and Storm Jameson to the *Evening News*; Margery Allingham, E. H. Young and H. G. Wells to the *Daily Express*; and Harold Nicolson, Arnold Bennett and George Moore to the *Evening Standard*. Perusal of the features pages of just one month (May 1930) of the *Daily Mail* reveals pieces by Evelyn Waugh, Edith Sitwell, Arnold Bennett, Daphne Du Maurier, Cecil Beaton, the dramatist Frederick Lonsdale, the author and dramatist Beverley Nichols and the popular novelist Mrs Belloc Lowndes. While newspaper ownership was consolidating, the number of newspapers was falling. Old-style, mainly Liberal papers such as the *Globe*, *Pall Mall Gazette*, *Westminster Gazette* and *Daily Chronicle* all either merged or closed within a few years of the end of the First World War, destroying, according to the contemporary commentator Denys Thompson, 'the last vestiges of the nineteenth century tradition in journalism'.[25]

Highbrow writers and the 'poison' of journalism

The contemporary commentator T. H. S. Escott argued in the *Quarterly Review* in 1917 that journalism had descended from a liberal profession to a mere commercial transaction, and this comment highlights a measure of how far, and how fast, the press had fallen in the eyes of the literary establishment. Escott, a leader writer for the *Standard* 1866–1873, was author, only a few years earlier, of a paean to the contemporary press, *Masters of English Journalism* (1911). Escott's *Quarterly Review* article identifies the year 1916 as the time when popular journalism changed from being an 'honourable profession' to an industry dedicated to the mass production of 'literary pemmican'.[26] Where once newspapers employed leader writers 'who could put their own ideas every morning before the world in a shape that gratified their readers, ideas that were talked about in Pall Mall and that even Downing Street could not afford to ignore', now 'there are today whole families innumerable owing all that they think, believe or say about the topics of the time to the leaderettes and paragraphs with which the halfpenny sheet abounds'.[27]

Like Escott, the novelist D. H. Lawrence locates the date on which both newspapers and the reading public changed character at the midpoint of the war as he writes in his 1923 novel *Kangaroo*: 'In the winter of 1915–16 the spirit of the old London collapsed ... and the genuine debasement began, the unspeakable baseness of the press and the public voice, the reign of that bloated ignominy, *John Bull*.'[28]

The idea that not only was the popular press guilty of sensationalism and intellectual slovenliness but that its mass appeal was somehow actively damaging the minds of readers and reducing the appetite for literature gained ground in the interwar years. In his recent study *Modernism on Fleet Street*, Patrick Collier argues that 'in the 1920s ... the sense of a crisis in British journalism was so widespread that taking a critical stance towards the degradations of the press was the clearest way to signal intellectual seriousness.'[29] Criticisms of the daily press were widespread and varied and were carried in the intellectual reviews and literary journals from T. S. Eliot's *Criterion*, John Middleton Murry's *Adelphi*, F. R. Leavis' *Scrutiny* as well as more general journals the *Fortnightly Review*, *Quarterly Review* and *Spectator*. It was argued that during the war the press and its proprietors had got too powerful; that the popular press was sensationalist; that its snappy headlines and reductive narratives 'reduced the popular mind to childishness'; that the press was in danger of ceasing to be a 'liberal profession', but instead had become 'a branch of business'; and that journalists practiced and promoted 'intellectual slovenliness'.[30] More seriously, in the immediate aftermath of the Great War, it was feared that aggressive attitudes of popular newspapers would distort the peace process and prevent a sustainable settlement from being reached. The journalist Sisley Huddleston, who represented the liberal *Westminster Gazette* at the 1919 Versailles Peace Conference, wrote as follows in the *Atlantic Monthly* in November 1920: 'Hate exudes from every journal in speaking of certain peoples – a weary hate, a conventional hate ... because I am a journalist myself I deplore the more this unconscious dishonesty of the press.'[31]

The immediate post-war period also saw the beginnings of the debate about a possible regulation of the press starting with the publication of Sir Norman Angell's *The Press and the Organisation of Society* (1922). In the book he describes a 'lynch press' which during the war came closer to governing the country than either the Church or politicians. He suggests as remedies both a 'Truthful Press Act' with harsh penalties for papers that printed untruths and inaccuracies and also a state press run along the lines of the new BBC, 'not as a monopoly or an exclusive substitute for privately-owned papers but as a supplement thereto'.[32] A career in journalism was viewed with disdain by upper-middle-class families who hoped their children might enter the Foreign Office, the law or academia, as prominent interwar journalist Claud Cockburn relates in his memoir *In*

Time of Trouble. He describes the horrified reaction by his family's friends at his decision, on graduating from Oxford in 1926, to apply for a job on the *Times*:

> To the advocates of a Foreign Office career, the notion of 'going in for journalism' was pitiably degrading. 'And mark you', as a friend of my father told me sternly, 'split what hairs you will, mince words as you may, in the last analysis *The Times* is nothing more or less than *sheer journalism*'.[33]

It is within this context of widespread criticism of the newspaper press that we must view the portrayals of journalists in fiction by writers seeking to establish their intellectual or 'highbrow' credentials. Take *Crome Yellow* (1921), the first (not very good) published novel by Aldous Huxley, for example. A partial satire of Lady Ottoline Morrell's Garsington Manor, which was a haven for intellectuals and pacifists and where Huxley worked during the war, the novel is careful to make distinctions between different genres of writing. The young hero, a poet, who can spend hours wondering about the connotations of a word such as 'carminative', is outraged when he and the egregious journalist Mr Barbecue-Smith, who prides himself in producing, in a state of self-induced hypnosis, 3,800 words in two and a half hours, are both described as 'writers' by their hostess: 'Denis was furious, and to make matters worse, he felt himself blushing hotly. Had Priscilla no sense of proportion? She was putting them in the same category – Barbecue-Smith and himself. They were both writers, they both used pen and ink.'[34]

Once again we see here the careful self-positioning of the 'writer' within his fiction, as we did in Chapter 1, and the consciousness of the exact place within the field of cultural production he aspires to occupy; and, for the artistic writer, the expression of the gulf that separates him and journalism.

Similarly the journalist, author and politician Harold Nicolson had spent an unhappy eighteen-month period on Lord Beaverbrook's *Evening Standard* in the late 1920s, editing the society pages. His *Diaries* reveal a growing sense of contradiction between his newspaper journalism and his aspirations to be taken more seriously as a literary writer and biographer. The 'clash' between the two worlds results in his leaving the *Standard* as a necessary precursor to his being able to write a novel – but not before he has three months of 'quarantine' from newspapers: 'I have been thinking during the last few days about my book. I have now had three good months of quarantine, and feel that I have at last got the poison of journalism out of my system. I can now settle down to write a book.'[35]

Predictably, the novel *Public Faces* (1932), a strange science fiction and political thriller, contains a few unpleasant scenes set in a newspaper office, the *Sunday Mail*, and several critical observations on the 'hysterics' of the 'Yellow Press'. Nicolson's most unsympathetic journalist character is the coldly ambitious, 'virginal' Miss Geraldine Smithers, home page editor of the *Sunday Mail*, a clichéd portrait of a blue-stockinged professional woman journalist out of her intellectual depth (see Chapter 7 for more unfortunate women journalists).[36]

Huxley and Nicolson used their novels as a crude way of announcing their literary difference from journalism. They were, in effect, suggesting to readers and critics their own preferred position within the field of cultural production, several rungs higher than that occupied by journalists, as if this deliberate self-positioning might help their reputations as 'highbrow' or 'intellectual'. Other interwar writers explored themes relating to journalism and the popular press more subtly. The cruelty of the reporter who cares nothing for human suffering in his haste to get a good story is vividly portrayed in Elizabeth Bowen's short story 'Recent Photograph' (1926). Bertram Lukin of the *Evening Crier* greedily takes down intimate details of the Brindleys, a suburban couple who have suffered a mystery double-killing. With a notebook full of quotes of a human tragedy and a 'recent photograph' of the pair, Lukin hurries back to his newspaper office, his heart 'like a singing bird'.[37] Motivated only by his desire to flesh out a mystifying story, Lukin regards the couple's young neighbour who may have clues as to why they died, 'with a look that yearned to violate her memory'. His divorce from ordinary concerned humanity is revealed as he looks at her again, after she has offered up her information, 'as though through a mile of ether'.[38] Upon discovering that Mr Brindley had lost his job a few weeks earlier, but had been pretending to his wife by going out every morning to a non-existent workplace, and that the discovery of this deception led Mr Brindley to kill both his wife and himself, Lukin is ecstatic. An otherwise baffling tale has now, with its themes of deception, discovery and jealousy, achieved an easily describable 'type' to be packaged and commodified for millions of readers, none of whom will have known of the Brindleys before Lukin's sensational report. Human suffering is cheapened and conveyed, through crass narrative, mass reproduction and dissemination processes. Lukin may have captured a 'story' of archetypal proportions, but in feeding it into the machine of the newspaper he is cheapening both the Brindleys' tragedy and the readers' experience. This idea is reinforced by Bowen's use of the final phrase 'his heart was like a singing bird', which must be an echo of the Christina Rossetti love poem 'A Birthday':

My heart is like a singing bird
Whose nest is in a water'd shoot.[39]

The simple romance of the poem ('the birthday of my life/Is come, my love is come to me') contrasts starkly with the Americanized drawl and horrible motivations of Lukin, who cynically manipulates the passions of a young girl to get his story. In contrast to the idea put forward by Edwardian journalist-novelists in Chapter 1 that because a newspaper story is 'true' it must be worth more to the reader than fiction, Bowen is saying something very different. The human misery that must inevitably be exploited in a newspaper story, by the journalist, to acquire evidence of human suffering in quotes and pictures is not some great self-sacrificing act but a horrible violation of private emotions. The newspaper which is never 'without its shriek of agony from someone', as recorded by Virginia Woolf in her diary just after the war, is now pushing the boundaries of the public–private realm, offering up slices of despair for a public that feasts on misery and trivia.[40]

For writers on the intellectual Left, the growth of the popular press presented a particular problem. On the one hand, popular newspapers democratized access to political, scientific and international information; they also offered, through the purchase and serialization of prominent writers' fiction, access to literature for a penny a day. However, the newspaper industry was increasingly becoming a part of an economic system that protected the interests of the rich and exploited the working classes. In addition, many intellectuals of the Left in the 1930s harboured an irrepressible disgust for Demos: 'The little men and their mothers, not plain but dreadfully ugly', as W. H. Auden so delightfully put it.[41] Many of Auden's poems and plays contain attacks on the toxic popular press, although, 'the public you poison are pretty well dumb'.[42] Similarly Auden's friend and collaborator Cecil Day Lewis adopts a patronizing tone to an unthinking newspaper-reading public in his lengthy diatribe aimed at press barons and the popular press in his *The Magnetic Mountain* (1933):

> Fireman and farmer, father and flapper
> I'm speaking to you, sir, please drop that paper;
> Don't you know it's poison? Have you lost all hope?
> Aren't you ashamed ma'am to be taking dope?
> It's a nasty habit[43]

The view from the middle

Interwar middlebrow writers elaborate on the joint complicity between readers and newspapers in the market for trivia. Former journalist A. S. M. Hutchinson's bestseller *If Winter Comes* (1921) relates events just before the war with the benefit of hindsight: 'These newspapers and these arguments you hear – it's all shouting and smashing. It's never thinking and building. It's all destructive; never constructive. All blind hatred of the other views, never fair examination of them.'[44] William Gerhardie in his novel *Doom* (1928) suggests that the continued jingoistic stereotyping of the German people during the 1920s was the fault of the *Daily Mail*. Here a woman who meets a real German is surprised by their culture and tolerance: 'It was not what she had read in the *Daily Mail*: "Tricking Huns. Once a German always a German. Blond Beasts," were the phrases that occurred to her.'[45] Gerhardie had some justification on this point, with popular newspapers carrying stories such as 'Huns demand 32,000,000 tons of food' (*Daily Mirror*, 8 March 1919) and 'Military Marches heard again in Berlin ... anti foreign sentiment openly expressed ... crowd sang "Deutschland Uber alles"' (*Daily Express*, 15 January 1923). Like the Brindleys' agony in 'Recent Photograph', the social goings-on of the rich and famous in Evelyn Waugh's *Vile Bodies* (1930) are just another commodity, emphasized by the 'social editress'' use of initials and ugly elisions in her boiled-down language: 'The social editress read ... "Can't have Kitty Blackwater," she said. "Had her yesterday. Others'll do. Write 'em down to a couple of paragraphs ... We've got to keep everything down for Lady M's party. I've cut out the D of Devonshire altogether."'[46]

Waugh wrote *Vile Bodies*, about London's 'Bright Young Things' and the gossip columnists who tracked their butterfly lives from party to party, following an unsuccessful trial on the *Daily Express* in Spring 1927. Having chosen to work on the *Express* in preference to getting down to his biography of Dante Gabriel Rossetti for which the publishers Duckworth's had paid him £20.00, Waugh was disappointed with his newspaper experience. He recorded initially finding the work 'exhilarating' in his diary, although two weeks later he wrote: 'I have got the sack from the *Express* ... Papers are full of lies.'[47] Bowen's Bertrand Lukin and the journalists in Waugh's *Vile Bodies* understand what the newspaper machine wants and unthinkingly try to provide it. Many of these novels blame both the newspapers, for supplying trivia, and the reading public, for demanding it. Here again, A. S. M. Hutchinson's novel examines why the Great War took so many people by surprise:

Why, if war – when war comes people will look back on this year, 1912, and wonder where the hell their eyes were that they didn't see it. What are they seeing? ... doctors and the Insurance Bill tripe, Marconi Inquiry, *Titanic*, Suffragettes smashing up the West End, burning down Lulu Harcourt's place, trying to toast old Asquith in the Dublin Theatre, Seddon murder, this triangular cricket show. Hell's own excitement because there's so much rain in August and people in Norwich have to go about in boats, and then hell's own hullaballoo because there's no rain for twenty two days in September and people get so dry they can't spit or something … That's what really interests the people.[48]

This list of 'news' – starting with the genuinely important Insurance Bill and Marconi Inquiry and finishing up with weather reports – suggests both the scattergun nature of the news providers, people in Norwich going about in boats in the same breath as the *Titanic* disaster, and also a descent from seriousness to trivia. The press is guilty of peddling reassuring trivia, yet the public is also guilty of preferring to read about the weather or celebrity weddings than portents of war. The blame must be shared. Here also in a popular novel, Hutchinson is stressing exactly the same absurdity of a world as portrayed in a newspaper as James Joyce does in the offices of the *Freeman's Journal* in *Ulysses*. In *Ulysses*, a litany of unconnected events, trivial and serious, without resolution and without end, are announced by bizarre headlines ('HIS NATIVE DORIC', 'ONLY ONCE MORE THAT SOAP') and thrown together simply because they happen on the same day.[49] Both writers foreshadow Bourdieu's analysis of the 'dehistoricized and dehistoricizing, fragmented and fragmenting' modern news presentation in *On Television and Journalism* (1996): 'The journalistic field represents the world in terms of a philosophy that sees history as an absurd series of disasters which can be neither understood nor influenced. Journalism shows us a world … full of incomprehensible and unsettling dangers from which we must withdraw for our own protection … this worldview fosters fatalism and disengagement.'[50]

Hutchinson's observations that while the Germans were building their army, British newspaper readers preferred to read about people in Norwich having to use boats are particularly pertinent in this respect. Neither Joyce, Hutchinson nor other interwar writers who commented in their fiction on the news packaging of global events had the benefit of Bourdieu's long view of a century of mass media. Their warnings of how a rampant 'entertainment' news industry might affect people's engagement in the world have powerful resonances today. Critics of internet journalism today similarly warn of the nature of social media news alerts, which make no differentiation between the *New York Times* and a trivial celebrity website.[51]

The independent periodicals

While popular newspapers enjoyed stability, literary periodicals in the interwar period were often on shaky footings, regularly closing or merging to survive. The failing *Athenaeum* merged with the *Nation* in 1921, the *Egoist* closed in 1919; *Art and Letters* and *Coterie* both folded in 1920.[52] Others were launched, most famously T. S. Eliot's *Criterion* in 1922 and John Middleton Murry's *Adelphi* the following year. F. R. Leavis launched his intellectually combative *Scrutiny* in 1932. These new interwar literary periodicals adopted a critical stance towards the mass circulation dailies, and core contributors regularly criticized the popular press. Consciously launched as 'platforms' from which the arts could establish their new role and purpose in a fundamentally changed world, these journals attacked daily newspaper journalism as a way of establishing their intellectual credibility.[53] In the *Adelphi*'s opening editorial, John Middleton Murry took pains to explain how the new magazine would bridge the 'gulf' between highbrow literary culture and the *News of the World*.[54] He watches crowds surging round newspaper billboards, eagerly checking the racing results in a state of bemusement at their difference from him: 'The chief difference between us, I suppose, is that his particular kind of dope, like insulin, needs to be injected every twenty-four hours, except on Sunday when there is the *News of the World*, while I keep myself going by looking for something more permanent.'[55]

Middleton Murry had written his own unsuccessful novel about a journalist ten years earlier, *The Things We Are* (1922). In the novel, Bettington, a struggling freelancer for popular periodicals unsuccessfully woos the beautiful intellectual Felicia. Realising he will never win her, he acknowledges sorrowfully, 'I don't suppose we belong to the same worlds, you know.'[56] While Murry sees the *Adelphi* as a bridge between these two worlds, its content suggests he is not prepared to reach particularly far across the intellectual and artistic divide. The second issue of the *Adelphi* magazine contains a short comic story about the press. It is not clear who authored the short story 'The Pressgoat', which, for reasons that become clear at the end, is only signed 'MZ 4796', but as a humorous story about 'Kiss 'n' Tell' – or rather 'Murder 'n' Tell' popular journalism, it deserves another airing.[57]

The journalist-narrator who works in a 'dusty corner in the office of a quiet trade monthly' tells readers he has a scandal. He has met an old friend, Smithson, who has lost several newspaper jobs due to his pedantry. Smithson was fired for spelling 'licence' with a 'c' rather than an 's', and sacked from the *Dictator* by insisting it should be 'the committee has' rather than 'the committee have'. Smithson tells the narrator about the 'Pressgoat' system: hard-up hacks are paid up to £1,000 by a syndicate of national newspapers on the understanding that, when there is a quiet news period, they 'would be called upon for a murder': 'Smithson was called upon for a first-class murder with mystery that meant he had to get away for a hue and cry, and keep up the interest by sending derisive postcards to Scotland Yard with duplicates to the syndicate in case the officials tried to hush them up; he received £500 and twelve months' grace.'

The 'Pressgoat' system benefits out-of-work journalists and the proprietors whose income from advertising now relies upon huge circulations and who fear that, after the war, sales would fall. In addition, readers get a great mystery story to read for a few weeks. Time is running out for Smithson and he knows he has to commit a murder soon. Smithson decides he will kill another journalist, as the victim will know the value of such a good story, for despite being a pedantic journalist, he is still at heart, a newspaperman: 'we must think of the headings, you know'.

'The Pressgoat' criticizes several aspects of the modern press and journalists, such as disrespect for the rules of grammar and spelling; the valuing of circulation above all other concerns; the venality and desperation of freelance journalists reduced to turning the contents of their lives into 'copy' for the papers; the need to please advertisers; and the hypocritical elitism of the 'quality' press (these papers are aware of the scandal, yet slavishly report the Pressgoats' stories rather than expose the system).

As well as literary periodicals, the interwar period was characterized by the establishment of other independent, often radical, literary and political papers (such as *Time and Tide*, *Left Review*, *Storm* and Claud Cockburn's *The Week*, the famous precursor to *Private Eye*). This real-life plethora is matched by fictional independent papers. Arthur Gideon's *Weekly Fact* in Rose Macaulay's novel *Potterism* (1920, discussed below) is joined by a fictional *The Week*, set up by wounded and idealistic First World War veterans in Storm Jameson's *Company Parade* (1934).[58] In John Buchan's novel *Castle Gay* (1930), the journalist Dougal Crombie writes for the newspaper magnate Thomas Carlyle Craw's popular papers, although, he says, 'I put nothing of myself into his rotten papers.' Instead, Crombie writes what he really thinks in the independent *Outward* 'every second Saturday'.[59] In these fictions it is revealed that writing for an independent paper instantly signifies a character's goodness and incorruptibility. When in Storm Jameson's *Mirror in Darkness* trilogy the initially earnest and campaigning socialist Louis Earlham stops writing for *The Week* and starts contributing to press baron Marcel Cohen's popular newspapers, he begins his long moral decline, which ends in his betrayal of everything he once held sacred.

Conflicting depictions from writers engaged with the newspaper press

While the general trend of interwar fiction is hostile towards the press, there are exceptions. Writers discussed below had all either spent time as staff writers on newspapers or were regular contributors. They use their fiction to work out their own, often contradictory, attitudes to the newspaper industry. Rose Macaulay, for example, who during the interwar years wrote for a wide range of publications from the *Daily Mail* to the *Spectator*, mounts a stout defence of both a pluralistic free press (*What Not*, 1918) and the role of the popular press in democratizing access to knowledge (*Potterism*, 1920). She is, however, also highly critical of its simplistic approach to catering for women readers (*Keeping up Appearances*, 1928, *Going Abroad*, 1934). Stella Gibbons, in the foreword to her sublimely comic *Cold Comfort Farm* (1932), obliquely defends newspapers by mocking the kind of highbrow writer who derides attempts by journalists to be literary: 'As you know I have spent some ten years of my creative life in the meaningless and vulgar bustle of newspaper offices ... The life of the journalist is poor, nasty, brutish and short. So is his style.'[60]

Perhaps Gibbons' four 'exhausting' years on the *Evening Standard* during the late 1920s helped her appreciate the difficulties a news reporter faces. Cecil Hunt's *Paddy for News* (1933), which idealizes the 'plucky' girl crime reporter, was also written by a press insider: Cecil Hunt spent eight years (1928–1936) as fiction editor of the *Daily Mail*.[61] Similarly the *Daily Mail* journalist Margaret Lane's novel *Faith, Hope and No Charity* (1935) gives a unique positive gloss on newspaper gossip pages. In this novel, lowly stableman Mr Viner is convinced he is a relative of Lord Viner, whose life he follows 'with furtive attention' in newspaper society pages.[62] This is the 'vicarious enjoyment' Northcliffe claimed newspaper readers obtained through reading about the luxurious lifestyles of the wealthy and titled.[63] John Buchan's relatively sympathetic portrayal of the newspaper business (he was a director of the Reuters news agency when writing the short story) in 'The Last Crusade' (1928) also reveals some dubious journalistic methods, while arguing that sometimes the press 'works out on the side of the angels' and therefore the end justifies the means.[64] Gilbert Frankau's *Life – and Erica* (1925) takes sides against literature, portraying journalists as honourable and sincere and literary writers as hypocritical.[65] In the novel, the villain is the novelist and playwright T. W. North, who tries to seduce the innocent newspaper cartoonist Erica Merryon. She is saved from ruin by her friend the journalist Honoria Watson, who persuades a gossip columnist colleague to suppress an article on the scandal.

Among the interwar writers, Rose Macaulay's treatment of the press, from highbrow weeklies to popular dailies, is the most thoughtful and comprehensive. By the end of the First World War, Macaulay had already written two novels discussing the press, *The Making of a Bigot* (1914), about a young man who wants to become a journalist, and *Non-Combatants and Others* (1916), discussed in Chapter 2. In *Potterism* (1920), the intellectual journalist Arthur Gideon disdains the popular press, much of it owned by self-made millionaire Percy Potter. From the ivory tower of his small circulation *Weekly Fact*, he condemns daily newspaper journalism catering for the masses. However, when the *Weekly Fact* itself goes downmarket to avoid bankruptcy, Gideon takes a long walk through London and has an uncomfortable epiphany:

> He saw, as he passed a newspaper stand, placards in big black letters – 'Bride's Suicide.' 'Divorce of Baronet.' Then, small and inconspicuous, hardly hoping for attention, 'Italy and the Adriatic.' For one person who would care about Italy and the Adriatic, there would, presumably be a hundred who would care about the bride and the baronet... 'Light Caught Bending', another placard remarked. That was more cheerful, though it was an idiotic way of putting a theory as to the curvature of the earth, but it was refreshing, that, apparently, people were expected to be excited by that too. And, Gideon knew it, they were. Einstein's theory as to space and light would be discussed, with varying degrees of intelligence, most of them low, in many a cottage, many a club, many a train... People were interested not only in divorce, suicide and murder, but in light and space, undulations and gravitation... Even though people might like their science in cheap and absurd tabloid form, they did like it. The Potter press exulted in scientific discoveries made easy, but *it was better than not exulting in them at all*.'[66]

This is the crux of Macaulay's argument: popular journalism may not be an ideal way of transmitting news of conflict and scientific discovery, but reading it is better than total ignorance. Her reference to the working-class 'cottage', upper-class 'club' and middle-class 'train' reflects her faith in the democratizing nature of the press, answering intellectuals' criticisms. Give people accurate information and trust them to do the right thing with it, she argues, and this is a thesis in fiction that reflects what interwar defenders of the press were also saying.[67]

Similarly J. B. Priestley trod a fine line between criticizing the excesses of the popular press, for which he wrote copious articles, and defending its readers against an intellectual elite who he despised just as much. Charlie Habble's unremarkable and instinctive actions in dousing a fire are blown into the performance of a 'Wonder Hero' by the *Tribune* newspaper in J. B. Priestley's *Wonder Hero* (1933), so it can create its own fantasy narrative. Charlie is bemused and uncomfortable at his treatment. He is an ingénu wrenched by journalist Hal Kinney from his small Midlands town and used as newspaper fodder: 'He was supposed to be a great hero, though he knew very well he was nothing of the kind. But there it was, in big print, in the *Tribune* … It made him feel excited, but it also made him feel ashamed.'[68] Priestley's argument is that the great London papers live in a fantasy world and have no notion of the struggles of ordinary people. Priestley expanded his theme in his non-fiction *English Journey*, written the year *Wonder Hero* was published:

> Just lately when we offered hospitality to some distinguished German-Jews who had been exiled by the Nazis, the leader-writers in the cheap press began yelping again about Keeping Foreigners Out. Apart from the miserable meanness of the attitude itself – for the great England, the England admired throughout the world, is the England that keeps open house, the refuge of Mazzini, Marx, Lenin[69]

However, unlike Auden and Day Lewis, Priestley was careful to avoid criticizing the readers of popular newspapers who were not 'dumb' at all, indeed were thoroughly aware that newspapers peddled make-belief. In *Wonder Hero*, Charlie's father reads the *Daily Tribune*, 'in a curious state of suspended belief or disbelief, the mood of a man at a conjuring entertainment … He felt it was a grand pennyworth, no matter whether it lied or told the truth'. This vision of the popular newspaper reader is the same as Rose Macaulay's in her novel *Keeping up Appearances* (1928; discussed more fully in Chapter 7). Mrs Lily Arthur, of East Sheen, instinctively understands that newspapers are works of fantasy, with their own language and worldview which is very different from that of ordinary people. These characteristics do not preclude her from thoroughly enjoying reading them, however. Mass Observation studies of newspaper reading from 1938 onwards reveal Macaulay and Priestley's assessment to be more accurate than that of the Auden Group. The spring 1938 reading survey asking people why they read papers reveals an amused detachment mirroring that of Lily Arthur and Charlie Habble's father, particularly from readers of popular papers. Here is just a sample:

> 'I read the *Daily Mirror* because I am insured with it and I like the pictures.'
>   '*The People*' always strikes me as rather low and common in style and none of us really like it although we have it.'
>   '[*Daily Mirror*] Plenty of sensation. It takes me away from this dull old place.'
>   '[*Daily Mail*] The ladies of my fiancée's family are chiefly interested in births, marriages and deaths, then needlework articles and cinema adverts.'
>   '[*Daily Mirror*] My opinion of newspapers is not very good on the whole. They all have a bad tendency to exaggerate.'
>   '[*Daily Express*] I think newspapers are an advantage to the world, but unfortunately all that is printed is not always true.'[70]

Interwar press defenders argued that for all the 'idiocy' of some of the stunts, popular newspapers rid the serious press of its pomposity, popularized science and religious and political ideas and 'gave the working classes and the half-educated news about themselves and their own world and about social conditions...which brought a remarkable change in the intellectual life of the people'.[71] The educated intellectual classes' underestimation of the British public and their appreciation of serious political events are vividly illustrated by an entry in Harold Nicolson's diary, 13 March 1938, after he had given a parliamentary speech warning against German aggression in the wake of Foreign Secretary Anthony Eden's resignation: 'Leicester [his constituency]...round to the Newfoundland Working Men's Club. They are all anti-Chamberlain, saying 'Eden had been proved right'. My own stock has gone up greatly over my speech... *it is amazing how many of them listen in to serious debates. It really encourages one*' (emphasis added).[72]

As the 1930s wore on, and it became clear that all over Europe when tyrants came to power one of their first moves was to take control of newspapers either by threat or coercion, these voices in defence of a free press would grow stronger (see Chapter 4).

Winifred Holtby and Ellen Wilkinson: Journalism and politics

Lovell Brown, journalist on the *Kingsport Chronicle*, both opens and closes Winifred Holtby's posthumous novel *South Riding* (1936). Holtby was a prolific journalist, described by Lady Rhondda, founder and editor of the interwar journal *Time and Tide*, as 'the most brilliant journalist in London' who wrote regular freelance articles for the *Yorkshire Post, Manchester Guardian, News Chronicle, Daily Herald* and *Evening Standard*.[73] Her subject matter, ranging from feminism, the plight of the poor, injustice in South Africa to the peace movement, underlines her conviction that journalism could be a force for good, a means to educate and inform people in the nineteenth-century liberal tradition. She disapproved of some of the most extreme activities of the popular press in the 1930s, as she writes in *Time and Tide* of 28 October 1933: 'Invasion of private decency, against which Mr St John Ervine made an able attack in his address... is not the only evil from which the modern press suffers. Equally serious is the suppression of inconvenient knowledge.' Her study of the journalist in *South Riding*, written as she knew she was dying, must surely be read as a warning to the press to stay on the side of right. Placing reporter Lovell Brown prominently in the Prologue and Epilogue underlines this emphasis, revealing the importance she gives to scrutiny and accountability to the workings of local democracy. In 'Prologue in a Press Gallery', journalists are discussing the drama of the election of the next county alderman. Among them is the cub reporter Lovell Brown, who, from his vantage point in the press gallery, sees everything happening on the floor of the council chamber:

> He saw below him bald heads, grey heads, brown heads, black heads, above oddly foreshortened bodies, moving like fish in an aquarium tank. He saw the semi-circle of desks facing the chairman's panoplied throne; he saw the stuffed horsehair seats, the blotting paper, the quill pens, the bundles of printed documents on the clerk's table, the polished firedogs in the empty grates, the frosted glass tulips shading the unignited gas jets, the gleaming ink wells.[74]

The level of detail Lovell perceives is impressive. The councillors, trapped beneath his gaze 'like fish in an aquarium tank', can do nothing without his seeing. Romantic and idealistic, Lovell, his heart beating fast with excitement, dreams of the stories he will cover: 'bridges, feuds, scandals ... bans on sex novels in public libraries, or educational scholarships, blighted hopes and drainage systems'. A local reporter whose heart quickens at the prospect of debates about drainage schemes is surely to be valued. But there is more: he will seek out and expose corruption, oppression and complacency. Brown, however, appears at crucial points in the novel; at each point, Holtby sets him a journalistic test, and each time he fails, missing the real corruption through growing hubris and self-importance.

In the Epilogue, Brown is seen flying high above South Riding in a monoplane, so that he can write a 'descriptive article' about the celebrations of the Silver jubilee of 6 May 1935. High above the countryside, he only gets vague images: 'Lovell was too high up to see and to describe the ingenuity of the loyal villagers who had chalked their flagstones red and white and blue.'[75] The contrast with his idealistic eye for the tiniest detail in the Prologue is obvious: he has placed himself far above the 'loyal villagers', and as a result sees nothing.

A parallel novel dealing with wilful blind-eyed journalism is Ellen Wilkinson's *The Division Bell Mystery* (1932). Ellen Wilkinson, the first woman Labour MP, elected for Middlesbrough East in 1924, wrote a number of books during her life, the most famous of which is *The Town That Was Murdered* (1939), her account of the decline of Jarrow after the collapse of the shipbuilding industry. She also wrote two novels, *Clash* (1929) and the less well-known *The Division*

Bell Mystery (1932), a thriller set in the House of Commons. *The Division Bell Mystery* concerns the attempts of Robert West, Conservative parliamentary private secretary to the secretary of state for home affairs, with the help of his journalist friend Sancroft, to solve the death of international financier Georges Oissel.

Wilkinson was from the start of her career at Westminster, aware of the power of the press to mould opinion and, as the first female Labour member, 'heralded by a fanfare of press trumpets', knew both the advantages and dangers of having the press interested in her life.[76] Most of the early reports of her in the House of Commons referred to her appearance, the *Daily Telegraph*, for example, describing her hair as of a 'stunning hue – auburn red … this shone like an aureole above the light Botticelli green of her dress' (*Daily Telegraph*, 11 February 1925). She worried that as a result she would not be taken seriously and that she would be sidelined into 'women's issues' rather than being able to fight for the unemployed of her constituency.[77]

She also used her fame to pursue her 'second love – journalism' and, from her early days in the House of Commons, wrote prolifically, mainly for the popular press, earning plaudits as 'a brilliant journalist' and a 'first-rate journalist … writing with verve and wit'.[78] After she temporarily lost her seat in 1931, she wrote for newspapers and magazines from the *Daily Herald* to *Pearson's Weekly*. She enjoyed the company of journalists, particularly 'sophisticated, well-informed and mainly left-wing' ones.[79] Her main themes were the dangers of the rise of fascism and the indignities of unemployment. She visited Germany in March 1933 immediately after Hitler came to power and, earlier than many other journalists, warned that 'The life of an Einstein or a Dr Zondek are at the mercy of hysterical lads of 18 or tough slum gangsters provided with revolvers with the warm approval and support of Captain Goering' and that it would be a dangerous mistake to treat 'Hitler as a bad smell, a temporary nastiness to be disinfected by boycott, or perfumed by legality'.[80]

Yet her fictional reporter, Sancroft of the *Daily Deliverer*, is neither fearless nor crusading, but a rather too comfortable friend of the powerful. Sancroft is a 'round, portly little person with twinkling eyes behind thick glasses'.[81] When West and others realize that the financier's 'suicide' is a murder and that an employee of the House of Commons may be to blame, Sancroft is kept in the dark – despite his helping with the investigation earlier on. He takes his bad luck meekly: 'That's all right. If you are in deep water I don't ask for confidences. You know where to find me if you want me. I'll just bring my little scraps of news and lay them at your feet like a good dog.'[82] The dog reference is appropriate. Sancroft may be a likeable character and a loyal friend, but as a journalist he is no good. He has become captivated by being so close to power and has forgotten what his main job should be. He wears West's slippers, has the key to his flat and helps himself to his tobacco: he is a pipe-smoking loyal lap dog, far too comfortable and tame.

In his history of the Lobby, veteran political correspondent James Margach warns against journalists getting too close to politicians: 'surveillance is eroded when newspapermen are treated as buddies, an arm of government manning an outstation in Fleet Street'.[83] In *The Division Bell Mystery*, all the papers can be relied on to keep quiet when leant on. There has been an embarrassing incident on the floor of the House when the lofty Conservative MP Lady Bell-Clinton has belittled a female Labour MP. After the session, Lord Dalbeattie, an early fictional spin doctor character, seeks out Robert West. 'Have a word with some of the pressmen', he tells West, 'They are very decent about incidents like that.'[84] The newspapers accept this censorship without question.

Claud Cockburn notes in his autobiography *In Time of Trouble* that in 1932 the time was ripe for him to establish his irreverent political weekly, *The Week*: 'It was [an] exhilarating [time] because the smug smog in which the press of that time enveloped the political realities of the moment was even thicker than I had anticipated.'[85]

The *Division Bell Mystery* is set during a Conservative administration in the middle of a recession. In one of the few scenes to take place outside the House of Commons, Robert West takes a taxi through London and passes a demonstration by the unemployed. He muses 'A bread march was not like England'.[86] Wilkinson was appalled by the plight of the working classes at a time of mass unemployment. There had been hunger marches in London throughout the 1920s, the first from Wales was as early as 1922 after unemployment passed two million in the summer of 1921.[87] West's uncomprehending and out-of-touch remark of course represents Wilkinson's attack on Conservative politicians, but Sancroft's demeanour is her attack on journalists. While he focuses on the death of a banker inside the House, the real story is happening outside, but he ignores it. Sancroft should have been covering the story of the bread marches, but was too busy helping himself to his political master's tobacco and warming himself by his fire. J. B. Priestley makes the same point in *Wonder Hero* (1933) when the popular press inflates and fabricates stories about heroes and beauty queens but ignores the reality of 1930s Britain and the lost town of Slakeby, where the shipbuilders have closed and young men have no hope of finding work.

'Intellectual Harlotry': Financial considerations and the clash between journalism and literature

That journalism often kept writers going financially was a source both of relief and resentment. Waugh records in his diary for 1930, when his agent secures him a monthly commission from the *Daily Mail* at £30 an article, 'I feel rather elated about it'.[88] He did not put his heart into it, however, recording: 'wrote *Daily Mail* article. Talked of lesbians and constipation' and his contract was not renewed.[89] Payment between the genres of journalism had by this time stratified with the popular press now being able to pay much more than 'highbrow' publications. Whereas 'highbrow' papers and journals in 1904 paid more or less the same rates as the new halfpenny ones, by the 1930s there was a definite pay gap between popular and highbrow papers, a situation that still persists today.[90] Waugh earned four guineas for an article on 'Consequences' for the *Manchester Guardian*, whereas a lighter one 'Too old at Forty' for the *Standard* earned him £10.[91] Similarly, Arnold Bennett records in his diaries that while the Liberal *Daily Chronicle* paid him six guineas a column in 1911, just three years later the latest Northcliffe paper, the *Sunday Pictorial*, with a circulation of 1.5 million, offered him £100 a column.[92] Perhaps the most poignant record is from William Gerhardie, whose 1928 novel *Doom* criticized the popular press for encouraging trivia and 'make-belief'.[93] In the early 1930s after his initial literary success waned, he submitted a list of articles he could write to the *Daily Express* including 'Why I am anti-dog', 'Why I love Children' and 'What I would do if I were king' and begged Beaverbrook to serialize his memoirs.[94]

In her memoir of Winifred Holtby, Vera Brittain notes that Holtby earned just £30 from Jonathan Cape for her novel *The Land of Green Ginger* in 1927, even though by now she was a well-established novelist, her earnings from journalism outstripping those from fiction: 'Many of the struggling writers who appealed to her for advice and envied her literary success would have been astonished to learn the modesty of her earnings apart from journalism.'[95] However, Holtby found her journalism a source of satisfaction and pleasure, as set out in a lecture she gave on 'Art and Journalism' a year before she died.[96] Rebecca West's letters also reveal a fairly equable attitude to her journalism although at times she expresses exasperation at having to churn out articles to subsidize her fiction. West wrote to the liberal journalist S. K. Ratcliffe in 1922: 'I feel dead beat and never want to write another line – I hate *hate* HATE journalism.'[97] Like Holtby, West earned more from her journalism than her literary work, noting in a letter of 1929 that she was paid £224 by her agent Pinker on publication of her novel

Harriet Hume, only slightly more than the £180 she was offered for a single article on 'Gossip' for the *Ladies Home Journal*.[98] Virginia Woolf described her literary journalism as her 'intellectual harlotry', and the fictional novelist Hervey Russell in Storm Jameson's novel *Company Parade* (1934) has a similar view, reflecting the author's own feelings of guilt over writing trivial articles for Rothermere's *Evening News*.[99] Storm Jameson's autobiographical *Mirror in Darkness* trilogy spanning the 1930s paints a detailed picture of interwar literary life of a group of writers and journalists not lucky enough to enjoy the Bloomsbury Set's private incomes. In *Company Parade*, the first of the trilogy, Hervey's husband, Penn, accuses her of writing a tawdry article that 'dripped with sentiment' for the *Daily Post* and tells her she won't do her literary reputation any good: "'I know," Hervey said. "But it was ten guineas."[100]

Apposite as ever, Rose Macaulay, another writer condemned as 'middlebrow' and always plagued with financial worries, simply referred to her newspaper articles as 'my Beasts'.[101]

No billet for Malone

Meanwhile the absence of journalist-novelists explaining and publicizing their glorious struggles in the manner identified in Chapter 1 is hard to ignore. An example of this change in attitude of writers who once extolled the virtues of the press is found in Arthur Conan Doyle's *The Land of Mist* (1926), a Professor Challenger novel featuring Edward Malone, reporter of the *Gazette*. *The Lost World* and *The Poison Belt*, discussed in Chapter 1, are told by Malone in the first person, and the stories are his own account of his adventures as published in the *Gazette*. *The Land of Mist*, Doyle's first post-war outing for Challenger, is told in the third person because 'Malone had lost his billet and had found his way in Fleet Street blocked by the rumour of his independence.'[102]

Modern Fleet Street is no place for a journalist of integrity and Doyle literally silences his erstwhile narrator. While for part of the novel Malone is engaged in journalistic activity, his newspaper office and his previously fondly drawn gruff Scottish news editor McArdle no longer feature. The newspaper system that formerly nurtured Malone is at first absent and then excluding, and he is rescued from impecuniousness by Challenger and the world of science. Perhaps in the aftermath of the First World War, publishers suspected there was no longer a market for stories starring heroic swashbuckling reporters. The large quantity of journalist memoirs published during this time suggests a public appetite for Fleet

Street nostalgia, although of course many of these are memories of a pre-war 'Golden Age'.[103] Perhaps the increasing demands of daily newspaper journalism now cramped would-be novelists' style and left them drained at the end of the day. Despite Stella Gibbons' defence of journalism in her preface to *Cold Comfort Farm* (1932), she confessed that while a reporter on the *Evening Standard* in the late 1920s, she found the work 'exhausting ... *You have to sell yourself to your paper*' (emphasis added), evoking the exhausted and compromised Hector Puncheon of Dorothy L. Sayers' *Murder Must Advertise* (1933).[104]

Writers and journalists between the wars, then, use their fictions to explore their own relationships with the newspaper press, as well as the role of commercial journalism in the age of mass newspaper reading. Whether, as in the case of Aldous Huxley, it is to differentiate his own writing from journalism or, for Harold Nicolson, to announce a break with popular journalism or, in the case of Stella Martin Currey, to negotiate writing for a suddenly competitive commercialised environment, writers for all genres clearly meditate deeply on where their writing 'fits in' in the field of cultural production. For Ellen Wilkinson and Winifred Holtby, journalism must be employed to hold politicians to account, if it is to have any social value. For Elizabeth Bowen and Dorothy L. Sayers, popular journalism must be exposed as an impostor in the literary field and expelled to where it really belongs: the field of commerce and advertising. All the fictions discussed here present newspaper journalism as a 'problem' for their authors, with those more closely engaged with newspaper work more keenly observing the transition of journalism from a liberal profession to a commercial transaction; none display the optimistic characteristics of the Edwardian age even though many do acknowledge benefits of wider access to political, social and scientific information. Writers engaged both in journalism and fiction are clearly struggling to straddle the two fast-separating worlds. The aggressive nature of the criticism of journalism in fictions studied here reveals, however, the regret, anguish and fear *all* writers felt towards the fast-changing nature of the field of cultural production.

Notes

1   The 'The Interview with the Cat Had Been Particularly Full of Appeal' in the title is from Dorothy L. Sayers' *Murder Must Advertise*, discussed below.

2   Many are referenced in this chapter. Others are referenced in Chapters 4, 5 and 7.

3   Sayers, *Murder Must*, pp. 221–222.

4   Sayers worked for the advertising agency Bensons 1922–1932 and her experience there owes much to the setting of this novel.

5   Sayers, *Murder Must*, pp. 225–226.

6   Political and Economic Planning (P.E.P.), *Report on the British Press*, p. 44.

7   Wells, H. G., *The Salvaging of Civilisation*, pp. 184 & 187.

8   Massingham, H. W., 'Journalism as a Dangerous Trade', pp. 839–840.

9   LeMahieu, D. L., *A Culture for Democracy*, p. 254.

10   Many of these writers and their works will be discussed later in the chapter. For a full list of authors and titles, see bibliography.

11   See particularly, Collier, Patrick, *Modernism on Fleet Street*; John Carey, *The Intellectuals and the Masses*; LeMahieu, *A Culture for Democracy*; Matthew Kibble, 'The Betrayers of Language: Modernism and the *Daily Mail*'; and Declan Kiberd '*Ulysses*, newspapers and modernism'.

12   Aldington, Richard, 'A Solemn Dialogue' in *Egoist*, pp. 105–106.

13   Currey, Stella Martin, *Paperchase End*, pp. 45–48.

14   J. P. Martin was author of the *Uncle* stories ('Uncle is an elephant. He's immensely rich, and he's a B.A.' J. P. Martin records in his diaries Stella's story-writing from a young girl.

15   Stella Martin Currey papers, privately held by her son, James Currey.

16   From F. R. Leavis' PhD Thesis 'The Relationship of Journalism to Literature' (1924), p. 336.

17   Wilson, Charles, *First with the News*, p. 322.

18   P. E. P., *Report on the British Press*, p. 5.

19   Ibid., p. 35.

20   From Cox, Howard, 'Mass Circulation Periodicals and the Harmsworth Legacy in the British Popular Magazine Industry', paper for the European Business History Association Annual Conference, Bergen, Norway, August 2008.

21   Figures compiled from http://www.magforum.com/glossies/womens_magazine _sales.htm (accessed 2 August 2015).

22   P. E. P., *Report on the British Press*, p. 157.

23   Leavis, F. R., 'Manifesto' in *Scrutiny*, 1/1, p. 2.

24   P. E. P. *Report on the British Press*, pp. 56–59.

25   Thompson, Denys, 'A Hundred Years of the Higher Journalism' in *Scrutiny*, 4/1, pp. 31–32.

26   Escott, T. H. S., 'Old and New in the Daily Press', p. 366.

27   Ibid., pp. 363 & 363.

28   Lawrence, D. H., *Kangaroo*, p. 250; *John Bull* was a libellous penny weekly edited by the notorious Horatio Bottomley, who was disgraced for the fraudulent selling of Victory Bonds.

29   Collier, *Modernism on Fleet Street*, p. 4.

30 See also *Spectator*, 23 February 1918, pp. 197–198, 'The Government and the Press'. 'The duty of the press is to inform the public … what the press cannot and must not do is try to rule the country'; *Nation and Athenaeum*, 19 August 1922, p. 677: 'So about thirty years ago the "New Journalism" was born. Headlines, scareheads, snappy pars and stunts took the place of literature, serious news and discussion …'; Baumann, Arthur, 'The Functions and Future of the Press' in *Fortnightly Review*, April 1920, pp. 620–627; Escott, 'Old and New in the Daily Press', p. 366; *Adelphi*, Vol 1 No 2 (July 1923, p. 155), 'The Contributor's Club'.

31 Huddleston, Sisley, 'The Human Spirit in Shadow' in *The Atlantic Monthly*, November 1920, pp. 596–601.

32 Angell, Norman, *The Press and the Organisation of Society*, pp. 28 & 61.

33 Cockburn, Claud, *In Time of Trouble*, p. 84.

34 Huxley, Aldous, *Crome Yellow*, p. 50.

35 Nicolson, Harold, *Diaries*, p. 116.

36 Nicolson, Harold, *Public Faces*, pp. 182, 210 & 218.

37 Bowen, Elizabeth, 'Recent Photograph', p. 220.

38 Ibid., pp. 218–219.

39 Rossetti, Christina, 'A Birthday', p. 780.

40 Woolf, Virginia, *A Writer's Diary*, p. 49.

41 Auden, W. H., 'Poem XVII' from *Look Stranger*, p. 34.

42 Auden, W. H., 'Beethameer, Beethameer, bully of Britain' in *The Orators*; collected in *The English Auden*, p. 86. 'Beethameer' is discussed at greater length in Chapter 5.

43 Day Lewis, Cecil, *The Magnetic Mountain*, Part Three, pp. 31–33.

44 Hutchinson, A. S. M., *If Winter Comes*, p. 148.

45 Gerhardie, William, *Doom*, p. 202. *Doom* is discussed in greater detail in Chapter 5 as its main character is a thinly disguised Lord Beaverbrook, Lord Ottercove.

46 Waugh, Evelyn, *Vile Bodies*, p. 87.

47 Waugh, Evelyn, *Diaries*, p. 284.

48 Hutchinson, *If Winter Comes*, p. 143.

49 Joyce, James, *Ulysses*, pp. 114–121.

50 Bourdieu, Pierre, *On Television and Journalism*, p. 8.

51 See for example Sessions, David, 'The State of the Internet is Awful and Everybody Knows it' in Patrolmag.com 25 August 2014 http://www.patrolmag .com/2014/08/25/david-sessions/the-state-of-the-internet-is-awful-and-everybody -knows-it/ (accessed 22 November 2015).

52 Harding, Jason, *The Criterion*, p. 7.

53 Ayers, David, *English Literature of the 1920s*, p. 107.

54 Edited by John Middleton Murry, priced one shilling, cheaper than T. S. Eliot's 7 shilling 6d *Criterion*, *Adelphi* achieved sales of 15,000 as opposed to the 800–1,000 achieved by the *Criterion* (Harding, *The Criterion*, pp. 19 & 27).

55   Murry, John Middleton, 'Editorial' in *Adelphi*, 1/1, pp. 2–3.

56   Murry, John Middleton, *The Things We Are* p. 126.

57   'MZ 4796', 'The Pressgoat' in *Adelphi*, 1/2, pp. 115–122.

58   This paper is loosely based on Jameson's own brief stint as subeditor on *New Commonwealth*, a short-lived and obscure paper as she describes it in her autobiography *Journey from the North* with offices on 'the top floor of a lean decrepit house in a square behind Fleet Street' (p.155).

59   Buchan, John, *Castle Gay*, p. 24.

60   Gibbons, Stella, *Cold Comfort Farm*, pp. ix–x. Stella Gibbons began her career at the British United Press Agency, before working at the *London Standard* 1926–1930. After being sacked in 1930, she then worked for a long time as editorial assistant on *The Lady* (Oliver, Reggie, *Out of the Woodshed*, pp. 62 & 82).

61   Hunt, Cecil, *Ink in My Veins*.

62   Lane, Margaret, *Faith, Hope and No Charity*, p. 149.

63   Bingham, Adrian, *Family Newspapers?* p. 232.

64   Buchan, John, *The Last Crusade*, pp. 61–62.

65   Frankau was a novelist and freelance journalist 1920s–1940s (from the introduction to 1947 edition of *Life – and Erica*).

66   Macaulay, Rose, *Potterism*, pp. 160–161. 'Light Caught Bending' was a headline in the popular Sunday *Weekly Despatch*, then edited by Bernard Falk, who explains the article in his memoirs: 'the witty sub-editor, John Rayner, having regard to the eccentric behaviour of the light rays when passing through the denser atmosphere close to the edge of the sun, headed "Light Caught Bending". This was about as much of the Einstein theory as we poor, benighted mutts could digest. Yet our heading seized the popular imagination, and like the Einstein theory itself, ran round the world' (Falk, 1931: 204).

67   See, for example, see Kennedy Jones' *Fleet Street and Downing Street* (1920), Harold Herd's *The Making of Modern Journalism* (1927) and A. J. Cummings' *The Press and a Changing Civilisation* (1936).

68   Priestley, J. B., *Wonder Hero*, p. 63.

69   Priestley, J. B., *English Journey*, p. 161.

70   Mass Observation Reading Survey No. 4 Spring 1938, Box 1/1B.

71   Cummings, A. J., *The Press and a Changing Civilisation*, pp. 35–36.

72   Nicolson, Harold, Diaries 1931–1939, p. 331.

73   Berry, Paul, and A. G. Bishop, *Testament of a Generation*, p. 17.

74   Holtby, Winifred, *South Riding*, p. 3.

75   Ibid., p. 483.

76   Vernon, Betty, *Ellen Wilkinson*, p. 78.

77   See, for example, her article in *Labour Magazine*, January 1925: 'Journalists seem to be more interested in whether I will quarrel with Lady Astor than with the solid hard work I have come to Parliament to do. Yet the Labour Party's having only one

woman in the House is not a matter of mere interest, but something for everyone of us to be ashamed of' (quoted in Vernon, *Ellen Wilkinson*, p. 79).

78   Vernon, *Ellen Wilkinson*, p. 132; Holtby, Winifred, 'Little Bo-Peep' in *Time and Tide*, 16 August 1930, p. 1049.

79   Vernon, *Ellen Wilkinson*, p. 134.

80   Wilkinson, Ellen, 'Thinking in Blood' in Time and Tide, 1 April 1933, pp. 381–384.

81   Wilkinson, Ellen, *Division Bell Mystery*, p. 28.

82   Ibid., p. 230.

83   Margach, James, *Abuse of Power*, pp. 4–5.

84   Wilkinson, *Division Bell*, p. 250.

85   Cockburn, *In Time of Trouble*, p. 207.

86   Wilkinson, *Division Bell*, p. 110.

87   Gardiner, Juliet, *The Thirties: An Intimate History*, p. 149.

88   Waugh, *Diaries*, p. 309.

89   Ibid., p. 310. The articles are not very good and were not considered worthy of inclusion in Gallagher, Donat (ed.), *The Essays, Articles and Reviews of Evelyn Waugh*, London: Methuen, 1983. There is no reference to lesbians or constipation in the finished versions that appeared in the *Daily Mail* May–June 1930, so either they were removed by a subeditor or Waugh was not writing his diary honestly.

90   Low, Frances, *Press Work for Women*, pp. 65–77.

91   Gallagher, *The Essays, Articles and Reviews of Evelyn Waugh*, p. 36.

92   Bennett, Arnold, *Journals Vol I*, p. 125.

93   Gerhardie, *Doom*, p. 78.

94   Davies, Dido, *William Gerhardie*, pp. 255 & 251.

95   Brittain, Vera, *Testament of Friendship*, pp. 275 and 307.

96   Ibid., p. 130.

97   West, Rebecca (ed.), Kime Scott, *Letters*, p. 52.

98   Ibid., pp. 113–114.

99   Underwood, Doug, *Journalism and the Novel*, p. 129.

100 Jameson, Storm, *Company Parade*, p. 317.

101 Letter to Victor Gollancz, Dame Rose Macaulay Papers ERM/5.

102 Doyle, Arthur Conan, *The Land of Mist*, p. 410.

103 Such as Philip Gibbs' *Adventures in Journalism* (1923), Russell Stannard's *With the Dictators of Fleet Street* (1934); Bernard Falk, *He Laughed in Fleet Street* (1931); Viscount Castlerosse *Valentine's Days* (1934); Mrs Alec-Tweedie's *Me and Mine* (1932); Tom Clarke's *My Northcliffe Diary* (1931); and Mrs Charle's Peel's *Life's Enchanted Cup* (1933).

104 Oliver, Reggie, *Out of the Woodshed*, p. 63.

Tinker, Tailor, Soldier, Hack: Journalism and Espionage in a Time of War 1933–1979

Newspapers and journalists have long offered writers methods of exploring concepts of secrecy, betrayal, duplicity and deceit. Times of war, both hot and cold, real and phoney, offer particularly fertile opportunities to writers exploring the dubious role of the journalist as spy, detective and adventurer, the mutability of the profession offering creative potential in the analysis of character and motivation. Incidents from the newly 'turned' Kim Philby using the Times as 'cover' in the Spanish Civil War, to the investigative reporter Phillip Knightley being courted simultaneously by the CIA and KGB reveal that truth and fiction are often intertwined. Newspapers and journalists, quite opposite from their stated claims on accuracy and impartiality, have always, both literally and metaphorically, blurred the truth at the edges.

It is 1936 and the freelance journalist Desmond d'Esterre Kenton is standing on a chilly platform in Nuremberg, Germany, waiting for the slow train to Vienna, when 'the Night Orient Express from Ostend came in, flecked with melting snow'. The man, an incurable gambler, is a consummate linguist, diffidently charming and always broke. His lack of funds makes him easy prey for an agent seeking to smuggle documents concerning the defence of Romanian oil installations out of Germany. When offered 300 marks to conceal the documents, 'at that moment, Kenton ceased for a time to be an impartial recorder of events and became a participator'.[1] So begin the adventures of Kenton in Eric Ambler's *Uncommon Danger* (1937), a novel that explores ideas of political commitment, journalistic engagement and of crossing borders as a way of recreating the self, wrapped up in a fast-paced thriller package. The arrival of the Orient Express, a modernist symbol of the literal and metaphorical breaking of arbitrary boundaries, is reinforced by its weight of 'melting snow', a substance transforming from one state to another as it travels from one country to another, a transformation that Kenton, too, will undergo during the novel. Kenton is an unlikely hero for a thriller on a number of levels. He 'had never regarded himself as a particularly courageous man' and violence upsets him.[2] His motivations are not always noble: he has previously sold information to military attachés for 'fabulous prices' and a darkening Europe offers opportunities to boost his meagre freelance income. Yet in 'the bad days of 1934' he had helped a Jewish instrument maker and his family escape from Munich to Vienna.[3] Not only has Kenton abandoned the so-called journalistic impartiality in the great ideological battles of the 1930s, but he has actively engaged in helping victims of Nazi brutality. This engagement has peeled back the skin of his persona as an objective, impartial journalist to reveal the human within: the committed activist not content to sit on the fence as Europe takes sides. In this 'Political Decade when the literary world turned *en masse* to the left', Ambler is leaving his readers in no doubt as to which side his hero, no matter his faults, is on.[4] Although not a member of the Communist Party, Ambler certainly had left-leaning sympathies. During the 1930s he attended radical literary evenings and listened to communist speakers in Hyde Park, and heard the poet Stephen Spender report back from Spain.[5] In his memoir *Here Lies Eric Ambler* (1985), he describes what his concerns were at the time of writing *Uncommon Danger*:

> The year was 1936, the year in which Italy invaded Abyssinia, Civil War broke out in Spain and Hitler ordered the German Army to reoccupy the Rhineland. It was a year of yet more refugees and of marriages arranged to confer passports. It was also the year in which the League of Nations was at last seen plainly to be impotent. Those were the things that I was trying, in my own fictional terms, to write about.[6]

Ambler's attitude mirrors that of other writers of the 1930s, including Graham Greene, Storm Jameson, W. H. Auden, Ellen Wilkinson and Evelyn Waugh, who used the figure of the journalist – as agent for good or ill – in their fictions to portray a quest for certainties and truths in a dangerous world on the brink of a second bloody conflagration. Other writers at this time, including James Hilton, Anthony Powell and Christopher Isherwood, saw creative possibilities too in the foreign correspondent operating abroad, alone, a small, yet often pivotal agent and buffeted by the great movements of history. The clear similarities between the information-gathering methods of journalists and spies, 'blood brothers separated at birth' and their ambiguous motivations offered writers the chance of exploring the grand themes of the time often in the vehicle of the popular genre of the spy or detective thriller.[7] The newspaper too, from the clichéd barrier behind which charlatans of all persuasions can hide in public places, to its conveying, in black and white, information both true and fabricated, both innocently acquired and cynically placed, is an image developed in fiction from the early days of classified advertising and, later, crossword puzzles and agony columns. We have already seen how Rudyard Kipling's first-hand experience of lovers' secret messages in the *Civil and Military Gazette* fired his imagination with the creative possibilities of the newspaper in his fiction. Writers now use this conceit in a variety of ways, the newspaper acting as some kind of secret doorway connecting the private and public realm. In Elizabeth von Arnim's *The Enchanted April* (1922) a group of dissatisfied women set off for romantic adventure in Italy after reading a classified advertisement to 'Those who Appreciate Wistaria and Sunshine' in *The Times*; In Ngaio Marsh's Inspector Alleyn mystery *Death in a White Tie* (1938) criminals communicate with each other via coded messages in the *Times* personal column: 'Childie Darling. Living in Exile. Longing. Only want Daughter. Daddy.'[8] In Robert Harling's *The Paper Palace* (1951), discussed below, a notice in the personal column is used as a way of forcing an agent to break cover.

Journalists and spies: Blood brothers separated at birth

The historian of appeasement Franklin Reid Gannon describes the 1930s as 'the age of the foreign correspondent … some became the veritable ideological James Bonds of their time.'[9] British newspapers, enjoying unprecedented circulations could afford to run networks of correspondents and stringers across Europe. The *Daily Mail*, with a circulation of more than 1.5 million kept at least three correspondents in Berlin alone. The *Daily Express*, at that time the newspaper with the highest daily circulation of more than 2.3 million kept no fewer than eight regular correspondents in Germany and a further four in other countries of middle Europe, despite its proprietor Lord Beaverbrook's policy of isolationism.[10] While the majority of the British press was pro-appeasement, many of their individual correspondents and stringers, seeing Nazi brutality at first hand, had other views. There was also, amongst some journalists as well as more literary writers, sympathy for communist ideas, which often put them at political odds with their capitalist proprietors. During the 1930s the Soviet travel agency Intourist, based in an office in Bush House encouraged month-long 'pilgrimages' to sympathetic, or wavering, journalists and intellectuals in the hope of swaying them during their tours of factories, theatre and cinema trips, a bargain at £31 for a twenty-eight-day tour.[11] On one such trip, described in a contemporary travelogue were 'a dozen' Fleet Street journalists: 'Hamilton Fyfe was their leader, whitehaired and benevolent-looking; Low the cartoonist was with them, silent, smiling, seeing everything; Smith the foreign editor of the *News Chronicle*; Yeats-Brown for the *Spectator*; Kingsley Martin, the editor of the *New Statesman*; Hughes of *Forward*; and several more.'[12]

Broadly speaking the *Times*, *Daily Mail*, *Observer*, *Sunday Times*, *Daily Express* and *Sunday Express* were the most pro-appeasement papers. The *Manchester Guardian* and *News Chronicle*, though opposed to Hitler, saw iniquities in the Treaty of Versailles and were suspicious of the French. The *Daily Telegraph*, *Daily Herald* and *Daily Mirror* were the most anti-German and anti-appeasement.[13] These papers, with news reports and cartoons (and Low's famous Hitler lampoons in the *Evening Standard*), made relations between Chamberlain's government and Hitler's regime difficult at times, leading to Goebbels' complaint to Lord Halifax in November 1937 about attacks on Hitler in the British Press. In contrast to this variety in the newspaper press, the BBC's coverage of Europe was effectively controlled by the Cabinet.[14] Churchill had enjoyed a platform for his anti-German views in the *Evening Standard* from 1936 to 1938 but in April 1938 he was sacked for being out of line with Beaverbrook's own views.[15] Churchill also had his platform in Parliament, and much of what he said in debates was reported in the next day's newspapers no matter their policy vis-á-vis German relations. For example, his speech in the House of Commons on 12 November 1936 that was reported the next day in the pro-appeasement *Times* described 'the vast process of German rearmament already in full swing ... Germany's rearmament expenditure of £800,000,000 in two years on warlike preparation'.

Europe in the mid-1930s was a world where spies and journalists often seemed to be doing the same job, and they sometimes were doing just that. The use of the newspaper as 'cover' for intelligence agents has a long history. The writer Somerset Maugham worked for British Intelligence in Moscow during the First World War, ostensibly a correspondent for the *Daily Telegraph*.[16] His mission 'to prevent the Bolshevik Revolution and to keep Russia in the war ... did not meet with success', he later wrote, somewhat understatedly.[17] Maugham used his experiences in Switzerland and Russia as material for his *Ashenden* stories (1928), about an early urbane spy and 'writer by profession' who, like a later and more famous fictional spy, drinks dry Martini: 'To drink a glass of sherry when you can get a dry Martini is like taking a stage coach when you can travel by the Orient Express.'[18] Kim Philby, who is generally thought to have been recruited by Russian Intelligence in Vienna in 1933 went to Spain in 1937 and succeeded in getting work as the *Times*' correspondent with General Franco. While in Spain he made his first tentative contacts with British Intelligence.[19] The committed communist Arthur Koestler has described how he used the *News Chronicle* as cover, 'the bona fide correspondent of a respectable English Liberal newspaper', to visit Franco's headquarters on behalf of the Comintern. For the British side, Claude Dansey's 'Z' Organisation, established throughout Europe during the 1930s, brought news of Hitler's rearmament programme to anti-appeasement politicians via anti-appeasement journalists: '[Claude] Dansey also had several British newspapermen working for him, most notably Gibson of *The Times*, Hillard of the *Manchester Guardian* and Maitland, second correspondent in Vienna and south-east Europe for the *Daily Express*.'[20]

During the mid- to late 1930s the Secret Services gradually began to realize that the threat to Britain lay more with Nazism and fascism than with communism and began to restructure its priorities accordingly. SIS and MI5 found Fleet Street and Grub Street fertile recruiting grounds, attracting among others David Walker, sports reporter of the *Mirror*, and John, Bingham columnist for the *Sunday Dispatch*, who was to become the inspiration for John Le Carré's 'George Smiley'.[21] The espionage expert Nigel West explains that due to a dearth of experienced military men, who were already otherwise engaged in defending the realm, 'MI5 and SIS found themselves recruiting some unusual characters, drawn mainly from the City, the universities, Fleet Street, the law ... the skills of these professions are ideally suited to the essential core activity of any security agency: the acquisition, collation, analysis and distribution of information.'[22] Whereas Bingham's recruitment was out of a simple patriotism, other journalists who held left-wing views saw working for the intelligence service as a way of fighting fascism. Left-wing writers for the *Spectator*, for example, Derek Verschoyle and Goronwy Rees, both worked for SIS.[23] Indeed the list of contributors to the *Spectator* in the 1930s reads like a 'Who's Who' of leftists, spies and intelligence operatives for both Britain and Russia: Anthony Blunt was arts correspondent; Guy Burgess wrote book reviews; and Ray Strachey, Graham Greene and Stephen Spender were all regular contributors. This author's own great uncle, Archibald Lyall, a freelance journalist, occasional *Spectator* contributor, linguist and travel writer, was recruited sometime in the 1930s and remained in SIS until long after the Second World War. He had been a journalist in Santander and Salamanca during the Spanish Civil War, spending some time in a Spanish jail and was credited with smuggling some of the first photographs of the war out of Spain in 1936.[24] He was later suspected of being a Soviet 'Mole' in the 1960s because of his friendship with Guy Burgess and because he had written a travel book, *Russian Roundabout*, in 1933, which, although critical of the communist system, ended on a sympathetic note.[25] Ian Fleming had acted as an agent for SIS while working for Reuters in Moscow in 1933.[26] Like Somerset Maugham, many literary spies would later write fictionalized accounts of their service, further emphasizing the shared characteristics between journalism and espionage. The making sense of apparently disconnected pieces of information, the forging of a 'story' out of a string of facts and events, the creation of a clear narrative from a superficially chaotic world and, yes, long periods of tedious legwork and boredom, often in far-flung places, while waiting for something to happen: all these are shared by the two professions.

Bulwarks against appeasement

While many British newspapers supported Chamberlain's policy of appeasement through the 1930s, sometimes their own correspondents, particularly those based in Germany, had very different views, often clashing fiercely with their editors, unable to ignore the 'orgy of cruelty' they witnessed being meted out on Jews and communists.[27] The then former Labour MP Ellen Wilkinson travelled to Germany as a journalist after losing her seat in 1931 and wrote in 1933: 'Some tribute ought to be paid to those pressmen who, in danger of physical violence … and equally in danger of their jobs on certain papers, yet managed to get the ghastly truth over to the world.'[28]

Correspondents Norman Ebbutt and Pembroke Stephens were expelled from Nazi Germany, in August 1937 and May 1934, respectively.[29] Pembroke Stephens' *Daily Express* despatches from Berlin ('New Hitler Blow at the Jews, Plan to Seize All They Possess?' *Daily Express*, 25 May 1934) revealed to a large audience that oppression and brutality were not only tolerated but encouraged under Hitler's regime. F. A. Voigt, respected diplomatic correspondent of the *Manchester Guardian*, was the target of a German SS assassination attempt at the end of 1933. Part of Dansey's Z Organisation, he continued writing well-sourced stories about the Gestapo and concentration camps throughout the mid-1930s.[30]

For journalists on the Left or even centre of politics, the growing threat in Europe made it impossible to sit on the sidelines and report. This, according to his biographer Michael Jago, is what prompted John Bingham to join MI5: 'Not for glory or for public recognition, but because he could not bear to stand idly by and merely write about momentous events.'[31] The journalist and writer Shiela Grant Duff records that she became a foreign correspondent for the simple reason that she realized, in 1934, that the main focus of her life should be 'preventing the outbreak of a major war'.[32] Having been rejected by Geoffrey Dawson of the *Times*, she went as a freelance to Paris in 1934 and then on to the disputed Saar territory, where she reported for the *Observer* on preparations for the vote on whether the region should stay within France or revert back to Germany. Her reports from the Saar in January 1935 reveal either courage or naivety, openly accusing the ascendant Deutsche Front of confiscating Jews' voting cards and 'brutally' handling activists campaigning for the Saar to stay neutral rather than revert to Germany (*Observer*, 13 January 1935). Unable to remain on the sidelines, at considerable personal risk, in Saarbrucken, she 'used [her] position quite shamelessly to ease the escape of anti-Nazis', using her persona as 'a liberal journalist' to be anything but impartial, something, she recalls, never concerned her at the time:

> Nor am I ashamed on humanitarian grounds, that I then held my liberal umbrella over [communist refugees]. As an English journalist I was able to cross easily into France. I did so whenever I was asked by friends I had made in the United Front. I carried their typewriters and their documents over the frontier. I guaranteed them a certain immunity in that interim period by being seen in public with them.[33]

Incidents such as these show how the role of the journalist can offer rich potential for writers interested in presenting Europe and politics and the role of the information-gatherers in a creative way during this time. They also suggest that journalistic 'impartiality' is a chimera and that the 'truth', a precious commodity at any time, particularly so during times of imminent war, is not something one should look for in newspaper reports. Many contemporary fictions address this point, from the Left and the Right, from the lying journalists willing to cover up anything for the powers that be in W. H. Auden and Christopher Isherwood's play *The Dog beneath the Skin* (1935) to Evelyn Waugh's famous novel of mendacious war correspondence, *Scoop* (1938). Lecture events and social gatherings in the small world of literary London meant that ideas and evidence could be easily circulated, even if journalists were prevented from reporting the truth in their newspapers. The influential Left Book Club, which by 1937 had over 40,000 members, organized discussion groups, week-end seminars, political rallies and cinema showings. By May 1938 it had several vocational discussion groups including an actors' group, musicians' group and influential journalists' and poets' groups, all circulating ideas and information.[34] In her memoir *Journey from the North*, the novelist Storm Jameson, for example, records that during the early 1930s she liked to gather journalists around her so that she could find out what was going on in Europe, particularly Germany, direct from the correspondent, not via the medium of his paper:

> The after-dinner gossip of foreign correspondents is the best in the world ... I listened to them with passionate attention. I could live happily in a cell, I told myself, so long as the messages continued to come in from all sides ... I was listening to Harrison Brown [a freelance correspondent], who had come back from Berlin with evidence – at that time new and barely credible – of what Hitler planned to do with the Jews living in Germany. I was still (in 1933) naïve enough to think that he had only to lay it before the editor of the *Times* to blow away for good every hopeful illusion about the Nazi regime. During the next two years that good man Ebbutt, the paper's Berlin correspondent, broke himself against his editor's wilful delusions.[35]

By the early 1930s, the *Daily Mail* had taken a pro-Hitler line and there were already complaints from Jameson's international correspondent friends that British politicians and newspapers were underestimating or deliberately downplaying the dangers ahead. Journalists, as well as writers, were taking sides. The left-wing journalist Claud Cockburn, for example, resigned from the Berlin office of the *Times*, frustrated at his inability to report the truth. Recording that 'a newspaper is always a weapon in somebody's hands', he started his own publication, *The Week*, with a very open left-wing agenda.[36] Malcolm Muggeridge, disgusted at the deliberate covering up of the Ukrainian famine by Moscow's foreign correspondents, quit the *Manchester Guardian* and journalism, and 'in a mood of anger' wrote a novel about it instead.[37] In the novel, *Winter in Moscow* (1934), while the Moscow-based Western correspondents aren't 'spies' in the classic sense, their journalism is pro-Soviet propaganda, deliberately downplaying food shortages. The greatest offender is Pye, correspondent for a 'great English Liberal newspaper' who refuses to see evidence of starvation during a tightly controlled visit to the Ukraine. With no little irony Muggeridge observes: 'Now at last, readers of the articles thought, we know what really is going on in Russia.'[38] The 'strong, unequivocal attitude' regarding Hitler's rise to power, reported by Muggeridge's fellow correspondent on the *Manchester Guardian*, F. A. Voigt, also 'made him an alien element in the *Guardian*'s measured columns'.[39] Voigt joined Claude Dansey's 'Z' organization, while Muggeridge would later join MI6.[40] With pro-appeasement editors unwilling to disturb Anglo-German relations and pro-Soviet journalists often wilfully covering up the harsh realities of the communist regime, interesting gaps between truth and fiction, engagement and impartiality, secrets and lies opened up for novelists and writers of both the Left and the Right.

Graham Greene's shady operatives

Ambler and Muggeridge's great contemporary Graham Greene employed the ambiguous role of the journalist reporting on foreign affairs in his early 'entertainments' *Stamboul Train* (1932) and *England Made Me* (1935). Greene had trained as a journalist on the *Nottingham Journal* before moving to the *Times* as a subeditor, where he recalls in his memoir being happy. After he left, in December 1929 to concentrate on his fiction, he would, during periods of creative frustration come 'bitterly to regret' leaving the quiet scholarly atmosphere and the 'gentle thud of coals as they dropped one by one in the old black grate' in the subeditors' room.[41] Greene's memoir *A Sort of Life* recalls *Times* reporters he met during his employment as subeditor, particularly Vladimir Poliakoff, the diplomatic correspondent, 'In a grey homburg hat with a very large brim, who would come into our room to consult the files, carrying with him an air of worldliness and mystery (why was he not reading them next door in the foreign room where he naturally belonged? Perhaps he wished to remain for obscure reasons of state incognito)'.[42]

This romantic description and suggestion of espionage illustrates the easy elision Greene makes between the spy and the journalist.[43] In *Stamboul Train*, Mabel Warren's work as a journalist seems indistinguishable from that of a spy or private detective. Before her determined interrogation of the socialist exile Dr Czinner, she steals into his compartment while he is out, reckoning she has three minutes to find some kind of clue among his belongings: 'First there was the mackintosh. There was nothing in the pockets ... She picked up the hat and felt along the band and inside the lining; she had sometimes found quite valuable information concealed in hats.'[44]

Both Mabel Warren and Ferdinand Minty, the lowly Stockholm stringer in *England Made Me*, are desperate creatures, operating out of 'the squalid necessity of earning money'.[45] Both cause the deaths of better people than themselves, for transient newspaper stories and a bit of money to allow them to continue living their limited lives. Both are self-imposed exiles from normal life. Mabel, a drunken, masculine lesbian lives a life on the move, her 'province' the region along the Rhine between Cologne and Mainz, where she makes a living out of interviewing 'brothel-keepers in their cells, the mothers of murdered children'.[46] Minty, 'the exile from his country and his class', scratches a living off tit bits other journalists discard, and keeps a spider trapped under a glass in his lowly lodging house, wondering how long it will live.[47] They both stumble across sensitive information, and both operate in a tinder-box Europe, where borders are contested and fluid and political swings or shifts in the balance of power in even minor countries have potentially major ramifications. They are small but significant catalysts in a wider game played by politicians, gangsters and international businessmen yet neither knows nor cares of the ripples spreading out from the small pebbles they cast. What interests Greene is their motivations for using the information that comes into their hands. For Mabel, the story of Dr Czinner's re-emergence and death in a Serbian railway station means the money to attract a girlfriend: 'Coral in pyjamas mixing a cocktail'.[48] For Minty, who 'had chosen his dump and stayed there', his passing on of information about the businessman Krogh's engagement is simply the chance to eke out his half-life of tepid coffees and cigarettes in Stockholm. What also interests Greene, for these, and his other journalist characters, is their privilege of having *access*, to people, to information, something which gives them, notwithstanding their lowly status, a particular type of power. It is this access, the ability to move between borders which are barred to most people – Mabel makes indiscriminate use of her 'reporter's pass' – which makes the journalist so interesting. It was this potential to move betwixt and between, to one day dine with kings and the next sleep on the ground, that so enchanted the young reporter Rudyard Kipling, who also used the image of the journalist to great creative effect (see Chapter 1). His observation, recorded in his 1936 memoir that, 'having no position to consider, and my trade enforcing it, *I could move at will in the fourth dimension*', echoes so much of the potential Greene sees in his fictional journalists.[49] Where Kipling's journalistic freedom of movement results in mischief-making, Greene's access goes further and, particularly with Mabel Warren, becomes invasive. She is most often described in terms of her smell: of gin and cheap powder; as she interrogates Dr Czinner, the train compartment fills with a 'smell of gas', and she is compared to the 'gross bouquets' of a field of defrosting cabbages through which the train is passing.[50] Like the transgressive journalist with her reporter's pass, her unwelcome smell crosses boundaries, invades bodies via noses and is at its most powerfully obnoxious as she corners her prey in a moving train carriage. (Mabel Warren will be discussed further in Chapter 7.)

Several of Greene's pre-war novels embody a sense of growing crisis. Around Mabel and Minty, Europe is darkening; an undemocratic evil is taking power from democratically elected governments. In *Brighton Rock* (1938) Greene eerily predicts an urban landscape destroyed by aerial bombardment: 'Half Paradise Piece had been torn up as if by bomb bursts; the children played about the steep slope of rubble.'[51] As with many other writers' work of the 1930s, these novels deal with the problems of public politics and private lives and how the former ask the latter for gestures of action and heroism. Neither Minty nor Mabel are prepared to give up their selfish, narrow goals for the greater good, something both could do with the information they have and the positions they occupy. In contrast to his shady characters operating on the sidelines, Greene would apply to join SIS after the outbreak of war although his service, by his own admission, was 'wholly undistinguished'.[52]

Foreign correspondence and the possibilities of the recreated self

While Greene's interest in the foreign correspondent in *Stamboul Train* and *England Made Me* is in the dreams and hopes of even shabby minor operatives, other novelists of the 1930s used the image of the foreign correspondent to evoke exoticism or glamour in the face of danger in their works. The correspondent Lushington commits careless sexual transgressions amid the deracinated diplomatic corps of a newly independent Baltic state in Anthony Powell's second novel, *Venusberg* (1932). The blithely anarchic Alcuin Chaddle, lately of the *Daily Mischiefmaker*, tracks blackmailers and kidnappers across the Balkans in Archibald Lyall's *Envoy Extraordinary* (1932). Ainsley Jergwin Fothergill, a social misfit, grasps at the chance to reinvent himself as a foreign correspondent and spy in revolutionary Russia in James Hilton's *Knight without Armour* (1933). Suppressing all traces of his previous life, Fothergill undergoes a series of transformations from correspondent to spy to Soviet revolutionary to peasant until he loses all sense of self: '*About himself* – that was the question. Who was he?'[53] Having unmade himself completely, he is now free, on the lawless forest roads of Soviet Russia, to find his authentic self. Helen Pratt is the tenacious and hard-drinking foreign correspondent in Christopher Isherwood's Berlin novel *Mr Norris Changes Trains* (1935), who tirelessly exposes Nazi thuggery against socialists and Jews until she is expelled from Germany. She seems to be partly modelled on Norman Ebbutt, with whom Isherwood socialized in Berlin taverns in 1933.[54] Pratt is a fearless reporter, coming into her own after the Nazis gain power in 1933, although her methods of obtaining information are occasionally hard-hearted:

> But not even Goering could silence Helen Pratt. She had decided to investigate the atrocities [the Nazis' ill-treatment of Jews and communists] on her own account. Morning, noon and night, she nosed around the city, ferreting out the victims or their relations, cross-examining them for details. These unfortunate

people were reticent of course, and deadly scared. They didn't want a second dose. But Helen was as relentless as their torturers. She bribed, cajoled, pestered. Sometimes losing her patience, she threatened.[55]

This mixture of approval and doubt about Helen's tactics reflects Isherwood's attitudes towards journalists, and his own lack of courage, at the time. Like Storm Jameson, he enjoyed journalists' company and spent time with the foreign press corps, but at the same time as he was writing *Mr Norris*, he was also working, with friend W. H. Auden, on their play *The Dog beneath the Skin*, which portrays utterly cynical journalists as collaborating with an oppressive state. As early as 1933, British newspapers had begun reporting the threat to the Jews posed by Hitler, with the *Daily Express* and *Daily Mirror* being the most outspoken. As a writer, Isherwood recognized it was his duty to report details of Berlin life during this turbulent time, and his memoir suggests he felt he had fallen short of his task considering his access, if he wanted, to 'Goering or even Hitler … he was a writer and could easily have been accepted as a freelance journalist … What inhibited him? His principles? His inertia? Neither is an excuse'.[56] Isherwood was given first-hand information about the brutal treatment of Jewish and homosexual prisoners after March 1933, but did not do anything about it himself. Instead he passed the information to Ebbutt. It was a timid and half-hearted action but Isherwood was aware that his widely known homosexuality made him particularly vulnerable. He records in his memoir that in Berlin foreign journalists and writers were watched by police spies.[57] He thus 'dared not' make his autobiographical narrator of *Mr Norris* obviously homosexual for the same reason. As a result 'the unlucky creature is no more than a demi-character'.[58] The public world of Nazi Germany thus penetrates, in the novel, the private world of Isherwood's imagination, illustrating well Samuel Hynes' thesis of the 'direct relation between literature and action in the public world' that becomes 'particularly close in times of crisis'.[59] Helen Pratt, however, is triumphantly expelled from Germany following a series of 'scalding articles … To hear her talk, you might have thought she had spent the last two months hiding in Dr Goebbels' writing desk or under Hitler's bed'.[60] Isherwood gives Helen more courage and journalistic *nous* than he possessed himself, and in portraying her as brave as well as ambitious reveals his admiration for some of the journalists he associated with in Berlin. Although Helen Pratt evidently guesses at Bradshaw's homosexuality, and although in the novel other characters are blackmailed on account of their own sexual transgressions, Helen, despite the fact that 'she was no more to be trusted with news than a cat with a saucer of milk', is loyal and disappears off to America, not having breathed a word.[61] She is an enthusiastic and vivid storyteller ('She had new stories about Roehm, about Heines, about Goering and his uniforms…She talked for hours…Helen brightened at the prospect of yet another story'), her verve and backbone atoning, to some extent, for Christopher Isherwood/William Bradshaw's pusillanimity.[62]

The vulnerability of correspondents and writers operating in Germany, and further east in Europe, presents writers with a further creative possibility. As we have seen, British journalists were subjected to observation, expulsion and assassination attempts and were targeted by rival regimes for recruitment. Many of the correspondents in the journalist-spy fictions discussed here are freelancers or stringers, and thus not enjoying the support or resources of their newspapers. Kenton, in Eric Ambler's *Uncommon Danger*, is a freelance journalist, as is Minty in Graham Greene's *England Made Me* and Ainsley Fothergill in James Hilton's *Knight without Armour*. In the Cold War journalist-spy fictions, discussed below, several more are too. The freelance status endows the journalist character a noble independence at a time when newspapers, particularly in the wake of the Abdication Crisis, were seen as an unquestioning arm of the state, as well as propaganda weapons for their capitalist proprietors' interests. Since the end of the First World War, journalists working for the mainstream press were depicted by the trade unions as being enemies of the working class; members of the National Union of Journalists (NUJ) were routinely abused at the Trades Union Congress. For instance it was reported in *The Journalist*, the union's paper, that at the TUC in Portsmouth, October 1920, the secretary of the Associated Society of Locomotive Engineers and Fireman said:

> It is necessary for every trade unionist at this Congress to put up with the general misrepresentation, vilification, and abuse of the capitalistic press…We know unfortunately that the brains of the members of the Journalists' Union here are bought and paid for to be used against members of their own class"…the statement was loudly resented at the press table.

In a critique of the press published in 1938, former *Times* editor Wickham Steed argues that the 'liberal profession' of the journalist by vocation is at odds with the interests of the newspaper business, which needs to manufacture and advertise a commercial product. In *The Press* Steed argues that by submitting to the proprietor's need for sales, journalists risk undermining their profession.[63]

Thus Kenton's freelance status is vital to our understanding his character as he roams across Germany and Vienna in the dying days of the interwar period. Kenton is outside the newspaper system, just as, when we first see him, he is outside the warm, lighted windows of the Orient Express. This must surely be

Ambler's mischievous reference to Mabel Warren in Graham Greene's *Stamboul Train* published just a few years earlier. Warren is inside the train and inside the corrupt journalistic network, a staffer on the *Clarion*. Kenton is outside, a penniless freelance. His vulnerability, and also his difficulty in getting his story published, is emphasized by the sinister agent Colonel Robinson, who warns him: 'I could, through my principals in London make it impossible for you to carry on your profession ... by having your name blacklisted by the proprietors of every important group of newspapers in England.'[64] Although Kenton ultimately succeeds in foiling the plot – a conspiracy between the Nazis and international oil companies to get a pro-Nazi government elected in Romania – he cannot get his story published. 'There was nothing he could do, except, he concluded bitterly, write to the *Times* about it', the proverbial gesture of ineffective protest. The use of the word 'to' rather than 'in' the *Times* reinforces Kenton's status as the powerless outsider, reduced to the status of ordinary citizen by 'Big Business', which maintains a stranglehold over the English press.[65] The role of the proprietor is further discussed in the next chapter.

Newspapers as unreliable texts

Before writing *Uncommon Danger*, Eric Ambler had already experimented with portraying a journalist in his first novel *The Dark Frontier* (1936). Casey is the wise-cracking communist-sympathizing 'ace foreign correspondent' from the American *Tribune*, who becomes the first journalist to report on the peasants' revolution in Ixania. While Casey the communist-sympathizer is rewarded with a scoop, an unnamed London daily newspaper carries an article denouncing Ixania's decision to disarm unilaterally, calling it 'idealistic folly gone mad. An unarmed Ixania is a potential cause of war'.[66] Ambler adds that after investigation, the author of the article is found to hold shares in a company that manufactures armaments (possibly a reference to Claud Cockburn asserting in his newssheet *The Week* in 1934 that the *Times* correspondents in Bucharest and Belgrade were both also agents for the arms manufacturer Vickers).[67] The contrast of Casey's honest self-exposure as partisan and the dishonest author of the article in the London paper confirms Ambler's approval of Casey's actions as well as being a wry comment on the mainstream press. *The Dark Frontier* also contains a humorous aside regarding the *Times*, which was regarded by 'radical newspapers, leftist dons and communist propagandists' as little more than an arm of Chamberlain's appeasing government, and its editor Geoffrey Dawson as a 'villain'.[68] The protagonist Professor Barstow is meeting the well-travelled Simon Groom, who brings him news from overseas: 'His [Groom's] knowledge of foreign affairs was remarkable. The Professor, an assiduous reader of the *Times* foreign page, heard for the first time of a major crisis just past.'[69]

This little, passing dig at the *Times* – suggesting its news coverage was patchy and partial – is a recurring motif in 1930s fictions. Writers are using their positions of public influence to attack a newspaper not, as we have seen before, as a rival in terms of cultural capital, but as a symbol of a political elite not functioning correctly. In this 'Political Decade', which saw the birth of the left-wing Group and Unity Theatre, even autonomous cultural producers try to influence the political field, Auden's 'poets exploding like bombs'.[70] Newspapers' role in conveying half-truths or lies, the 'racket' that Auden and Isherwood's journalists describe in *The Dog beneath the Skin* (1935), becomes a common theme in the work of writers of the Left.[71] In the play the 'racket', the connivance of the press and big business, is symbolized in the shady 'financier' spotted aboard a train travelling through Europe, 'half-hidden by his newspaper' which is both literally and metaphorically protecting his interests.[72] Likewise John Lehmann, writer, journalist and friend of Isherwood and Auden, set his novel *Evil Was Abroad* (1938), dedicated to Isherwood, in a darkening middle Europe. In the novel, Dick of the *Daily Cable* is sent to Berlin to cover the Reichstag Fire, and notes wryly that the version of events that appears in his paper is not how he reported them. In Storm Jameson's *In the Second Year* (1936), which imagines life in Britain after a fascist coup, the *Times* has become in the novel the prime source of propaganda, a mouthpiece of dictator Frank Hillier. It is an apt fate for a paper Jameson singled out in her autobiography for criticism in supporting the government's policy of appeasement and of smothering journalists' despatches from Germany. While avoiding any overt description of how the *Times* has capitulated to Hillier's and his propagandist Thomas Chamberlayn's control (while left-wing journalists and writers are incarcerated in work camps), casual asides allow us to fill in the dots. The dissident professor Robert Tower concludes that a Hillier loyalist has gone secretly to meet Hillier in Scotland, because 'If you look in *The Times* you'll find he is supposed to be speaking in London today'. Similarly after the narrator hears Tower being murdered by Hillier's men while he is speaking to him on the phone, he reads of Tower's 'suicide' in *The Times*.[73] The literary writer Stevie Smith commented in her experimental *Novel on Yellow Paper* (1936) on the *Times* downplaying the German threat: 'How deeply neurotic the German People is, oh how it goes right through and isn't just the leaders, like they pretend in *The Times*'.[74] 'Pretend' suggests a deliberate misleading rather than the more neutral alternatives such as 'report' or 'state'. Stevie Smith had made regular trips to visit Jewish friends in Germany from 1929 to the early 1930s and had reacted strongly to the rise of the Nazis; she also had German Jewish friends among her Palmers Green circle and was well placed to assess coverage of Germany in the *Times*.[75]

How during wartime the press censored information, on the one hand, and circulated untruths, on the other, had been a concern since the First World War. Commentators in the mid-1930s, when another war loomed, quite rightly started asking whether the press could be trusted a second time around. Denys Thompson, one of the journal *Scrutiny*'s editors, raised this issue in 1935, discussing a *Times* pamphlet urging schools to use the newspaper as an educational tool. Thompson quotes the pamphlet: 'Pupils should be told in particular that an editor's duty is to see that accuracy permeates the whole organisation.' He then comments: 'Pupils should also be asked in particular how far was the *Times* scrupulous in publishing atrocity stories during the War; and then whether it is possible to accept without reservation the accounts of atrocities alleged to have been committed by the Spanish rebels more recently; and finally why this newspaper is tendentious and in what direction?'[76]

Mass Observation records of newspaper reading habits in the late 1930s also show that ordinary readers too took much of the political news they read in the press with a large dose of scepticism. Observers recorded comments, for example: 'I object to papers generally because of the Tory political bias,'; 'unfortunately all that is printed is not always true' and '(a reader of the *Times*): Does not believe all it says as he is quite aware that it represents the official view'.[77] This idea, that newspapers, particularly at a time of war, could not be relied on for the truth, was so pervasive that in the mid-1930s it was already a familiar theme as *Spectator* reviewer Derek Verschoyle noted in his review of *The Dog beneath the Skin*: 'So far from being new, many of Mr Auden's targets – the press, the pulpit, the armament manufacturer, the party politician and the rest – have been familiar objects of intellectual ridicule for a decade.'[78]

Nevertheless, cliché or no cliché, the role of the newspaper in a time of war is something that concerned all writers, not only those on the Left, and the image of the newspaper correspondent during this time will forever be linked to Evelyn Waugh's dark comedy *Scoop* (1938). In *Scoop* there is no seeking of 'truth'. When ingénu William Boot, mistakenly wrenched from his rural obscurity to cover a foreign war, tries to tell another reporter what eventually becomes the real 'scoop' of the novel, his colleague doesn't want to know, preferring the 'fake' story of the Russian agent to the real one: 'The false beard was a very pretty touch. His story was better than yours all round.'[79] This idea that 'an exclusive lie was more valuable than a truth which was shared with others' is a reiteration of Waugh's perceptions on the coverage of the Abyssinian war as described in his non-fiction account *Waugh in Abyssinia* (1936).[80] Waugh had already dedicated a chapter of a previous travel book *Remote People* (1931) to how the world's press covered Haile Selassie's coronation:

> My surprise in reading the Press reports of the coronation was not that my more impetuous colleagues had allowed themselves to be slapdash about their details or that they had fallen into some occasional exaggeration of the more romantic and incongruous aspects of the affair. It seemed to me that we had been witnesses of quite a different series of events.[81]

Although *Scoop* is a humorous novel, it must be read as part two of a trio of books about corruption of public life, the other two being non-fiction works *Waugh in Abyssinia* (1936), and *Robbery under Law* (1939). Both the non-fiction books are intensely pro-Catholic and anti-liberal; they express a yearning for quiet restraint and are fearful of the 'anarchy' that is fostered when the public is fed the distorted reality of a popular press and sensational newsreels. *Waugh in Abyssinia* justifies the Italian invasion of Abyssinia as bringing a classical civilizing law and order to an essentially barbarous country stuck in the Middle Ages: 'They [the Abyssinians] built nothing; they squatted in the villages in the thatched huts ... dirty, idle.'[82] He blames the 'Socialists of Europe', beguiled by newsreels contrasting bellicose Italian movements in East Africa with barefoot Abyssinians, for nearly succeeding in 'precipitating world war in defence of an archaic African despotism'.[83] He expanded his thesis in a review of Guy Chapman's history of the First World War *Vain Glory* (*Spectator*, 29 July 1937): 'It should be the proper function of an intelligentsia to correct popular sentiments and give the call to order in times of hysteria. Instead the editors and publishers, whose job it is to exploit the intelligence of others, see it as their interest to indulge and inflame popular emotion.' *Robbery under Law* is an attack on the Mexico of General Cardenas, which had expropriated European and American oil concessions and persecuted the Catholic Church. Waugh cannot understand why the British public did not protest more at these events and also why it appeared to have sided with the Republican cause in the Spanish Civil War. For all these ills, he blames distortions of the truth circulating in the media, 'the deliberately fostered anarchy of public relations and private opinions that is rapidly making the world uninhabitable'.[84]

Here he expands a theme begun in *Waugh in Abyssinia*, that public opinion on issues as important as foreign policy and international commerce is often based on inaccuracies, and sometimes downright lies, fed to Fleet Street by untrustworthy foreign correspondents. Correspondents make up stories, Waugh argues, rely on mercenary locals or allow their 'copy' to be influenced by propagandists. In *Waugh in Abyssinia*, he describes sacking an unreliable 'spy' who then sells his stories to other correspondents: 'He had no difficulty in finding other correspondents and, as the situation became darker and reporting more speculative, Wazir Ali Beg's news service formed an ever-increasing part of the morning reading of the French, English and American newspaper publics'.[85] In *Scoop*, even Boot, a reporter for just a few weeks, learns the rules about allowing commercial interests to doctor newspaper copy, in the sinister scene late in the novel, where Boot allows the businessman Baldwin to put his own commercial spin on the truth:

> 'If you would not resent my co-operation, I think I can compose a dispatch more likely to please my good friend Copper' … Mr Baldwin sat at William's table and drew the typewriter towards himself. He inserted a new sheet of paper, tucked up his cuffs and began to write with immense speed: MYSTERY FINANCIER RECALLED EXPLOITS RHODES LAWRENCE TODAY.[86]

Just as portrayed from the left in *The Dog beneath the Skin*, so also here from the right, the British newspaper press works only in the interest of money and only an elite few know how to 'read between the lines', able to detect the 'little grit of fact, like the core of a pearl' among so much obfuscating ornament.[87] Newspapers are thus a secret code, hidden in plain sight, a means of allowing politicians and financiers to communicate with each other while carving up the world. Waugh's – and Boot's – response is to retreat to the country, Boot to the plashy fens of Boot Magna and Waugh to Piers Court, the house he and his new wife Laura had just moved into, where, like Voltaire's Candide, he took special joy in planning the planting scheme for the garden.[88]

Journalist-spies in the Cold War era

When the Second World War broke, the intelligence services needed qualified men, so, 'each officer tore around to rope in likely people; when they knew of none themselves, they asked their acquaintances.'[89] This rather amateurish-sounding way of recruiting agents resulted in many Fleet Street journalists, wanting to do something for their country, recruited into government service. In addition, secret service operatives were given journalistic 'cover' by helpful newspapers, particularly the *Observer, Times* and *Daily Telegraph*.[90] The *Times* 'Madrid correspondent', for example, in reality SIS officer Lieutenant Colonel Dudley Wrangel Clark, was arrested in Madrid on 17 October 1941 dressed 'down to a brassiere, as a woman'.[91] Retaining close links with the security service after 1945 would clearly benefit editors and journalists, especially diplomatic, political and foreign correspondents, with access to leaks and exclusive information. For the government's part, selective information could be 'placed in the public sphere but without attribution', which allowed it a cosy relationship that, of course, undermines the very foundations of journalistic impartiality.[92] These links continued into the late twentieth century and beyond. The *Observer's* former home affairs editor, David Rose, for example, has recently admitted to getting too close to his MI6 contact during the run-up to the Iraq invasion in 2003, which, 'to my everlasting regret', he unquestioningly supported on account of strong reassurances from his contact that weapons of mass destruction would be found.[93]

On 20 December 1968 the Russian newspaper *Izvestia* published a list of British editors, journalists and newspaper proprietors it claimed were working for SIS, thus proving 'that Britain's free press is a myth' ('Russia Accuses Fleet Street', *Times*, 21 December 1968). Many of the journalists named in the *Izvestia* report, who denied vehemently their involvement in the intelligence game, admitted to having been SIS agents much later.[94] A similar flurry of accusations that British foreign correspondents were working for SIS in the mid-1970s led *Times* foreign editor Louis Heren to warn of 'this dangerous game that could put a gun at the head of British reporters abroad'.[95] The journalist and author Eric Clark was the target of a number of recruitment attempts while working for the *Observer* in 1965–1975. 'People will ask you to do tiny things, pass on tiny scraps of information. Then they, in return, will help you.' On another more recent journalistic assignment, he was asked by a Russian oligarch to try to gauge whether the finance minister of a small country was open to bribery, but Clark refused the request. 'The oligarch vanished soon after and only his clothes and some blood were found in a hotel room.'[96] During the Cold War, it seems, being tempted by secret agencies of either side was something of an occupational hazard for foreign correspondents. In his memoir *A Hack's Progress*, former *Sunday Times* investigative reporter Phillip Knightley reveals how he was 'recruited by the CIA and KGB' while in India in 1960–1962. The rather clumsy Igor's KGB overtures towards Knightley, complete with copious quantities of vodka, flattery and financial inducements, read like something out of a second-rate thriller, the hapless 'Igor' a dead ringer for one of Ian Fleming's fictional KGB fixers.[97] As previously noted, the secret services were a particularly attractive area of work for both journalists and novelists. With so many 'literary men' either active or former secret service agents, it is hardly surprising that, despite the Official Secrets Act, writers with detailed insider knowledge, from Somerset Maugham to Ian Fleming, produced spy genre novels, pitching murky, knuckle-headed Reds against suave British spies. Or, as in the case of John le Carré, pitching terrifyingly competent Russian agents against apparently amateurish British ones. In his novel *The Honourable Schoolboy* (1977), the amiable journalist Jerry Westerby's public school jollity, however, masks the 'part of him that never ceased to watch'. One of life's outsiders, the part-time spy occupies 'the vaguer spaces in-between' without arousing attention.[98] Expert on the intelligence world Nigel West asserts: 'Contrary to what has commonly been assumed, the British intelligence community has entered the public sphere often since its creation, primarily in the form of memoirs, fictionalised memoirs and classic spy fiction.'[99] Often in these fictions, the worlds of journalism and espionage collide. Ian Fleming, who had worked for Naval Intelligence during the Second World War, returned to his original career in journalism, as foreign manager of the *Sunday Times*, running a network of foreign correspondents across Cold War Europe. References to his newspaper experiences are sprinkled through the James Bond novels, from his very first, *Casino Royale* (1953), where Bond's Jamaica-based contact Fawcett's cover is picture editor on the *Daily Gleaner*, 'the famous newspaper of the Caribbean' to *The Spy Who Loved Me* (1962), where Vivienne Michel's early career is as a cub reporter on the *Chelsea Clarion*, a 'glorified parish magazine'.[100]

Fleming's references to journalism are, however, little more than a slight autobiographical seepage, a grateful nod to the training that rendered his writing 'neat, correct, concise and vivid ... far more valuable to me than all the English literature education I ever had'.[101]Other Cold War and post-war spy novels, written by one-time or practising journalists, use the figure of the journalist in more interesting and creative ways. He is the intensely curious noser-out-of-truth, who cannot resist the urge to track a mystery back to its roots (John Bingham, *Fragment of Fear*, 1965; Robert Harling, *The Paper Palace*, 1951, and *The Enormous Shadow*, 1955). He is the foreign correspondent whose deep history as a Soviet 'Sleeper' agent is used by MI5 (Eric Clark, *The Sleeper*, 1979). He is the down-on-his-luck anti-establishment freelancer who stumbles across an East German plot to control the minds of people in Western Europe through clandestine mass communications (J. B. Priestley, *The Shapes of Sleep*, 1962). While these fictions discuss for a wide audience global politics, particularly the

Soviet 'threat' and Britain's decline on the international stage, they do not, l their 1930s counterparts, seek to influence the political field by asking readers to 'take sides'. There is, in most of these fictions, a faintly patriotic message that for all her faults – and they are many, including unappetizing landladies, horrible coffee and eye-burning London fog – at least post-war Britain is a place where the odd, the anti-establishment and eccentric are free to operate without fear of unjust imprisonment. The journalist, driven by his passion to unravel mysteries, and his ability to perceive a narrative where others cannot, thus becomes a bulwark against oppression in all its forms as well as a decidedly amateurish detective-cum-spy who often stumbles into schemes of which he is only dimly aware. The journalist and designer Robert Harling's second Fleet Street novel *The Enormous Shadow* incorporates all these themes and is partly based on the author's own wartime experiences. Working with Ian Fleming in Naval Intelligence, one of his roles after D-Day was to make a lightening dash across Germany to pick up German scientists engaged in atomic research.[102] Harling, having trained at the *Daily Mail* before the Second World War, became a renowned typographer and newspaper designer afterwards, as well as architectural correspondent for the *Sunday Times*. He loved 'the pace and gossip of the newspaper world'.[103] In the novel the unnamed narrator, correspondent for an unnamed popular Fleet Street newspaper, tracks the attempted defection of a Labour MP and a British nuclear scientist, catching them as they escape to the Soviet Union in a Polish merchant ship, the *Polski Robotnik*. As well as being a Cold War thriller, the novel is a meditation on the role of the journalist as trespasser on other peoples' lives: 'I think I hate investigating anybody. In this dusty world we're all too vulnerable in some way or another', and the access members of the public give journalists to their private selves: 'I had time to be puzzled again by the readiness with which so many people answered a newspaper's queries.'[104] In John Bingham's *A Fragment of Fear*, the crime writer James Compton becomes a threat to Soviet Intelligence because he, 'bumbling along, obstinately, began to creep up on things' that had eluded the police investigators in Italy and Britain.[105] In J. B. Priestley's *The Shapes of Sleep*, freelancer Ben Sterndale identifies the plot before any of the intelligence agents because, as he says, 'I *am* a reporter ... I'm the sort of man who hates loose ends in a world that now offers hardly anything else ... My job is digging out facts and then putting them together to make an honest story.'[106]

Priestley is no uncritical admirer of the newspaper press, however. The mass newspaper 'deceives the men and rapes the women, by the million, every morning and evening'.[107] In the novel Priestley pursues a thesis he had been building for a number of years: that public life is overly influenced by commercial mass communications and individuals are being 'brainwashed' out of the capacity for original, independent thought. He had visited this topic in fiction in a previous 'newspaper' novel *Wonder Hero* (1933, see Chapter 3) and in his supernatural thriller *The Magicians* (1953), depicting an evil magnate seeking to control the world through mass communications and mind-bending drugs. In a 1957 essay 'Mass Communication' Priestley notes that television pundits have taken the place of writers like George Bernard Shaw and H. G. Wells. Modern media consumers are 'flattered and never disturbed' by purveyors of mass media.[108] In *The Shapes of Sleep*, East German communists are trying to steal an experimental psychologist's discovery that people can be controlled if they sleep with certain geometric shapes pinned on their bedroom walls. The British Secret Service is trying to foil the communists and the freelancer Ben Sterndale beats all the agents to it. The irony is, of course, that in the so-called 'free' west, minds are already controlled by 'propaganda, public relations, advertising' – much of the action is set in an advertising agency – and when Sterndale examines the 'shapes' and pins them to his own wall, he is not affected – his western mind has already been corrupted.[109] Similarly in John Bingham's *Fragment of Fear*, the price paid for democracy seems to be almost too high. Despite having been an intelligence agent himself, the author sets out the irony that in order for democracy to defend itself against totalitarianism, 'the greater the cause, in the end, the greater the tyranny which it erects to defend itself... now he was boxed in by frontiers, passports, and visas and walls and interdicts, and laws, and police, to preserve the liberty and freedom of the individual.'[110] Individual journalists try to make an individual impact but they are submerged by a system – the newspaper enterprise, social mores, the Establishment – bent on homogenization and a biddable public. This theme, that the Establishment, of whatever political persuasion, has an ultimate goal of crushing the individual is a central one in Eric Clark's *The Sleeper* (1979). James Fenn, a foreign correspondent recruited as a KGB sleeper agent when very young, is bullied, abused and terrified by a paranoid MI5 desperate to please the CIA. Ultimately all the journalist can do is stir a little trouble and make facetious comments. Any notions of 'making a difference' are mere pipe dreams.

Graham Greene's Thomas Fowler:
The journalist as unreliable narrator

In a review of the 2001 film adaption of *The Quiet American* for the *New York Times*, Martin Nolan quotes the American war correspondent David Greenway, who says the novel became some kind of talisman for reporters in Vietnam during the 1960s: 'Every reporter had one. Many carried *The Quiet American* and *Scoop* by Evelyn Waugh' (*New York Times*, 30 January 2003).[111] Both novels are undoubtedly marvellous reading but the war correspondents could hardly have chosen two novels which undermine more claims by their profession to be dealing in the truth. Waugh's black comedy reveals journalistic mendacity on a grand and obvious scale. *The Quiet American* (1955) is a far-more devious proposition as the protagonist-narrator Thomas Fowler presents himself as an utterly professional, detached reporter, dismissive of leader-writers and their nuanced opinions as well as the rest of the foreign press corps which willingly swallow lies at organized press conferences. While the foreign press pack drinks safely out of the reach of grenades on the upper terrace of the Hotel Continental, Fowler deliberately risks his life on lone reporting missions to military outposts. On the surface, Thomas Fowler's unflinching observations of war suggest an almost obsessive urge to report the unvarnished truth: 'The canal was full of bodies: I am reminded now of an Irish stew containing too much meat. The bodies overlapped: one head, seal-grey, and anonymous as a convict with a shaven scalp, stuck out of the water like a buoy... *we* ran on a shoal of bodies and stuck' (emphasis added).[112]

Some of the novel's reportage is taken almost word for word from Greene's own Indo-China journalism. The section above was used twice: 'here and there the canal was filled with a thick gruel, heads floating above the accumulation of bodies below' in 'Indo-China: France's Crown of Thorns' (*Paris Match*, 12 July 1952) and 'It was very present in the canal so laden with bodies that they overlapped and a punt of parachutists stuck on a reef of them' in 'Before the Attack' (*Spectator*, 16 April 1954).[113] In his real-life reporting, particularly in the second article, Greene suggests he was not on the punt, but merely observing. In the novel, Fowler is on the vessel, riding the thick tide with the soldiers. This subtle change in Fowler/Greene's position in the novel emphasizes the veteran foreign correspondent's professionalism: he is part of the action. Indeed he wears his willingness to see the action up-close and personal like a badge of honour even though he knows his paper will only use a small paragraph buried deep in the foreign pages, for ' if one writes about war self-respect demands that occasionally one shares the risks'.[114] This distinguishes him from the other foreign correspondents who on a press trip are 'flown over the late battlefield at a height of 3,000 feet (the limit of a heavy machine-gun's range) and then delivered safely and noisily back, like a school-treat, to the Continental Hotel in Saigon'.[115] Their reports back to their papers, one infers, are little more than fabrications, their main interest in the press trip being that the barman at the Hanoi press-camp 'was the best in Indo-China'. Fowler's work also distinguishes him from Pyle, his love rival and the American intelligence operative, for whose death Fowler is indirectly responsible. While Fowler prides himself on being the detached reporter, on not being '*engagé*' – the existentialist term appears several times in the text – Pyle's meddling in a world he does not understand renders him 'responsible for at least fifty deaths' in his short time in Saigon.[116]

The novel, which shifts between two time frames, one beginning, and the other ending, on the night of Pyle's death, is supposed to be Fowler's confession for his involvement in Pyle's murder at the hands of the communists. His 'justification' for knowingly sending Pyle into a trap is Pyle's responsibility for a bomb attack in central Saigon, which killed dozens of civilians. It is a useful smokescreen and Fowler repeats the words of his communist contact Heng as his justification: 'Sooner or later one has to take sides. If one is to remain human.'[117] Superficially, Fowler sticks to his story – that after a lifetime of not getting involved, the bomb at Place Garnier was the last straw and forced him to become, finally, *engagé*. In thus making Pyle's death a political act, Fowler can assume the mantle of the existentialist hero who takes responsibility for his actions, carrying him triumphantly towards personal redemption. This common reading of the novel, that after a lifetime of non-commitment the bomb finally forces Fowler to choose sides, is, however, erroneous.[118] Greene is never that simple. Pyle's involvement with the bomb is a convenient excuse for Fowler to kill off his love rival, as one Greene scholar points out: 'It is difficult to read Thomas Fowler as a portrait of political commitment without doing serious violence either to the text or to the rational conception of political commitment.'[119] This reading challenges Fowler's pretence of justifying his actions as his finally becoming *engagé*. The key part of his 'confession' that could help him find the inner peace he so desperately seeks – the true nature of his motivation for sending Pyle to his death – remains unacknowledged by Fowler. But it is nevertheless there in the text. It is through his occasional slip-ups, particularly recounting the night of Pyle's death under cross-questioning from the impressive French detective Vigot, and through his account of events running up to the bomb, that Fowler's deep and unerasable guilt can be discerned.

Critics have compared *The Quiet American* with Greene's previous novel *The End of the Affair*, highlighting thematic similarities but suggesting that *The Quiet American*, at least, has a 'happy ending at least in the sense that Fowler does not lose Phuong'.[120] I suggest there will be no happy ending for Fowler. The guilt that will plague him for the rest of his life is indeed already eating away at him as he tells his story. Fowler tells Vigot that on the night of Pyle's death, he went to see a film. 'What was it? *Robin Hood*?' asks Vigot. '*Scaramouche*, I think', Fowler replies.[121] Greene was interested in how narrative structures can help define the state of mind of the protagonist and here we have a deliberate clue into the inner life of Fowler. Fowler sees and records faithfully every tiny detail he observes as a reporter. Why can he not remember decisively the title of the film he went to see? It is unlikely to have been *Robin Hood*, as that film came out in 1938. It is far more likely to be *Scaramouche*, which came out in 1952, within the time frame of the novel. This slight doubt over the film he saw is a deliberate ploy by Greene to hint at Fowler's unacknowledged guilt. When we come to Fowler's account of the fateful night, his confusion over what he actually saw is amplified: 'I said good night to him and went to the cinema next door – Errol Flynn or it may have been Tyrone Power (I don't know how to distinguish them in tights).'[122] If he went to see *Robin Hood*, it would indeed have been Errol Flynn. However, if it was *Scaramouche* it would have been neither Flynn nor Power, but a third actor, Stewart Granger, who played the starring role in *Scaramouche* (a film about mistaken identity). This slip is all the more odd as just before he goes to see the film, Fowler meets fellow journalist Wilkins and they discuss a third correspondent who shares the name of *Scaramouche*'s lead actor, Granger. Indeed Granger's name is spoken twice just before Fowler takes up the narrative and recounts his visit to the cinema. To forget the name of the actor of the film he has seen just after he has recorded the name twice is not credible. Fowler's terrible, unacknowledged guilt has interrupted his usually clinical power of recall. Fowler's narrative then becomes even odder. He describes the film: 'He rescued a girl and killed his enemy and led a charmed life. It was what they call a film for boys, *but the sight of Oedipus emerging with his bleeding eyeballs from the Palace at Thebes would surely give a better training for life today*' (emphasis added).[123] This bizarre insertion of the Oedipus myth into the narrative, at about the exact point in time when Pyle is being murdered, cannot go unremarked. Rather like *Scaramouche* – or was it *Robin Hood* – Fowler has rescued the girl (Phuong) and killed his enemy (Pyle) yet he rejects the happy ending of the film and instead conjures the terrible image of Oedipus at the moment he is confronted with his epic crime. Surely the limp that Fowler acquires on the Tanyin Road after spending the night with Pyle in the watchtower is another Oedipal reference as is his confession to Granger, on the night Pyle dies: 'I've been blind to a lot of things.'[124] Despite Fowler's continual protestations throughout the novel that he is a reporter whose job is to 'expose and record', he has only unconsciously revealed the extent of his guilt and no amount of dressing up his involvement in Pyle's death as a political act can cover up the truth.[125]

As a reader, then, one begins to suspect all of his testimony. He does not report the random atrocity of Captain Trouin's extermination of a tiny sampan on the Red River ('it was of no more value to my paper than my excursion to Phat Diem'); he doesn't even write up the Place Garnier bomb incident, even though he was a witness. Instead he leaves it to Dominguez, his factotum, admitting, 'I was less capable than Dominguez of telling truth from falsehood.'[126] A reporter who has, finally, become *engagé* would surely leap at the chance of detailing the horrible civilian casualties caused by Pyle's bomb: the 'woman sat on the ground with what was left of her baby... the legless torso'. As he waits for Pyle to come to his apartment on the night of his death, he observes a trishaw rider out of his open window, 'presumably he was waiting for a client in one of the shops'.[127] This is a clumsy lie. The reader already knows – as does Fowler – that the trishaw rider is waiting for Fowler, part of a pre-arranged plan with Pyle's assassins.

This novel begins from the narrator's assertion that as a reporter he writes what he sees, and thus his testimony must be believed, and ends with ultimately the complete unravelling and dismantling of his 'confession'.[128] It is not just the journalist Fowler whose evidence we cannot trust. The other reporters don't get anywhere near the theatre of war to be reliable witnesses. Newspapers print partial, truncated and doctored accounts of the war. Fowler's colleagues report that the 'Bicycle Bombs' incident was a communist outrage, when it was the responsibility of the American-backed General Thé's 'Third Force'; Fowler's report was originally correct, yet, he notes dispassionately, 'my account was altered in the office'.[129] Just as his newspaper's texts are unreliable, so is Fowler's 'confession'. He yearns for peace of mind, but his guilt will not allow it. Greene's mid-century novel stands out from most of the fictions in this study as a literary masterpiece. However, it pursues a theme common to other contemporary novels about journalists, that 'unfortunately, all that is printed is not always true'.[130] In addition, many mid-century fictions about journalists, by Greene, Harling, Clark and others, exhibit a particular kind of post-war malaise, a consciousness of the absurdity of one's existence in a terrifying world. These themes are explored further in Chapter 6.

Notes

1   Ambler, Eric, *Uncommon Danger*, pp. 10 & 15.
2   Ibid., p. 43.

3   Ibid., p. 10.

4   Gallagher, Donat, 'Introduction' to *The Essays, Articles and Reviews of Evelyn Waugh*, p. 10.

5   Ambler, Eric, *Here Lies Eric Ambler*, p. 124.

6   Ibid.

7   Dover, Robert and Michael Goodman, 'Spooks and Hacks: Blood Brothers', pp. 58–59.

8   Marsh, Ngaio, *Death in a White Tie*, p. 300.

9   Gannon, Franklin Reid, *The British Press and Germany 1936–1939*, p. 3.

10   Ibid., pp. 34–36.

11   Lyall, Archibald, *Russian Roundabout: A Non-Political Pilgrimage* (1932).

12   Ibid., p. 8.

13   Gannon, *The British Press*, pp. 33–88.

14   Adamthwaite, Anthony, 'The British Government and the Media 1937–1938', pp. 283–284.

15   Griffiths, Dennis, *Fleet Street*, pp. 258–260.

16   Atkins, John, *The British Spy Novel*, pp. 165–167.

17   Maugham, Somerset, 'Preface' to *Ashenden*, p. ix.

18   Maugham, Somerset, *Ashenden*, p. 225.

19   Page, Bruce, David Leitch and Phillip Knightley, *Philby: The Spy Who Betrayed a Generation*, pp. 86 & 112–115.

20   Read, Anthony and David Fisher, *Colonel Z*, p. 174. Dansey had been involved in espionage in much early twentieth-century conflict and in the Second World War ran MI6 and MI9.

21   For a comprehensive list of journalists who joined SIS during the 1930s and 1940s, see West, Nigel, *The Faber Book of Espionage*.

22   West, Nigel, *Espionage*, p. 13.

23   West, Nigel, 'Fiction, Faction and Intelligence', p. 124.

24   Clarke, Patricia and David Footman (eds), *In Memoriam Archie*.

25   Ibid., pp. 159–162; also Wright, Peter, *Spycatcher*, p. 338.

26   West, 'Fiction, Faction and Intelligence', p. 124.

27   Wilkinson, Ellen, 'Thinking in Blood', pp. 381–384.

28   Ibid.

29   On 25 May 1934 Stephens had written a particularly caustic attack on the Nazis' treatment of German Jews in the *Daily Express*: 'German Jews are facing their darkest days – Denied a Living – Savings Gone – Friends Dare not Greet them – their children play at home'. This led to his expulsion, but did not have the desired effect of shutting him up: *Daily Express* 2 June 1934, p. 1: 'My Expulsion by the Nazis – Article about Jews that angered Hitler – *Daily Express* to prove its truth'. He had been arrested on May 31 and made his way back to England via Amsterdam.

30   Gannon, *The British Press*, pp. 81–82.

31   Jago, Michael, *The Man Who Was George Smiley*, p. 83.

32   Grant Duff, Shiela, *The Parting of Ways*, p. 66.

33   Ibid., p. 84.

34   Samuels, Stuart, 'The Left Book Club', pp. 67 & 73.

35   Jameson, Storm, *Journey from the North*, pp. 318–320.

36   Cockburn, Claud, *Time of Trouble*, pp. 192–193.

37   In his memoir, Muggeridge records that his despatches from Ukraine to the *Manchester Guardian* were severely cut by W. P. Crozier, the editor. He wrote to him: 'From the way you've cut my messages ... I realise you don't want to know what's going on in Russia, or to let your readers know. If it had been an oppressed minority or subject people valiantly struggling to be free, that would have been another matter' ... I was finished with moderate men of all shades of opinion for evermore. (Muggeridge, Malcolm, *Chronicles of Wasted Time Part I*, p. 268.)

38   Muggeridge, Malcolm, *Winter in Moscow*, p. 145.

39   Muggeridge, Malcolm, *Chronicles of Wasted Time*, pp. 190–191.

40   Dorril, Stephen, 'Russia accuses Fleet Street', p. 214.

41   Greene, Graham, *A Sort of Life*, pp. 125 & 143.

42   Ibid., p. 131.

43   Where Poliakoff was concerned, Greene may well have been right about his suspicions. While diplomatic correspondent on the *Evening Standard*, he made some uncannily accurate predictions about Lord Halifax's supposedly secret visit to Germany in November 1937. It was widely suspected he was being 'used' by sources in the Foreign Office. Gannon, *The British Press and Germany*, pp. 129–131.

44   Greene, Graham, *Stamboul Train*, p. 48.

45   Greene, Graham, *England Made Me*, p. 71.

46   Greene, *Stamboul Train*, p. 28.

47   Greene, *England Made Me*, pp. 180 & 67.

48   Greene, *Stamboul Train*, p. 176.

49   Kipling, Rudyard, *Something of Myself*, p. 30.

50   Greene, *Stamboul Train*, pp. 36 & 57.

51   Greene, Graham, *Brighton Rock*, p. 153.

52   West, *Espionage*, p. 280.

53   Hilton, James, *Knight without Armour*, p. 87.

54   Isherwood, Christopher, *Christopher and His Kind*, pp. 96–97.

55   Isherwood, Christopher, *Mr Norris*, p. 180.

56   Isherwood, *Christopher*, pp. 94–95.

57   Ibid., pp. 96–97.

58   Ibid.

59   Hynes, Samuel, *The Auden Generation*, pp. 9–14.

60   Isherwood, Christopher, *Mr Norris*, p. 185.

61   Ibid., p. 186.

62 Ibid.

63 Steed, Wickham, *The Press*, pp. 12–16.

64 Ambler, *Uncommon Danger*, p. 71.

65 Ibid., pp. 211 & 76.

66 Ambler, Eric, *The Dark Frontier*, p. 221.

67 *The Week*, 28 March 1934, number 52: 3–4 'Several years after the War, Mr Bryce, a nephew of Lord Bryce was simultaneously the *Times* correspondent in Belgrade and business agent for Messrs Vickers. Similarly the *Times* correspondent in Bucharest was a Mr Boncesco and oddly enough he also was a Messrs Vickers agent … inexplicable association of a great newspaper and Messrs Vickers.'

68 Gannon, *The British Press*, p. 64.

69 Ambler, *The Dark Frontier*, p. 15.

70 Auden, W. H., 'Spain, 1937' in *Selected Shorter Poems 1930–1944*, pp. 189–192; there is more on political theatre and its relationship with newspapers in Chapter 8.

71 Auden, W. H. and Christopher Isherwood, *The Dog Beneath*, p. 40.

72 Ibid., p. 82.

73 Jameson, Storm, *In the Second Year*, pp. 163 & 200.

74 Smith, Stevie, *Novel on Yellow Paper*, p. 102.

75 Spalding, Frances, *Stevie Smith*, pp. 81–84.

76 Thompson, Denys, '*The Times* in School', p. 380.

77 Mass Observation records, 'Newspaper Reading' 1938 Box 1/1B TC61.

78 Verschoyle, Derek, 'Review', p. 211.

79 Waugh, *Scoop*, p. 102.

80 Waugh, Evelyn, *Waugh in Abyssinia*, p. 157.

81 Waugh, Evelyn, *Remote People*, p. 40.

82 Waugh, *Waugh in*, p. 26.

83 Ibid., p. 34.

84 Waugh, Evelyn, *Robbery Under*, p. 3.

85 Waugh, *Waugh in*, p. 124.

86 Waugh, *Scoop*, p. 177.

87 Auden, *The Dog Beneath*, p. 40; Waugh, *Scoop*, p. 170.

88 Waugh, Evelyn, *Diaries*, pp. 427–428.

89 Report by Sir David Petrie, National Archive ref KV/88.

90 See West, *Faber* and Jeffrey, Keith, *MI6: The History of the Secret Intelligence Service 1909–1949*.

91 Jeffrey, Keith, *MI6*, p. 406.

92 Lashmar, Paul, 'Urinal or Conduit? Institutional information flow between the UK intelligence services and the news media', p. 1027.

93 Ibid., p. 1032.

94 For a comprehensive analysis of the *Izvestia* claims, see Dorril, 'Russia Accuses Fleet Street'.

95　*Times*, 14 January 1976.

96　Interview with Eric Clark.

97　Knightley, Phillip, *A Hack's Progress*, pp. 83–97.

98　Le Carré, John, *The Honourable Schoolboy* pp. 42 & 129.

99　West, 'Fiction, Faction and Intelligence', p. 122.

100　Fleming, Ian, *Casino Royale*, pp. 5–6.

101　Quoted in Bennet, Tony and Janet Woollacott, *Bond and Beyond*, p. 89.

102　Barker, Nicholas, 'Robert Harling' obituary, *Independent* 8 July 2008, http://www
.independent.co.uk/news/obituaries/robert-harling-typographer-designer–house
–garden-editor-and-author-of-riveting-novels-of-old-fleet-street-862014.html
(accessed 10 August 2015).

103　MacCarthy, Fiona, 'Robert Harling' obituary, *Guardian* 2 July 2008, http://www
.theguardian.com/media/2008/jul/02/pressandpublishing1 (accessed 10 August
2015).

104　Harling, Robert, *The Enormous Shadow*, pp. 134 & 78.

105　Bingham, John, *A Fragment of Fear*, p. 164.

106　Priestley, J. B., *The Shapes of Sleep*, pp. 81 & 211–212.

107　Ibid., p. 222.

108　Priestley, J. B., 'Mass Communication', p. 10.

109　Ibid., p. 247.

110　Bingham, *Fragment of Fear*, p. 167.

111　The film was released the day before the September 11 attacks on New York but
was then withdrawn and postponed until November 2002.

112　Greene, Graham, *The Quiet American*, pp. 43–44.

113　Both these articles are reproduced in the collection of Greene's journalism,
Reflections.

114　Greene, *The Quiet*, pp. 139–140.

115　Ibid., p. 15.

116　Ibid., p. 13.

117　Ibid., p. 166.

118　See for example Bergonzi (2006): the bomb explosion 'shakes Fowler out of his
habitual detachment … he decides Pyle will have to go before he does any more
damage' (147).

119　Thompson, Brian Lindsay *Graham Greene and the Politics of Popular Fiction and
Film*, p. 182.

120　Hoskins, Robert, *Graham Greene: An Approach to the Novels*, p. 156.

121　Greene, *The Quiet*, p. 163.

122　Ibid., p. 173.

123　Ibid., p. 174.

124　Ibid., p. 177.

125　Ibid., p. 80.

126 Ibid., pp. 139 & 114.

127 Ibid., pp. 154 & 167.

128 In this aspect the novel bears remarkable similarities to Alain Robbe-Grillet's *Les Gommes* (1953), another unreliable text with Oedipal references and the unravelling of accounts of a murder. The minute observations of the books in Dupont's study by the assassin Garinati just before he shoots him are particularly resonant with Fowler's observations in Pyle's study after his death.

129 Greene, *The Quiet*, p. 134.

130 From Mass observation Newspaper Reading survey 1938, see Chapter 3.

'I call my cancer – the main one in my pancreas – Rupert':[1] The Press Baron from Northcliffe to Murdoch

The figure of the press baron in fiction is quite distinct from that of the journalist. In early portrayals he flexes his new and unusual muscle, threatening to upset the social and cultural order. In later portrayals his desire for money overtakes his desire for social acceptance. Unlike more nuanced portrayals of journalists we have seen, the press baron is deliciously bad, a thorough-going villain, receiving perhaps his best portrayal in Anthony Hopkins' role as Le Roux in David Hare and Howard Brenton's Pravda *(1985) stalking the stage with his 'carnivorously affable smile'. For early twentieth-century writers it is his control of the written word, and his ability to corrupt it, that poses the greatest threat. For more contemporary writers he is at the heart of all that is wrong with modern Britain.*

In Edwardian playwright James Bernard Fagan's 1909 play *The Earth*, newspaper proprietor Sir Felix Janion is 'a man over fifty, of huge burly frame ... His face is enormously powerful, and his mouth shuts like a steel trap ... His movements are quick and resolute'.[2] Nearly 100 years later, Lennox Mark, aged fifty-three, proprietor of the *Daily Legion* in A. N. Wilson's newspaper novel *My Name Is Legion* (2004), is similarly described: 'His face was fleshy, but not especially fat. He had a very big head with a massive jaw ... In the massiveness, even the monstrousness of his skull, the eyes always seeming slightly sore, as if mild conjunctivitis could not be banished, looked small.'[3]

Both men epitomize the power they wield, and both, eventually, are brought down by their lack of self-awareness and thoughtless cupidity. Janion uses the power of his newspapers to try to influence politics, and takes microscopic interest in his papers' appearance down to the length and headlines of individual stories. Lennox Mark uses his power to settle personal scores and keep himself and his wife in their luxurious lifestyle. Perhaps curiously for a newspaper proprietor, he takes no interest in his papers' journalism, unless it has a direct impact on his business interests and his political manoeuvring. Janion and Mark's divergent approaches speak to changes, and constants, in over a century of popular newspaper ownership, finance and management.

The new fictional figure of the millionaire press baron, with the opinions of millions of readers at his disposal, emerged shortly after Lord Northcliffe bought the *Times* in 1908, and has been a fascination for writers interested in politics, social comment and the exercise of power ever since. While nineteenth-century newspaper proprietors enjoyed access to politicians, their papers' circulations were limited by high cover price and low levels of literacy. Theirs was a closed, if influential, world. Described in 1930, the mid-nineteenth-century *Times* of John Walter II and his editor Delane was 'the sphere of the men who governed ... meanwhile outside those well-lighted windows ... there stood a vast mass of men and women whom the Education Act had endowed with a power to read but who could find nothing in contemporary journalism that they could understand.'[4] It was the twentieth-century proprietors' access to the breakfast tables of millions of readers, including the newly literate, newly enfranchised classes, which made the figure of the press baron an interesting one for writers. In real life, as in fiction, the press baron often treats writers with contempt and his papers devalue artistic expression, reducing 'culture' to yet another commodity. Yet writers of all genres, from journalists and playwrights to novelists, are drawn to his gaudy light: he is the resented gatekeeper to the sacred wells of public opinion, fame and success. Writers respond by portraying him variously as deluded (Lord Copper in Evelyn Waugh's *Scoop* (1938)); murderous (Victor Kingsbrook in David Drury's film *Defence of the Realm* (1985)), the victim of an assassination plot by his own reporters (Lord Carpenter in Christopher St John Sprigg's *Fatality in Fleet Street* (1933)) and vaporized in an atomic reaction (Lord Ottercove in William Gerhardie's *Doom* (1928)).

Portrayals of Lord Northcliffe

In 1909 two plays, opening within weeks of each other, introduced a new fictional character: the modern press baron.[5] Both plays, *The Earth* by James Bernard Fagan and *What the Public Wants* by Arnold Bennett, portray this new figure in British society as coarse and brilliant. In Arnold Bennett's *What the Public Wants*, he is Sir Charles Worgan, proprietor of a new popular paper, the *Mercury*.

Worgan is 'Brusque. Accustomed to power. With rare flashes of humour and of charm...Strong frame. Decided gestures. Age 40'.[6] That Worgan is a thinly disguised Northcliffe becomes apparent when the foreign secretary dismisses Worgan's *Mercury* as 'written by errand boys for errand-boys', a reference to Lord Salisbury's famous put-down of the *Daily Mail* as being 'written by office boys for office boys'.[7] The stage direction for Worgan contrasts sharply with Bennett's first impression of Northcliffe (then Alfred Harmsworth), when he sees him at a theatre on 17 October 1896, five months after the successful launch of the *Daily Mail*:

> Harmsworth (director of 14 weeklies reaching 3,300,000 copies, and three daily papers) with the head of a poet and thinker; blond hair; quiet, acute, self-contained; a distinguished look about him. One would take him for...a contemner of popular taste and of everything that caught the public fancy.[8]

The change in Bennett's opinions on Northcliffe over a decade and a half reveals much about the gradual shift in Bennett's view of the popular press, from novel experiment in educating the newly literate lower classes to a literary bully and a threat to good taste. Bennett was a prolific journalist as well as novelist and playwright and, at the end of 1908, the year he wrote *What the Public Wants*, recorded that he had written sixty newspaper articles, including a regular column for the *Manchester Daily Despatch* at six guineas per column. Bennett's diaries in the early years of the twentieth century reveal a gleeful interest in popular press coverage of high-profile criminal and libel cases ('Great fun reading the account of the 200-million franc *krach* by a financial swindler in all the papers today') although he begins to record distaste for increasing sensationalism: 'Continental *Daily Mail*...was full of its third anniversary and of the horrible agonies of a man in USA who died slowly of hydrophobia.'[9]

Both Bennett and Fagan were left-leaning: Bennett was temporarily a Fabian and also sympathized with the Liberal cause, and Fagan, an Irishman, was a political sympathizer with George Bernard Shaw; he was also a supporter of Irish Home Rule, including the severance of Protestant Ulster from the United Kingdom, something that Northcliffe and his papers opposed.[10] *The Earth* examines how a man who despises ideas of social justice uses his newspapers' circulations to manipulate public opinion. Janion uses this power to try to destroy Liberal cabinet minister Trevena's Wages Bill that would end sweated labour for women and children. Janion opposes Trevena's Bill as he feels it would curtail Britain's industrial expansion: 'The circulation of my morning papers alone is close on four million a day; and its going to be more. I disapprove of your Bill. I'll smash it if I can.'[11]

He threatens Trevena with evidence of his adulterous affair in order to get him to drop the legislation. He does not take into account the fact that Trevena's mistress, Lady Killone, would rather be publicly humiliated than see the Wages Bill fail. When confronted with such nobility of spirit, his words – mimicking the hack journalese of his papers – are inadequate: 'You've beaten me – this time. You're a plucky woman.'[12]

In *What the Public Wants*, Sir Charles Worgan's motives are social rather than political: raised by a provincial middle-class family, he wants acceptance from 'your intellectual, your superior people' who have snubbed him at a time when wealth alone was no guarantor of social status.[13] In an effort to gain respect from the intellectual elite, he subsidizes a production of the *Merchant of Venice*, saving a failing theatre. Yet despite the huge box-office success, the highbrow theatre manager is not grateful as anything that achieves commercial success in his eyes is an artistic failure. Both plays discuss the new pared-down language of popular newspapers, and both barons defend their papers' interest in sensation and trivia as being what the public wants. As if confirming writers' fears over this new brusque guardian of public opinion, both plays received poor newspaper reviews and consequently had short runs. Arnold Bennett complained of the 'cold, carping tone' of most of the reviews of *What the Public Wants* in his diary.[14] *The Times*, then owned by Northcliffe, was particularly spiteful, commenting: 'It never rains but it pours. On stage it is just now pouring Newspaper Kings. Mr Fagan gave us one the other day. Mr Arnold Bennett gives us now another, and if there is a difference between them it is that "twixt Tweedledee and Tweedledum."'[15]

Letters written to Northcliffe by writers as prominent as the bestselling novelist Hall Caine as well as less successful freelancers reveal helpless resentment at the way their words are treated by the proprietor and his subeditors. Perhaps most pathetic is Twells Brex, a popular author and journalist who had written a regular full column on the leader page of the *Daily Mail* since the paper's launch. In 1917, the column was cut in half to make way for more war news and to mark its curtailment, Brex wrote an article: 'Mr Half Column Introduces Himself... Mr Whole Column, whom you have known in this page day after day for twenty-one years, will talk to you less often.'[16] He later wrote a letter to Northcliffe: 'I am carefully studying your present page four and I note that nearly all the articles are articles of movement or actions and that you have no room now for the [humorous] sort that I have always done.' The letter ends with a despairing realization that his brand of writing cannot compete with sensational news articles.[17] Another writer, John Foster Fraser, wrote, in June

1911: 'I would break my heart if my stuff were cut to ribbons and to paragraphs by sub-editors in the interests of space, it kills good work.' His request for 'one thousand words a night' was met with a terse reply from Northcliffe, who informed Fraser he was 'staggered' by the demand. The golfing writer Henry Leach, who had written twice the number of words Northcliffe required in a feature 'Golf in Paris', was told: 'The article is too long and therefore in accordance with what usually happens in such cases, has had to wait... I think we had better hold this article until the Spring' (the letter is dated 12 February 1912).[18] Even bestselling author Hall Caine had battles with Northcliffe over space for his work, writing in 1908, when his star was on the wane: 'You cannot have meant to insult me by sending me the sub-editor's message to cut down an article out of which nobody living could remove a line without injuring it.'[19] Only a writer of the stature of Arnold Bennett appeared able to turn the tables. In his letters he rejects an invitation from Northcliffe in 1913 to write an article in the *Evening News*. He tells his agent J. B. Pinker: 'I haven't the time and my ideas would not perhaps rouse sympathy in his noble breast and even at one shilling a word it would not pay me.'[20]

This power over writers' words is explored both in Bennett's *What the Public Wants* and in Keble Howard's *Lord London* (1913), a fictionalized account of Northcliffe's life up to the early years of the *Daily Mail*. In *What the Public Wants*, the dramatic critic Simon Macquoid is furious that Worgan has not only added lines to his signed article but committed the sin of including split infinitives: 'If you imagine, Sir Charles, that because you pay me thirty pounds a month you have the right to plaster my work with split infinitives, you are tremendously mistaken.' After Macquoid resigns, Worgan reveals his disdain for 'these cultured johnnies... they're mad every one of 'em'.[21] This attitude closely reflects that of Northcliffe himself, who in a 1903 guidance to would-be journalists disparaged literary writers as 'bohemians... drunken, irregular rascals' favouring instead 'strong and healthy' reporters.[22]

In *Lord London* Hannibal Quain is an energetic genius determined to provide reading matter for the lower middle classes. To this end, for example, a journalist on the *Little Daily* is given the task of 'boiling down' a fiction writer's short story from 8,000 to 1,500 words.[23] Howard, however, portrays this action, and the shortening of all newspaper genres from news reports to dramatic criticism to make room for 'sufficient advertisements to make the paper a financial success', as a stroke of entrepreneurial genius:

> Hannibal, as we now know, solved it by... keeping his literary matter, such as dramatic criticism and literary reviews down to the smallest possible limits... the

lesson that he found hardest to teach his staff [was] the absolute necessity of boiling down every paragraph to the smallest possible limit.[24]

Evidently annoyed at his portrayal, Northcliffe was able to delay the book's publication for several months as he threatened Howard's publishers Chapman and Hall with legal action. This obstruction bewildered the writer, who had been a dramatic critic on the *Daily Mail* between 1908 and 1911, and who claimed that his portrait of Northcliffe was entirely fair. 'What earthly good could accrue to me from antagonising the most powerful newspaperman in the Kingdom?' he asks in his memoirs.[25] While dominion over the written word and the proprietors' willingness to flex their new muscles was a concern for writers, Worgan and Janion are both eventually undone, suggesting a perceived vulnerability and a limit to the press baron's power. Worgan is a vain and insecure man who loses his lover and the respect of his family through his vulgar pursuit of sensational crime stories for his evening paper. Janion is vanquished by the power of love. But the steady rise of newspaper proprietors' wealth and political influence during and after the war would gradually change writers' perceptions and representations of the press baron.

Barons between the wars

As we have seen in Chapter 3 the growing influence of the popular press became a major concern to writers during the interwar years. The popular press had ceased to be a novelty that could be made mild fun of: its circulation was on a seemingly endless upward parabola. For many in politics, the elevation of the press lords to wartime government positions was a deeply troubling departure.[26] In *The Press and the Organisation of Society* (1922), the writer and politician Norman Angell argued that the newly commercialized press 'does not in fact guarantee freedom of discussion', pointing to a relative lack of dissent in the press over the conduct of the war.[27] Indeed, Angell asserted, it was the newspaper proprietors who governed England during the war, not 'Commons or Cabinet, Church or Trade Union'.[28] Many saw the *Daily Mail*'s publication of the infamous 'Zinoviev' letter, suggesting communist control of the Labour Party, just before the 1924 General Election, as a deliberate attempt by Lord Rothermere to swing the outcome of a democratic vote.[29] Fears over the intentions of the press barons were realized when Rothermere and Beaverbrook joined forces to launch the United Empire Party in opposition to Stanley Baldwin's Conservatives and provoked Baldwin's famous 'power without responsibility' by-election speech in March 1931.

Rose Macaulay's early post-war novel *Potterism* (1920) describes how the popular Potter Press, which, 'like so many other presses, snubbed the militant suffragists, smiled, half approvingly on Carson's rebels, and frowned, wholly disapprovingly on the strikers' follows a similar trajectory to the press of Northcliffe and Beaverbrook.[30] Macaulay's ironic description of Percy Potter's ennoblement during the war is a comment on Lloyd George's relationship with Northcliffe and Beaverbrook: 'The Potter press surpassed itself... With energy and wholeheartedness it cheered, comforted, and stimulated the people... So glad were the Government of it that Mr Potter became, at the end of 1916, Lord Pinkerton.'[31]

Potter exerts a profound influence on mass reading matter, appealing to a public aspiring to better itself. Ascertaining, for example, that there is a 'fourpenny' public, whose brains 'could only rise with effort to the solid political and economic information and cultured literary judgements meted out by the sixpennies', but which also avoids 'the crudities of our cheapest journals', he produces the *Wednesday Chat*, a fourpenny weekly which rapidly reaches a circulation of millions.[32] Macaulay is here portraying a system of producing written matter which relies as much on its marketing and packaging – for a sixpenny or fourpenny, or cheaper readership – as it does on its content. While *Potterism* certainly contains criticism of the popular press and its proprietors' methods, Macaulay, an unmarried woman, was always uncomfortably aware of her financial reliance on newspapers, churning out 'trivial topicalities' to pay the bills.[33] Like her contemporary J. B. Priestley, Macaulay was as critical of snobbish intellectuals as she was of the popular press. Lord Pinkerton is allowed a happy ending. Despite his papers' demonization of suffragettes and strikers, Macaulay allows him to enjoy a peaceful old age, spending time in the garden with the grandson he dotes on. Gideon, however, the highbrow intellectual and outspoken critic of Potter is killed in Russia, bizarrely both by Whites and Reds. Ironically, his final act is to become 'a placard for the press' because of the odd nature of his death: 'his murder was in a little paragraph on the front page' of one of Potter's newspapers.[34]

Margaret 'Storm' Jameson, another 'middlebrow' interwar author, was more passionately committed to left-wing politics than Macaulay. Her wide-ranging *Mirror in Darkness* trilogy (1934–1936) examines the role the press plays in the failure of the Left to make political headway in the 1930s. Like many contemporary writers, she blames in her novels the press baron Marcel Cohen, not the individual journalist who is often bullied or muzzled by his proprietor, for the malign influence of the press.[35] As the trilogy progresses,

Jameson's attitude towards Cohen hardens. In the first novel *Company Parade* (1934) Cohen is described as 'handsome' with 'dark, brilliant and womanish' eyes.[36] His willingness to commission the heroine Hervey Russell (as Rothermere did Jameson) to write about liberal causes is rewarded with an initially generous portrayal. In *Love in Winter* (1935), however, he now has a 'brutal temper' and begins to politicize his paper's news coverage to suit his business needs.[37] We learn from Jameson's autobiography *Journey from the North* that up until 1933 she had a generally optimistic view of newspapers and journalists.[38] However, from 1933, as the discrepancy between what foreign correspondents told her in private and what newspapers published grew, she became increasingly disappointed with the mainstream press (see Chapter 4).[39] Jameson wrote *Love in Winter* during this period of gradual disillusionment. In the novel Cohen's *Daily Post* publishes the 'Russian letter' – a reference to the Zinoviev letter – knowing it is fake, not out of political conviction but because he has lost money under a Labour administration and wants a return of a Conservative government more sympathetic to his business needs.[40] For Jameson, who was passionately committed politically, this is an even worse crime than any ideologically inspired gesture. Cohen's punishment is the slow and painful death of his wife from cancer. Cohen's attitude to journalism is portrayed as similarly thoughtless and equally damaging as his political meddling. He neither knows nor cares of the consequences of his actions beyond the desire to sell more papers. To that end, he creates a culture, through his papers, that supports and reflects his business interests. His paper criticizes strikers, promotes trivial, human interest articles, suggests the poor only have themselves to blame for their misfortune and reduces coverage of serious political and literary topics. Cohen hires the egregious journalist William Ridley to write 'something you're not ashamed of writing, but it will have to please a million readers'.[41] Cohen's direction to Ridley to make readers 'stare and chuckle but once in a while don't forget the lump in the throat' summarizes the approach of the popular press, which was to elevate human interest stories and 'talking points' over more serious or 'difficult' content. Writers on the Left saw this as part of an elaborate smokescreen to distract peoples' attention from social inequality and their exploitation by the capitalist system: 'We're not really a newspaper, we're a circus in print, a vaudeville show' is how one of the journalists in J. B. Priestley's *Wonder Hero* describes the *Daily Tribune*.[42] Similarly, in William Gerhardie's novel *Doom* (1928), based on his unequal relationship with Beaverbrook, 'Lord Ottercove' boasts of his newspapers peddling 'illusions in a world of appearances'.[43]

Gerhardie was an aspiring young writer who, in 1925, was suddenly brought into Beaverbrook's dazzling orbit, the proprietor being convinced Gerhardie was 'the next big thing'.[44] In *Doom*, the protagonist, Frank Dickin, a struggling young writer, feels obliged to pay homage to Ottercove like some Jacobean courtier. As Beaverbrook did to Gerhardie, Ottercove promises Dickin what he craves: a commission for writing his novel, and the promise of publication. After their initial champagne-soaked meeting, like a painted marionette: 'In the glass lift he saw red patches on his cheeks. He thought that unless he steadied his thoughts he might have a stroke... he walked unsteadily on his feet past the braided commissionaire'.[45]

In the mid-1920s Beaverbrook, now owner of the *Daily* and *Sunday Express* and the *Evening Standard*, which he was quickly transforming from a minor London paper to a high-quality one with enormous literary clout, was a fascinating, magnetic social figure. He had a wide circle of literary friends including Rudyard Kipling, Arnold Bennett, H. G. Wells and George Moore and an even wider circle of other influential acquaintances including Bertrand Russell, the Aga Khan, John Middleton Murry and Lloyd George, who drank and partied at his London residence, Stornoway House.[46] During these years the writer Rebecca West briefly interrupted her long-running love affair with H. G. Wells to have a passionate and unsatisfactory one with Beaverbrook. After the affair was ended, rather abruptly by Beaverbrook, West wrote her own Beaverbrook novel *Sunflower*, in which she described 'Francis Pitt': 'With his ape's mouth and over-large head, and his over-broad shoulders he had an air of having been created before the human structure had added to itself such refinements as beauty and shapeliness'.[47]

William Gerhardie describes Beaverbrook's magnetism in his memoirs: 'The man at once attracted me irresistibly. He was irresistible. His force and charm were irresistible'.[48] The 'lovable peer', wrote Gerhardie in 1930, 'has inspired all the novelists of his day to create newspaper proprietors in his image'.[49] This may have been a slight exaggeration, but, as well as *Doom*, Arnold Bennett's affectionate portrayal of *Lord Raingo* (1926) and H. G. Wells' Sir Bussy Woodcock in *The Autocracy of Mr Parham* (1930) are certainly inspired by Beaverbrook. Perhaps wanting to show his highbrow admirers (D. H. Lawrence, a critic of the popular press was a 'mentor') that he could not be 'bought', Gerhardie ends *Doom* by having Lord Ottercove vaporized in an atomic reaction.[50] Beaverbrook, either reading the manuscript of the novel himself or being told of its contents, declined to serialize it as previously promised. As Northcliffe before him, Beaverbrook thus confirmed the baron's control over the artist's access to an audience – Gerhardie had to wait another three years before a publisher took the novel on. The press baron, who by the late 1920s now controls dozens of newspapers, magazines and even publishing houses exerts a severe distorting influence over the field of cultural production. From the vulgar economic pole he can reach out to influence the cultural pole and even, on a whim, silence the artist completely.

The intellectuals and the proprietors

Writers who did not need, or want, a press baron's patronage were able to be more directly critical. F. R. and Q. D. Leavis encouraged aggressive attacks on popular journalism and the press barons in their journal *Scrutiny*, launched in 1932. For them, popular journalism and its proprietors represented the forces of darkness against which they pitted themselves. Q. D. Leavis described press barons as pre-Christian monsters, 'figures from an underworld that rise out of the mud for a moment's ironical contemplation', in an article for *Scrutiny*.[51] Her influential *Fiction and the Reading Public* (1932), although ostensibly about the modern degradation of literature, with the lower classes reading their 'worn and greasy novels' as a 'drug habit' rather than a reading habit, critiques in detail Northcliffe and the rise of the popular press. She blames Northcliffe, Pearson (founder of the *Daily Express*) and Beaverbrook for turning serious daily journalism into 'pre-digested food', rendering the lower classes incapable of reading anything, either fiction or non-fiction, that was difficult.[52] Similarly in a 1933 *Scrutiny* article, the poet and critic Geoffrey Grigson makes a distinction between the journalist and the industry that employs him: 'Moral values are kicked into Fleet Street gutters by the existence of each newspaper as a vast capitalistic enterprise, depending on selling itself as widely as possible and greedy for profits... Every journalist is not a rogue; but every journalist is a half-marionette jerked by the newspaper industry (which is nine tenths a rogue).'[53]

Left-wing writers contributed to the debate, particularly after Rothermere's newspapers *Daily Mail*, *Sunday Pictorial* and *Mirror* embraced Oswald Mosley's fascists with a rash of horrible figures: W. H. Auden's 'Beethameer Beethameer bully of Britain' in *The Orators* (1932), the 'Scavenger Barons' of Cecil Day Lewis' *The Magnetic Mountain* (1933) and Lord Carpenter in Christopher St John Sprigg's *Fatality in Fleet Street* (1933). In 'Journal of an Airman', book two of Auden's *Orators*, the pilot-poet is planning his immediate activities after his revolutionary conquest of Britain thus: '*After Victory*. Few executions except for the newspaper peers – Viscount Stuford certainly'.[54] His enemy is clearly identifiable, and follows a tradition, started by the provincial and Scottish papers referring 'to "Beavermere and Rotherbrook" as though they were a double turn in a music hall'.[55] Auden's 'Beethameer, Beethameer, bully of Britain' has insinuated his influence, 'In kitchen, in cupboard, in club-room, in mews/In palace, in privy ... nagging at our nostrils with its nasty news'.[56] The image of Beethameer and his paper invading not only the sanctuary of the home and privy but the body too crystallizes the press baron's image as an uninvited malign influence polluting society. While in Rose Macaulay's *Potterism*, Percy Potter's influence is diffused through the bank of editors, news editors and journalists (including his own daughter Jane, who is able to argue for women's rights in the Potter Press even though his press as a whole campaigns against women's suffrage), Beethameer has no such braking mechanism. He delivers his 'nasty news' direct to people's nostrils. 'Beethameer' is followed immediately by the following line: '10,000 Cyclostyle copies of this for aerial distribution', a reference to an incident the year before *The Orators* was published when the Italian revolutionary poet Lauro de Bosis scattered thousands of anti-fascist leaflets over Rome from an aeroplane, before crashing and dying on his way back to Corsica (there is an account of this incident in the *Times*, 15 October 1931). This reference underlines the doomed airman-poet's political commitment. Direct action, meeting social and economic violence with physical violence, is for Auden's airman, the only way now to excise this cancer at the heart of British politics.

Similarly the Marxist writer Christopher St John Sprigg resorts to having his fictional press baron murdered as the only way to prevent him from realizing his dastardly plans. Bysshe Jameson, Charles Venables and Andrews, journalists on the *Daily Mercury* in Sprigg's *Fatality in Fleet Street* (1933), are all sympathetic characters 'who formed the conversation and conscience of democratic England' and are sickened by their proprietor Lord Carpenter's megalomaniacal plans to start a war with communist Russia.[57] The writer, who also took the name Christopher Caudwell, was a Marxist who was killed fighting for the Republicans in the Spanish Civil War. He had trained as a reporter on the *Yorkshire Observer* and supported his more literary writing by publishing several detective novels, 'merely his pot boilers'.[58] Through the late 1920s and early 1930s his politics became increasingly left-wing, until he joined the Communist Party in 1934.[59] The 'pot boilers' nevertheless contain a political message beneath the easy prose. For Sprigg/Caudwell, criticism of the likes of Lord Carpenter, who observes 'London's roofs tossing in a troubled sea below the lemon yellow and gilt heights of the *Mercury*'s gaudy building', is not enough.[60] He must be destroyed. Bysshe, the paper's star descriptive writer, stabs Carpenter in a desperate bid to prevent his plans being realized, only to find that the paper's put-upon librarian has got there first. In this instance, as in others quoted in the previous chapter, the journalists' goal on their paper – that is, peace, a liberal-left agenda and telling the public the truth – is the opposite of that of the proprietor – war, extreme libertarianism and manipulation of the facts. Studies by journalism scholars have concluded that journalists experience a very particular kind of professional tension: journalists believe that ideally news coverage should make society a better place, but actual news is dictated by a story's sensationalism and whether it involves famous people. Another study concludes that ethical journalists are often restrained from their role as truth-tellers because this role clashes with the interests of the organization they write for.[61] Unlike other professions such as law and medicine, journalists lack 'monopoly over their worth' and, for obvious reasons, the prestige of compulsory licensing. Therefore, there will always be 'ambiguity surrounding the status of journalism as a profession'.[62] Although Sprigg's plot is extreme, he is, however, illustrating a major source of tension for journalists working for powerful proprietors who often have other major interests, particularly financial and political. We shall see another example of this tension, again taken to the extreme, in the film *Defence of the Realm*, discussed below. Sprigg's novel is a warning of how a newspaper proprietor with access to '36, 563,271 readers', of whom even the prime minister is terrified, can dictate a nation's foreign policy.[63] In *Scoop* Evelyn Waugh's Lord Copper of *The Daily Beast* has a similar – although less potent – megalomania, telling William Boot as he departs for Ishmaelia: 'The British public has no interest in a war which drags on indecisively. A few sharp victories, some conspicuous acts of personal bravery on the Patriot side and a colourful entry into the capital … We shall expect the first victory about the middle of July.'[64] It is not clear, however, who is the more dangerous: the man who actually brings Britain to the brink of war with Russia through engineering a massacre of British subjects in a remote Soviet or the man who thinks that his journalists can make things happen just because they say it is so.

Writers here are beginning to construct a critique of the modern popular newspaper which will later acquire a robust theoretical framework, particularly from the early 1970s onwards, concerning the news media's tendency to distort facts to suit its own agenda.[65] That critique is based on the concept that newspapers construct an alternative version of reality for their readers, which in some cases bears no relation to actual events: Gerhardie's 'illusions in a world of appearances' and Priestley's 'circus in print'. These writers should be praised for their prescience. News providers, according to contemporary commentator Stephen Coleman, 'do more than tell daily stories; they frame and shape a common sense of the world, both distant and local' on which modern audiences increasingly rely in an increasingly mediated society.[66] When trivial stories about celebrity adultery are given the same prominence as the launch of a new Government White Paper or when an entire news system fails to scrutinize politicians' assurances (during the run-up to the second Gulf War) or the bankers' dealing in subprime mortgages 2004–2007, then it is difficult to understand what journalism is for any more. Writers were beginning to ask these questions, in particular in relation to newspaper proprietors, more than eighty years ago.

The rise of Rupert Murdoch

The figure of the press baron fades from early post–Second World War newspaper fictions due to a combination of factors including wartime paper rationing and a generally accepted perception that newspapers had had a 'good war' (see Chapter 6). By the end of the war, with the success of the BBC's radio coverage, newspapers had also lost their monopoly on information.[67] The baron himself had lost some of his newspaper empire: by 1947, the three most powerful proprietors controlled a smaller section of the British press than ten years earlier.[68] By the mid-twentieth century the press baron in the likeness of a Northcliffe, Rothermere or Beaverbrook was 'virtually extinct' due to a number of reasons, including the rise of boardroom governance, organized labour, more 'arms length' proprietors and competition for advertising from radio and television.[69] There was concern over newspaper attacks on Clement Attlee's 1945 Labour Government but the consensus politics of the following three decades largely blunted this issue for writers. The proprietor returns in fiction with a vengeance after Rupert Murdoch takes control of *The Times* and *Sunday Times*, the jewels of the British newspaper crown, with Chris Mullin's novel *A Very British Coup* (1982), the film *Defence of the Realm* (1985) and, most memorably, in Howard Brenton and David Hare's play *Pravda* (also first performed in1985).

Murdoch had been running British newspapers since he bought the *News of the World* and the *Sun* in January and November 1969, respectively. By 1978 the *Sun* had overtaken the previously dominant *Mirror*, reaching sales of four million copies a day – from under one million when Murdoch took over. Murdoch and his editor Larry Lamb achieved this by adding more sex, sensationalism and populist politics than the *Mirror*.[70] During the 1970s there was considerable intellectual concern, as ever, over the further decline in standards of the popular press. However, Murdoch and the image of the proprietor escaped writers' particular interest until after 1981, when he pulled off the breathtaking coup of acquiring the *Times* and *Sunday Times*, without being referred to the Monopolies Commission, and in secret negotiations with the new prime minister Margaret Thatcher.[71] Murdoch's smooth acquisition of the *Times*, in return for political favours, triggered three waves of what Tony Harcup describes as 'principled resignations' from prominent journalists: the first in 1981–1982 after the initial takeover, then in 1986 after Murdoch moved his newspapers to Wapping (the 'Wapping refuseniks') and again in 1988 after what was seen as a politically motivated attack in the *Sunday Times* on the Thames TV programme *Death on the Rock*.[72] Among the casualties was Harry Evans, editor of the *Sunday Times*, and briefly the *Times*, and generally accepted as having been the greatest 'broadsheet' newspaper editor of the second half of the twentieth century. In his memoir *Good Times Bad Times*, Evans describes his failure to fight against the acquisition of *Times* newspapers by a proprietor who had already 'debauched the values of the tabloid press' as 'the worst [judgement] in my professional career'.[73]

Chris Mullin's portrayal of Sir George Fison is not, in fact, an accurate depiction of Murdoch's *modus operandi* – already a knight, Fison is very much part of the traditional British establishment, drinking in its leather-chaired clubs and accepting his peerage when the left-wing prime minister is brought down. The novel, dealing as it does with the idea of unaccountable institutions, including newspapers, infecting legitimate democratic processes, served, however, as a prescient warning of the extent of Murdoch's steady insinuation into British public life, the extent of which only became really apparent after the collapse of the *News of the World* and the Leveson Inquiry (2011–2012).

Pravda opened at the National Theatre in May 1985 and was an immediate box-office success. The protagonist, Le Roux, is a South African newspaper proprietor who gradually buys up Fleet Street and, in so doing, changes the nature of British journalism. Anthony Hopkins, who played Le Roux, was praised by the *Times* theatre critic Irving Wardle as producing 'as spellbinding performance as I have yet seen on this stage' despite the obvious connections between the South African Le Roux and Wardle's new employer Rupert Murdoch: 'Adopting a slight stoop and a feline walk, he confronts adversaries and underlings alike with a carnivorously affable smile; always generating uneasiness; exploding into fearful foul-mouthed abuse, and then switching to soft reassurance.'

Wardle's review begins with a disarmingly honest confession of his difficulty in reviewing the play: 'They [Brenton and Hare] nail up their message in the main title: signifying truth but meaning lies, and they are out to give offence, rattle skeletons, and give people like me a hard time in writing this notice' (*Times*, 3 May 1985). Le Roux's easy corruption of lawyers and bishops in persuading them he is the right man to buy *The Victory* is a fruitful theme for Hare and Brenton, part of the alliance between theatre and Left politics since they began Portable Theatre in the 1960s.[74] *Pravda* was seen by fellow dramatist David Edgar as part of a continuum of post-war dramaturgy, 'anatomising the nation's decline' from a left-of-centre perspective, from *The Entertainer* (John Osborne, 1957) onwards.[75] The ownership of the newspaper press by predominantly Conservative-leaning businessmen had been a concern for the Left for decades, but after Rupert Murdoch acquired the *Times* and *Sunday Times* and their 'cherished independence', 70 per cent of British newspaper circulations were now pro-Conservative.[76]

Newspaper ownership and the Conservative Party is not, however, the main interest of the play. The main interest is Le Roux's easy exploitation of journalists, 'whose lack of both spine and mutual solidarity contrasts with the behaviour of workers in happier, healthier professions', and his elevation of trivia over 'real' journalism, something ex-Murdoch employees have long complained about but which now appears enormously prescient.[77] Hare commented on the play's prescience in 1986: 'various pieces of wild satire have transformed themselves effortlessly into prophesy', something he calls the 'eerie coincidence of life in art'.[78] As years rolled by, both these issues have achieved greater clarity particularly in the operation of Murdoch's tabloids. The Leveson Inquiry and its fallout have shown how easily some journalists, particularly on the *News of the World*, accepted that breaking the law in order to obtain stories about celebrity antics was part of their job as a tabloid reporter. The revelation that Murdoch was first offered, but rejected, the parliamentary expenses material also fits into his 'Let somebody else annoy them' approach to journalism.[79] While the *News of the World* certainly scored its fair share of exclusives, these were mostly about celebrity antics and the Royal Family, and not the kind of 'risky altruism' that really places a newspaper and its journalists in jeopardy. Bruce Page, former investigative journalist on the *Sunday Times*, puts it thus:

> Newscorp distinguished itself by frantic boasting about its devastating scoops, and pitiless skills in criminal investigation. For the most part this was just bar-room hype, rarely if ever involving engagement with targets showing a damaging capacity to shoot back. Many of these scoops involved hunting members of the Royal Family: a sport best practised by the kind of people who will shoot at tethered game.[80]

The journalist Suzie Fontaine in *Pravda* has assimilated this Murdoch philosophy. She conducts an investigation into the pork content of pâté with the help of the 'Depth-Probe' team, a reference to the *Sunday Times* famous Insight investigative journalism unit. Insight had made a name for itself in the 1970s particularly in the Thalidomide story, often referred to as British journalism's answer to the celebrated Watergate exposé painstakingly uncovered by the *Washington Post*.[81]

> We've got four reporters at the Ritz – photo session, as well – eating sixty different brands … The whole Depth-Probe team is on it … Kitchens. Consumer objects. Holidays. Microchips. Show-biz gossip … Keep it all frothy. The world's ten leading film stars, just how much bran is in their breakfast? (*She smiles*). Funny, everyone used to be so frightened of investigative journalism.[82]

When a real investigative story about potentially dangerous containers that were used to carry plutonium from power stations is brought to the paper, Le Roux stifles it as it would damage his relations with the government. Journalists who can't accept the Le Roux way either resign or are fired including the new editor of the broadsheet *Victory*. Good journalism, says Le Roux, is too expensive: 'All that writing. Why go to the trouble of producing good [papers], when bad ones are so much easier? And they sell better too.'[83]

A subtext of the political thriller *Defence of the Realm*, set in the offices of the fictional *Daily Dispatch*, is what happens to journalists when they want to go against their proprietor's interests. Two shabbily dressed investigative journalists unravel a plot between their sharp-suited proprietor and the secret service to cover up the near-miss of a nuclear accident at an American air base in Norfolk. As in Christopher Sprigg's *Fatality in Fleet Street*, the tension lies between the journalists' idealistic view of what their job should be and the reality of working for a man who also has a stake in the lucrative defence industry. The script writer Martin Stellman, like Hare and Brenton, and Sprigg before them, puts the spotlight on the ambiguity of the journalistic profession and the irreconcilable differences between the aims of journalists and the interests of the proprietor. Not only does Victor Kingsbrook (another 'Beethameer' construction from Cecil Harmsworth King, former chairman of the *Daily Mirror* and Lord Beaverbrook) 'spike' Nick Mullen's story, but he also has him, and fellow correspondent Vernon Bayliss, murdered by the secret service. Martin Stellman, who had been a freelance features writer for *Time Out* magazine and the underground magazine *Ink*, wanted to explore what a morally dubious, yet essentially honest, reporter would do, when faced with the 'Big Story' that had to be told and his 'Murdoch-style proprietor' was trying to obstruct him:

I think some of us sensed in the early 80s that there was something crooked in the manner Thatcher cleared the way for Murdoch to take over the Times Group though we didn't really get the full story until Harold Evans spelt it out properly some years later. The idea that Murdoch, a man with a billion dollar portfolio of newspaper and media interests in both Australia and the US could make a smash and grab raid on the major opinion-forming 'serious' newspaper of the day was deeply worrying. A big beast like Murdoch with many and varied outside interests seemed to put journalists with integrity immediately under notice that there would inevitably be some no-go areas and editorial independence could well suffer.[84]

Writing the script in 1984, however, Stellman was also inspired by the recent takeover of the 'fiercely independent liberal' *Observer* by R. W. 'Tiny' Rowland of Lonrho, a famously aggressive operator with huge mining and agri-businesses in southern Africa: 'I asked myself, what would it be like if a reporter uncovered a story which unfavourably implicated one of Lonrho's many interests?'[85]

It is of note that while Northcliffe and Murdoch were 'only' owners of popular newspapers (notably the *Daily Mail* and *Daily Mirror* for Northcliffe, although he owned several other titles, and the *News of the World* and the *Sun* for Murdoch), writers saw no need to present a monstrous image of the press baron for the public. In both cases, it is the purchase of the *Times* that seems to prompt major portrayals. It could be that writers have little concern for the press baron until he begins to pollute the reading matter of the elite; it could be that in both cases, acquisition of the *Times*, in purely numerical terms, is one paper too many.

Of further note is that these later portrayals of the proprietor are in film and theatre, and not in the pages of a novel. His malign influence also runs through two more contemporary dramas about the press, Doug Lucie's *The Shallow End* (1997) and Richard Bean's post-Leveson *Great Britain* (2014). Paschal O'Leary, the proprietor in *Great Britain*, however, is a confused hybrid: part Murdoch, part Richard Desmond (owner of *Express* Newspapers) and part Barclay Brothers (owners of the *Daily* and *Sunday Telegraph*). As such he loses some of the focused power of Le Roux: O'Leary is a pornographer whose papers also publish the M.P.s' expenses story.[86] These plays are discussed further in Chapter 8. As in the early portrayals of Northcliffe by Bennett and Fagan, the monstrous figure of the proprietor appears to lend itself more to theatrical rendering rather than through words alone. Indeed in an introduction to a collection of essays, David Hare writes that in imagining a contemporary newspaper newsroom, he and Howard Brenton 'wanted to re-write *Richard III* and ask again the old question about why and how evil is so attractive'.[87] Film, television and theatre too have more immediate social impact than a novel. Certainly both *Pravda* and *Defence of the Realm* attracted much contemporary commentary and both won significant accolades. The reactions of an audience in a public venue such as a cinema or theatre are easy to gauge: the laughter, the groans, the level of chatter, the box-office takings night by night. David Hare notes that the 'National Theatre had to take on four extra staff to cope with the demand' after the announcement of an end to *Pravda*'s run. To journalists watching the play, 'it must have been a disconcerting experience to come and sit in an auditorium where they were forced to breathe in the heady air of revenge. A readership was expressing (loudly) their view of the papers they read, and of their fawning relationship with Government'.[88] Martin Stellman talks of the 'explosive impact' he was looking for when writing *Defence of the Realm* for a cinema audience.[89]

In these later depictions of the press baron, writers are not concerned with their predecessors' turf wars over ascendancy in the field of cultural production. There are a number of reasons for this, the most important one being that from the middle of the late twentieth century journalism and literature had completed their messy divorce and began living apart, now in separate fields. Although occasional pot shots are still sent over from time to time, there is some kind of a fragile truce. This is discussed in the next few chapters. What concerns these later writers is not so much how journalism will impact their market but how this new style of newspaper proprietor is distorting the political field and 'polluting' British political and cultural life. And so to Dennis Potter's cancer called Rupert, the epithet that opens this chapter. In his interview with Melvyn Bragg, the critically acclaimed writer expands on his reasons for so naming the disease that is killing him:

> There is no one person more responsible for the pollution of what was already a fairly polluted press, and the pollution of the British press is an important part of the pollution of British political life, and it's an important part of the cynicism and misperception of our own realities that is destroying so much of our political discourse ... How can we have a mature democracy when newspapers and television are ... so interlaced with ownership?[90]

There are of course within politics and journalism supporters of Rupert Murdoch who credit him with saving British journalism by ridding it of the cost and waste of the pre-Wapping days and this is discussed further in Chapter 8. British imaginative writers, however, are not among his fan club.

Notes

1   Dennis Potter to Melvyn Bragg in an interview published in the *New Left Review* 1/205, p. 131.

2   Fagan, James Bernard, *The Earth*, p. 27.

3   Wilson, A. N., *My Name Is Legion*, p. 18.

4   Evans, B. Ifor, 'The Rise of Modern Journalism', *Fortnightly Review* 127 (1930), pp. 233–234.

5   *The Earth* was first performed at the Kingsway Theatre, April 1909; *What the Public Wants* at the Aldwych Theatre May 1909.

6   Bennett, Arnold, *What the Public Wants*, p. 7.

7   Ibid., p. 37.

8   Flower, Newman (ed.) and Newman Flower, *The Journals of Arnold Bennett, Volume 1*, p. 19.

9   Ibid., p. 270, 283 & 291.

10 Innes, Christopher, 'Bernard Shaw and James B. Fagan, playwright and producer', *Shaw* 30.

11 Fagan, *The Earth*, p. 46.

12 Ibid., p. 153.

13 Bennett, *Public Wants*, p. 143.

14 Flower, *Journals Arnold Bennett*, p. 317

15 *Times*, 4 May 1909.

16 *Daily Mail*, 21 February 1917.

17 Twells Brex to Lord Northcliffe, 29 May 1918, Northcliffe Papers Add 62220.

18 Lord Northcliffe to Henry Leach, 12 February 1912, Northcliffe Papers Add 62219.

19 John Foster Fraser to Lord Northcliffe 14 May 1912; Hall Caine to Lord Northcliffe 8 May 1908, Northcliffe Papers Add 62178. Hall Caine's great bestsellers had been published several years before: *The Christian* (1897) and *The Eternal City* (1901).

20 Bennett, Arnold, *Letters* Vol I, p. 195.

21 Bennett, *Public Wants*, p. 30.

22 Harmsworth, Alfred, 'The Making of a Newspaper', pp. 178 & 168.

23 Howard, Keble, *Lord London*, p. 209.

24 Ibid., pp. 234–240.

25 Howard, Keble, *My Motley Life*, pp. 185–186.

26 Beaverbrook directed the Ministry of Information and Northcliffe the Department of Enemy Propaganda.

27 Angell, Norman, *The Press and the Organisation of Society*, p. 7.

28 Ibid., p. 9.

29 Margach, James, *The Abuse of Power*, p. 38. Rothermere, Northcliffe's brother, had taken over running his newspapers after his death in 1922.

30 Macaulay, Rose, *Potterism*, p. 5.

31   Ibid., p. 21.

32   Ibid., p. 177.

33   Rose Macaulay to her mother 26 January 1921, ERM 9/1.

34   Ibid., p. 181.

35   For example, the socialist journalist Louis Earlham in the *Mirror in Darkness*.

36   Jameson, Storm, *Company Parade*, p. 53.

37   Jameson, Storm, *Love in Winter*, p. 273.

38   Jameson, Storm, *Journey*, p. 318.

39   Ibid., p. 320.

40   The letter, purportedly written by Zinoviev, president of the Communist International contained instructions to the British Labour Party to carry out 'seditious activities' (Taylor, A. J. P., *English History 1914–1945*, pp. 219–225).

41   Jameson, *Company*, p. 283.

42   Priestley, J. B., *Wonder Hero*, p. 288.

43   Gerhardie, William, *Doom*, p. 78.

44   Gerhardie, William, *Memoirs of a Polyglot*, p. 226.

45   Gerhardie, *Doom* (published as *Jazz and Jasper*, 1928, later as *Doom*, p. 58).

46   Davies, Dido, *William Gerhardie*, pp. 153–154.

47   West, Rebecca, *Sunflower*, p. 48; *Sunflower*, although written during the mid 1920s, was published only after West's death.

48   Gerhardie, *Memoirs*, p. 240.

49   Ibid., p. 252.

50   Ibid., pp. 254–255.

51   Leavis, Q. D., 'Fleet Street and Pierian Roses', *Scrutiny* II/4, p. 388.

52   Leavis, Q. D., *Fiction and the Reading Public*, pp. 7, 87 & 178–186.

53   Grigson, Geoffrey, 'Review', p. 416.

54   Auden, W. H., *Orators*, p. 66.

55   Margach, *The Abuse of Power*, p. 24.

56   Auden, W. H., *The English Auden*, p. 86.

57   Sprigg, Christopher St John, *Fatality in Fleet Street*, p. 15.

58   Strachey, John, 'Introduction' to the 1938 edition of Caudwell's *Studies in a Dying Culture*.

59   Mulhern, James, 'The Marxist Aesthetics of Christopher Caudwell', p. 38.

60   Sprigg, *Fatality in Fleet Street*, p. 9.

61   Stromback, Jesper, 'Determinants of News Content' in *Journalism Studies* 2012, p. 722; Harcup, Tony, 'Journalists and Ethics' in *Journalism Studies*, 2002, pp. 111–112.

62   Elsaka, Nadia, 'New Zealand Journalists and the appeal of "professionalism"' in *Journalism Studies* (2005), p. 73.

63   Sprigg, *Fatality in Fleet Street*, p. 9.

64   Waugh, Evelyn, *Scoop*, p. 42.

65   See for example Hall, Stuart et al., *Policing the Crisis*; Coleman, Stephen et al., *Public Trust in the News* and Davies, Nick, *Flat Earth News*.

66 Coleman, Stephen et al., *Public Trust in the News*, p. 7.

67 Households with radio licenses increased from two million in 1927 to nine million by 1939; Briggs, Asa, *The Golden Age of Broadcasting*, pp. 253–254.

68 Seymour-Ure, Colin, *Prime Ministers*, p. 99.

69 Brendon, Piers, *Life and Death*, pp. 1 & 251–256.

70 There are several good accounts of Murdoch's proprietorship of the *Sun*. For several insiders' points of view, see Peter Chippendale and Chris Horrie's *Stick It Up Your Punter*. More analytical is the 'Trading Tabloid Places' chapter in Bruce Page's *The Murdoch Archipelago*.

71 Although there was at the time plenty of unease over the way Murdoch managed to acquire the *Times*, the extent of the secret contact between Murdoch and Thatcher was not revealed until, first, the publication of go-between Woodrow Wyatt's Journals 1998–2000 and, second, by evidence that Murdoch and Thatcher *did* actually meet in January 1981, contrary to all previous denials, to discuss his bid for *Times* newspapers. This evidence came to light in 2012. The memos regarding the meeting can be seen here: http://www.theguardian.com/media/interactive/2012/mar/17/rupert-murdoch-thatcher-meeting-letters.

72 Harcup, 'Journalists and Ethics', p. 108.

73 Ibid.

74 Bull, John, *New British Political Dramatists*, p. 16.

75 Edgar, David, 'Why Pay's the Thing', *Guardian* 28 June 1985.

76 Evans, Harold, *Good Times*, p. xxiv.

77 Hare, David, 'Sailing Downwind: On *Pravda*', p. 134; see for example Page, Bruce, *The Murdoch Archipelago*, pp. 7–9.

78 Ibid., p. 133.

79 The phrase is what Murdoch is reported to have said when he submitted to Beijing's demand for censorship in the wake of the Tiananmen Square massacre. Page, Bruce, *The Murdoch Archipelago*, p. 7.

80 Ibid.

81 See for example Evans, *Good Times*, pp. 60–82.

82 Brenton, Howard, and David Hare, *Pravda*, p. 68.

83 Ibid., p. 118.

84 Interview with Martin Stellman.

85 Ibid.

86 The Parliamentary expenses scandal, revealed in the *Daily Telegraph* in 2009, exposed widespread misuse of expenses claims by politicians.

87 Hare, 'Sailing Downwind', p. 135.

88 Ibid., p. 133.

89 Interview with Martin Stellman.

90 Dennis Potter to Melvyn Bragg in an interview published in the *New Left Review* 1/205, p. 131.

'A journalist's finished at forty, of course': Alienation, Disenchantment, Irrelevance in the Post-War 'Age of Anxiety'[1]

With the 'battle of the brows' all but over, writers with first-hand connections to the world of newspapers astutely identify deep, structural weaknesses of a monolithic press years before editors and circulation managers will. Against a backdrop of post-war Austerity followed by economic renaissance and the arrival of the 'swinging sixties' journalist-novelists address themes of commercialization, slipping standards and the growing irrelevance of an industry that appears stuck in the past even as it enjoys record circulations. During this period too, novels about journalism gradually cease to be about writing and the literary marketplace, focusing more on characteristics of a new and separate journalistic field. This change suggests that at some point during this period the final breaks between literature and journalism occurred.

The immediate post–Second World War literary landscape was an unutterably gloomy one. For George Orwell, hallways 'smelt of boiled cabbage and old rag mats'; Graham Greene saw 'black leafless trees … like broken water pipes' which gave no protection from the continual rain; and for Monica Dickens, meals in miserable boarding houses 'tasted of gravy powder'.[2] Post-war writers were not just expressing a physical gloom caused by the air raids, rationing and the ruinous expense of waging war for six years, but a moral crisis, a realization of the depths of man's capacity for evil, summed up most succinctly in Theodor Adorno's famous comment that 'to write poetry after Auschwitz is barbaric'. Accompanying these philosophical attitudes was the pervasive fear that 'World War Three was round the corner' and that Britain and Europe would be 'probably this time destroyed utterly'.[3] How would writers present reality against a backdrop of rapid social change and fears of an apocalyptic future? What would be their attitude towards the press, now so pervasive that newspaper sales had virtually reached saturation point, and which was for the first time seriously under scrutiny by Parliament in the guise of the Royal Commission on the Press (1947–1949)?

Contemporary literary commentators initially criticized the conservatism of post-war writing, comparing it unfavourably to the flamboyant experimentation of the 1920s and 1930s; as if six years of war, and more of grim belt-tightening, had, according to the contemporary critic Cyril Connolly, 'enslumbered the arts, like a skilled anaesthetist, into final oblivion'.[4] This assessment may have been apt for the times. However, the social realism employed by the new generation of 'angry young men' was partly a reaction against the perception that interwar experimentation had largely been the preserve of a social and cultural elite and that Modernism 'generally sounded in an upper middle class accent'.[5] Young working-class and lower-middle-class writers like Keith Waterhouse, John Braine and Alan Sillitoe achieved something new in the characters, cityscapes and social themes they portrayed, however narrowly focused they now appear in retrospect. Just as great an achievement was their success in challenging the existing literary and cultural hegemony thanks to the 1944 Butler Education Act, which established the right to a secondary education for all. Keith Waterhouse, who would become a hugely successful journalist, notes in his memoirs: 'There had been a revolution – although quietly, and without anyone really noticing that it had started until it had taken hold … [an]upstart generation which instead of becoming factory fodder had come up through the grammar schools and the redbricks and the drama schools and the art colleges and was now ready to take the world on.'[6]

While there are certainly difficulties in grouping the many apparent disparate literary trends of the 1950s and 1960s into one movement or idea, Malcolm Bradbury suggests the umbrella terms of 'anti-authoritarianism' or 'anti-Establishment protest' may be a useful starting point.[7] This attitude, though broadbrush, can include the ideas of class and social upheaval of the angry young men and the rejection of a metropolitan Oxbridge elite in the flowering of the provincial and 'campus' novels as well as those fictions which explore new philosophical and literary ideas imported from a war-bruised Continent such as existentialism and the French *nouveau roman*.

Fictions featuring newspapers and journalists written during this time can also be broadly categorized as 'anti-Establishment': a general theme is the enormous power of a monolithic press but a press which is becoming stale, over-commercialized and failing to reflect the eddies and undercurrents of seismic change in society. One contemporary author and journalist puts it: 'The

Daily Mail hated – and still hates – the 1960s and all that decade stood for'.[8] Writers unconnected with journalism and viewing the press from a distance see mainstream newspapers as contributing to the cultural conservatism which characterized England of the 1950s and 1960s. Mass-produced newspapers, like the mass-produced new 'Subtopian' housing estates and the mass-produced consumer goods, contribute to a suffocating standardization where everyone lives in the same kind of house, wears the same kind of clothes and reads the same kind of newspaper.[9] Fictional journalists created by writers with first-hand experience of newspapers tend to be vulnerable outsiders who question the shady and immoral practices of their employers. The *Sunday Sun*, for example, in Murray Sayle's novel *A Crooked Sixpence* (1961), set in a 1950s tabloid newspaper office, sets itself up as a crusader against vice, its hollowed-out editor Cameron Barr knowing only too well that the resultant salacious headlines attract 'nasty readers of his nasty paper'.[10] Meanwhile the rookie reporter James O'Toole, who takes a principled stance against the paper's cynicism, ends up jobless and penniless.[11]

This post-war criticism may seem somewhat surprising in that the British press is generally perceived to have had a 'good war' in terms of the reliability and veracity of its coverage of the conflict. George Orwell, always a fierce critic of his some-time profession, decided a year after the German occupation of Norway in April 1940 that 'the tone of the popular press has improved out of recognition during the last year … all of them print articles which would have been considered hopelessly above their readers' heads a couple of years ago, and the *Mirror* and *Standard* are noticeably 'left'. He concludes: 'as to the accuracy of the news, I believe this is the most truthful war that has been fought in modern times … there is certainly nothing to compare with the frightful lies that were told on both sides in 1914–1918'.[12] The remarkable absence of fictions criticizing the press written during the Second World War (apart from a few barbed references in Evelyn Waugh's *Put Out More Flags* (1942) and the stolidly prosaic 'Mr Page the reporter, licking his pencil', taking dull notes of an artistic pageant in Virginia Woolf's *Between the Acts* (1941)) upholds Orwell's view. As during the Boer War, where fictional journalists were thin on the ground, this absence confirms a lack of concern among the literary classes of press behaviour (see Chapter 2). There may be several reasons for this apparent improvement in standards since 1914–1918. First, the severe shortage of newsprint during the war limited newspaper pages to as few as four per issue. Not only did this force advertisers to purchase space in less profitable newspapers with smaller circulations, but also, instead of chasing sales with promotions and sensationalism, editors actively tried to avoid raising circulations. Frank Waters, manager of Express Newspapers in Scotland, recorded in his diary in April 1940: 'Newsprint has become rarer than gold. Sizes of paper have been further limited to 8 pages. Now actually embarrassed by extra sales.'[13] When in 1941 newsprint became even scarcer, reducing pages to four, the *Daily Telegraph* opted to keep its pagination to six by means of lowering circulation. In a letter to readers the *Telegraph* proprietor Lord Camrose asked those 'who are fortunate enough to get their copies regularly' to 'share them wherever practicable, with less fortunate friends', which under normal circumstances is commercial suicide.[14] George Orwell pointed out: 'Ultimately this will bankrupt the newspapers and compel the State to take them over, but at the moment they are in an interim period when they are controlled by journalists rather than advertisers, which is all to the good in the short time it will last.'[15] On top of the newsprint shortage, patriotic proprietors were enlisted in the war effort. The most popular newspaper of the day, the *Daily Express*, lost its interfering proprietor's laser-like attention when Lord Beaverbrook was appointed minister of aircraft production by Churchill within days of his becoming prime minister. When Beaverbrook did interfere, it was not to urge editors to boost sales, as he had done before the war, but to discourage sensationalism in favour of sober reporting: 'The front page should be a document of the war. You do not want any more net sales, and you should make no popular appeal whatsoever.'[16] Perhaps also the 'fight to the death' nature of the conflict, when after May 1940 Britain stood alone against Nazi Germany, meant there was little public appetite for sensationalism or trivia.

Post-war circulation boom

In the immediate post-war years, however, after restrictions on newsprint were lifted, the newspaper press reached its zenith in terms of sales and readership despite the firm establishment of radio as a news medium during the war and the steady growth in sales of television licenses: four million in 1955, more than ten million by 1960.[17] Popular newspapers once again engaged in a circulation war, not with insurance schemes and offers as in the interwar years, but with increasingly sensationalist reporting. This led Randolph Churchill, severe critic of the popular press, in tone remarkably similar to many contemporary post-Leveson criticisms, to observe in 1956:

> Some papers have definitely built up mammoth circulations by consciously degrading the public taste. They set their sights on the gutter and invite the public

to go down and roll about with them in it and join them in the task of intruding into other people's private lives and spattering anyone who has achieved any degree of eminence or notoriety with filth and slime.[18]

In 1956 the total readership of the main daily and morning newspapers was forty-nine million out of a population of fifty-one million.[19] Proprietors of even popular newspapers were now at the very heart of the British Establishment. The historian Dominic Sandbrook, for example, quotes research from the early 1960s to show that descendants of four Victorian peers (Devonshire, Lansdowne, Abercorn and Marlborough) 'included the Prime Minister, the Foreign Secretary, the Lord Chancellor and six other government ministers, the British Ambassador to the United States, the Governor of the Bank of England...and the owners of the *Times*, the *Observer* and the *Daily Mail*...the owner of the *Daily Express*' as well as major regional chains.[20] It is no accident that the opening scene of the period's most important play, John Osborne's *Look Back in Anger* (1956), portrays two young men slumped in armchairs literally pinned down by the Sunday newspapers, with only their legs being visible. The floor is awash with Sundays and weeklies; the men's oppression and the suffocating banality of a provincial English Sunday afternoon is framed by this dead weight of newsprint which, as Jimmy Porter observes in the first line of the play, 'seem[s] to be the same as last week's'.[21] Always questing through pages to find something of interest, he is bored by everything the press has to offer. He observes that popular papers are becoming ever more sensationalist: 'Reconstructions of midnight invocations to the Coptic Goddess of fertility' and the 'posh' ones are disappearing into intellectual irrelevance: 'there's a particularly savage correspondence about whether Milton wore braces or not'.[22] And yet still he and Cliff devour their papers, searching for some kind of satisfaction from them, something that will speak to them. The papers, however, always disappoint, being part of the powerful establishment inertia: Cambridge, the Athenaeum, Roedean and All Souls, against which Jimmy Porter vainly kicks. The irony is of course that the 'angry young men' are afraid of a changing society which apparently offers young working-class men more opportunities but which beguiles them into an overeducated cul-de-sac and where women, like Helena, are becoming sexually liberated and financially independent. The papers' reports of a changing world – stories of sexual promiscuity in the 'dirty' ones and the threat of the 'H Bomb' in the 'posh' ones – thus pose a twofold danger: the Establishment of which Jimmy will never be part and frightening change which threatens even the small kingdom – his wife, sweet stall and his flat – over which he exercises doubtful control. A decade later, the mainstream papers are still dismaying and oppressing Bob, the young writer with literary aspirations working for an exhausted Fleet Street newspaper in Michael Frayn's *Towards the End of the Morning* (1967): 'the sight of the newspaper, still greyly excited about the daily trivia of six months before, made him feel suddenly dismal'.[23]

Francis Williams, one-time editor of the left-wing *Daily Herald* and later Clement Attlee's press adviser, when he first became prime minister after the 1945 Labour landslide, wrote a wide-ranging critique of his industry during the mid-1950s, in the aftermath of the Royal Commission: *Dangerous Estate*.[24] In describing the phenomenon of British newspaper readership, Williams marvels: 'No other product of modern civilisation has achieved so complete a saturation of its potential market ... the frontier can be pushed no further – 88 per cent of the adult population reads a paper every day.'[25] What Williams saw as dangerous was not so much the huge success of newspapers in finding readers, but that at the same time as newspapers had never been more read, their numbers of individual titles had never been fewer.[26] Since 1921 more than 300 weekly papers had closed; the number of towns with more than two morning papers had reduced from thirteen to three and the number of towns with more than two evening papers from twenty-three to eight.[27] Since the end of the First World War, nearly a dozen 'national' or London-based daily and Sunday papers, including the *Morning Post, Pall Mall Gazette, Daily News, Daily Graphic, Daily Dispatch* and *Daily Chronicle*, had either closed or merged with other titles.[28] The *News Chronicle* and *Sunday Chronicle, Daily Herald* and *Daily Sketch* would shortly follow in 1960, 1964 and 1971 respectively. With every newspaper that died, the mainstream press became more weighted towards a Conservative viewpoint, something which has alarmed Labour politicians for decades, and which led Aneurin Bevan to describe British newspapers as 'the most prostituted press in the world, most of it owned by a gang of millionaires'.[29] The failure of the Liberal and middlebrow *News Chronicle*, which, with a circulation of more than a million, was still losing more than £300,000 a year by 1960, was particularly concerning, as distinguished *Chronicle* journalist James Cameron said: 'it stood for something outside the Establishment', a 'warhorse ridden by grocers'.[30] The journalist and author Michael Frayn, who was brought up on the *Chronicle*, describes it as a 'decent Liberal paper which died of decency or Liberalism or both'.[31] As Williams points out, with such a vast industry dominated by just a few enormous organizations the production of newspapers was becoming like any other mass-produced item: 'readers have to be fought for by the millions to make popular journalism viable'.[32] As a result, conservative, mainstream views are dominant, leading the popular press to 'de-legitimise radical or politically deviant groups'.[33] So, for example, although popular newspapers were on the whole restrained in their coverage of the decriminalization of homosexuality in 1967, throughout the 1950s and 1960s gay men were variously described as 'poofs', 'perverts', 'pansies' and 'sick'.[34] Newspapers thus represented conservatism, commercialism, homogenization and social control, back to the position in the 1930s, but with larger circulations and fewer titles. Small wonder, then, that writers wanted to kick against them.

Winston Smith, an extreme parody of the 'good' journalist

George Orwell's *1984* (1949) opens this post-war debate with his horrid vision of a society where news, both its current and its historic production, is controlled by the Party. Two-way 'telescreens' monitor access to information. Protagonists Winston and Julia are employed within the Ministry of Information, which produces the *Times* for Party members as well as 'rubbishy newspapers which contained almost nothing except sport, crime and astrology' for the 'proles'.[35] Winston works in a parody of a newspaper newsroom where, instead of producing original news copy, Winston and his colleagues either doctor *Times* archives to suit the Party's agenda or fabricate pieces of news to fill gaps left by the excision of articles whose existence would question Big Brother's authority. Instead of vying with each other to produce a dozen different original reports, Winston and 'as many as a dozen people' were trying to produce the best fabricated story to replace one excised one. Just as a reporter is sure his 'scoop' will make it into the paper because it is factually accurate and tells the world something new, Winston is sure that his story, a piece of fantasy about a 'Comrade Ogilvy', will be the chosen piece from the many submitted precisely because it is entirely fabricated with no awkward links to real events which might make further amendments to the *Times* necessary. In a typically Orwellian piece of irony, Winston's only 'original' articles for the *Times* are in 'newspeak', a language developed to destroy not only words but the power of independent thought in its users. George Orwell, although best known as the author of *Animal Farm* and *1984*, was also a prolific journalist, contributing regularly to the *Observer* and *Tribune* as well as other publications including the *New Statesman* and *Time and Tide*. Despite his war-time forgiveness quoted earlier, Orwell's usual attitude to newspapers and journalism was one of constant disappointment, particularly after he had seen at first-hand during the Spanish Civil War how newspapers on either side – and within warring factions on the Republican side – had suppressed the truth to suit their own ends. 'One of the dreariest effects of this war has been to teach me that the Left-wing press is every bit as spurious and dishonest as that of the Right', he wrote in *Homage to Catalonia*, which recounts his experiences fighting for the POUM militia.[36] Orwell himself had nearly become victim of the suppression of the news that the POUM had been outlawed while he was at the front, blithely returning to Barcelona on leave not realizing he was liable to be arrested. 'All word of it was kept out of the Barcelona papers. This kind of thing is a little difficult to forgive', he observes mildly:

> I know it was the usual policy to keep bad news from the troops, and perhaps as a rule that is justified. But it is a different matter to send men into battle and not even tell them that behind their backs their party is being suppressed, their leaders accused of treachery and their friends and relatives thrown into prison.[37]

Orwell also became a victim of censorship of his own work when the *New Statesman* refused to publish an article 'because it contravened the paper's editorial policy'.[38] While working at the BBC during the war, he accepted that working for such an institution during wartime 'one rapidly becomes propaganda-minded and develops a cunning one did not previously have', before confessing to broadcasting information he did not believe to be true.[39] In *1984* no one has reliable information and in their ignorance the workers at the Ministry of Information even are not sure whether what they are rectifying was itself 'merely the substitution of one piece of nonsense for another'.[40] While the novel is only tangentially about the press, it must be borne in mind that Orwell was writing *1984* during the Royal Commission hearings when some of the most resounding criticisms of the British press submitted to the inquiry focused on its failure to fulfil its most fundamental duty in a liberal democracy: to help produce, through articulating divergent views of public opinion, an enlightened public which could conduct its civic duty in full knowledge of events. The then home secretary Herbert Morrison was particularly outspoken of the 'gramophone press' where local papers owned by the same proprietor as far apart as Cardiff, Newcastle and Glasgow 'carried identical leading articles written by one hand in the London office'.[41] The Royal Commission found this accusation of a single leader writer for multiple papers partly true, though not practiced in all newspaper chains. The commission's strongest and most damning conclusion was, however, that 'newspapers, with few exceptions, fail to supply the electorate with adequate materials for sound political judgement', as concluded by Winston.[42] In *1984* the culprit is not a monolithic commercial press but the Party, but the results are the same: in *1984* the 'vast disregarded masses' are fed a diet of sex, popular music, gambling and superstition to keep them from organizing rebellion: 'Until they become conscious they will never rebel,' writes Winston in his diary.[43]

Journalism and literature: Rapidly separating worlds

In this chapter a wide range of fictions approach the ideas of rebellion and difference from different philosophical standpoints. What is of note is that most fictions regarding the press published during this period are authored by former or practising journalists, as in the Edwardian period (see Chapter 1). The Bourdieusian struggle between literature and newspaper journalism appears to be ending, as the two genres have now moved too far apart for literary writers to feel threatened by the growth of the mass press in the way they had in the first decades of the century. Divorces are, of course, always messy, and writers, still today, have professional relationships with newspapers. In the early post-war period newspapers employed, or regularly commissioned, literary authors and cultural critics. Norman Mailer, Richard West, Philip Norman and Nicholas Tomalin, all writers who successfully straddled the worlds of journalism and literature, wrote for the *Sunday Times* magazine. The new *Sunday Telegraph* magazine, launched in 1964, commissioned contributions from Laurie Lee, Edna O'Brien, John Betjeman, John Braine and Anthony Burgess.[44] The *Observer's* dramatic critic Kenneth Tynan was the most influential arbiter of theatrical taste for a decade, and later crossed between two worlds when he joined the National Theatre.[45] The leading establishment literary commentator Cyril Connolly wrote for the *Sunday Times*, and classical music expert William Mann for the *Times*. Mann's enthusiastic review of the Beatles' *Sergeant Pepper* album – 'George Harrison's *Within Without You*... is recognisably mixolydian ... the intriguing asymmetrical music of *Lucy in the Sky*... and the hurricane glissandi of *A day in the Life* ...' – assumes in his readers a high level of classical and musical knowledge (*Times*, 29 May 1967).

During this period the 'new journalism' and 'gonzo' journalism movements were being pioneered by American writers including Tom Wolfe, Hunter S. Thompson, Norman Mailer and Gay Talese. The 'new journalism', which borrowed techniques from the novel, such as multiple viewpoints and interior monologues, stirred up resentment equally among journalists and literary writers, explains Tom Wolfe, because 'in some vile Low Rent way [their] output was *literary*'.[46] The movement had an impact on 'long form' newspaper journalism, particularly the new *Sunday Times* magazine launched in 1962. The magazine became an icon of 'swinging London', with men in 'plum dark hipsters' commissioning pioneering photo-journalism and long-form articles both on lifestyle and celebrity subjects and also on Vietnam, Northern Ireland, South American drugs cartels and the pop art movement.[47] The writer Philip Norman remembers days of excess: excessive expenses claims and excessive amounts of time in which to research and write articles: 'I spent weeks travelling Route 66 with a photographer for an article on it, and then asked the magazine editor for some "thinking" time before I wrote it, so I got permission to sail back to England first class on the QE2.'[48] The magazine, however, was a source of enormous frustration for *Sunday Times* editor Harry Evans, who took control of the paper, but not the magazine, in 1967.[49] 'The magazine was spectacular but it completely failed to relate to the newspaper reading public of the 1960s which was still very conservative', says Philip Norman, who as a young journalist desperately wanted to work for the 'chronicler of double cream-gorging "swinging" Britain'. In his novel about his days on the *Sunday Times* magazine, 1966–1976, he depicts his younger self's desire 'to be published not in smudgy newsprint "pars" but in the colour supplement's lovely chaste type, in book-length paragraphs set in double measure, with dropped capitals and starred copybreaks'.[50]

The polarizing newspaper market

The loss of the middle market *News Chronicle* and the middlebrow magazine *John Bull* in the same year was symptomatic of the polarizing of the current affairs print market, with a small highbrow and intellectual end, and a large and steadily lowering lowbrow end. This led to the dismayed observation of the author and journalist Robert Holles in August 1960: 'We are left with a magazine and Sunday newspaper coverage which presupposes that the population is composed of 10 per cent articulate egghead and 60 per cent sniggering halfwit, with a balance of women who are obsessed with frustrated romance and the latest knitting patterns.'[51] This observation is of course a prejudiced generalization. However, he did have a point when he observed that the death of *John Bull*, hot on the heels of *Illustrated* in 1958 and *Everybody's* in 1959, had at one stroke destroyed the short-story market for new fiction writers. Holles, who had written for *John Bull* since 1956, noted that every week the magazine had received more than 150 short stories from up-and-coming writers. The last of the general interest magazines, *John Bull* 'carried virtually all the short stories published in Britain outside the women's magazines'.[52]

The *Daily Mirror* in 1951 had offered a job to the talented young writer Keith Waterhouse, who, nearly sixty years later, was still writing 'deathless dispatches' for the *Daily Mail*.[53] His first job interview with the *Daily Mirror*'s news editor consisted of these questions: 'Who were my favourite authors? Did I read *The Times*? Did I go to the theatre at all?'[54] Authors Celia Haddon and Elizabeth Jane Howard wrote for the *Daily Mail* in the 1970s, and the historical novelist Jean Plaidy reported for the paper from the typhoid-hit liner the *Oronsay* in 1970. However, the days when 'highbrows' like Edmund Gosse and Ford Madox Ford wrote for the *Daily Mail's* literary pages were over (see Chapter 1), although the critic and Graham Greene scholar Kenneth Allsop still brought perceptive insights into the new literary scene to readers of the *Daily Mail* book pages.[55] His review of Keith Waterhouse's first novel ascertains that something new and important is brewing in the housing estates of the north, and assumes readers' knowledge of Orwell's *1984*:

> a brick and concrete desert of a place, a bleak, die-stamped method of putting the population under roofs, where a sensitive individualist child might, from the stage of feeling vaguely parched, pass into passivity. As so many young Britons do now grow up in these Orwellian proles-quarters, [KW's childhood] is drawn almost as perfect as a snapped off dandelion. (*Daily Mail*, 21 March 1957)

Popular newspapers still occasionally published verse and serialized important new works of fiction (the *Daily Express*, for example, published John Braine's *Room at the Top* in a lengthy serialization during 1957),[56] although this was an increasingly rare event and news of new plays or poems by leading writers failed to make front-page news in the way they did in the early years of the century. The gulf between the 'quality' press and the burgeoning tabloids was widening in terms of literary and news content and presentation. The contemporary observer Dwight Macdonald commented that quality publications such as the *Observer*, *Times*, *Manchester Guardian* and *New Statesman* remained resolutely highbrow: 'It is taken for granted that readers [of broadsheets] will know what and where the Trucial States are, what is the difference between an Emir and an emu, and that what was Benares in Kipling's day is now called Banaras.'[57]

Popular papers were in a process of steady 'degradation', however. Keith Waterhouse also noted this in his second set of memoirs *Streets Ahead* that during the 1950s 'there was then an iron curtain between the popular and the 'serious' press, with little or no border traffic between them'.[58] Coverage of the definitive medical evidence of the link between smoking and lung cancer in 1957 is a case in point. 'Serious' newspapers emphasized the dangers of smoking, but popular papers, for whom tobacco advertising was a vital source of income, scandalously misled their readers. The *Daily Sketch* headlined 'SMOKUS POCUS: Gimmick men cash in on cancer scare' (17 June 1957); and the *Daily Express* stated: 'SMOKING: The "scare" school gets some new facts to think about', quoting '11 independent research teams' insisting 'there is still no proof that smoking causes lung cancer' (12 July 1957). The *Daily Mirror* ingeniously found some 'research' which suggested that 'English cigarettes are less likely to produce lung cancer than American cigarettes' with the headline: 'Are English cigs safer?' (12 July 1957). This gulf would become wider following Rupert Murdoch's purchase first of the *News of the World* and then the *Sun* in the dying months of the 1960s. On the first anniversary of his purchase of the *Sun* in autumn 1970, the first Page Three picture was published.[59]

The story of the newspaper press is not one of unrelieved long decline and reaction during this time. Newspaper coverage of the Suez crisis has been described by historians as 'a model of how it should operate in a liberal democracy, with independent newspapers "freely" articulating the divergent views of public opinion'.[60] The introduction of lay membership onto the Press Council after the second Royal Commission on the Press (1962) strengthened its ability to deal with complaints – up from dozens a year in the 1950s to hundreds in the 1960s – although standards would again tumble disastrously throughout the 1970s and 1980s, and beyond.[61] During the 1950s and 1960s, the *Daily Mirror* under Hugh Cudlipp was an enormously successful and much-admired newspaper which, despite its popularity – at one point selling more than 5.5 million copies a day – was intellectually aspirational and socially progressive. The paper employed several female political and diplomatic journalists including Diana Houstoun-Boswall and Shirley Williams, daughter of Vera Brittain, and campaigned against poverty during the 'never had it so good' era, pointing out the deprivations suffered by those still living in back-to-back tenements even as the glossy image of Swinging London took hold. Its famous columnist Cassandra boldly demanded the abolition of the death penalty just before the hanging of Ruth Ellis: 'And if you feel that way – and I mourn to say that millions of you do – [it's] a fine day for a hanging.'[62] The response to the decriminalization of homosexuality in 1967 was mostly measured and sensitive, and in the 1960s newspapers began investing in investigative journalism, starting with the *Sunday Times* 'Insight' team first under Denis Hamilton and then reinforced under Harold Evans.[63]

In addition, literary culture in general was on the wane as the visual and technological era began. The influential sociologist Richard Hoggart accurately forecast in 1961 that 'literature will have relatively a much smaller place in the society which is now emerging'.[64] Newspapers and weekly journals devoted less space, as a proportion of their contents, to book and theatre reviews than they had in the interwar years. Writers were no longer the cultural celebrities they had been – these were now the visual 'pop' artists, film and television stars, models and popular musicians.[65] In the age of television and mass communications, journalism no longer directly competes with literature although through reviews it still controls access to public opinion.[66] We can see this in attitudes to writing expressed in journalist-authored novels produced fifty years apart. In the Edwardian novels, journalists standing on the shoulders of Coleridge, Dickens and George Eliot, and inspired by correspondents like Charles Hands and G. W. Steevens, emphasized the literary qualities of their craft: 'This was the journalist's sense – a sixth sense – which urges its possessor to set down everything he observes ... It did not content him to think that a street lamp was merely a lamp. He would ask himself, almost unconsciously, "What does it look like?" and search for a simile. His thoughts ran in metaphors and symbols.'[67]

In his novel *Mightier than the Sword*, *Daily Express* journalist Alphonse Courlander is making these claims for journalism: that it is a literary genre and it shares characteristics with poetry and the novel (see Chapter 1). By the time former *People* reporter Murray Sayle came to write *A Crooked Sixpence* (1961), the language of popular newspapers has moved into its own specific and immediately recognizable genre:

> How about this: 'My survey of the seamy world of London vice has turned up an army of parasites who are growing fat on the shame of fallen women: even a man who has debased the profession of public relations by cynically advertising every kind of perversion and vice.'
>
> 'It's long for the fourth par of the lead,' said O'Toole. 'Let's break it up into two sentences. We've got one "fat" already so let's say they're growing rich on the shame of et cetera.'
>
> 'The filthy ponces,' said Knight. 'Get it down.'[68]

Virtually every phrase is a cliché: 'seamy world', 'London vice', 'army of parasites', 'fallen women', 'filthy ponces', designed to alert readers, with as little effort as possible, to the nature of the information being transmitted to them. In an echo of Winston Smith's 'newspeak' articles in *1984*, here the journalists'
is information delivery rather than providing a pleasing reading ex
Headlines are now reduced to non-language; words are used in ter

number of letters they contain, not the meaning they carry. This is a habit commented upon by the American author Dwight Macdonald in an essay contrasting American and British journalism in *Encounter*, November 1956. Criticizing the popular press for carrying 'myriads of tiny trivial items swarming confusedly over the front page', he observes: 'the *Evening News* hit the jackpot with fifty different front page stories, including such enigmatic headlines as THEY STOLE SHIRTS'.[69] Murray Sayle's bewildered protagonist James O'Toole observes the activities of the subeditors: 'As the sub-editors worked, O'Toole noticed that their left hands were periodically busy on the table, the fingers thumping in order like practising pianists'. They were counting letters, reducing political turmoil in far-off republics to RED GRAB BID'.[70]

Keith Waterhouse, one of the last figures to straddle the worlds of journalism and literature successfully, and whose hero, Edgar Wallace, had also managed to do so fifty years before him, notes, in the early 1960s, the increasingly rare event of a writer linking the two fast-separating worlds:

> You only had to spend an hour in this red plush melting pot [the Salisbury Tavern] to see a 'movement' forming before your very eyes. There were several routes into it: from the BBC, from RADA, from Joan Littlewood's Stratford East, from the film studios, from Soho, from St Martin's School of Art, from the workshop theatres of the north and Wales, from the new commercial television stations, from the universities ... Strangely, or perhaps not so strangely, given that it always was *a deeply conservative community* – Fleet Street was a little-used gateway into this stimulating company; but that is the one I took. (emphasis added)[71]

Irresistible forces of commercialization

Journalists, as they have always done, still took to fiction to describe their world. From Monica Dickens' *My Turn to Make the Tea* (1951), James Lansdale Hodson's *Morning Star* (1951), Murray Sayle's *A Crooked Sixpence* (1961), Gordon M. Williams' *The Upper Pleasure Garden* (1970) and Peter Forster's *The Spike* (1965), the themes of irrelevance in a rapidly changing world and moral degeneration among journalists forced to work in an increasingly competitive and cut-throat industry are pursued. The physical and spiritual exhaustion of journalists and editors in these novels culminate in the utterly worn out staff and newspaper in Michael Frayn's *Towards the End of the Morning* (1967). This fatigue, this world-weariness, is a curious leitmotif for an industry which, although just beginning its long, slow decline in circulation, was nevertheless a hugely influential force in politics and society.[72] In addition – apart from the stagnant years of the early 1960s – from about the mid-1950s onwards Britain was going through her own mini-renaissance, from the 'never had it so good' Macmillan era to the swinging 1960s and Harold Wilson's 'white heat' re-conceptualization of British industry.[73] Had these journalist-novelists, all of whom spent several years, sometimes lifetimes, immersed in their profession, unconsciously apprehended the seeds of their industry's decline decades before the press scandals of the late twentieth and early twenty-first centuries? Is this weariness a symptom of the pressures put on journalists in this competitive world where a newspaper selling more than a million copies a day is still uneconomic? James Lansdale Hodson's *Morning Star*, which draws on many of the findings of the 1947 Royal Commission on the Press, portrays the last of a breed: an independent local newspaper serving Greycastle, an industrial town in the north-west of England. A beacon of fearless Fourth Estate journalism, it is struggling to survive against an attempted buyout by the millionaire proprietor of a chain of 'newspapers of varying repute'.[74] The staff of the *Morning Star*, led by the courageous editor Oliver Blackwood, valiantly battle to raise the £500,000 needed to match Samuel Sedgwick's bid in the belief that 'a newspaper like [the *Star*] isn't merchandise'. Although 'a trifle austere' it gives its 70,000 readers something of immeasurable value in the form of unbiased reviews, detailed political news and campaigns against injustice – 'our lost causes'. With only hours to go, the paper is saved, with money from readers, local politicians, the Bishop and a wealthy Liberal politician. Yet even as the reporters are celebrating in the newsroom symbolically under the statue of Shakespeare, they learn that Sedgwick is launching his own provincial paper in Greycastle, the *Daily News-Letter*, 'written for those who can't damn-well think – with pictures for them who can't read'.[75] The shadow of impending doom thus looms over the sherry-fuelled celebrations and Blackwood, whose old wound from the First World War is causing him pain again, collapses exhaustedly into his editor's chair. He may have temporarily saved his paper, but he knows that it is only a matter of time before the public's changing reading habits will ultimately destroy it. This is the same theme of the author and journalist A. J. Cronin's 1958 novel *Northern Light*, which is about a family-owned regional newspaper struggling against the brash new arrival, owned by a large combine headed by Vernon Somerville. While the *Northern Light* is 'set inflexibly against sensationalism' and has built up a reputation for 'fair mindedness and sound news presentation', Somerville's national daily the *Gazette* deals in crime, sport and sensation: 'Spread over the front page, was a luridly retouched flashlight of three blood-splashed corpses, two men and a pitifully half-naked woman, sprawled on the floor of a tenement room, while above, in inch-high type, screamed the headline THE PRICE OF PASSION.'[76]

Again drawing on the Royal Commission's findings, particularly the rapid closure of dozens of local and regional newspapers, the novel highlights the bleak and vain attempts of the older, independent liberal newspapers to survive the onslaught of the slick, money-making chains. Somerville's greasy representative, Nye, tells Henry Page, editor of the *Northern Light*, some uncomfortable home truths about the reading public: 'some of our citizens like to see little floosies in bikinis; they dream of going to bed with them instead of with their fat old woman ... what do you think a working man wants with his morning cup of tea at six o'clock on a foggy morning? Not the smarmy, soapy sermon that you serve up.'[77] Ultimately there is no answer to this conundrum in either novel. This, essentially, is the debate that has been confounding intellectuals since the birth of the mass press, and crystallized in the conclusions of the 1947 commission: 'In order to maintain, and, if possible, increase, its circulation in the face of strong competition, a popular paper concentrates on publishing what it knows from experience a very large public will buy.'[78] The commission warned that unless this practice of chasing after the lowest common denominator ended, standards would continue to fall.

Sensationalism, corruption, trivia

For journalists working on popular newspapers, the issue was not economic survival, but surviving in savagely competitive newsrooms led by 'vicious immoral children' who 'stab and maim and mutilate' to give their paper the edge over their rivals as the former journalist Peter Forster observes in his grim Fleet Street novel *The Spike* (1965).[79] To keep their jobs, reporters must produce titillating and occasionally fabricated copy for their readers. James O'Toole, new recruit to the *Sunday Sun* in Murray Sayle's *A Crooked Sixpence*, is horrified by what his editor asks him to do. He spends several days making up the story of 'an innocent mill girl from Bradford' who has been lured to the 'BRIGHT LIGHTS OF THE WEST END', only to become a fallen woman: 'How much I'd give to be back at my loom, to change my DIAMONDS AND FURS for my old cotton overalls and my clogs.'[80] On another occasion he is ordered to 'doorstep' society debutantes who have acquired illegal abortions after being seduced by a group of predatory aristocrats. The men, 'public school boys with titles', will be kept out of the paper as the editor does not want to risk angering the Establishment. O'Toole finally cannot take it anymore and quits after being asked to traduce a vulnerable transvestite into becoming just another piece of fodder for the paper which prides itself as 'hammer of homosexuals and champion of sound, clean British sex'.[81] During this period, the amount of editorial space dedicated to current affairs news plummeted, and the amount dedicated to human interest stories grew. A survey of popular newspaper content conducted in 1978 concludes that current affairs content of *The People*, the newspaper Murray Sayle models the *Sunday Sun* on, fell by 51 per cent between 1936 and 1976. While in 1946 current affairs news took up 26 per cent of *The People*'s editorial space, by 1976 this figure had dropped to 8 per cent.[82] Meanwhile current affairs content of 'broadsheet' newspapers barely changed, staying at just over 30 per cent. It is interesting to compare Sayle's barely fictionalized reminiscences with Michael Frayn's memories of working on the much gentler *Manchester Guardian* at the same time:

> I was sent to cover a case in which a bank manager had run amok, attacked his wife, children and mother-in-law with an axe and left them to die slowly overnight, then attempted to commit suicide by stabbing himself in the chest with a pair of rusty scissors. 'Don't do anything silly,' said the News Editor anxiously. 'Don't try to get your foot in anyone's front door, or steal their wedding photographs. Just go to the police press conference, look at the *outside* of the bank, and come back to the office.'[83]

Another journalist, Andrew 'Ming' Menzies, is the 'door-step body snatcher', star reporter of the downmarket *Hamport Recorder* in Gordon M. Williams' *The Upper Pleasure Garden* (1970), a powerfully dark vision of mid-century popular journalism. Ming's editor crudely asserts: 'some people sell cabbages, some sell their cunts, we sell papers. It ain't art and it ain't the community soul, it's business'.[84] Ming, revealing growing mental distress through the novel, gradually succumbs to alcohol and nervous breakdown in his restless quest to find the sensationalist angle in every story he covers, from car crashes to bird shows:

> Was he different from other people? ... Trying to see yourself honestly was like watching for your face in the windows of passing cars – you got a glimpse, just enough to tell you it was yourself you were seeing, but never long enough for a second glance. Was he some kind of maniac, some demented person who couldn't see things in their right proportion?[85]

Whereas O'Toole makes his excuses and leaves, Ming, after a brief departure from the paper, is lured back, like a moth to the flame, pausing, for a moment of transient introspection to confess: 'I wish I could go back to everybody I ever wrote about and tell them I was sorry'. However realizing there is no other job he can do, he grimly returns to the paper – not before selling another victim's pictures to the *News of the World* for 'fifty-sixty quid' – aware he will need to rely on alcohol to 'stay sane'. Long since out of print, *The Upper Pleasure Garden*, though crudely told, is a raw, Faustian tale of a man who knowingly sells his soul to survive in 'the only job where they paid you a wage for finding men who built the Taj Mahal out of empty beer bottles'.[86] Ming's plight is reminiscent of the Edwardian journalists in Chapter 1, the pioneers in the new popular daily press who are surprised at what they are asked to do in the name of the public interest. For Humphrey Quain in Alphonse Courlander's *Mightier than the Sword* (1912):

> The reporter...is a fit subject for tragedy. He is a social outlaw...He is a trespasser in private places, a Peeping Tom, with his eye to a chink in the shuttered lives of others. His inner self wrenches both ways; he loathes and loves his duty. The human man in him says 'This is a shocking tragedy!' The journalist subconsciously murmurs, 'This will be a column at least'.[87]

In the fifty years between Courlander and Williams, competition has got stiffer, what is considered acceptable in terms of subject matter and taste has become broader and thus the journalist's jeopardy is increased. Not even the establishment in 1953 of the first General Council of the Press could curtail the irresistible forces sending newspapers downmarket. For journalists working on overstaffed popular newspapers, competition between colleagues for space was particularly fierce. A study of journalists and newspapers conducted in 1965 reveals that on average a *Financial Times* journalist got 19.8 inches of copy into the paper each day, compared with just 3.2 inches for a *Daily Express* journalist and only slightly more for a *Sun* and *Daily Mirror* journalist.[88] This 'aggressive' treatment of work on which reporters have spent 'their whole day' must surely contribute to the manic newsgathering behaviour that Ming exhibits in Gordon Williams' novel. Is it a reaction, as Jean Chalaby suggests in his important study of the newspaper industry, *The Invention of Journalism* (1998), to creating text which is just commodity like tins of beans? Indeed the nameless protagonist, the 'Editor', of a popular paper in Peter Forster's *The Spike* (1965) encourages his journalists 'to think in three-sentence paragraphs, ideally the first sentence leading compulsively to the second' to avoid being disappointed when they see their work in print.[89] In his foreword to the novel, Forster explains his motivation for writing it: 'Fleet Street is a mentality as much as a noisy, grubby London thoroughfare...what fascinates me is the nature of the job, and the conditioning effect upon the nature of the person who does it.' The Editor has a miserable, short-lived reign, losing his wife, his mistress and his job in a few months to a man prepared to put more 'tits on show'. There is no crisis of conscience, a seeing of the light, however, just a grinding implosion.[90] The Editor and many other characters discussed here are unknowing victims of the very kind of profit-hungry economics that their newspapers promote. Their post-Thatcherite successors, discussed in Chapter 8, don't just resort to drink or adultery, they completely fall apart.

'It's not our news, is it?' Irrelevance in a changing world

Another strong theme of novels written during this time is that newspapers have failed to keep pace with rapid change, and many that once were a force for progressiveness, a breath of fresh air, are now stuck in the past and are acting as a brake on new ideas and creativity. Mr Corby-Smith, for example, editor of the *Farbridge Weekly Record* in J. B. Priestley's *Festival at Farbridge* (1951), 'was a tall elderly man with a narrow skull and a pince-nez, a high stiff collar and a spotted bow tie; and suggested a minor character having a shot at the editor of *The Times* in an Edwardian play'.[91] Corby-Smith instinctively sides with the forces of conservatism in Farbridge ranged against the colourful characters who want to enact their own version of the Festival of Britain. Here Priestley, very much in support of the Festival, is taking a swipe at, as Michael Frayn described them in a contemporary essay, 'the carnivores, the readers of the *Daily Express* ... led by the Beaverbrook press' who opposed the Labour Government's attempt at cheering up a nation ground down by years of austerity.[92]

In his own newspaper novel *Towards the End of the Morning* (1967), Frayn evokes a soporific atmosphere at the daily newspaper where Bob, John Dyson, egregious picture editor Reg Mounce and a cast of other characters somehow manage to bring out a paper every day. In the Foreward to the 2000 edition of the novel, Frayn, who began his newspaper career on the *Manchester Guardian* in 1957, tries to describe the atmosphere on Fleet Street in the late 1960s, which contrasts sharply with the excitement evoked in the Edwardian novels: 'By that time, Fleet Street was coming towards the end not just of the morning, but of the afternoon as well, and the shades of night were gathering fast ... the appearance of anything new in this run-down world seems as unlikely as the birth of a baby in an old-folks' home. Even when the *Daily Telegraph* did manage to give birth to the *Sunday Telegraph* in 1961 the new infant had a suitably grey and elderly air.' In the novel there is a 'vaguely wartime air' about the newspaper office, despite the war having ended more than twenty years previously; photographers bring in pictures of 'restored Cathedrals, Cotswold villages, sunsets over lakes' apparently unaware of swinging London, Beatlemania, anti-war demonstrations and the mini-skirt; beery lunches in the pub are followed by endless sleep-filled afternoons. By eight o'clock, when the presses judder into life, everyone has gone home:

> Here and there light shades and other thin metal fixtures burred faintly, or ticked, or rattled. In Dyson's department, deserted, and lit only by the yellow sodium light coming in through the windows from the street-lamps in Hand and Ball court, a ruler sticking out over the edge of old Eddy Moulton's desk moved itself slowly sideways until it over-balanced and fell on the floor.[93]

Compare this rather feeble effort – a faint rattling and ticking, a ruler dislodged – to the elemental, orgasmic power of the presses in Philip Gibbs' *The Street of Adventure* (1909): 'In a moment the machine came to life with a sudden and miraculous activity. The great roller went round, steel rods plunged to and fro with beautiful rhythm, a frame rose and fell with perfect regularity, and at each heart-beat, as it were, of those mighty organisms a batch of complete newspapers was ready for the world.'[94]

Similarly in Ferdinand Mount's *The Clique – A Novel of the Sixties* (1978), Fleet Street journalists Gunn Goater and Rory Noone are put in their place by the fashionable young hippies whose house they both end up staying in. Asking whether he can watch the television news, Gunn is asked by Clara: 'It's not *our* news, is it?' Happy, a performance artist who lives the archetypal counter-culture lifestyle, adds:

> 'News is a non-event. News is olds… the real news is what doesn't get into the news. God is dead. News is dead.'
>
> Happy's contempt made Gunn both indignant and ashamed. He could not deny it – there was something old fashioned about newspapers.[95]

This observation punctures Gunn's confidence and is an astute observation by Mount, whose 1970s novel is a reflection on his days as a reporter for the *Daily Sketch* in the 1960s, but seems to look forward to the twenty-first-century world of multimedia news, when newspapers, in terminal circulation decline, are now described as a 'legacy' or 'twilight' industry and whose authority is in constant question by users of social media.

Gunn's newspaper office, like John Dyson's in *Towards the End of the Morning*, seems to belong to another age:

> Underneath successive coats of cream and pale green paint, behind the ramparts of back numbers and flaking, dark-green cabinets, the more grandiose materials in which the founder had built were still to be seen: pilasters of marble, recessed

and moulded panelling in some rare wood, Nigerian, perhaps, which still retained its strange ginger colour and whorled grain, window frames of bronzed metal opened and closed by elaborate handles, all in that same founder's mixture of Babylonian, Egyptian and Roman styles.[96]

The classical references only serve to underline that inhabitants of this 'cut-price rabbit warren' are but the feeble inheritors of a once-glorious empire, even at a time when newspapers still enjoyed vast circulations. Again the contrast with the thrilling modernity of newspaper offices in the Edwardian novels is inescapable. In *Mightier than the Sword* (1912), the *Day* office 'with its arrogant dome-tower (lit up at nights), its swinging glass doors, where *The Day* is jewelled in electric lights across the dark sky' and where people never dawdle but are in constant action is 'typical of the modern newspaper world'.[97] Whereas here *The Day* is compared favourably to the 'hopelessly out of date' journal *Nineteenth Century*, by the late 1960s and 1970s newspapers are themselves outdated. Newspapers were of course reflecting the views of their readers who were slower to catch on to the chic of 'Swinging London' than the avant-garde artists of the capital. Rather than being cool, plum-coloured hipster-wearers, readers were more likely to be the thousands who rang up the BBC to complain about irreverence on its late night show 'BBC3' as reported in the *Sunday Times*: 'There were protests about a sketch in which Alan Bennett, as a clergyman dealing with the adultery of a parishioner, used a crucifix on his study desk as a pipe rack' (28 November 1965).

The new 'alternative' publications such as *Oz*, *Ink* and *International Times*, as well as the new listings magazine *Time Out* and the re-launched *New Musical Express*, provided more targeted reading matter for a younger audience. In fiction they are publications like *The Maggot* and *Toilet Paper*. *The Maggot*, a fictional *Private Eye* 'produced by a gang of freaks and anarchists', features in the comic novel *Harris in Wonderland* (1973), loosely based on the life of freelance journalist Richard West.[98] *Toilet Paper* is edited by the anti-establishment Quiggin Twins, part of the new generation taking over from the old Establishment in Anthony Powell's *Hearing Secret Harmonies* (1975), the last novel in his series *A Dance to the Music of Time*. This was a fecund time for 'alternative' magazines, of which *Oz* and *International Times* were only the most famous. The magazines supported and encouraged avant-garde poetry movements as well as sexual liberation, drugs and rock and roll. Several such as *Time Out* and the *New Musical Express*, re-launched in 1968, developed large-enough circulations to make them financially viable and offered ambitious young journalists an alternative career path from the traditional one of provincial to national newspapers.

Set against these irreverent, edgy publications how could the popular behemoths of Fleet Street not appear outdated particularly when newspapers like the *Daily Mail* and *News of the World* appeared deliberately to set themselves against this bold new youth culture? Indeed the *News of the World* exposed drug-taking antics at the underground UFO club and instigated the famous police raid on Keith Richards' house in February 1967.[99] It is no surprise that the most influential popular music album of the late 1960s, launched in June 1967, the Beatles' *Sergeant Pepper*, contains, in its final track 'A Day in the Life', references to the incomprehensible banality of newspapers, 'I read the news today, Oh Boy/About a lucky man who made the grade', and the means by which to escape from their world into a more meaningful inner one: 'I'd love to turn you on.' By 1973 even Fleet Street traditionalist Bernard Levin was starting to wonder whether tabloid and mid-market newspapers' obsession with sex scandals wasn't somewhat outdated. Commenting on a recent incident where the *News of the World*, the *People*, *Daily Mail* and *Daily Express* had hysterically competed for photographs of a prostitute and her pimp on their wedding day, he admits that contemplating the story of an epic Fleet Street struggle, he 'caught a whiff of mothballs ... an echo from a faded, sepia-tinted past' where papers 'staged great battles with their rivals ... yet somehow, amid all the excitement, failing to notice the hands of the clock going round' (*Times*, 7 June 1973).

This sense that newspapers have somehow failed to keep up with modern life is a theme of Keith Waterhouse's novel *Billy Liar* (1959), where the youthful protagonist, desperate to get out of his depressing northern home town and find success in the bright lights of London, scoffs at the *Stradhoughton Echo*'s columnist 'Man o' the Dales' nostalgic characterization of his town: '"The very name of Stradhoughton," Man o' the Dales had written in the *Stradhoughton Echo* one morning... "conjures up sturdy buildings of honest native stone, gleaming cobbled streets, and that brackish air which gives this corner of Yorkshire its own special *piquancy*" ... The cobbled streets, gleaming or otherwise, had long ago been ripped up.'[100]

For young Billy, Man o' the Dales and his clichéd – and in Billy's eyes, incorrect – observations are a symbol of everything that is wrong with his life in Stradhoughton: the prim resistance of the girls to his advances, his employer, the decrepit Councillor Duxbury, and his parents' mean council house. The pages of the *Stradhoughton Echo* reflect a town he does not recognize: 'I had a fairly passionate set piece all worked out on the subject of rugged Yorkshire towns, with their rugged neon signs and their rugged, plate glass and plastic shop fronts, but so far nobody had given me the opportunity to start up on the theme.'[101] In Waterhouse's recently discovered memoir, *How to Live to Be 22*, written when he was just a little older than Billy, he records being delighted at being offered a job on the *Yorkshire Evening Post*. However, in his more mature reminiscence of those days, *City Lights* (1994), he reports that very quickly he realized his job on the *Post* could only be temporary. He must escape to London, to Fleet Street and, ultimately, literary fame. In order to achieve enough notoriety to make that move easier, Waterhouse took on the job as the 'Walking Reporter' for the *Yorkshire Evening Post*, admitting his prose 'tended towards the purple'. He quotes some in his memoirs, sounding uncannily like Man o' the Dales: 'The wind that blows tin cans down the city streets is the same wind that moans tonight along the crags and heather of the Dales, howling round peak and scar, and wresting piccolo tunes from the reed patches near Kettlewell, nestling under great Whernside's protective wings.'[102]

Man o' the Dales, then, is Keith Waterhouse's gentle rebuke to his younger self, for producing clichéd, nostalgia-inducing visions of the 'dark satanic housing estates' of Leeds, even as he well knew 'there was a civic restlessness about, a growing clamour for clearing away the old'.[103] At the end of the novel when Billy finally comes face to face with Man o' the Dales, he is dismayed to find he is a young man, not much older than himself, bizarrely sporting a handlebar moustache: a warning to Waterhouse the writer, how thin is the line between success and failure, and originality and cliché.

The journalists in Michael Frayn's *Towards the End of the Morning* also have ambitions to leave the newspaper – either into more intellectual publications such as the *New Statesman* or *Spectator* or, increasingly, into the glittering new world of television, which, after a slow start, was now an exciting, culturally influential medium since Sir Hugh Greene's arrival as director-general of the BBC in 1960. Many of the novels examined here refer to the attraction of television for journalists who dream of being pundits on current affairs shows. Arthur Christiansen, the hugely successful mid-century editor of the *Daily Express*, after leaving his paper in 1961, devoted his time to television, observing: 'One medium of communication is new. The other is old.'[104] In *Towards the End of the Morning* John Dyson is desperate to break into television, imagining himself talking cleverly in smoke-filled studios, but he is a vain and limited man and all his efforts end in failure. By the time he wrote the novel, Michael Frayn was already hoping for more literary departures than his humorous column on the *Observer*. He admits he found journalism much harder than fiction as writers of fiction have the luxury of being able to mould and reshape reality to fit the demands of their imagination. Reporters must use only what they see in front of them:

> Out there in the world it's very different. Nothing, for a start, is in words – nothing is the right shape to be *put* into words. Nothing has its cause or its result written upon it. Even when you find witnesses who supply you with a testimony already in verbal form, their impressions of the same things and recollections of the same event are dismayingly various.[105]

Perhaps like Keith Waterhouse's Man o' the Dales and Ferdinand Mount's Gunn Goater, in John Dyson's pathetic efforts at journalism, Frayn was already signalling the end of his newspaper apprenticeship, which had served him well but which imposed too many limits to his creativity.

From man of letters to hardboiled hack

In concluding his wide-ranging study of literary fashions, *The Rise and Fall of the Man of Letters* (1969), John Gross describes the technological, scientific post-war era as being of a completely different character to the more literary culture of the time before 1939 and that the role of the 'literary man' had, by the late 1960s, been all but squeezed out.[106] While the novelist or poet will always occupy some elevated position in the field of cultural production, Gross argues, other agents, particularly critics and journalists, are being displaced in terms of intellectual status by sociologists, anthropologists, linguists and psychoanalysts, leaving for the 'man of letters' a marketplace very diminished in terms of cultural capital and economic reward. The scarcity of writers engaged both in the newspaper press and more literary endeavours during this period may explain the absence of the journalist in more literary fictions of the post-war era. Whereas in the interwar period literary writers had seemed interested to the point of obsession with the newspaper press, which they viewed as a rival within the same field (see Chapter 3), their mid-century equivalents, namely Kingsley Amis, John Wain, Doris Lessing, Angus Wilson and Margaret Drabble, all but ignored newspapers and journalists in their fictions apart from to provide occasional background chatter. Contemporary literary writers had wider concerns than the degradation of the language of popular newspapers. As Ronald Sukenick observed in *The Death of the Novel and Other Stories* (1969), 'God was the omniscient author, but he died; now no one knows the plot.'[107] Literary writers were busy grappling with modern literary theory and crises of representation: Iris Murdoch's much-quoted 'opacity of persons' which questioned the fundamentals of the novel tradition.[108] Whereas previously literary authors used their fiction to define how their writing was different from newspaper journalism, literary authors of this period do not even bother to make this distinction. The conclusion must be that by this time journalism and literature were functioning, although not wholly, certainly mostly, in separate fields.

What stands out, however, is that during this early post-war era, fictions which do feature journalists – Graham Greene's *The Quiet American* (1955, Chapter 4), James Lansdale Hodson's *Morning Star* (1951), Murray Sayle's *A Crooked Sixpence* (1961), Gordon M. Williams' *The Upper Pleasure Garden* (1970) and Monica Dickens' *My Turn to Make the Tea* (1951, Chapter 7) – contain the most interesting and complex characters of the entire 100-year period covered in this book. The intensity and complexity of characterizations suggests this is a pivotal moment for agents, particularly for those with literary aspirations, operating in the journalistic field. Yes, these characters' lives are difficult; they struggle, often vainly, with a rapidly commercializing marketplace, but also, their being journalists lends interesting nuances to their authors' take on the human condition. They are, if you like, a final cry of agony as the worlds of literature and journalism move from uncomfortably sharing different areas of the same field to journalism moving into its own highly commercial field of modern communications. Novels written after this time give up investigating the complex inner lives of their journalist characters and certain instantly recognizable journalistic stereotype will emerge. Writers will begin to use a kind of shorthand for journalist characters, used in films as well as fiction: scruffy, cynical, shambolic, bad mannered and fond of expletives. One of his first iterations is seen in Galpin, the foreign correspondent propping up the Athenee Palace bar, Bucharest, in Olivia Manning's *Balkan Trilogy* (1960), set during the Second World War:

> Galpin's dark, narrow face hung in folds above his rag of a collar. Elbow on bar, sourly elated by his return to his old position, he kept staring about him for an audience, his moving eyeballs as yellow as the whisky in his hand. As he drank, his yellow wrist, the wrist-bone like half an egg, stuck out from his wrinkled, shrunken, ash-dusty dark suit. A wet cigarette stub clung, forgotten, to the bulging purple softness of his lower lip and trembled when he spoke.[109]

From the 1970s onwards this stereotype (and his even more two-dimensional female version) will totter crazily into ever-more ludicrous caricature as literary writers finally take their revenge on the tabloid press.

Notes

1   'The Age of Anxiety' is the title of W H Auden's book-length poem first published in 1947 encapsulating all the uncertainty of the post-WW2, post–atom bomb world.

2   These quotes are from three groundbreaking mid-century novels, all published within two years of each other respectively, from George Orwell's *1984*, p. 3, Graham Greene's *The End of the Affair*, p. 2 and Monica Dickens' *My Turn to Make the Tea*, p. 38. This latter, although less well known than the other two, is a brave and honest portrayal of a female reporter battling sexism and entrenched corruption on a local paper. It is referred to at greater length in the next chapter.

3   James Lansdale Hodson (see Chapters 1 and 2) had by now lost his youthful optimism. His 1951 novel *Morning Star* (discussed later in the chapter) evokes an 'end of an era' despair over the future of a liberal, educative provincial press in the face of irresistible commercialization of the press (p. 135).

4   Cyril Connolly, quoted in Pryce-Jones 'Towards ...' (p. 212). See also Taylor, D. J., *After the War* (p. xiv).

5   Bradbury, Malcolm, *The Modern British Novel*, p. 304.

6   Waterhouse, Keith, *City Lights*, p. 227.

7   Bradbury, *British*, p. 319.

8   Interview with Eric Clark.

9   See for example T. R. Fyvel's essay 'The Stones of Harlow: Reflections on Subtopia' published in *Encounter*, June 1956, which quotes the architect Ian Nairn's famous diatribe against universalization, 'Outrage'.

10   Sayle, Murray, *A Crooked Sixpence*, p. 202.

11   The novel is based on Murray Sayle's experiences on the *People* in the late 1950s. Murray Sayle left the *People* but went on to be a respected foreign correspondent for the *Times* and *Sunday Times*, reporting throughout the 1960s and early 1970s, on among other stories, Sir Francis Chichester rounding the Horn in Gypsy Moth, the Vietnam War, communist guerrillas in Bolivia and the Soviet Invasion of Czechoslovakia.

12   Orwell, George, 'London Letter to *Partisan Review*', 15 April 1941.

13   Griffiths, Dennis, *Fleet Street*, p. 287.

14   Ibid., p. 288.

15   Orwell, George, 'London Letter ...'

16   Griffiths, *Fleet Street*, p. 267.

17   Sandbrook, Dominic, *Never Had It So Good*, p. 384.

18   Churchill, Randolph 'The Daily Newspaper: Notes on the Press in Britain and America', *Encounter*.

19   Shaw, Tony, *Eden, Suez and the Mass Media*, p. 198.

20   Sandbrook, *Never Had It*, pp. 561–562 & 569.

21 Osborne, John, *Look Back in Anger*, p. 10.

22 Ibid., pp. 76–77.

23 Frayn, Michael, *Towards the End of the Morning*, p. 24.

24 The term 'Fourth Estate' was used to describe reporters in the Commons Press Gallery after they were first given access in the early nineteenth century. The definition of the role of the Fourth Estate is taken from Delane's famous *Times* leader of 7 February 1852:

> The duty of the press is to speak, of the statesman to be silent, we are bound to tell the truth as we find it without fear of consequences ... the duty of the journalist is ... to seek out truth, above all things, and to present to his readers not such things as statecraft would wish them to know but the truth as near as he can attain it.

For a more detailed discussion of the idea of the Fourth Estate see Boyce, 1978, pp. 19–40. See also note 6 in Chapter 1 of this book.

25 Williams, Francis, *Dangerous Estate*, pp. 1 & 240.

26 Ibid., p. 4.

27 Royal Commission on the Press, 1949, pp. 187–189.

28 Williams, *Dangerous*, pp. 3–4.

29 Quoted in Margach, James, *The Abuse of Power*, p. 86.

30 Griffiths, *Fleet Street*, pp. 333–334.

31 Frayn, Michael, *Travels with a Typewriter*, p. 2.

32 Williams, *Dangerous*, p. 278.

33 Curran, James, 'The Press as an Agency of Social Control', pp. 74–75.

34 Sandbrook, *Never Had It*, p. 636. The *Daily Mail*, for example, had carried a piece by the pro-legalization bishop of Southwark on 11 February 1966 titled 'Must I bury yet another man because of this hypocrisy and humbug?' The day after legalisation the paper carried an article by the Earl of Arran who wrote: 'Any form of ostentatious behaviour now or in the future, any form of public flaunting would be utterly distasteful ... while there may be nothing bad in being a homosexual, there is certainly nothing good.'

35 Orwell, George, *1984*, p. 50.

36 Orwell, George, *Homage to Catalonia*, p. 208.

37 Ibid., p. 162.

38 Slater, Ian, *Orwell: The Road to Airstrip One*, p. 154.

39 Ibid., p. 210.

40 Orwell, *1984*, p. 48.

41 Quoted in Margach, James, *The Abuse of Power*, p. 93.

42 Royal Commission on the Press, 1949, p. 154.

43 Orwell, *1984*, p. 81.

44 Greenslade, Roy, *Press Gang*, p. 152.

45   Tynan, Kathleen, *The Life of Kenneth Tynan*.

46   Wolfe, Tom, *The New Journalism*, p. 27.

47   Norman, Philip, *Everyone's Gone to the Moon*, p. 83.

48   Interview with Philip Norman.

49   Griffiths, *Fleet Street*, p. 321.

50   Norman, *Everyone's Gone to the Moon*, p. 22.

51   Holles, Robert, 'Death of a Magazine', p. 42.

52   Ibid., p. 43.

53   Forster, Peter, *The Spike*, p. 67.

54   Waterhouse, *City Lights*, p. 244.

55   Allsop was indeed a scholar of English literature, author of a Graham Greene monograph and of a culturally important book *The Angry Decade: A Survey of the Cultural Revolt of the 1950s* (1958).

56   *Daily Express*, 22 April 1957:

> As a holiday fiction bonus the *Daily Express* today hands over Page Three for the opening instalment of the most praised first novel of recent years. Is there anyone in your family who knows what it feels like to work in a glum and dreary town and dream of the days when all the things money can buy will be theirs?

57   Macdonald, Dwight, 'Amateur Journalism', p. 15.

58   Waterhouse, Keith, *Streets Ahead*, p. 240.

59   Griffiths, *Fleet Street*, p. 361.

60   Shaw, *Eden, Suez*, p. 14.

61   Shannon, Richard, *A Press Free and Responsible*, p. 13.

62   Horrie, Chris, *Tabloid Nation*.

63   Griffiths, *Fleet Street*, pp. 318 & 321.

64   Hoggart, Richard, 'Mass Communications', p. 457.

65   Hewison, Robert, *Too Much*.

66   Bourdieu, Pierre, *On Television and Journalism*, p. 46.

67   Courlander, Alphonse, *Mightier than the Sword*, p. 62; see Chapter 1.

68   Sayle, *A Crooked Sixpence*, p. 159.

69   Macdonald, 'Amateur Journalism', p. 17A favourite of mine is the intensely opaque 'TADPOLE CRASH GIRL WAS FLYING MAD' from the *Daily Sketch*, 30 April 1957.

70   Sayle, *A Crooked Sixpence*, p. 132.

71   Waterhouse, *Streets Ahead*, p. 230.

72   For a flavour of how assiduously prime ministers and politicians cultivated the press and how obsessively they read the newspapers to see how they were being portrayed during this time, see Margach's, *The Abuse of Power*, particularly, pp. 100–156.

73   See for example Dominic, *Never Had It*.

74   Hodson, *Morning Star*, p. 12.

75   Ibid., pp. 43, 35 & 321.

76   Cronin, A. J., *Northern Light*, pp. 27–28.

77   Ibid., p. 46.

78   Royal Commission on the Press, 1949, p. 152.

79   *The Spike*, p. 226.

80   Sayle, *A Crooked Sixpence*, pp. 66–67.

81   Ibid., pp. 164 & 202.

82   Curran, James 'The Human Interest Story' in *Newspapers and Democracy* (1980). Sayle's novel was pulped shortly after publication because a character recognized himself in the thinly veiled fiction.

83   Frayn, *Travels with*, pp. 6–7.

84   Williams, Gordon M., *The Upper Pleasure Garden*, p. 184.

85   Ibid., p. 182. Gordon M. Williams trained as a reporter on the *Johnstone Advertiser* in Glasgow, earning £2.00 a week in the early 1950s. After moving to London he worked for the *Daily Mail* as a sports correspondent in the 1960s. Another of his novels, *The Siege of Trencher's Farm* (1969), became the basis of the controversial film *Straw Dogs* (1971).

86   Ibid., 342, 364 & 353.

87   Courlander, *Mightier than*, p. 94.

88   Tunstall, Jeremy *Journalists at Work*, pp. 32–33.

89   Forster, *The Spike*, p. 43. Peter Forster was literary critic of the *Daily Express* in the 1950s (frontispiece to his novel).

90   Ibid., pp. 9, 221 & 226.

91   Priestley, J. B., *Festival at Farbridge*, p. 227.

92   The 'Multi-Million Pound Baby' was a headline in Beaverbrook's *Evening Standard*, August 1949. Michael Frayn, 'Festival', p. 319–320.

93   Frayn, *Towards the End of the Morning*, pp. vi, 7 & 17.

94   Gibbs, Philip, *The Street of Adventure*, p. 48.

95   Mount, Ferdinand, *The Clique*, p. 86.

96   Ibid., p. 88.

97   Courlander, *Mightier than*, pp. 47–48.

98   The novel, an amusing period piece, is by 'Philip Reid', pen name for Richard Ingrams and Andrew Osmond.

99   There is an excellently detailed section on the alternative magazines of the 1960s and 70s in Robert Hewison's *Too Much*, pp. 81–133.

100 Waterhouse, Keith, *Billy Liar*, p. 16.

101 Ibid.

102 Waterhouse, *City Lights*, p. 214.

103 Waterhouse, Keith, *Billy Liar*, p. 117; Waterhouse, *City Lights*, p. 209.

104 Quoted in Griffiths, *Fleet Street*, p. 331.

105 Frayn, *Travels with*, pp. 10–11.

106 Gross, John, *The Rise and Fall of the Man of Letters*, pp. 202–203.

107 Quoted in Bradbury, *British*, pp. 348–349.

108 Murdoch, Iris, 'Against Dryness', p. 293.

109 Manning, Olivia, *Balkan Trilogy*, p. 299.

From Plucky Pioneers to 'Dish Bitches': The 'Problem' of Women Journalists[1]

The number of women entering newspaper journalism increased through the early twentieth century, although their progress until the 1970s was slow. Traditional newsroom practices and, later, union-imposed restrictions confined most to either writing freelance at home, for low pay, or being 'pigeonholed' in the new women's pages, primarily established as a vehicle to attract advertising. Fictions written by and about women journalists express complex attitudes from the rewards of financial independence, to the idea that women journalists are somehow 'deviant', to discussions of the 'problem' of women's journalism, which is often described as 'soft' and too closely linked to advertising and commerce. Contemporary representations tend to foreground women journalists' vulnerability: ingénues who have strayed into a dangerous world.

In Ella Hepworth Dixon's novel *The Story of a Modern Woman* (1894), the protagonist Mary Erle, sitting nervously waiting for an interview with the editor of *The Fan*, realizes she is an outsider in the clubby male world of newspapers at the end of the nineteenth century:

> Ten minutes, fifteen minutes, twenty minutes went slowly by. The murmur of voices, the baritone laughter in the next room continued to be audible. At last, when Mary had finally made up her mind to go, the door was flung open and a young man with a high colour stumbled out. 'Ta ta old chap, thanks awfully. See you in the club tonight', and, bestowing on Mary a prolonged stare, he disappeared down the long glass corridor.[2]

Ella Hepworth Dixon's semi-autobiographical novel about a woman freelance journalist portrays the acute discomfort 'Mary' feels as an unwanted interloper. The laughter is 'baritone', and the editor and the egregious young male journalist have clearly been drinking together. Their 'insider' status is reinforced by the man's use of the informal and masculine 'old chap' and his mention of the 'club' they will meet at later on. His 'prolonged stare' underlines that she is something out of the ordinary in this world. Although Ella Hepworth Dixon was a talented and reasonably well-connected writer, she never surmounted the obstacles before her and her career was restricted to light society sketches and 'women's page' articles.[3] Forty years later, another woman journalist's novel about her profession, Rachel Ferguson's *The Brontes Went to Woolworths* (1931), portrays the freelancer Deirdre Carne struggling to write serious journalism against her editor's wilful stereotyping. Deirdre wants to write a profile of a High Court judge but she, being 'that rather unclassifiable creature which Fleet Street sometimes chooses to write descriptive signed articles on people and "movements"', is frustrated. Her request baffles her editor. He frets, he runs his hands through his hair and he names the male reporters who do court reporting and serious profiles. He blocks all her entreaties, then states: 'By the way, I'd like you to do us something bright on "Is the Bank Holiday Girl Naughty?" About a thousand [words].'[4]

Deirdre agrees, but only if the editor will lend her pencil, paper and 'a rather large basin', presumably for Deirdre to be sick in, a violent physical reaction to her oppression. The novel is based on Ferguson's own experience as a freelance journalist in the mid-1920s, when she was mainly commissioned to write descriptive sketches of balls and Royal events, and 'those would-be controversial articles of the type I've always called Do Women Make the Best Wives?'[5] Twenty years later, Poppy, the female journalist in Monica Dickens' *My Turn to Make the Tea* (1951), is just too much trouble for her editor to handle. Her gender makes the all-male newsroom uneasy; she is gently, and not-so gently, bullied by the other reporters who see her conscientiousness as a threat; she points out the corrupt power structure of back-scratching between the editor and his well-connected friends and the content of the newspaper; when she tries to exercise her own censorship to save a friend's reputation, she is fired: 'It made quite a friendly transaction, and we agreed that women were a nuisance in an office, anyway ... 'We'll miss you,' [the editor] said, and they got a promising young lad, fresh from school, to take my place on the *Downingham Post*.'[6]

Over a period of some sixty years, the main theme of these novels – and others – written by women journalists is the same: journalism is a man's world; women are intruders who either can't or won't play by the rules. If they want to retain even a toehold in this so-desired world, then they must be content with writing 'soft' features and celebrity trivia. While the content and personnel of newspapers have changed much more rapidly in the past sixty years than the previous sixty, women journalists writing about their profession still explore the twin themes of the 'outsider' in a man's world and the stereotyping of women readers and writers. Susan Street in Julie Burchill's *Ambition* (1989) has to accept sexual humiliation as the price for becoming a Fleet Street editor; Tamara Sim in Annalena McAfee's *The Spoiler* (2011) is condemned to write articles in the popular Sunday supplement *Psst!* with titles like 'Top Ten Soap Star Love Rats; Telly Catfights; Best and Worst Boob Jobs'.[7] These novels do explore other aspects of journalism and society (Ella Hepworth Dixon and Rachel Ferguson both discuss the welcome financial independence journalism brings their heroines; Annalena McAfee's novel is also a commentary on the changing nature of newspaper journalism in the digital world). It is, however, hard to ignore the key theme that runs through more than a century of fictions by and about women journalists and one which severely disrupts Bourdieu's model of the field of cultural production. Bourdieu's model of writers jockeying with other writers and genres for their chosen position within the field holds good, broadly, until the years following the Second World War. The field still operates, in an albeit weakened way, even a few decades into the post-war period as the once-close and competing genres of journalism and literature break apart in a haphazard fashion, with 'quality' papers still retaining links with traditional ideas of the world of letters in some of their sections. We have seen the model of the field disrupted in Chapter 4, as a cataclysmic war and the threat first of fascism and then of communism diverts some writers into investigating the dynamic activity between the journalistic and the political sphere more thoroughly. We have also seen, in Chapters 5 and 6, how themes of newspaper morality and even criminality, and the press baron's interference in the political and economic sphere, also divert writers from their main focus within the field. However, for women, the issue of gender and the struggle for equality more severely distort the conventional operation of Bourdieu's model. The writers discussed here still use their fictions as a way of mirroring the structure of the actual social space they inhabit, but these novels are not about whether their writing is 'bourgeois' or 'autonomous', 'commercial' or 'artistic'; they are about 'that awful business, sex'.[8] Bourdieu's concept of 'the field', while widely praised as an elegant way of examining both broadbrush social structures and detailed dispositions, has always been controversial among feminist scholars for its 'androcentric' view of the world.[9] This chapter reinforces those arguments when applied to the status and struggles of women journalists, although the picture is often complex and confusing as resistance among dominated groups is often difficult to map. It may seem counter-productive to discuss women journalists' 'otherness', perceived or actual, at a time when they are still struggling for parity with male colleagues both in terms of pay and prestige.[10] However, it is impossible to ignore the twenty-five novels written by women journalists – as well as the dozens of others by men – which provide intense discussions of women's experiences in journalism and their contested place within the media industry.

The social and cultural context

Women faced multiple obstacles to entering the professions (apart from nursing and teaching) in the early twentieth century: notably a lack of educational opportunities, the prevailing view that a woman's place was in the home and fierce resistance from male colleagues.[11] Women journalists' antecedents, 'lady writers' who contributed essays and sketches to the nineteenth- and early twentieth-century periodical press, were certainly numerous. The celebrated nineteenth-century journalist Barbara Bodichon claimed that at one stage two-thirds of the contributors to the prestigious *Chambers Edinburgh Journal* were female – although most wrote under male pseudonyms.[12] Even Mrs Pearl Craigie, the first president of the Society of Woman Journalists, founded with 200 members in 1894, wrote under the pseudonym of John Oliver Hobbes.[13] The Newspaper Press Directory for 1897 indicates that by the beginning of the twentieth century every London paper had at least one female writer on its staff.[14] An essay in the *Englishwoman's Review* in 1904 refers to 'women newspaper reporters almost as numerous as men'.[15] Apart from the short-lived failure of the *Daily Mirror*, however, launched in November 1903 initially with women-only writers, women reporters on Fleet Street newspapers were highly unusual. Several women did report for the large quantity of women's suffrage papers at the start of the twentieth century; however, these had low circulations and, if anything, emphasized women's marginalization from mainstream journalism.[16] According to census figures for England and Wales, in 1861 around 145 females and 1,525 males called themselves as journalists; by 1901, the number of women journalists had risen to 1,249, around 9 per cent of the total, and by 1931, that figure had risen further to 3,213, around 17 per cent. By 1961, the proportion of female journalists stood at just over 20 per cent and at just under a quarter by 1971.[17] The reasons for this lengthy period of stagnation in women's participation in journalism at a time of rising news consumption and expansion of the BBC include the introduction of the Marriage Bar at the BBC in 1932 and, in other news organizations without a formal Marriage Bar, the convention that a woman journalist would leave work after marriage because the antisocial hours were contrary to the demands of a wife and mother.[18] The former *Guardian* journalist Mary Stott, who began her career in 1926, recalls in her memoirs her early struggles for advancement at the *Co-operative News*: 'The job of editing the *Co-operative News* ... was NOT offered to me for the specific reason, I was told by the editor ... that it would not do to have a woman.'[19] Again, in 1950 she left the *Manchester Evening News* after an awkward encounter worthy of Dickens' *My Turn to Make the Tea*, being told 'plainly and honestly' by the editor 'that I could not expect promotion ... the successor must be a man.'[20] By the outbreak of the Second World War, apart from a few high-profile women such as Margaret Lane of the *Daily Mail*, Shiela Grant Duff of the *Observer* and Rebecca West, most British women journalists were confined to features departments or women's pages or were precariously freelance. This compares to the American 'newspaperwoman' who, following on from the high-profile 'stunt girl' of the late nineteenth century, became 'one of the most recognisable popular images of the woman writer in America.'[21] Real-life groundbreaking American women reporters like Ida Tarbell of *McClure's* and the foreign correspondent Martha Gellhorn, who made her name in the Spanish Civil War, inspired a series of mostly affectionate black-and-white films during the 1930s and 1940s such as *A Woman Rebels* (1936), starring Katharine Hepburn, the Torchy Blane film *Smart Blonde* (1937); and the perennially popular *His Girl Friday* (1940) and *Woman of the Year* (1942), starring Rosalind Russell and Katharine Hepburn, respectively.[22] In England, when Shiela Grant Duff asked *Times* editor Geoffrey Dawson to send her to Europe in 1934, he and the foreign editor 'explained to me at once that it was quite impossible for a woman to work on the editorial side of a newspaper ... If on the other hand, I was going to Paris anyway, perhaps I would like to send them some fashion notes.'[23] Even when Margaret Lane was sent by the *Daily Mail* to Berlin in 1933 to interview Frau Goebbels (flying in a two-seater plane with a drunken pilot), her article was confined to Frau Goebbels' anodyne views on beauty: 'Marriage First; But Beauty is a Duty.'[24] Women in the 1930s were also denied the traditional route into mainstream journalism by provincial newspaper editors who were unwilling to recruit girls into apprenticeship schemes.[25] The profession was strongly unionized until the late twentieth century (although the first national pay agreement in 1917 covered men only). During the 1960s and early 1970s the National Union of Journalists (NUJ) failed to challenge discriminatory workplace policies, which included suppressing female wages and imposing limits on the number of females accepted onto training schemes, despite the rise of the women's movement during this time. In 1972, when female to male membership of the NUJ stood at

4,000 to 21,000, around 1:5, the union began a detailed investigation into discrimination against women journalists, but improvements both in pay and attitudes were slow. Unofficial bans on women entering the composing room where subeditors, section editors and printers worked on the final version of the paper in the pre-computerisation 'hot metal' days meant that until, in some cases, the early 1980s it was impossible for women to hold senior editorial positions.[26] When the NUJ elected its first woman president in 1975, Rosaline Kelly was still barred from visiting the Central London (Fleet Street) branch. She recalls speaking at conferences during the 1970s and being greeted by calls of 'Get 'em down' by the male delegates. The 2001 census shows the numbers of women journalists now almost reaching parity with men, with 32,000 males and nearly 28,000 females.[27] In 2003 the number of new women entrants to the NUJ reached parity with the number of men for the first time.[28] Despite this, an analysis of national newspaper front page bylines in 2012 showed that just over one in five (22 per cent) were female, suggesting the decades-long legacy of discrimination and of stereotyping women as 'soft' features writers rather than news reporters perpetuates on what is still known as Fleet Street.[29] The difficulty of asserting oneself in an overwhelmingly male preserve, and, once inside fighting against being pigeonholed into feature-writing is a constant theme in fiction portraying woman journalists of the period. However, despite women journalists being in a minority throughout the twentieth century, the profession did offer wider access than others. While women made up over 50 per cent of teachers and 17 per cent of journalists in 1931, they made up less than 1 per cent of architects and lawyers, 2 per cent of dentists and about 7 per cent of doctors.[30] As a comparison, women dentists have yet to reach numerical parity with their male counterparts, and are not expected to reach 50–50 status until 2020.[31] Although most journalists (62 per cent) today have university degrees, having a degree has never been a prerequisite of becoming a journalist, unlike medicine or the law.[32] In effect, then, journalism has presented opportunities for women, as well as obstacles – a theme that also emerges in the fictions discussed here. The exclusion of women from mainstream Fleet Street journalism, and from mainstream journalistic arenas such as the House of Commons Press Gallery, had an additional effect, in the early twentieth century, of provoking a vibrant 'alternative' women's press, focused particularly around the suffrage campaign.[33] As well as providing women journalists a platform for the discussion of news and politics, the alternative women's press cemented the idea of women's 'otherness' within the journalistic sphere. This was both a positive and an exciting departure and one which captured novelists' imaginations but one which also accentuated the 'deviant' nature of women journalists. To this day women journalists in newspaper newsrooms report feeling like an 'interloper' and the need to become more 'macho' to fit in.[34]

Deviants

Women journalists have been characterized by social scientists as 'deviants' in the same way female politicians were up until the late twentieth century.[35] By choosing journalism, they were both deviating from the accepted role of homemaker and also diverging from acceptable female professions of nursing and teaching. While, as in any profession there have been a small number of flamboyant rule-breakers – such as the interwar *Evening Standard* journalist Edith Shackleton, who conducted a very public affair with the poet W. B. Yeats or, more latterly, the columnist Julie Burchill, whose private life has provided as much comment as her columns (see below) – the sheer quantity of wildly imagined fictional women journalists belies the ordinary, hard-working lives most women journalists lead. Fictional female journalists created by both male and female writers deviate from the socially accepted norm in a surprising number of ways. Tommy, of Jerome K. Jerome's novel *Tommy and Co* (1904) is at first mistaken for a boy and is treated like one through her teenage years; Christina Stanton, the heroine of Cecil Hunt's *Paddy for News* (1933), is given the masculine and/or diminutive nickname 'Paddy', as this is the only way she can be accepted into the newsroom of the *Sentinel*.[36] (This author was called 'Bert' in the late 1980s by a provincial news editor who could not accept the idea of a competent female reporter.) Katherine Halstead in Philip Gibbs' novel *The Street of Adventure* (1909) is an unnatural woman in that she chooses a career in Fleet Street over marriage and babies:

> 'I pray God there may be babies,' said Frank
> 'No,' said Katherine, 'not on £120 a year. I am not cut out for it.'[37]

Daisy Simpson in Rose Macaulay's *Keeping up Appearances* (1928) is a social transgressor, a lower-middle-class woman who dares to stray into the intellectual upper-middle-class household of the Folyots and pays a terrible price when she is unmasked. Mabel Warren in Graham Greene's *Stamboul Train* (1932) is a sexual deviant, a tweed-wearing predatory lesbian who, despite her masculine characteristics, is nicknamed 'Dizzy' by her male colleagues. Helen Pratt in Christopher Isherwood's *Mr Norris Changes Trains* (1935), although 'fair-haired and fragile-looking', she '[takes] sex seriously', has a university education, unusual for a woman in 1935, talks like a man and can drink anyone under the table.[38] Ailsa Brimley, editor of the *Voice* in John Le Carré's *A Murder of Quality* (1962), is a 'ridiculous spinster' who travels the escalators of the 'Unipress' building where she works 'like a drab parcel on a luxury liner'.[39] Susan Street in Julie Burchill's *Ambition* (1989) abandons her son in order to pursue her career. Honor Tait, the veteran foreign correspondent in Annalena McAfee's *The Spoiler* (2011), is also 'the most unnatural of mothers', unable to have children of her own and adopting a German orphan as a 'project' but whom ultimately she cannot care for.[40] Rita Skeeter in J. K. Rowling's *Harry Potter* novels is 'that foul Skeeter woman' who has 'large, mannish hands' and a 'heavy-jawed face' at odds with her 'scarlet-taloned fingers' and 'curiously rigid curls'.[41] Rowling's overwhelmingly negative portrayal of journalism in her bestselling series was to some extent influenced by her own treatment at the hands of the tabloid press, which she described in detail to the Leveson Inquiry 2011–2012 (see Chapter 8). Rowling's suggestions of transvestism/transgender are not unique. 'Henry Beechtree', the protagonist of Rose Macaulay's *Mystery at Geneva* (1922), who is the 'pale and melancholy' correspondent of the *British Bolshevist* covering a League of Nations assembly in Geneva, is unmasked as Miss Montana, burning with resentment and unrequited love, in the last few pages of the novel.[42] Mabel Warren in *Stamboul Train* refers to herself in her copy as a male correspondent. It is interesting to note also that in the affectionate American films *Smart Blonde* and *His Girl Friday* the female journalists both describe themselves as a 'newspaper*man*'.[43] The photojournalist Agnes in Tim Finch's *The House of Journalists* (2013) is another sexual deviant. She is the only named female inhabitant of the House of Journalists, a refuge for displaced writers fleeing oppressive regimes from around the world, and is the only one who, apparently, has sex, enjoying noisy sessions with a man from outside the House to the embarrassment of its other occupants. While Agnes' 'otherness' is ultimately her salvation in that she manages to escape the increasingly sinister House, it is of note that her independence is asserted in sexual terms. She is sexually voracious, while her male colleagues lead, apparently, lives of monkish celibacy.

The negative stereotyping of journalists generally in fiction, and particularly film, in the past thirty years has become a source of concern to some commentators who fear that the modern 'credibility crisis' of journalists has to some extent been stoked by 'the depiction of journalists by entertainment media as "exploitative jackals"'.[44] While there is certainly debate over that particular 'chicken or egg', what is clear is that women journalists have suffered disproportionately. Modern stereotyping of male journalists tends to depict them as shabby, yet still somehow loveable rogues (Nick Mullen in *Defence of the Realm*, discussed in Chapter 5, Galpin in the TV dramatization of Olivia Manning's *Fortunes of War* (1987) and Cal McAffrey in the more recent film *State of Play* (2009), discussed in Conclusion). In the past thirty years a tedious litany of fictional women journalists sleep with editors or contacts to enhance their careers: Julie Burchill's *Ambition* (1989) opens with Susan Street sitting triumphantly astride the man she has just despatched to become the first woman editor of *Sunday Best*; in Michael Dobbs' *House of Cards* (1989) Mattie Storin, in her first iteration, sleeps with the deputy editor of her newspaper. Tamara Simm (*The Spoiler*, 2011) sleeps with a man for her story ('This was front line reporting'); the 'honey-haired' Fran Dyson, employed as a secretary on the *Sunday Dispatch* magazine in Philip Norman's *Everyone's Gone to the Moon* (1995), mysteriously starts getting journalistic commissions after sleeping with first the features editor and then the editor. When it comes to women journalists in contemporary film and television portrayals, it is the ones who *don't* sleep with their contacts who are out of the ordinary. Since 2000, *Trainwreck* (2015), *House of Cards* (2013), *Rock of Ages* (2012), *Crazy Heart* (2009), *Thank You for Smoking* (2005), *Three Kings* (2000), *Nightcrawler* (2014), *Anchorman* (2004) and *Adaptation* (2002) – and this list is not exhaustive – all feature women journalists who find that sleeping with contacts is part of the job, thus portraying them as both thoroughly unprofessional and, of course, sexually available 24/7.[45] This phenomenon, however, has much more to do with Hollywood's long-standing misrepresentation of women and the 'pornographification' of contemporary entertainment media – unfortunately outside the scope of this book – than it has about women journalists.[46] However, some of these screen representations reflect a highly problematic theme, which has its roots in earlier written fictions: that is, that women journalists are out of their depth in the male world of power, the world of soldiers, politicians and business magnates – as well as male journalists – and if they want to be 'rubbing shoulders with the big boys', then the price of entry into this forbidden realm is to be paid with their bodies, or even their lives.[47] Prejudices against women journalists appear to stem from deeply entrenched attitudes towards the 'Killer Bimbos of Fleet Street'.[48] The comparative treatments meted out to 'medusa-haired' Rebekah Brooks, who was compared to a witch following her appearance at the Leveson Inquiry, and Andy Coulson, who has so far escaped similar personal, if not professional, attack, are a case in point.[49]

Opportunities

Despite myriad obstacles, journalism provided women with financial independence and an opportunity to contribute to political debate many years before they acquired universal suffrage. Pioneering nineteenth-century writers such as Harriet Martineau, Clementina Black and Eliza Cook had exposed wife beating and sweated labour, and argued for women's equality in the periodical press.[50] The Quaker campaigner Emily Hobhouse's investigation into the treatment of Boer women and children in the 1899–1902 conflict 'caused uproar in parliament' after she published it in the radical press.[51] Early *Mirror* reporter Alison Settle's pride in her job is evident in this recollection from the First World War:

> I do recall in the First War having my hair done at Mr Gerard in Victoria Street, and the sirens went off when my hair was wet. I got up and said, 'Would you mind lending me a towel? I've got to get back to the office immediately.' 'We're going to the cellar,' he said. 'I can't because I'm a reporter on the *Mirror* and shall be wanted.'[52]

In 1924 women journalists Stella Wolfe Murray and Edith Shackleton became parliamentary correspondents for the *Daily Sketch* and *Evening Standard* respectively, permitted for the first time to sit with men in the Lords and Commons press galleries 'with all the usual privileges'. Rebecca West joined them for the *Daily News* the following year.[53] For women who had to earn a living, journalism offered reasonable pay, the chance to work from home and more flexible hours than alternatives such as teaching and governessing.[54] A female contributor to the writer Frances Low's 1904 advice booklet *Press Work for Women* encourages: 'I do my work when and how I like, the sole condition being that my copy shall be good and punctually delivered. When I see the tyranny to which governesses and nurses are obliged to submit, I count it a great gain that in journalism the woman is entirely her own mistress.'[55] The memoirs of one turn-of-the-century woman journalist reveal that, after her husband's death, journalism paid for her home and her sons' education: 'I thank the Press from my heart. It served me well and largely educated my sons.' Although after fifteen 'years of grind', she 'still shudders at the recollection of working against time to get some particular article ready for the "printer's devil" who would call at 10.00 pm to take it off to the machines'.[56]

Early twentieth-century fictions by women engaged in journalism and portraying the female reporter explore a world of work, bedsits and boarding houses much earlier than the prevailing convention that places this genre in the post–Second World War writings of Margaret Drabble and Muriel Spark and as such are an important resource for exploring early attitudes towards women and work. The women journalists in *The Pathway of the Pioneer* (1906), for example, are proud to pay their own rent and buy their own clothes even though they wear dark colours all year round because 'office and writing-desk soil them in an hour'.[57] For the journalist Stella Hammond in the short story 'The Eleventh Hour' (1917), the financial independence afforded by journalism has allowed her to rent Virginia Woolf's famous 'room of her own ... a quiet room' so essential for the woman writer.[58] Although it is a tiny cramped flat under the eaves of an apartment block, and although she mostly 'did for herself', the open window represents a delicious freedom she cannot enjoy at home. On a summer's night she can climb out onto the roof and roam freely. As in other stories featuring women journalists, Stella is a transgressor – but this might help her career: 'I suppose ... the law-abiding person might say: "Thou shalt not walk upon thy neighbour's roof at night!" But here I might get a column or two by getting arrested for attempted burglary!'[59]

The exciting world of opportunity that journalism could offer to an educated woman is portrayed in Arnold Bennett's novel *Hilda Lessways* (1911), which is about a young woman who flouts convention in her small provincial town. Stiflingly bored, her introduction to the wider world via the offices of the *Five Towns Chronicle* is to have a profound effect on the course of Hilda's life: 'Her life became grand to her. She knew she was known in the town as "the girl who could write shorthand"'.[60] The journalist and novelist Gilbert Frankau's novel *Life – and Erica* (1925) paints a Fleet Street world populated by independent working women, whose 'keen wits clashed like proverbial rapiers' at their club. The company of female journalists in *Life – and Erica* includes heroine Honoria Watson of the *Afternoon Herald* and

> a socialist leader writer ... a high tory 'sub', the financial expert of a non-committal monthly review, and two flappers who were respectively 'Auntie Mabs' of the *Daily Picture* and 'Our Young Man About Town' of the *Weekly Metropolitan* ... she heard tales to make the mouth water of single women earning their two thousand a year, and tales to make the heart sink of married women earning less than their two hundred.[61]

The economic freedom journalism brings these women is not just the freedom to escape home. It is also the freedom to escape marriage altogether or, if married, to escape the drudgery that married life brings. For Eleanor Denbigh, the journalist-heroine of Adeline Sergeant's *The Work of Oliver Byrd* (1902), her first cheque of 30 shillings for an article in the *Phonograph* represents an escape from her mother's plans for her: 'Nothing would seem so utterly ludicrous to Lady Frances as the refusal of a good offer of marriage. And [Eleanor], bound as she was by the traditions of her life, had not hitherto seen a way out for herself. But now she thought she saw a way.'[62]

Eleanor, a journalist in the Harriet Martineau mould, writes campaigning articles about 'the condition of children in certain London slums; and she had gathered together a mass of facts and details ... which was becoming very useful to the statisticians and philanthropists of her time'.[63] Elizabeth Grey, the women's page editor in Stella Martin Currey's *Paperchase End* (1934), has escaped not only her talkative widowed mother and stepfather but marriage, through her journalism: 'She didn't want to get married, she only wanted to be left alone and be allowed to make her own pattern out of life ... When she escaped ... the relief had been so great that she had been almost intoxicated.'[64] In Fay Weldon's *Darcy's Utopia* (1990), features writer Valerie Jones finds work much easier than her domestic duties and leaves homes to dedicate herself to her work and her lover: 'Compared to home, in fact, work is a piece of cake. Many women report the same thing. It is easier to please an employer than a family: a liberation to have a job description, a joy to be free of the burden of peace-keeping ... And because I am not anxious, I do well. Me, Valerie Jones, Features Writer of the Year!'[65]

Whether 'public good' or 'soft', journalism is portrayed in these fictions as bringing for women an intoxicating freedom. What, in effect, their journalism is helping them do is resist their subjugated social role, even though, ironically, to do this they often have to accept a subjugated position within the hierarchy of journalism. There is the further question, discussed below, of whether much of 'women's journalism', through its close links with advertisements for fashion and consumer goods, re-enforces traditional gender roles. Through the very tools of their freedom, then, are women journalists in fact constructing, as the author and journalist Rose Macaulay put it, a 'cage of print' for women with less social and educational capital than them?[66] These examples also highlight a problematic aspect of Bourdieu's social structure which does not seem to have considered gender as an important factor in dispositions of agents in the field of cultural production, which is a rather serious omission.

The 'problem' of women's journalism

Critics associated the arrival of women journalists in significant numbers with the disintegration of values in the press. In an ostensibly helpful guide for aspiring women journalists written in 1897, the author Arnold Bennett thus begins, somewhat discouragingly: 'Of the dwellers in Fleet Street, there are, not two sexes, but two species – journalists and women-journalists – and the one is about as far removed organically from the other as a dog from a cat.' His guide also derides women's cavalier attitude to punctuation and grammar.[67] In 1920 the commentator Arthur Baumann complained at how 'feminised' the press had now become, stating bluntly: 'For the majority of women there is but one topic of real interest, namely clothes. It must be obvious that women have exercised a deteriorating influence on the Press.'[68] A 1930 article in the *Spectator* by the essayist and critic St John Ervine complains: 'Articles by, and about women prevail in these papers and editors, without any embarrassment will print "powerful articles" by young ladies not long enlarged from school on the reform of Marriage or the reorganization of sex or the overhaul of religion.'[69] The inanity of the reading subjects in the popular press by and for women is parodied as early as 1907 in the comic fantasy *Signs of the Times* by E. V. Lucas and C. L. Graves. The satirical volume is laid out like a lengthy early *Private Eye* Magazine and during the August 'silly season' the *Daily Mail* initiates a heated debate titled 'Should Women Eat?'[70]

While it is certainly true that the majority of journalism produced by women in the early years of the twentieth century was focused on domestic topics, we must ask, first, whether women produced this kind of journalism because that is what they were commissioned to write, usually by male senior editors, and second, whether the best examples of this kind of journalism in fact perform an important social function and should not be so lightly dismissed. In answer to the first question, we have the testimony of Mrs Charles Peel, women's page editor of the *Daily Mail* 1916–1920 who wrote an entertaining memoir of her time working for Northcliffe:

> They [male editors] expected women to be interested solely in knitting jumpers, in caring for their complexions, in looking after babies, in cooking, in a 'good' murder and in silly stories about weddings … I wished to be treated as a person doing a job, instead of which some people were kind to the poor woman, some people were jealous of the damned woman and some people thought the tiresome woman had better go home and make way for a man.[71]

Despite these prejudices, Mrs Peel did in fact produce an enormously important contribution to the 'war effort' with her *Daily Mail* Food Bureau, answering 'millions' of letters from housewives and British prisoners of war in Germany wanting recipes for meagre food rations.[72]

Rose Macaulay, who by 1920 had established herself as a thoughtful novelist commenting on important social issues, also suffered from stereotyping when it came to newspaper journalism. In her collection of essays, *A Casual Commentary* (1925), Macaulay writes:

> Some time ago for instance the literary editor of a newspaper wrote to me asking if I would write an article for his paper on 'Why I Would not Marry a Curate.' I rang him up and gave him a suitable reply. He said, well then, would I write about a caveman ... Shortly afterwards another editor inquired if I would write on 'Should Clever Women Marry?'[73]

Although Rose Macaulay did indeed turn out dozens of 'soft' pieces of journalism (such as 'A Recipe for Happiness' (*Daily Mail*, 20 August 1929), 'People Who Should Not Marry' (*Daily Mail*, 26 October 1929) and 'Why I Dislike Cats, Clothes and Visits' (*Daily Mail*, 2 November 1929)), she never felt comfortable doing so. Her frustration at being 'one of those vulgar little journalists who write popular feminine chit-chat' is channelled into what is perhaps her best interwar novel, *Keeping up Appearances* (1928).[74] Like Macaulay, the novel's protagonist Daisy Simpson is confined to writing newspaper articles about 'Women' and feels trapped because of her sex: 'Why would they not let her write about inhuman things, about books, about religions, about places, about the world at large, about things of which intelligent persons had heard? "A subject for you, Miss Simpson: Can Women Have Genius? You might make something good of that, I think."'[75]

Daisy Simpson is the embodiment of the complex attitude felt towards the press by the increasing numbers of women journalists: they needed the income that freelance journalism provided, yet they were frustrated in what they were allowed to write about and very often wrote for newspapers and magazines that took an anti-feminist stance overall. Magazines like *Good Housekeeping* energetically promoted the 'return to home' theme, recommending women, who worked during the First World War, to now retreat back behind their front doors and make their homes cocoons of domesticity for their menfolk. However, these magazines provided both a voice and an income for some of the interwar period's most original, outspoken and feminist writers, including Vera Brittain, Storm Jameson, Rose Macaulay and Winifred Holtby.[76] Daisy Simpson's response to these stresses is a personality that fractures into three different characters: Daphne, the smart middle-class girl about town, Daisy the woman journalist and Marjorie the popular novelist. As her carefully constructed persona cracks, she is exposed as the gendered 'cheap and babbling authoress'.[77]

The modernist novelist and poet Stevie Smith shares similar views to Macaulay's when writing about the inside workings of women's magazines in her *Novel on Yellow Paper* (1936). The narrator Pompey Casmilus, who works for magazine publishing magnate 'Sir Phoebus Ullswater', reports of an occasion when a young girl writes in to the paper asking for advice about how to excite the interest of a young man at a tennis club she has joined. The answer – 'arrange to play the last set with him, and then linger hopefully and perhaps he will see you home' – disturbs Pompey: 'Oh how I could not have thought of that phrase it is so rich and full and so pictorial in quality... I do not think it is at all good advice... there is also that *White Girl* that Whistler painted, very wan she is now. She is lingering now but not hopefully'.[78]

During the 1930s Stevie Smith worked as a secretary for Neville Pearson, the son of the famous Arthur Pearson, who founded the *Daily Express* in 1900. By then the Newnes-Pearson group had divested itself of all its newspaper titles, but published a diverse array of magazines, from Newnes' original *Tit-Bits* to newer titles such as *Women's Own* and *Amateur Gardening*.[79] Although loyal to her boss, Pompey Casmilus has a conflicted attitude to the women's magazines his company churns out. They are responsible, she knows, for 'the idea these funny asses [suburban women]' have of matrimony: 'God loves a cheerful buyer of twopenny weeklies, and so do we. These are the girls who believe everything our contributors tell them. They put a spot of scent behind the ear, they encourage their young men to talk about football, they are Good Listeners, they are Good Pals, they are feminine'.[80]

Smith's *Novel on Yellow Paper* is about the power of language both to trap and circumscribe, as does the language of the women's magazines in whose production the heroine is implicated, but also to liberate, beyond the bounds of the material and the humdrum:

> This is a foot-off-the-ground novel that came by the left hand. And the thoughts come and go and sometimes they do not quite come and I do not pursue them to embarrass them with formality to pursue them into a harsh captivity.[81]

Pompey's rift with her fiancé Freddy is expressed in language differences between the two. While Pompey loves literature and poetry and flights of fantasy, Freddy's language is simpler, plainer, the language of the popular magazines Pompey despises. Freddy represents a 'little home', 'their furniture, their radiogram, their famous washing-up machine' that the magazines she works with tell their readers to aspire to.[82] After the First World War, women's magazines increasingly relied on advertising revenue and thus concentrated on articles which reinforced the gender stereotyping of women, offering advice on issues such as child-rearing, dealing with servants and the latest fashion and electrical items – advertisements for which complemented the editorial copy.[83] In the interwar years, the vast proportion of women's magazines degenerated into the kind of 'cloying, patronising journalism which has brought the women's press its indifferent reputation', with articles such as this one from the *Lady's Companion* advising 'the busy little housewife' that 'hubby likes you to keep that girlish prettiness'.[84] This contribution from a male reader of *Home Chat* is reminiscent of Freddy's matrimonial goal: 'I married … because I knew she would see to it that every detail was perfect in my home, from taking care that there was always a sheaf of fresh shaving papers in the bathroom, to having exactly the right sort of dinner for the evenings I'd been kept late at the office' (*Home Chat*, 22 February 1930).

Popular journalism, magazines and newspapers are a leitmotif in *Novel on Yellow Paper*, representing suburbia, stuffiness and limitation compared to the freedom Pompey craves, and expresses through her poetic prose. For Pompey (and Stevie), the tragedy for so many young girls is that they have swallowed the trite articles and advice in these magazines and newspapers and are thus doomed to keep their feet on the ground and their minds in 'harsh captivity'. This thesis persists in contemporary fiction with Annalena McAfee's *The Spoiler* contrasting the political, bold and masculine journalism of veteran foreign correspondent Honor Tait with the trivial, celebrity-obsessed scribbling of Tamara Sim, who is both shallow and ignorant. Tamara has been sent to interview Honor for the upmarket glossy magazine supplement *S*nday*; it was her first big break and she brought with her both tape recorder and notebook as a precaution:

> 'Very wise dear,' said [Honor]. 'It would be disastrous if one of your stories were to be lost to the reading public. Like Alexandria's library all over again.'
>
> Tamara caught the hostility but not the reference … In her notebook she wrote: *Chk: who is Alexandria? What happened to her library?*[85]

While the 'cloying, patronising' nature of much women's journalism is certainly regrettable, it would be wrong to dismiss all domestically focused journalism as 'soft' or 'irrelevant'. There has been a tendency among journalism scholars to construct an 'ideal' definition of journalism as that which covers politics and international debate and contributes to the 'public sphere', a place where rational arguments among well-informed citizenry are conducted.[86] Feminist critics of this ideal have pointed out that the profoundly male origins (the Greek city state and eighteenth-century 'coffee house' culture) and characteristics of this 'public sphere' necessarily exclude women from what is defined as legitimate political debate. The domestic sphere, traditionally inhabited by women, is as much about politics, finance and labour (albeit underpaid or unpaid) as the public sphere. 'Soft' features and 'lifestyle' journalism, by bringing domestic issues to a public arena, can thus help women participate in political debate.[87] During the First World War, for example, women feature writers wrote about new and important topics such as food rationing, how to grow vegetables in townhouse gardens and how to cope with losing young sons and fiancés to war.[88] Their vivid descriptions of working women, normalizing their participation in the public life of the country, contributed to the campaign for women's suffrage, such as this feature in the *Daily Mail*:

> It was at the end of the night shift in a munitions factory. Through the open door of the workshop I could see the meagre grey light of a winter's morning, and the rain falling like threads of steel – the cold raw wind driving in cut like a knife across the vitiated air, tainted with the smell of stale food, sweat and fumes from the braziers we had breathed all night... the smell of fruit, the smell of cough lozenges, the musty smell of damp clothes steaming in the warmth of the gas overhead, cheap scent and cigarette smoke... an icy draught playing around our swollen feet. ('The Real Life of the Girl Worker', *Daily Mail*, 1 January 1917)

Describing the women workers, virtually absent from portrayals in the press, despite their working in large numbers before the war, in such sensory terms with their stale sweat, cheap scent and breath heavy with cough lozenge vapour is groundbreaking.[89] Here we have on the leader page of a daily newspaper, working women stepping into the public realm revealing this type of well-written feature as a text where women can see important aspects of their life treated on an equal footing with that of men. It is this attempt to convey the reality of civilian life in the stress of war that the journalist Martha Gellhorn took up in the Spanish Civil War twenty years later, and which then became a respected genre of war journalism throughout the twentieth century.[90] The Irish journalist Nell McCafferty, who has won many plaudits for writing about life on the 'Home Front' in the Irish 'Troubles', explains how she tried to do the same thing for readers of the *Irish Times*:

> It is the modest ambition of every journalist to write a front page story – the big one at the top left hand side, with large headlines, that tells the world the main event of the day... I discovered early on, that I'd never be able to write a front page story. I'd be inclined to argue with the person in charge... I discovered this particularly on Bloody Sunday in Derry, while I was lying on the street while other people around me got shot dead... the other reporter, rightly, wrote the

front page story because somebody had to establish the name of the officer in charge ... My version appeared on the inside pages. I wrote about how the rest of us felt, lying on the ground.[91]

The idea that features or 'soft' journalism, often written by women, is an important contributor to public debates has been discussed in fictions since the First World War. The short story 'Cupid Wields a Pen' (1917) by the author and journalist Betty Maxwell describes how reading an article by a woman journalist about losing her wounded fiancé's love helped women come to terms with their sense of loss.[92] While Rose Macaulay's *Non-Combatants and Others* (1916) is generally critical of the press and the reading public (see Chapter 2), the role newspapers play in helping people make scant food rations stretch and 'making do and mending' old clothes is treated positively.

The feminist author Fay Weldon made this idea the central theme of her novel *Darcy's Utopia* (1990), in which two journalists, one male political correspondent and one female feature writer, try to understand the source of a recent national economic catastrophe. Hugo Vansitart, the respected political journalist writing for the *Independent*, and Valerie Jones, the features writer for *Aura* magazine, both interview Eleanor Darcy, the wife of a senior economist, whose advice to the Treasury has resulted in economic chaos. While Hugo concentrates on Eleanor's bizarre political and economic theories (that neighbours should vet people's suitability for parenthood, television and money should be banned), Valerie concentrates on Eleanor's unusual upbringing and personal life. Valerie begins with a timid disclaimer: 'We're intelligent enough, I hope, but, naturally, considering our market, are more concerned with matters of human interest than anything particularly intellectual.'[93] Throughout the novel Valerie deprecates her 'just human interest, women's magazine', although her carefully detailed account of Eleanor's childhood brings us nearer to understanding her subject than Hugo's economic account, which he himself gives up on.[94] Despite this contribution, however, most women journalists are depicted as longing to cover the traditionally masculine areas of politics and foreign correspondence as a way of proving their legitimacy. This is part of the hierarchy of journalism that places male 'newshounds' over female 'features bunnies' with foreign and political correspondents at the top.[95] Travelling the world or conducting interviews with the powerful is, of course, a magnificently exciting way of earning a living. The foreign correspondent Christina Lamb remembers, as an intern on the *Financial Times* in 1987, observing the international correspondents when they returned to the newsroom bringing with them 'the smell of the desert, or tang of the sea, dressed in crumpled linen suits ... They were glamorous, rugged ... They were all men and to me they were all gods'.[96] In the final section of this chapter, however, we will see that contemporary fictional portrayals of female foreign and political correspondents tend to emphasize their vulnerability and also reinforce negative gender stereotypes.

Icarus on the cookery page

While the goal for many female journalists, both in real life and in fiction, is access to the masculine public sphere, contemporary fictions foreground the dangers facing these women, as if they don't understand the rules of the forbidden realm into which they have strayed. We have already seen how women newspaper journalists who turn to fiction emphasize feeling like an interloper in a man's world. While the world of the women's page does not tend to pose too many risks, women have recently made inroads into the traditionally male areas of politics and foreign correspondence, although they are still very much in a minority. In a poll of Britain's 'Top 100 Political Journalists' by the political website totalpolitics.com, just five women made it into the top fifty (Laura Kuenssberg and Emily Maitlis of BBC television, Martha Kearney of BBC radio, Cathy Newman of Channel Four News and Ann Treneman (*Times* political sketch writer).[97] Seventeen made it into the top 100. Only five (Ann Treneman, Rachel Sylvester, Polly Toynbee, Anne McElvoy and Isabel Oakeshott) are print journalists. Recent commentators have suggested that while women started to make headway in political journalism in the 1990s, today the lobby is more like a 'gentleman's club' than ever.[98]

Into this dangerous world of men strays, like a little lamb that has lost her way, Mattie Storin/Zoe Barnes, the female fictional journalist at the centre of a story about power and the media so compelling that it has received three different representations. In her first outing, Michael Dobbs' novel *House of Cards* (1989), Mattie does not sleep with the ambitious Chief Whip Francis Urquhart (or the House Majority Leader Frank Underwood) as she does in her screen iterations, although like any career-minded modern female fictional journalist she does sleep with her boss, the deputy editor of the *Daily Telegraph*.[99] When her investigations threaten to upset the cosy power relationships between her paper's proprietor and the Conservative Party, her editor threatens the ultimate sanction: 'Put her on the cookery page.'[100] Similarly in the BBC television series (1990) her editor warns: 'I've been thinking about your next career move Mattie. I'd like to see some new thinking in our cookery and home interior pages ... "What's bright and sparkly in the shops for her indoors … twenty things you never thought you could do with a Wok'".[101]

In all three versions of *House of Cards*, Mattie/Zoe quits her paper and enters either the uncertain world of the freelance or, in the most recent Netflix version (2013), joins the fledgling online news site *Slugline*. While her tenuous foothold in newspapers was always contested, once freelance without the protection and access of her newspaper, she is both vulnerable and powerless, as Urquhart points out to her in the BBC series: 'You now have evidence of a conspiracy, but you don't have access to a newspaper to publish it.'[102] Throughout the BBC series Mattie is seen as a lone woman struggling unsuccessfully against a phalanx of male reporters and photographers for access to politicians outside Number 10 and in the House of Commons. Only through sleeping with Francis Urquhart/ Frank Underwood can she gain any kind of access to power, a transaction both she and her US counterpart Zoe Barnes willingly and knowingly make, as we have seen in a pervasive contemporary stereotype. This may be part of the trend that *Guardian* journalist Hadley Freeman has derided as 'film-makers' tragic sexual fantasies'.[103] However, considering the high number of women journalists who have experienced unwanted sexual advances from contacts, with a significant proportion either from interviewees, government officials or the police, this representation of the woman journalist is highly problematic.[104] If a dominant cultural conception of the woman journalist is that of someone prepared to exchange her body for a story, then this not only undermines women journalists' professionalism in the public's eye but also emphasizes her interloper status. She is only tolerated in the corridors of power because she is prepared to 'put out'. At the end of the BBC series, Mattie is symbolically ejected from the male seat of power when Urquhart throws her off the roof of the House of Commons. Like Icarus not content to stay on the ground, Mattie is not content to settle for the cookery page and, as a result, falls from the sky; her death is a warning to other women journalists hoping to break the gender barriers of journalism and politics.

There is a similar contemporary theme of fictional women journalists' vulnerability in war zones and in crime reporting, two other traditionally male areas where women have recently made inroads. Whereas in reality, women journalists only make up a small proportion (7 per cent) of journalists killed in the course of their work, they are over-represented in fictions where journalists come to grief.[105] The female victim of the predatory male, of course, is as pervasive a cultural trope as the mendacious 'cow' (Rita Skeeter) or the woman who sleeps her way to the top (Mattie Storin, Susan Street). As a journalist in

Minette Walters' *The Devil's Feather* wryly notes, 'There's a lot of mileage to be made out of female journalists... women under fire make good copy.'[106] According to this survey, with the exception of Valerie Jones in *Darcy's Utopia* (1990), the last time an interesting and nuanced female journalist appeared in a novel was 1951 (Monica Dickens' *My Turn to Make the Tea*), whereas fiction of the first four decades of the twentieth century was full of them.[107] Ironically, then, as women journalists have become more numerous and successful, their cultural representations have become increasingly negative and stereotyped. The 'dish bitches' may be in front of the camera now but that only makes them easier targets.

Notes

1 In broadcast journalist Martin Bell's memoir *Through Gates of Fire* (p. 175) he recalls how male correspondents, using satellites to transmit their despatches were known as 'dish monkeys', a gender neutral term, while women correspondents were known as 'dish bitches'.

2 Dixon, Ella Hepworth, *The Story of a Modern Woman*, p. 45.

3 For more on Ella Hepworth Dixon's career in journalism, see her memoir *As I knew Them*.

4 Ferguson, Rachel, *The Brontes went to Woolworths*, pp. 16–17.

5 Ferguson, Rachel, *We Were Amused*, p. 163.

6 Dickens, Monica, *My Turn to Make the Tea*, p. 222. The novel is based on Dickens' experience at the *Herts Express*, which she joined shortly after the end of the Second World War.

7 Julie Burchill is a successful journalist and commentator, having started work at the *New Musical Express* in the late 1970s. She has written for the *Guardian*, *Sunday Times*, *Daily Mail* and *Spectator*. Annalena McAfee spent thirty years on newspapers, mainly the arts pages of the *Financial Times* and *Guardian*. She was founding editor of the *Guardian Review*. McAfee, Annalena, *The Spoiler*, p. 291.

8 Macaulay, Rose, *Potterism*, p. 2. In this passage the female journalist Jane Potter is meditating on the unfairness of her less talented brother being given a head start in life because of his gender.

9 See for example Adkins, Lisa and Bev Sheggs (eds), *Feminism after Bourdieu* (2005) and McCall, Leslie, 'Does Gender Fit?' (1992).

10 See for example Franks, Suzanne, *Women and Journalism*.

11 See for example, Holloway, Gerry, *Women and Work in Britain* and Beddoe, Deirdre, *Back to Home and Duty*, pp. 44–88.

12 Onslow, Barbara, *Women of the Press*, p. 12.

13　Kent, Sylvia, *The Woman Writer*, pp. 11–14. Unfortunately early archives of the Society of Women Journalists, containing minutes and correspondence, were lost in 'fires, floods and during several wars' (p. 13).

14　Hall, Valerie, *Women in Journalism: A Sociological Account*, p. 96.

15　'An Old Oriental' *Englishwoman's Review*, 1904, pp. 151–153.

16　Tusan, Elizabeth Michelle, *Women Making the News*.

17　Categories vary, from 'author, editor, writer' in 1861 to 'author, editor, journalist, reporter and shorthand writer' in 1901; 'publicist' is added in 1921; from 1971 the category is 'authors, journalists and related workers'. Source: Office of National Statistics.

18　Murphy, Catherine, *On an Equal Footing with Men?* p. 3; Hall, *Women in Journalism*, pp. 322–324.

19　Stott, Mary, *Before I Go*, p. 199.

20　Ibid., p. 200.

21　Lutes, Jean-Marie, *Front Page Girls*, p. 2 & 161.

22　Ida Tarbell exposed corruption in the American oil industry, particularly Rockefeller's Standard Oil in a series of articles for *McClure's* 1902–1904, now called 'the greatest business story ever written' (Starkman, Dean, *The Watchdog That Didn't Bark*, p. 19).

23　Duff, Shiela Grant, *The Parting of Ways*, pp. 66–67.

24　Interview with Selina Hastings, Margaret Lane's daughter; *Daily Mail*, 3 July 1933.

25　Hall, Valerie (1978, 321–326) collates letters from provincial newspapers outlining news editors' resistance to hiring 'girls'. Reasons include fears they would put male reporters off their work, a perceived lack of female interest in news and low appreciation of female literacy skills.

26　Page, Bruce, *The Murdoch Archipelago*, p. 113.

27　The 2001 census shows also, for the first time, the total numbers of journalists at a lower level than the previous decade (approximately 60,000 compared to nearly 80,000 in 1991). Source: Office of National Statistics.

28　Gopsill, Tim and Greg Neale, *Journalists*, pp. 36–44.

29　Franks, *Women and Journalism*, p. 21.

30　Beddoe, *Back to Home and Duty*, pp. 77–78.

31　Pacey, Laura, 'Investigation: Have Women Changed the Dental Workforce?' in *British Dental Journal*, 216, pp. 4–5, http://www.nature.com/bdj/journal/v216/n1/full/sj.bdj.2013.1266.html (accessed 1 September 2015).

32　Sanders, K. and Mark Hanna, 'British Journalists' in Weaver, David and Lars Wilnat (eds) *The Global Journalist*.

33　Women were banned from the Press Gallery of the House of Commons until after the First World War. See Macdonagh, Michael, *The Reporter's Gallery*, p. 10; see Tusan, *Women Making the News*.

34　See for example Ross, Karen, 'Women at Work'.

35 See for example Hall, *Women in Journalism*, p. 6; Currell, Melville, *Political Woman*.

36 Cecil Hunt was fiction editor of the *Daily Mail* 1928–1936 (Hunt 1948).

37 Gibbs, Philip, *The Street of Adventure*, p. 314. 'Katherine Halstead' was based on the journalist Emilie Peacocke, who began her career on her father's paper the *Northern Echo* in 1898 and who worked with Gibbs on the *Tribune* 1906–1908. She rose to become woman's page editor of the *Daily Telegraph* in the 1930s.

38 Isherwood, Christopher, *Mr Norris*, p. 38.

39 Le Carre, John, *A Murder of Quality*, pp. 11 & 17.

40 McAfee, Annalena, *The Spoiler*, pp. 431 & 418.

41 Rowling, J. K., *Harry Potter and the Goblet of Fire*, pp. 266, 269 & 393.

42 Macaulay, Rose, *Mystery at Geneva*, p. 1.

43 *His Girl Friday*, directed by Howard Hawks, is an adaptation of an earlier stage play, *Hold the Front Page*, where the Hildy character is male.

44 Stewart, Daxton, 'Harry Potter and the Exploitative Jackals', p. 1.

45 *Trainwreck* (2015) dir. Judd Apatow; *Crazy Heart* (2009) dir. Scott Cooper; *Three Kings* (2000), dir. David O'Russell; *Adaptation* (2002) dir. Spike Jonze; *House of Cards* (TV, 2013) dir. David Fincher; Nightcrawler (2014) dir. Dan Gilroy.

46 See for example Paul, Pamela, Pornifed: How Pornography Is Damaging Our Lives, Our Relationships and Our Families.

47 Skorsky, Janine, White House correspondent of the *Washington Herald* to Zoe Barnes, an ambitious young blogger at the paper in *House of Cards* (US, Netflix) Series One.

48 See for example, Chambers, Deborah, Linda Steiner and Carole Fleming, *Women and Journalism*; Ross, 'Women at work: Journalism as an En-Gendered Practice' and Carter, Cynthia et al., *News, Gender, Power*.

49 Tulloch, John, 'A Little Bit Salem': Rebekah Brooks of News International and the Construction of a Modern Witch' in Ethical Space, 10/1, pp. 4–7.

50 Onslow, *Women of the Press*, pp. 159–182.

51 Hudson, Miles and John Stanier, *War and the Media*, p. 35.

52 Quoted in Hall, *Women in Journalism*, p. 184. Alison Settle went on to become the third editor of *Vogue* magazine, 1926–1935.

53 These 'firsts' were recorded in the journal *The Woman Journalist* in November 1924 and January and March 1925

54 Onslow, *Women of the Press*.

55 Low, Frances, *Press Work for Women*, p. 83.

56 Alec-Tweedie, Mrs., *Me and Mine*, pp. 117 & 62.

57 Wyllarde, Dolf, *The Pathway*, p. 41.

58 Woolf, Virginia, *A Room of One's Own*, p. 61.

59 Bretherton, Eva, 'The Eleventh Hour', p. 885. Eva Bretherton was a freelance writer who contributed both fiction and non-fiction to a range of periodicals including *The Quiver* and *The Sussex County Magazine*.

60 Bennett, Arnold, *Hilda Lessways*, p. 81.

61 Frankau, Gilbert, *Life – and Erica*, pp. 80–81.

62 Sergeant, Adeline, *The Work of Oliver Byrd*, p. 10.

63 Ibid., p. 224. Adeline Sergeant worked on the staff of the *People's Friend* magazine 1885–1887 and was a contributor until her death in 1904.

64 Currey, Stella Martin, *Paperchase End*, p. 55.

65 Weldon, Fay, *Darcy's Utopia*, p. 21.

66 Macaulay, Rose, *Keeping up Appearances*, p. 131.

67 Bennett, Arnold, *Journalism for Women: A Practical Guide*, p. 8.

68 Bauman, Arthur, 'The Functions and Future of the Press', p. 626.

69 Ervine, St John, 'The Future of the Press', *Spectator*, 29 November 1930.

70 Lucas, E. V. and C. L. Graves, *Signs of the Times*, p. 90.

71 Peel, Mrs Charles, *Life's Enchanted Cup*, pp. 227–229.

72 Ibid., p. 222.

73 Macaulay, Rose, *A Casual Commentary*, p. 213.

74 Macaulay, *Keeping up Appearances*, p. 18.

75 Ibid., p. 22.

76 Briganti, Chiara and Kathy Mezei, *Domestic Modernism, the Interwar Novel and E H Young*, pp. 4–6.

77 Macaulay, *Keeping up Appearances*, p. 156.

78 Smith, Stevie, *Novel on Yellow Paper*, pp. 147–148.

79 Spalding, Frances, *Stevie Smith*, p. 49.

80 Smith, *Novel on Yellow Paper*, p. 151.

81 Ibid., p. 38.

82 Ibid., pp. 242–243.

83 White, Cynthia, *Women's Magazines*, pp. 79–115.

84 Ibid., pp. 100–101.

85 McAfee, Annalena, *The Spoiler*, pp. 65–66.

86 See for example Habermas, Jurgen, *The Structural Transformation of the Public Sphere*; Chalaby, Jean, *The Invention of Journalism*; Curran, James, *Power without Responsibility*.

87 See for example Fraser, Nancy, 'What's Critical about Critical Theory?' and Lonsdale, Sarah, 'Roast Seagull and other Quaint Bird Dishes'.

88 Lonsdale, Sarah, 'Roast Seagull'.

89 Braybon, Gail, *Women Workers in the First World War*, pp. 26–32.

90 See Gellhorn, Martha, *The Face of War*.

91 McCafferty, Nell, *The Best of Nell*, p. 14.

92 Maxwell, Betty, 'Cupid Wields a Pen' in *The Quiver*, June 1917.

93 Weldon, Fay, *Darcy's Utopia*, p. 13.

94 Ibid., p. 212.

95 Franks, *Women in Journalism*, p. 23.

96   Lamb, Christina, *Small Wars Permitting*, p. 12.
97   http://www.totalpolitics.com/print/5638/top-100-political-journalists-the-results. thtml (accessed 15 September 2015).
98   Veeneman, Alex, 'Should There Be More Female Journalists at Westminster? http://www.kettlemag.co.uk/article/should-there-be-more-female-journalists-westminster (accessed 15 September 2015).
99   See also Burchill, Julie, *Ambition* and McAfee, Annalena, *The Spoiler*.
100 Dobbs, Michael, *House of Cards*, p. 228.
101 *House of Cards* BBC television, episode three.
102 Ibid., episode four.
103 Freeman, Hadley, 'Don't Believe Hollywood's Sexual Fantasies about Female Journalists', *Guardian*, 29 July 2015.
104 International Women's Media Foundation Survey of 683 Women Journalists, http://www.iwmf.org/sexual-harassment/ (accessed 15 September 2015).
105 The death of the crime reporter Veronica Guerin inspired two screen representations of her life and untimely end: *When the Sky Falls* (2000) and *Veronica Guerin*. In the movie *Manticore* (2005), a female war correspondent is torn apart by a mythical beast. Although the war reporter Connie Burns in Minette Walters' *The Devil's Feather* (2005) is not killed, her sexual humiliation at the hands of her captor is brutal, graphic and degrading. The Committee to Protect Journalists, which compiles statistics on journalist deaths, reports that of the 1147 journalists killed in 1992–2015, 7 per cent were female. https://www.cpj.org/killed/ (accessed 15 September 2015).
106 Walters, *The Devil's Feather*, p. 207.
107 Screen representations are mixed. Maddy Bowen in *Blood Diamond* (2006), Della Frye in *State of Play* (2009) and Ellis Kane in Channel Four's *Secret State* (2012) are hard working, serious-minded reporters but they tend to be drowned out by the lazy stereotypes discussed earlier.

'Now we don't even have anyone in fucking Manchester': Falling Apart in the 'Last Chance Saloon'[1]

The cracks in the newspaper edifice apprehended by writers in Chapter Six become first fissures and then huge tectonic movements as continued circulation declines, the arrival of the Internet and further falls in standards of tabloid and middle market newspapers combine to create a 'perfect storm'. The end result would be the Leveson Inquiry 2011–2012; the dismal collapse of the Press Complaints Commission (which had replaced the abject failure of the Press Council twenty years previously); the closure of the News of the World; and the arrest, trial and imprisonment of several tabloid reporters and editors. Novels about newspapers written during this period reflect a frenzied, crazy world of crisis: not just economic and moral but also, more fundamentally, many writers question the journalist's ability to report on a world that defies neat, sound-bite summary. Not only this, but, as journalism faces its greatest challenge, writers raise a deeper, more existential question about the intangible nature of journalism's benefits to society.

Sometime during the mid to late 1970s, between unemployment reaching one million in 1975 and Mrs Thatcher becoming prime minister in 1979, Britain moved from the post-war period into the late twentieth century. For many contemporary writers the changes which severed the earlier post-war period from this later one were engineered by the economic and social consequences of Thatcherism, which first distorted and then undermined 'the communal values prized by an older generation', unleashed the full powers of the City and prized individual gain over the common good.[2] Similarly the end of the post-war consensus after Mrs Thatcher became leader of the Conservative Party in 1975 marks the dividing line between 'post-war' and 'contemporary' fiction.[3] It may be still too early to achieve a historical perspective on the current literary period with the fragmentation of genres from post-colonialism to 'steampunk'; and of forms from postmodernism to magical realism. However, no matter the form or genre, the complex, symbiotic relationship between literature and social, political and historical movements and events still maintains during this period. Writers will attempt to critique and propose a role for journalism in advanced liberal society even as the trade, Proteus-like, changes shape and function with increasing rapidity.

For the newspaper industry, a new era began when, in early 1981, within days of having installed Kelvin Mackenzie as new editor of the *Sun*, Rupert Murdoch gained control of the *Times* and *Sunday Times*, the jewels in the British newspaper crown.[4] Mackenzie's aggressive, confrontational style made the *Sun* a dubious national icon, with headlines such as 'GOTCHA' celebrating the sinking of the Argentinean cruiser the *General Belgrano*, with the loss of 300 lives, and 'UP YOURS DELORS', an invitation to Britons to send a collective 'V' sign to the then president of the European Commission.[5] Mackenzie's robust editorial stance, and his introduction of newspaper Bingo, raised *Sun* daily sales to over four million, where they stayed for the entire decade, which is a considerable feat.[6] For many journalists and commentators, however, this was also a time when the *Sun* went beyond the pale, with Joe Haines of the *Mirror* calling the rival publication a 'coarse and demented newspaper' which had 'fallen from the gutter to the sewer'.[7] In 1988, Hugh Cudlipp, for many journalists the personification of the mid-twentieth-century 'Golden Age' of the British popular press, accused modern proprietors and editors of having decided that 'playing a continuing role in public enlightenment was no longer the business of the popular press'.[8] In conjunction with the steady march downhill of the tabloid press another deeper structural change was taking place as Rupert Murdoch sought to break up the powerful print unions and move his newspapers to Wapping, east of the Tower of London. The move, which began in January 1986, would lead, over the next decade, to most national newspapers leaving their cramped offices in and around Fleet Street to new homes in Clerkenwell, Docklands, Battersea and Kensington: literally scattered to the four winds. The loss of their clubby, centuries-old home 'where eccentric adventurers or literary men occasionally climbed off barstools to write deathless dispatches',[9] with its pubs, restaurants and even its own Parish Church of Saint Bride's, coincided with a slew of late twentieth- and early twenty-first-century fictions portraying journalists and editors as either dangerously unstable, mentally vulnerable, morally compromised and even deranged, murderous or suicidal. Some fictions even mark in their narratives the start of the downhill trajectory as the time when their featured newspapers leave Fleet Street and the glory days when newspaper hell-raisers, wild, excessive drinkers and literary men like Keith Waterhouse, Jeffrey Bernard and Christopher Hitchens held court in El Vino's, 'where leftwing lambs and rightwing lions downed their differences in bottles of champagne'.[10] In A. N. Wilson's horribly dark newspaper novel *My Name Is Legion* (2004), the *Legion's* moral decline begins after its takeover by colonial businessman Lennox Mark and its move from 'the piratical jollity of the old *Legion* in its Fleet Street manifestation' to its new home, a plate glass tower in Bermondsey.[11] While a move of physical premises could not in itself precipitate widespread moral and mental breakdown, either imagined or real, the re-location from Fleet Street was a symptom of the ongoing changes in journalism economics and practice where even eccentric millionaire proprietors now have to justify expenses to their boardrooms. Although some newspapers maintained circulation for long periods and new newspapers, most notably the *Independent*, were launched during this time, the general trend would hereafter be always downwards.[12] High staff costs and the sharp rise of newsprint prices rises particularly from the mid-1970s, when they almost doubled overnight, meant that high circulation newspapers particularly saw profits slashed.[13] The average annual cost of bringing out a national newspaper rose from nearly £1.6 million in 1946 to more than £28 million in 1974.[14] Since the mid-1980s, technology has replaced many of the traditional skills previously needed to bring out a paper, first in the printing and composing sectors, and, latterly, the arrival of the Internet has given IT engineers, search engine optimizers and 'Twitter Twats' as much status as expert specialist correspondents.[15] Novelists tackling the character of the journalist and the nature of news during this time are among our finest contemporary writers and literary innovators: Martin Amis, Gordon Burn, Ian McEwan, Iain Banks, Pat Barker and James Meek. These writers seek, and find, creative possibilities in contemporary journalistic themes, which are also the themes of current modernity: the cult of celebrity and the technological revolution, which packages 'the poignant details of your life, your plain statements coleslawed into something weightless, sizeless, and travelling at the speed of light within information networks depending ... on minute components, invisible processes, intangible, incomprehensible technologies'.[16] Other writers, all having worked in newspapers, including A. N. Wilson, Andrew Martin, Revel Barker, David Nobbs, John Preston, Julie Burchill and Annalena McAfee, have also written 'newspaper' novels of varying quality during this period. Some of our most important modern playwrights including Arnold Wesker, Howard Brenton, David Hare, Tom Stoppard and Richard Bean take on the subject of newspapers and their role in society, suggesting widespread intellectual interest in, and concern for, this at-once-threatening, and threatened, medium. Another area of interest for contemporary novelists is the role of journalists in reporting international conflicts and the effect war reportage has on them. Very different from the pistol-packing Victorian and Edwardian adventurer who portrays war as heroic sacrifice and as an opportunity to write purple-tinged 'prose poems', late twentieth- and early twenty-first-century war reporters are seen as highly vulnerable agents, prone to damaging emotional attachment to the atrocities they witness and questioning journalism's ability to represent human suffering.[17]

Journalism moves to a different field

Now writers' concern for the way contemporary journalism is practiced, and their portrayal of the mental state of its practitioners, presents a very different kind of criticism from the early twentieth-century struggles of literary and journalistic agents engaged in a turf war over the nature of cultural capital. Writers appear to acknowledge that modern journalism now occupies a more commercial field, that of advertising, communications technology and public relations.[18] Although journalist characters in these modern novels do occasionally nod to their once belonging to a more literary field, there is an acceptance that this is no more than a faint echo from the past. Ghosts from journalism's more literary age are used, in these fictions, to emphasize differences rather than similarities. In Iain Banks' *Complicity* (1993), the reporter Cameron Colley tries, and fails, to emulate his hero Hunter S. Thompson. In Gordon Burn's *Fullalove* (1995), tabloid hack Norman Miller acknowledges the irony of his name, 'four brick dull, plain artisanal syllables' being a near-duplication of 'the champ of writers' Norman Mailer. While Mailer, when the same age as Miller had already published three novels, Miller refers to a novel he had once conceived: 'a book of course that I have never written, and have now lost all ambition to write'.[19] Meanwhile the shades of Ernest Hemingway and Graham Greene are briefly conjured, before vanishing like will-o'-the-wisps. L. P. Watson, the columnist on the *Daily Legion* in the journalist and author A. N. Wilson's novel, had once been a literary writer before his 'Faustian Pact' with 'more lucrative' journalism. Now, decades on from his fall, a volume of poetry 'was laid aside. So, too, was a vague idea that he might write a study of the philosophy of Heidegger ... In fact he had reached a stage of his career where it was no longer possible for him to read.'[20] Watson's creator A. N. Wilson admits the cynical and prolific fictional columnist is 'a sort of nightmare-projection of what A.N.Wilson might have become, or perhaps was in some ways. As far as published work is concerned, I began as a novelist, and hope to end as a novelist. If my novels had sold well, I probably would not have written the other stuff – or not so much – but I have always needed to be a breadwinner.' He has, however, always 'found journalism enormously enjoyable. Addictive. I absolutely loved writing at speed, seeing one's words in print almost instantly... I love the company of other journalists'.[21]

In these contemporary fictions, when characters attempt a piece of more original literary journalism, their news editors criticize them for not covering what all the other reporters are covering. The newspaper organization's goal is homogeneity. Difference is not prized, and it is seen as a weakness, a sign that the organization's reporter has missed the story that everyone else has got. The result is a bland sameness, which does little to spread enlightenment to the reading public. In James Meek's *We Are Now Beginning Our Descent* (2008), the foreign correspondent Adam Kellas writes a long piece about musicians barely surviving in an Afghanistan where the Taliban has outlawed secular music, but his news desk only wants to know why he didn't send them an article about a missile attack on a market 'which was in the rival papers that morning'.[22] In *Fullalove* Norman Miller sends his desk 'colour' pieces from Zaire, where he has been sent to cover the boxing match between Mohammed Ali and George Forman, but 'The dispatches were ruthlessly pruned... pretty soon I fell in with requirements: I rarely left the pack of reporters and filed little that couldn't as easily have been lifted from the morning's press handout'. This is different from the aims of the press pack in Evelyn Waugh's day when, in Waugh's view, 'An exclusive lie was more valuable than a truth which was shared with others'.[23] Both practices, that is, the manufacture of the exclusive lie and the bland repetition of known facts are worlds away from idealised notions of journalism. Both place the journalist who wants to write the truth in jeopardy: he is at once a vulnerable outsider, taking risks to seek out the truth while his colleagues concoct lies in hotel bedrooms.

James Meek's novel contains autobiographical elements from when he was a *Guardian* correspondent, including the incident involving the out-of-work Afghan musicians. Meek's view is that the 'good' journalist who wants to do a decent job in conveying the truth of what he sees is confronted with the double indifference of the news desk who only wants the same as everyone else and the audience who 'is only ready to apprehend events from a war zone through a set of clichés' and who isn't interested in making the commitment to learn about day-to-day life in a war zone.

There are peaceful days in war zones, there are days when nothing at all happens and I wanted to learn about life in the villages on these days. But in doing so I missed a rocket attack on a market place, something that happened all the time. It had no significance, apart from as a news event that other papers carried. In some ways I was a bad reporter.[24]

In the novel, Adam Kellas reacts to the 'disconnect' between what he was trying to do as a journalist and the smug satisfaction of his north London readers with a violent outburst, smashing glasses and crockery at a dinner party attended by representatives of a metropolitan intelligentsia. For Kellas – and Meek – it is the moment of realization of the limitations of journalism – mainstream, mass journalism, anyway – as a means of conveying the truth of war. Meek has solved this problem personally, by writing literary fiction, where he examines ideas on politics, society and journalism in greater depth, but also by writing for the highbrow journal the *London Review of Books* and 'a discriminating audience, people who make the time to read and understand'. In order to write the way he wants to write, he has thus deliberately removed himself from the field of commercial journalism and re-occupied the literary field. The trade-off – losing a large audience for the sake of cultural capital – for this writer is a price worth paying.

Tabloid ethics and the problems of celebrity

In early 2015 another British tabloid newspaper, the *Daily Mirror*, was prosecuted for hacking celebrities' phones on 'an industrial scale' similar to the practice at the *News of the World*, revelations of which led to that newspaper's closure in 2011.[25] The phone-hacking scandal came after four decades of ever-more public Establishment hand-wringing over press standards, from the conclusions of the Third Royal Commission's Final Report in July 1977, that newspapers committed 'flagrant breaches of acceptable standards' to the *Sun* being denounced in the House of Lords in April 1989 as 'one of the nastiest newspapers published in any Western democracy' following its coverage of the Hillsborough football stadium disaster.[26] There was so much shocking content in British tabloids then that Channel Four even commissioned a series, *Hard News*, also in 1989, in which *Financial Times* journalist Raymond Snoddy delivered a weekly guilty verdict on Britain's 'Red Tops'. The Calcutt Committee on Privacy and Related Matters was convened later that year. When it reported in 1990 it proposed a Code of Practice by which all newspapers should abide. The code, covering journalistic practice from accuracy, respect for privacy, harassment and intrusion into grief, is taught to trainee and student journalists but has been so severely undermined that its monitoring by the Press Complaints Commission was held up to widespread ridicule during the Leveson Inquiry. Tabloid newspaper excesses from the politicized demonizing of the miners during and after the 1984 Miners' Strike, the *Sun*'s coverage of the Hillsborough tragedy through to the obsession with Princess Diana particularly after the announcement of her separation from Prince Charles in December 1992 are now a matter of historical record.[27] While Diana was often an accomplice to her exposure, she was also many times a victim of deeply intrusive and often illegal press behaviour.[28] Media observers have been especially concerned over the overwhelmingly pro-Conservative bias of British newspapers since the early 1980s, as well as the continuing polarization between the 'quality' press and mass-market newspapers.

While 'broadsheet' newspapers have maintained their coverage of international and current-affairs news, the mass market press devotes less and less space to current affairs, and more and more to 'human interest' stories, trivia, sports news and celebrity gossip, a trend which began in the 1950s but which accelerated through the 1970s and 1980s.[29] The use of celebrity news as a way of selling newspapers in a fiercely competitive market led inevitably from the paparazzi stalking of the glamorous and famous to the widespread hacking of mobile phones, a practice which revealed the moral vacuum at the heart of modern tabloid newspaper journalism. It is this moral vacuum that has preoccupied many contemporary novelists and produced characters such as Martin Amis' robotic Clint Smoker (*Yellow Dog*, 2003), Ian McEwan's empty Vernon Halliday (*Amsterdam*, 1998), Annalena McAfee's monstrously stupid Tamara Sim (*The Spoiler*, 2011), J. K. Rowling's mendacious Rita Skeeter (in various *Harry Potter* novels 2000–2007) and most of the staff of the *Legion* in A. N. Wilson's *My Name Is Legion* (2004), among others.

Martin Amis, who has found source material in many major contemporary social and political concerns from the globalized publishing industry to the modern crisis of masculinity, has, in *Yellow Dog*, imagined the character and motivations of the tabloid newspaper reporter. Clint Smoker, who writes for the *Morning Lark*, is the personification of the sociologist Jean Chalaby's tabloid journalist who has been subsumed into his newspaper's industrial process. This market-conscious agent produces, unthinkingly, a commodified discourse that is closer to a mass-produced product on a factory line than it is to a carefully reasoned, painstakingly researched piece of writing aimed at enlightening the lay person on a current affairs topic. Chalaby's important work on the development of a mass commercial newspaper press, *The Invention of Journalism* (1998), contends that journalists working for the popular newspaper press are 'a new breed of discursive producers whose only apparent reason to work in the press was "to give the public what it wants"'.[30] Clint Smoker's prose, a hideous mix of cliché, titillating innuendo, puns and euphemism, is a kind of parallel language not used in ordinary written or spoken discourse:

> The Duke of Clarence played Prince ChowMein last night... Yes, Prince Alf wokked out with his on-again off-again paramour, Lyn Noel, for a slap-up Chinese. But sweet turned to sour when photographers had the sauce to storm their private room. Wan tun a bit of privacy, the couple fled with the lads in hot pursuit – we'll cashew! What happened, back at Ken Pal? Did Alf lai chee? Did he oyster into his arms and give her a crispy duck?[31]

Smoker, who calls *Lark* readers 'wankers', does not trouble himself with concerns over the impact of his 'journalism'. He knows his market: 'The upmarket tabloids are aimed at the Bourgeoisie. The downmarket tabloids are aimed at the proletariat. At the *Lark* our target wanker is unemployed.' He constructs his pornographic copy with the interest and mental capacity of his imagined reader in mind: 'and have your bogroll handy for when gueststar Dork Borgarde pumps his lovepiss over the heaving norks of our very own Donna Strange'.[32] This journalese is reminiscent of the excruciating copy produced by Olyett in Rudyard Kipling's short story 'The Village That Voted the Earth Was Flat' (1914; see Chapter 1): 'the crepuscular penumbra spreading her dim limbs over the boskage', another example, written nine decades earlier of how authors imagine popular newspaper journalists perceive, and cater for, the tastes of their readers.[33] In a typically Amisian piece of irony, Clint falls for a woman, 'k8', who not only writes but speaks in a language more denuded than his own: '@ last – the dex r clearing! He's not a gr8 hint-taker, orl&o, & he hasn't noticed i've stopped talking 2 him, but he has noticed i've stopped making his t.'[34]
Smoker may be at the very lowest rung of the word-production ladder, but there is still a complicity between his devalued industry and that of Amis, which now relies on media packaging, book signings and well-publicized lecture tours to shift units: 'you arrive in each city and present yourself to its media; after that, in the evening, a mediated individual, you appear at the bookshop and perform'.[35]

The cross-currents circulating between writing and celebrity are complex and often murky and *Yellow Dog* as well as other Amis fictions reveal his 'ongoing and uneasy negotiation of the terms of his own celebrity brand'.[36] *Yellow Dog* examines the idea of the celebrity-as-martyr to the tabloid newspaper industry. Smoker's victim is Ainsley Car, once lauded for his prodigious talent and now past his prime: 'One of the most talented footballers of his generation … now up to his armpits in decline'.[37] Smoker assiduously courts Car, standing him cocktails in night clubs and setting him up with a glamour model in a hotel. But Car's demise and imprisonment, engineered by Smoker, when it comes, is barely mentioned: it is just a headline, discussed for a minute by minor characters in the novel before they move on to other subjects. A life destroyed for a brief talking point and an inch or two of newsprint. In *Yellow Dog*, as in Ian McEwan's *Amsterdam* (1998), fame makes a person vulnerable. In *Amsterdam* the Foreign Secretary Julian Garmony, a love-rival to the newspaper editor Vernon Halliday, is exposed as a transvestite because his is a face that everyone recognizes and the black-and-white pictures of the prominent politician in lacy lingerie need no further explanation. Another intrusion into a celebrity's personal agony is depicted in the author and journalist Gordon Burn's *Fullalove* when television star Scott McGovern, lying in a coma, is 'papped' by Norman Miller and the photographer Heath Hawkins. The scene is an echo of the 1990 real-life incident when journalists from the *Sunday Sport* photographed popular television actor Gordon Kaye in Charing Cross Hospital, where he was recovering from head injury. Just weeks before the Calcutt Committee began taking evidence, the incident became 'a landmark in atrocious intrusiveness' although the paper's editor described it as a 'great old-fashioned scoop'.[38] After Miller and Hawkins' intrusion, the dying celebrity's face now looks like a photograph as if the act of taking his picture has changed the human being into a mediatized image of himself. The modern treatment of celebrity was always interesting to Gordon Burn, whose last piece of journalism before he died was an essay for the *Guardian* on the 'famous for being famous' Jade Goody, 'pilloried in the press for her gluttony and ignorance', the minutiae of her short and tragic life played out to the 'crash of the camera shutters'.[39]

The 'quietly famous' actor and author Xan Meo in *Yellow Dog* offers further intimations of Amis' own feelings about his celebrity and a press that will make headlines out of his £20,000 dental surgery.[40] Meo's newly published collection of short stories, *Lucozade*, is still promoted in his High Street bookshop, something which gives Meo quiet satisfaction. But he is vulnerable because of his recognizability: 'Every five minutes someone would smile his way – because they thought they knew him.'[41] Meo's book has caused offence to a ruthless gangster, and the hitman easily identifies the famous writer ('"Are you *the*?" … "Yes I'm *the*"') and inflicts a near-fatal head injury.[42] *Yellow Dog* takes Amis' ongoing meditations on ideas of literary celebrity to absurd and brutal extremes – and the idea of the author's own complicity in the commodification of both his work and his self.

The writer viewed by the public as 'unique visionary' to whom the rest of us look for inspiration and the answers to life's problems has a long history.[43] But until the growth of literacy and the mass media in the late nineteenth century, the public was a select group of the highly educated middle classes. The rise of mass readership 'was accompanied by a growing unease and sense of doom' by writers and intellectuals.[44] Rudyard Kipling, for example, often described as the first 'global' literary celebrity, was uncomfortable with his fame, particularly when it crossed into his private life.[45] He had experienced Boston newspaper reporters making up quotes by him when he refused them an interview and newspaper placards announcing his wedding left him feeling 'uncomfortable and defenceless'.[46] Much of the content of his short story 'The Village That Voted the Earth Was Flat' can be read as an examination of media and celebrity (See Chapter 1). Huckley, the village at the centre of a press storm, is exposed to the 'impersonal and searing curiosity' of the whole world:'in all the zealous, merciless press, Huckley was laid out for it to look at, as a drop of pond water is exposed on the sheet of a magic-lantern show'.[47]

Once again, Kipling's eye for modernity has identified a characteristic of the mass media as it was still in its infancy. Huckley is a passive victim of an 'impersonal' public's curiosity, which does not seek to understand but only to view as one views a curio or spectacle. The image of the drop of water dehumanizes the villagers as well as suggesting their innermost thoughts, secrets and even their bodies, down to a cellular level, are available to view as under a microscope. Similarly Arnold Bennett, another celebrity author, describes press intrusion in his novel *The Pretty Lady* (1918). In this scene, Lady Queenie Paulle, 'who appears nearly every week in either *The Tatler* or the *Sketch*', emerges from the courthouse having given evidence in a notorious trial:'At that moment a press-man with a camera came boldly up and snapped her. The man had the brazen demeanour of a racecourse tout'.[48]

The clearly socially inferior 'pap' has no regard for manners nor indeed class barriers. While *The Tatler* may be an appropriate space for images of society ladies to be reproduced, the newspaper press clearly is not. The ease with which the pressman is able to cross social boundaries to take, and reproduce, Lady Paulle's likeness for the delectation of millions speaks to the 'sense of doom' and powerlessness of those caught in the limelight. Nearly 100 years later, the pursuit of celebrity has become even more aggressive, from the motorbike chase through Paris that led to Princess Diana's death to the terrifying stalking revealed by actress Sienna Miller during her testimony to the Leveson Inquiry.[49]

One literary celebrity who has suffered notorious tabloid intrusion is J. K. Rowling, author of the *Harry Potter* books. In her evidence given to the Leveson Inquiry, Rowling acknowledges 'media interest in my story and my work must have had some beneficial effects on the sales of the first Harry Potter book and every one thereafter'. Her testimony reveals some early kindness from journalists who could see better than she, what was about to hit her. However, most of her testimony dwells on the intrusions, particularly into her children's privacy. At one point during her testimony she revealed: 'I felt as though I were under investigation for a crime I had not committed', a feeling which parallels Harry's persecution by Rita Skeeter.[50] Harry Potter the 'boy wizard' is also a celebrity victim. His experiences at the hands of Rita Skeeter of the *Daily Prophet* mirror those of Rowling herself after she became suddenly famous. Harry is misquoted by Rita and vilified in the *Daily Prophet*. His mediatized image, when presented to his peers at Hogwarts, causes him to be shunned by most students of the school. They are readier to believe the false newspaper image of Harry than the real Harry. Rowling has confessed that after introducing Rita in Book Four (*Harry Potter and the Goblet of Fire*, 2000), she had 'more fun' writing her character because of the experiences she had suffered.[51] As a result, Rowling's series of novels, which have sold more than 400 million copies worldwide and, according to one analysis, have been read by half of all children aged nine to seventeen in 2010, have 'taken numerous unsubtle digs at the credibility and decency of journalists for more than a decade'.[52] An author of J. K. Rowling's stature and reach has the power to mould the public image of the journalist in an act of literary revenge that puts Rita Skeeter not far below the Death Eaters in the hierarchy of evil in the books. The lying, intrusive, manipulative journalist has joined such archetypes as the Jesus-figure (Dumbledore/Harry Potter) and the ideal mother (Mrs Weasley).

War correspondents in crisis

The journalists in a quartet of contemporary novels about war reporters have all been affected by their work in recent conflicts: The first Gulf War (*Complicity* by Iain Banks (1993)), Bosnia (*Double Vision* by Pat Barker (2003)), Afghanistan (*We Are Now Beginning Our Descent* by James Meek (2008)) and the second Gulf War (*Devil's Feather* by Minette Walters (2004)). The novels all emphasize the modern war correspondent's limitations and/or vulnerability in the theatre of conflict. In *Complicity*, the hero Cameron Colley's descent into drug-assisted breakdown stems from his inability, when faced with the horrors of the Basra Road slaughter, to report what he has witnessed. In *Double Vision* Stephen Sharkey's breakdown is prompted by the horrific vision of a dead Bosnian girl in a bombed-out apartment in Sarajevo. In *We Are Now Beginning Our Descent*, Adam Kellas experiences a delayed breakdown when, during a smug dinner party for the liberal-left intelligentsia, the war in Afghanistan, from whence he has recently returned, is lightly dismissed. In *Devil's Feather* Reuters correspondent Connie Burns herself becomes the victim of a serial rapist mercenary in the ungoverned mayhem of Baghdad following the US-led 'Shock and Awe' assault (see Chapter 7).

While fiction about war reporters has been a familiar subgenre of 'newspaper' novels for more than 100 years, emphasis in previous periods has been on the 'manly' virtues of the intrepid adventurer not afraid to wield his own pistol and endure multiple hardships in a *Boy's Own* kind of way (see, particularly, Chapter 1). Even Thomas Fowler in Graham Greene's *The Quiet American*, while unwittingly letting us into his subconscious, has a typically macho approach to the dangers he faces: 'It occurred to me that if something happened to me in this street it might be many hours before I was picked up: time for the flies to collect' (see Chapter 4).[53] An efflorescence, then, of novels portraying a very different kind of war correspondent needs exploring. It can partly be explained by the emergence of what has now been labelled as 'the journalism of attachment', a phrase coined by former BBC journalist Martin Bell after the Bosnian war (1992–1995). Marking a dividing line between correspondence from previous conflicts, Bell describes this new kind of war journalism as 'a journalism that cares as well as knows' as opposed to an earlier kind of war correspondence he calls '"bystanders journalism" – being on stage and shedding light on events, but not affecting or being affected by them'.[54] He continues that previous conflicts – Vietnam and Israel in the 1960s – were about 'strategies, military formations and weapons systems', but that after Bosnia, 'it was about people – the people who wage war and the people who suffer from war'.[55] This is nonsense of course. One only needs to read the deeply engaged despatches from war zones revealing the extent of civilian suffering – Martha Gellhorn from a bomb-torn Finland during the Second World War, Wilfred Burchett from the Hiroshima aftermath, John Burrowes from Vietnam, Nell McCafferty from Northern Ireland – to see how far from the truth Martin Bell's assertions are.[56] There is even a limited amount of journalism from the First World War which details the effects of war on civilians (see Chapter 7).[57] Journalists' memoirs from earlier conflicts, too, reveal that being affected by what they witness is not just a modern phenomenon.[58]

Where Bell may have a point is in the rise of real-time television journalism from war zones, which places the flak-jacketed correspondent right in the centre of the viewer's gaze, which is very different from the impersonal newspaper byline. In addition, in the Balkan Conflicts particularly, the suffering of civilians was emphasized over military tactics. Indeed in this conflict, where journalists arrived before UN peacekeepers, it has been argued that the 'emotional attachment' shown by reporters compelled politicians to act. For analysts Miles Hudson and John Stanier, 'The catalyst which finally compelled the world to react was the combined force of the world's press and television. Probably never before had the influence of the media been more powerfully felt by the governments of the world.'[59] Since the first Gulf War (1990–1991), television had finally asserted its dominance over the written press, beaming its images 'by satellite to waiting multitudes whose hunger for news was insatiable.'[60] It was 'the first war to appear on TV screens as a kind of *son et lumiere* display, the first where the bombardment of enemy forces acquired the bloodless precision of a video game' as portrayed in one novelist's account.[61] Since then, the correspondent, often in quasi-military gear, delivering his or her report against a backdrop of destruction, ducking every so often as a shell whizzes past, has trumped, for mass audiences, even the finest written report. In a recent study of the representation of war correspondents in fiction and memoir, Barbara Korte argues that the characteristics of fictional correspondents are shaped by the dominant medium through which the public gains experience of the war correspondent at work: 'Representations provide material for a cultural reading of war correspondents: they indicate dominant cultural conceptions of correspondents.'[62] The image of the war correspondent has thus been shaped in recent years by television, even though, curiously, the four fictional correspondents surveyed here are all press reporters. This may be because a press reporter, with only his or her notebook and pen, or laptop, is for the creative writer a more vulnerable agent than a TV correspondent, who is often seen with cameraman, sound crew and hefty jeep to cart all the expensive equipment around in.

Bell's genre of journalism has been criticized by fellow correspondents including his former BBC colleague John Simpson, as well as other contemporary commentators.[63] Bell and his kind stand accused of 'turning the world's war zones into private battlefields where troubled journalists can fight for their own souls'.[64] However, it was imitated by many of his colleagues, including ITN correspondent Michael Nicholson, who went so far as adopting a girl orphaned by the conflict and who famously discarded the 'so-called objectivity' in favour of displaying 'emotional anguish'.[65] This 'attached' way of reporting, actively expressing emotion and seeking to evince emotional reaction in viewers has clearly had an impact on the way novelists portray the character of the journalist. If the journalist is no longer an impervious bystander, the opposite must be true: that he or she is powerfully affected, indeed traumatized, by the horrors he or she is witnessing. This, combined with the military's increasingly sophisticated public relations techniques, and the impact of real-time images of warfare on both the viewing public and the reporter have, says commentator Greg McLaughlin, contributed to 'a crisis in the role and function of the war reporter … these all put into question the ability or willingness of the journalist to be imaginative, to say something meaningful about the nature of modern warfare'.[66] The clearest examples of this effect in fiction are Pat Barker's *Double Vision* and Iain Banks' *Complicity*. As in previous historical periods (see particularly Chapters 2, 5 and 6), these contemporary writers have also apprehended a moment of important change, a cultural shift long before scholars and historians have constructed a theoretical framework for its study. Iain Banks' novel *Complicity* is constructed around a single incident, 'the one place I've hidden from myself' that has occasioned the narrator Cameron Colley's breakdown. This incident happened on the Basra Road, where coalition air forces had destroyed an enormous column of Iraqis – civilians and military – fleeing Kuwait, a slaughter which had been described by the pilots themselves as a 'turkey shoot'.[67] Faced with having to make sense of what he sees, Colley is lost for words:

> it was put right there in front of me practically screaming at me to *fucking write something* – I couldn't do it … I just stood there, awestruck, horrorstruck, absorbing the ghastly force of it with my inadequate and unprepared *private* humanity … My body shook, my ears rang, my eyes burned, my throat was raw with the acid-bitter stench of the evaporating crude, but it was as though the very ferocity of the experience unmanned me, unmade me and rendered me incapable of telling it.[68]

Colley's body is invaded by war through the ears, eyes and mouth, leaving him unable to do the one thing he was sent to Iraq to do: to tell the truth about the conflict. The blinking cursor on the blank screen taunts him, a reminder that despite technological advances, a reporter is nothing if he or she can't distil words out of events made up of noise, images and smells. Compare Colley's late twentieth-century self-doubt to that of Rudyard Kipling's Gilbert Torpenhow and Dick Heldar, brave foreign correspondents covering British-Egyptian forces and their battles with the Mahdi in Sudan:

> The Soudan campaign was a picturesque one, and lent itself to vivid word-painting. Now and again a 'Special' managed to get slain – which was not

altogether a disadvantage to the paper than employed him – and more often the hand-to-hand nature of the fighting allowed of miraculous escapes which were worth telegraphing home at eighteenpence the word.[69]

Pat Barker's novel *Double Vision* takes Banks' idea of the correspondent rendered wordless by what he has seen as a starting point from which to examine the ways human suffering is represented in journalism and the arts, and the limitations of both. The foreign correspondent Stephen Sharkey has been traumatized by the sight of a dead Bosnian girl in Sarajevo: 'Eyes wide open, skirt bunched up around her waist, her splayed thighs enclosing a blackness of blood and pain.'[70] Sharkey leaves journalism and goes to convalesce in the wide open spaces of Northumberland, where he works on a book which examines the way wars are represented in painting, photography and film.[71] The novel explores several methods of conveying human cruelty and suffering, and asks us to assess whether any representations can adequately express the pain and humiliation we inflict on each other. Four images dominate: Goya's Prison Scene from the Spanish Peninsular War, which several characters in the novel go to see at the Bowes Museum; the picture taken of the raped girl by Sharkey's now-dead photographer friend; television news footage of American bombing raids in Bosnia and Iraq; and an enormous sculpture of the crucified Christ which is taking shape throughout the timeline of the novel. The sculptor Kate finds the Goya painting more powerful than any photographic image:

> The interior of a prison, seven men in shackles, every tone, every line expressing despair ... she wondered how any photograph, however great, could prompt the same complexity of response as this painting. Photographs shock, terrify, arouse compassion, anger, even drive people to take action, but does the photograph of an atrocity ever inspire hope? This did ... seeing this scene through Goya's steady and compassionate eye it was impossible to feel anything as simple or as trivial as despair.[72]

These meditations then lead her to question her dead photographer husband's reckless efforts to obtain war pictures, efforts which ultimately led to his death from a sniper's bullet in Afghanistan. But Kate has her own form of 'Double Vision': choosing only to sculpt male figures, as she believes women have the 'wrong body' to explore heroic pain and suffering, a position undermined by her own husband's war photography and the woman in Sarajevo whose violent death has prompted Sharkey's breakdown.[73] Modern television news appears to be the least satisfactory medium of all in helping people understand the human cost of warfare as it presents a 'sanitized' version of warfare to make it palatable to Western audiences: 'on the television screens, puffs of brown smoke appeared underneath the cross-hairs of the precision sights. Doubly screened from reality, the audience watched, yawned, scratched... And all the while, under the little spurts of brown dust, this. A child torn to pieces. Human bodies baked like dog turds in the sun.'[74]

Technology has a lot to answer for in all these novels. It gives pilots the ability to claim 'surgical strikes' on human targets and it satisfies the viewing public's thirst for information about war without asking people to contemplate the suffering caused: 'Nothing as vulgar as blood was ever allowed to appear.' It also contributes to journalists' unwitting dehumanization of 'the enemy' who, in James Meek's novel, is reduced to mere pixels by a long lens digital camera: the 'black vertical a few pixels high... Kellas couldn't be sure. Maybe it was a gap in the rock. Sheryl had lenses the size of buckets.'[75]

A gap in the rock or a human being: either way the Californians viewing the image in the morning, over coffee, would be more interested in 'the exact monumental broccoli shapes their bombs made in the sky' rather than what was underneath them. In *We Are Now Beginning Our Descent* the impersonal, distant B-52 bombers, chalking white stripes across the blue sky, contrast with a few 'good' journalists' attempts to get close to the people on the ground and report their suffering. Kellas realizes it is ultimately a doomed exercise, and his best efforts will never come close to conveying the truth of human suffering, due to the limitations of journalism and the public's fragmented attention span. To that extent, Kellas ultimately concludes that reporters who stand by and watch are as culpable as the pilots. Astrid, the magazine journalist, who becomes Kellas' lover and also his conscience, also realizes this: '"Oh it was my bomb," said Astrid absently. "They're all my bombs."'[76]

These contemporary novels then deliver a bleak assessment of journalists' attempts to report modern warfare. Although Cameron Colley still believes that for all journalism's faults 'it's still better than nothing,'[77] James Meek and Pat Barker, for different reasons, are not so sure, or at least not about instant-reaction, mass-produced television and online journalism. The trouble is, that is how most of us receive information about foreign conflict. Whether or not journalism's benefits outweigh the problems it creates is also a theme of several contemporary playwrights' work, discussed below.

Journalists on stage

Eight dramas written between 1972 and 2014 chart the history of newspaper journalism over the past forty years and together they construct a narrative of decline. Arnold Wesker's *The Journalists* (1972) and Tom Stoppard's *Night and Day* (1978) both problematize aspects of the trade, particularly the journalist's need to fit complex events into a simple narrative. However, both also temper criticism with acknowledgement of the importance of a 'free press' in informing the public of world events and the existence of 'good' journalists who genuinely aspire to report accurately and fairly, sometimes at great personal risk.[78] Stoppard gives his famous lines, 'it's worse in places where everybody is kept in the dark, it really is. Information is light', to veteran war photographer George Guthrie, as a last word following two hours of discussion on newspapers' strengths and weaknesses.[79] Certainly the cacophonous, irreverent and occasionally crude British press is seen as preferable to the single newspaper run by Dictator General Mageeba's relative in the fictitious Kambawe, where the action is set. Similarly Michael Frayn's *Alphabetical Order* (1975), although a satire on the journalist's vain attempts to impose order on a disordered world, presents the staff of a provincial newspaper as sympathetic, if pedantic logophiles: (John) 'With gold I associate words like endomorphic, somatic, meridional, holistic. Silver I tend to locate in a cluster which contains ectomorphic, cerebral, nocturnal, analytic.'[80] In *The Journalists*, during periods of inactivity, members of the arts pages discuss the relative merits of D. H. Lawrence, Shakespeare and Tolstoy, echoes of Philip Gibbs' erudite newsroom of 1909. The well-financed *Sunday Paper*, based on Harry Evans' *Sunday Times*, attracts 'the best minds' in the country and has correspondents in every foreign capital and its business staff cover: 'Industry subdivided into heavy, light, state-owned and private. Economic management. Industrial relations. International monetary control. The stock market, takeovers, interpretations of balance sheets, the impact of new technology.'[81] Forty years later in *Enquirer* (2012), 'Maureen' complains:

> There's nobody here. No staff, no coverage, no planning, no support. No fucking notepads. They took away the stationary cupboards. This paper used to keep a desk in Timbuktu, in Vladivostock, in Papua New Guinea. We used to keep a man and a phone in Alice Springs, just in case a UFO suddenly dropped from the sky. Now we don't even have anyone in fucking Manchester.[82]

David Edgar's *Wreckers* (1977), written for the 7:84 Theatre Company, although earlier than *Night and Day*, carries criticism of the press more in keeping with the later dramas. As the enemy of progressive politics, the mainstream press is accused of commodifying human misery as 'Sob Story/A glorious gory story/A darn good yarn' and of being a 'lie-factory', abusing language in pursuance of ideological ends: (Paul) ' how odd it is that when the Right's active it's healthy democracy, but when it's the Left it's a sinister conspiracy.[83] Criticism then mounts through the decades, in David Hare and Howard Brenton's *Pravda* (1985), Doug Lucie's *The Shallow End* (1997) and Richard Bean's post-Leveson *Great Britain* (2014). These three dramas, when read as a trio, chart the advance of a pornographic, hubristic industry and demands the mesmerized audience to acknowledge its complicity in creating a monster at the heart of public life. As the Leveson Inquiry was taking evidence the National Theatre of Scotland's *Enquirer* (2012) asks us to consider what a world without newspaper journalism, despite its shortcomings, would look like.

Playwrights operate within an interesting sphere vis-á-vis newspapers. Although they are part of the same broad field of cultural production as novelists and poets, Bourdieu contends that writers for the theatre operate further from the cultural pole because of their interest in immediate political and social events, their dependence on an audience coming to watch and the relatively high production costs of theatre compared, say, with poetry.[84] These distinctions, particularly in terms of cost, are of course blurred by subgenres such as the amateur theatre groups of the Left which emerged during the 1930s and from which much of the political theatre of the later twentieth century took inspiration.[85] Theatre, when it is about social and political issues, is more powerful when it has a hot-off-the-press immediacy, giving it contemporary impact as well as sometimes a short shelf life. Its topicality, particularly in asking an audience to confront a disquieting social or political issue, is a source of political theatre's strength, says Howard Brenton: 'It's important to make connections with what the audience already knows. I don't think of myself as writing plays to last, but to be performed at the time I write them.'[86]

David Hare also asserts that (unsurprisingly, perhaps), particularly since 1945, the theatre is the best venue for social and political discussion: 'If you want to study the social history of Britain since the war, then your time will be better spent studying the plays of the period ... than by looking at any comparable documentary source.'[87] One review of *Great Britain*, which draws heavily on the Leveson hearings and the trials of former *News of the World* executives Andy Couslon and Rebekah Brooks, praises it precisely for its immediacy: 'The really good thing is that it's here. Rat-a-tat satire on the South Bank. No other art form has reacted with such speed, stealth and pizzazz to recent news.'[88]

The 1930s Unity Theatre 'Living Newspaper' productions were written, ᵉarsed and staged within weeks of important political events, sometimes, in ˙se of *Crisis*, in reaction to the Munich Crisis, within hours.[89] Journalism's like political theatre, is linked to its close connection with actual events, a source both of its strength and its perceived weaknesses. These similarities make for theatre's complicated relationship with newspapers and, in particular, the newspaper critic. Arnold Wesker acknowledged the high dependence theatre has on the newspaper critic, who can make audiences disappear, or throng to a production, with words 'made seductively omnipotent by print'. Unlike poetry, a highly autonomous art form, a play, like a newspaper, is nothing without an audience for the moment it is delivered. After a particularly bruising series of reviews of his play *The Friends*, Wesker proposed that newspaper critics should read manuscripts of plays, attend rehearsals and come to productions one at a time rather than en masse to avoid a play becoming submerged under an avalanche of poor reviews all published on the same day.[90] In his diary of *The Journalists'* incubation, he records that 'my own zest for work, public actions, and myself had become eroded by reviews, journalistic profiles and columnists' attacks'.[91] It was with these feelings of personal affront that Wesker decided to investigate whether the figure of the journalist might be an interesting subject for a drama:

> To what extent does the journalist damage himself when he engages in constant attack of others? Is there an element of self-destruction in him which is sufficiently true of other people to make him a subject for drama? Doesn't he reflect a special kind of mentality – which might be called Lilliputian – which operates in all of us when we feel ourselves to be failures?[92]

Here then is an example of an agent positioned in one part of the field of cultural production engaged in close combat with other agents occupying adjacent positions within the field. Wesker is acknowledging that journalistic agents, although inferior to playwrights in terms of cultural capital, have, in their role as gatekeepers to public opinion, the power to bestow both cultural and economic capital on agents such as he. David Hare makes similar observations over newspaper critics' reactions to *Pravda*, in an essay which asserts both the theatre's greater cultural capital and the jealous actions of journalistic agents who are aware of their inferiority:

> In Britain a great deal of what appears in the newspapers about the theatre and television is motivated by simple jealousy. By and large American tourists do not pile off planes at Heathrow and ask how soon they can buy a hot edition of the latest *Sunday Times*. They ask the way to *Cats* and the National Theatre. Journalists know this and it annoys them.[93]

Wesker spent two months visiting the *Sunday Times* in order to garner material and ideas for characters for his play. Reality, however, clashed with imagination when Wesker discovered 'the *Sunday Times* under Harold Evans was an enlightened place. I was really quite surprised when I spent two months in their offices, that most of the journalists I met were impressive and honourable. I came away thinking that I was going to end up with a positive portrait'.[94] In the play, which was never produced commercially, the 'Liliputian' columnist Mary Mortimer is thus disparaged, restrained and disliked by the editor, and other journalists working on the *Sunday Paper*.[95]

A key change between *The Journalists* and *Pravda*, written ten years later, is the transformation of the newspaper from primarily a vehicle for the discussion of ideas and spreading political influence to a money-generating business. The two later plays, *The Shallow End* by Doug Lucie (1997) and *Great Britain* by Richard Bean (2014), also make this point. The pre-Murdoch *Sunday Paper* in *The Journalists* is staffed with 'brilliant left-wing journalists' trying to undermine the conservative Establishment from within.[96] Wesker was writing *The Journalists* during the *Sunday Times*' famous campaign to win bigger compensation for the victims of Thalidomide from the Distillers conglomerate, manufacturers of the drug. Harold Evans' diary notes that when he told the advertising manager of the articles about to be published, the manager first pointed out that Distillers was the paper's biggest single advertiser, spending £600,000 a year, and then added: 'I know that won't stop you and it shouldn't.'[97] Newspapers were of course more profitable in the 1970s than they are now, but if we compare this incident to the famous *Telegraph* repression of criticism of the banking giant HSBC in 2015, it is clear we are operating in very different worlds. In *The Shallow End* the unnamed Sunday newspaper exists only really to promote the owner's new cable television channels. In *Pravda*, Le Roux chooses Andrew May as the new editor of *The Victory* for his policy of jettisoning news pages and replacing them with pages of classified advertising, a successful policy and one which, apparently, the reading public either doesn't mind or doesn't notice. In the Britain of Lambert Le Roux and Margaret Thatcher, people's minds are 'fogging … clogging … decaying … silting up … with falsehood', a resuscitation of the intellectual anxiety of the interwar years (see Chapter 3).[98] These dramas all raise the question of press standards, what *Guardian* reviewer Michael Billington, in his review of *Great Britain*, calls 'the thorniest question'.[99] In *Night and Day*, the gutter press is a sign that a free press is in a healthy condition: 'evidence of a society that has got at least one thing right, that there should be nobody with the power to dictate where responsible journalism begins'.[100] The later plays are more critical and force the audience to confront its support of vast media conglomerates through its purchase of semi-pornographic material and propaganda dressed up as political journalism. In *The Shallow End*, this effect is achieved literally by staging an apparently live sex act between a journalist and a waitress during an entire scene. In *Pravda*, the hyperactive Le Roux contrasts with the passive reading public that has allowed its watchdog of democracy to sink into the abyss. When his corrupted editor questions Le Roux of how he apparently effortlessly accrues power and influence, Le Roux answers, 'People like you'; although the answer is directed at his editor, it is certainly for the audience too.[101] In *Great Britain*, Paige Britain, although only a news editor, is in energy and power a twenty-first-century Le Roux: 'Every morning I have to give the public what they want. And what do they want? Tits, bingo and the death penalty for paedophiles.'[102] Her final and direct address to the audience also asks them as newspaper readers to confront their hypocrisy over phone hacking: nobody complained when celebrities' sexual indiscretions were exposed, apart from the celebrities themselves, she points out. Similarly in *Enquirer*, Gabe says: 'I think the group of people who haven't been on trial in the Leveson Inquiry are the British Public, you know, three million of whom bought the *News of the World* every fucking week, because they wanted to read that stuff – how do they think they fucking got those pictures?'

What exactly is journalism *for*?

The period under review here was marked, particularly in the early phase, by newspapers of all types pursuing investigative journalism, which exposed for readers the ways in which power works to maintain its grasp over politics, industry and finance. With its roots in the 1960s, investigative journalism flowered in the 1970s but continues as a strong part of newspapers' appeal today. In the 1970s newspapers invested heavily in investigative journalism, most notably the Insight team on Harold Evans' *Sunday Times*. On television, Granada's *World in Action* provided viewers for the first time with a physical image of the investigative journalist. Initially the programmes were a simple airing of contemporary issues by a disembodied narrator, rather than an investigation by an on-screen reporter, but the reporter began to be a more permanent fixture in the 1970s, beginning with John Pilger's award-winning *The Quiet Mutiny* about GIs in Vietnam in 1970. His image, and that of other *World in Action* reporters, open-necked shirts, shoulder-length hair, manly-yet-sensitive persona, would provide a model for film portrayals of journalists on both sides of the Atlantic from the 1970s onwards.[103] While fictions of this period contain justifiably savage attacks on tabloid newspaper standards, there is little acknowledgement in the novels of the important role newspapers play in a liberal democracy, particularly, latterly, as circulations continue their rapid descent. Novelists on the whole choose to highlight the trade's obvious shortcomings and are almost silent on the role of newspapers in holding power to account, which many, particularly the *Guardian*, *Sunday Times* and *Daily Mail*, still do on a regular basis. This may be because, as James Meek says, 'It's very difficult to present in a novel a crusading journalist who is going to change the world. A sympathetic journalist would be kind of preachy today. Journalists in fiction make particularly unpleasant characters.'[104] This may also be because in recent years journalism has been seen to have failed in its biggest challenges: the lack of scrutiny of Tony Blair's prospectus for the second Gulf War in 2002–2003 and the failure of financial journalists to foresee the banking crisis of 2008.

Theatre at least pays grudging respect. During the 1970s, playwrights including Trevor Griffiths, Barry Keeffe and David Edgar 'borrowed' investigative journalism techniques in their exposés of British life from the fate of borstal boys to striking dock workers and the rise of the National Front, an example of how journalism occasionally influences other genres within the broader field of cultural production. This has happened before, in the way vivid eyewitness reportage of battlefields and urban poverty in the late nineteenth and early twentieth centuries influenced writers of fiction (see Chapter 1), and, in America, when the 'new journalism' of Tom Wolfe, Truman Capote and Hunter S. Thompson influenced fiction techniques (and vice versa, see Chapter 6).[105] The plays in addition ask more questions about the future of newspapers, highlighting differences in the way journalism is represented in prose and in the theatre. The playwright David Edgar had spent three years on the *Bradford Telegraph and Argus*, where he had acquired some experience of investigative journalism covering local authority corruption.[106] While Edgar ultimately rejects the 'journalistic mind' that only retains, like a colander, immediately useful information, he appreciates the discipline, and results, of investigative journalism. Similarly in *The Journalists*, *Night and Day* and the *Shallow End* investigative journalism and foreign correspondence are deliberately singled out as parts of the trade that are worth both praising and saving. By the time of Richard Bean's *Great Britain*, investigative journalism has sunk into hacking celebrities' phones and rifling their rubbish bins.

Many of the fictions discussed here raise the problem of representation: how journalism can adequately represent such a confusing, complex and irrational world. These problems range from the business reporter Dominic in Wesker's *The Journalists* suggesting that all newspapers should carry a disclaimer on their front page – 'Warning! The selective attention to data herein contained may warp

your view of the world' – to the editors of Adam Kellas' newspaper
Now Beginning Our Descent preferring 'the punchy certainties of una
sources' far from Afghanistan to his 'nuanced inconclusive........ ... the
uncertainties of the journalist who actually was [there]'.[107] Far from the bold
confidence of the Edwardian self-styled 'truth-tellers', contemporary fictions
reflect a vast well of self-doubt, on the one hand, and, a cynical hubris, on the
other. One of the problems of journalism is that its benefits to society are so
intangible. The benefits of medicine can be seen in waiting lists, cancer survival
rates and life expectancy increases. The benefits of the legal justice system can
be measured in recidivism rates, miscarriages of justice and crime statistics; and
that of education, in GCSE pass rates and world ranking tables of numeracy
and literacy. How can we measure the benefits of good journalism? In political
scandals exposed? In electoral participation? These questions, however, raise a
second and fundamental problem with most forms of journalism: we expect it
to operate like a public service such as education and the law, but it is, in fact,
a private enterprise. With declining sales and profitability, it appears that only
billionaire proprietors, cross-subsidy, an exclusive readership willing to pay to
read behind the paywall or liberal doses of sex and scandal can save them.

Notes

1   From *Enquirer* (2012). David Mellor MP's memorable phrase: 'I do believe the
    popular press is drinking in the last chance saloon', spoken on Channel 4's *Hard
    News* Programme on 21 December 1989 has now become shorthand for criticism of
    British tabloids. The phrase of course has achieved a degree of irony, and received
    several embellishments some 25 years on. For example, media academic Tom
    O'Malley, in criticizing another Parliamentary Select Committee for ducking the
    issue of press behaviour writes: 'The Select Committee ... has left the music blaring,
    the lights glaring, and the Lords, tycoons, conglomerates and their hired hands free
    to carry on getting drunk and disorderly in the Last Chance Saloon.' Blog posted on
    the Campaign for Press and Broadcasting Freedom website 23/1/2010 http://www.
    cpbf.org.uk/body.php?id=558&selpanel=1 accessed 10 April 2015.
2   Mengham, Rod, 'General Introduction: Contemporary British Fiction', in Bentley,
    Nick (ed.), *Contemporary British Fiction*, pp. 11–12.
3   Bentley, Nick, *Contemporary British Fiction*, p. 2.
4   Griffiths, Dennis, *Fleet Street*, pp. 362 & 357.
5   'GOTCHA' 4 May 1982; 'UP YOURS DELORS' 1 November 1990.
6   Horrie, Chris, *Tabloid Nation*, pp. 165–166.

7   *Daily Mirror* 8 May 1982.

8   Quoted in Leapman, Michael, *Treacherous Estate*, p. 14. Hugh Cudlipp. Cudlipp, at twenty-four, had been the youngest editor of a Fleet Street newspaper, the *Sunday Pictorial*, before being editor of the *Sunday Express* and then editorial director of the *Mirror* and *Sunday Pictorial*. He had been at the heart of the British popular press from the mid-1930s to his retirement in 1973.

9   Forster, Peter, *The Spike*, p. 21.

10 Polly Toynbee, 'Ghastly Man', obituary of Auberon Waugh 19 January 2001. http://www.theguardian.com/books/2001/jan/19/news.comment (accessed 21 April 2015).

11 Wilson, A. N., *My Name Is Legion*, p. 86.

12 The *Independent*, staffed with many Wapping 'refuseniks', was launched in October 1986. For more detail see Griffiths, *Fleet Street*, p. 372.

13 See Wingate, Pauline, 'Newsprint' in *Newspapers and Democracy* (1980). Wingate quotes newsprint costs as having risen from £59.06 per tonne in 1957 to £229.36 per tonne in 1976, with the sharpest rises occurring between 1973 and 1974 (p. 71). This meant that the average annual cost of bringing out a national newspaper rose from nearly £1.6 million in 1946 to more than £28 million in 1974.

14 Curran, James, 'The Human Interest Story', p. 299.

15 See the conclusion for more on the print-digital dilemma. The phrase 'Twitter Twat' is used pejoratively in the American Netflix series *House of Cards* (Series One, 2013) by traditional *Washington Herald* political correspondent Janine Skorsky in describing new reporter Zoe Barnes. Both journalists end up moving to the online news outlet *Slugline*. The impact of digital changes to newspapers was highlighted by the public resignation of Peter Oborne as the *Daily Telegraph*'s chief political commentator in February 2015. In his resignation letter he decried the loss of the newspaper's editor Tony Gallagher and his replacement with a 'Head of Content' the American Jason Seiken. Oborne's resignation letter: https://www.opendemocracy.net/ourkingdom/peter-oborne/why-i-have-resigned-from-telegraph (accessed 2 March 2015).

16 Burn, Gordon, *Fullalove*, p. 1.

17 Gibbs, Philip, *Street of Adventure*, p. 47.

18 Journalism and the theatre, however, still share some fundamental characteristics such as the need for an immediate audience and are still thus engaged in struggles with each other. These will be discussed later on in the chapter.

19 Ibid., pp. 5 & 13.

20 Wilson, A. N., *My Name Is Legion*, pp. 153 & 158.

21 Interview with A. N. Wilson.

22 Meek, James, *We Are Now Beginning Our Descent*, p. 115.

23 Waugh, Evelyn, *Waugh in Abyssinia*, p. 157.

24 Interview with James Meek.

25 *Guardian* 3 March 2015.

26 Shannon, Richard, *A Press Free and Responsible*, pp. 14–15.

27 See for example Milne, Seamus, *The Enemy Within* (1994), Williams, Granville, *Shafted: The Media, the Miners' Strike and the Aftermath* (2009) and Mayes, Tessa, *Disclosure: Media Freedom and the Privacy Debate after Diana* (1998).

28 See for example Shannon, *A Press Free*, particularly Chapter 7, pp. 135–153.

29 See for example Curran, 'The Human Interest Story', pp. 305–306.

30 Chalaby, Jean, *The Invention of Journalism*, pp. 184–185 & 187.

31 Amis, Martin, *Yellow Dog*, p. 22.

32 Ibid., p. 77.

33 Kipling, Rudyard, 'The Village …', p. 172.

34 Amis, *Yellow Dog*, p. 172.

35 Amis, Martin, *Experience: A Memoir*, p. 275.

36 Mickalites, Carey James, 'Martin Amis's *Money*: Negotiations with Literary Celebrity' in *Postmodern Culture* 24/1.

37 Amis, *Yellow Dog*, p. 40.

38 Shannon, *A Press Free*, p. 28.

39 http://www.theguardian.com/books/2009/mar/07/gordon-burn (accessed 25 September 2015).

40 The dental procedure to straighten and whiten Amis' teeth was widely reported in 1995 http://www.independent.co.uk/life-style/health-and-families/health-news/the-price-of-perfect-teeth-525488.html (accessed 20 September 2015).

41 Ibid., p. 9.

42 Ibid., p. 13.

43 Ommundsen, Wenche, 'From the Altar to the Market-Place and Back Again: Understanding Literary Celebrity', p. 250.

44 Demoor, Marysa, *Marketing the Author*, p. 2.

45 See for example Montefiore, Jan, *Rudyard Kipling*, p. 125.

46 Kipling, Rudyard, *Something*, p. 55.

47 Kipling, 'The Village …', p. 191.

48 Bennett, Arnold, *The Pretty Lady*, pp. 87 & 246.

49 http://webarchive.nationalarchives.gov.uk/20140122145147/http://www.levesoninquiry.org.uk/wp-content/uploads/2011/11/Witness-Statement-of-Sienna-Miller.pdf (accessed 28 March 2015).

50 http://webarchive.nationalarchives.gov.uk/20140122145147/http://www.levesoninquiry.org.uk/wp-content/uploads/2011/11/Witness-Statement-of-JK-Rowling2.pdf (accessed 28 March 2015).

51 http://www.ew.com/article/2000/09/07/jk-rowling-explains-why-harry-potter-and-goblet-fire-was-hardest-write (accessed 27 March 2015).

52 Stewart, Daxton, 'Harry Potter and the Exploitative Jackals', pp. 1–2.

53 Greene, Graham, *The Quiet American*, p. 42.

54 Bell, Martin, *Through Gates of Fire*, pp. 152 & 158.

55   Ibid., p. 163.

56   For Martha Gellhorn's despatches from Finland see her collection *The Face of War*. For Burchett's despatch from Hiroshima see his collection *Rebel Journalism: The Writings of Wilfred Burchett*. For the effects of visiting a Vietnamese children's hospital, see John Burrowes' *Frontline Report: A Journalist's Notebook*, pp. 30–31. For Nell McCafferty's despatches from the Irish Troubles, see *The Best of Nell*.

57   See for example *Daily Telegraph* Saturday 8 January 1916 'The Human Side' by John Raphael.

58   John Burrowes' memoirs of covering the Vietnam War refers to a 'war happy' photographer who would come back to Press Centre 'raving' from what he has seen during the day. 'The war affects us all some way. That's just the screwy way it's got to him,' observes another journalist (pp. 57–58).

59   Hudson, Miles and John Stanier, *War and the Media*, p. 278.

60   Ibid., p. 209.

61   Barker, Pat, *Double Vision*, p. 241.

62   Korte, Barbara, *Represented Reporters*, p.17.

63   Bell, *Through Gates*, p. 152.

64   McLaughlin, Greg, *The War Correspondent*, p. 153.

65   Bell, *Through Gates*, p. 152; Nicholson, Michael, *Natasha's Story: Welcome to Sarajevo* (1992) was made into a film directed by Michael Winterbottom. His comments about objectivity are quoted in McLaughlin, *The War Correspondent*, p. 154.

66   McLaughlin, *The War Correspondent*, p. 4.

67   Hudson and Stanier *War and the Media*, p. 237.

68   Banks, Iain, *Complicity*, pp. 290–291.

69   Kipling, Rudyard, The Light That Failed (1891), Chapter 2 (accessed via Project Gutenberg http://www.gutenberg.org/files/2876/2876-h/2876-h.htm).

70   Barker, *Double Vision*, p. 52.

71   Ibid., p. 57.

72   Ibid., p. 152.

73   Ibid., p. 156.

74   Ibid., p. 131.

75   Meek, *We Are Now Beginning*, p. 9.

76   Ibid., p. 21.

77   Banks, Iain, *Complicity*, p. 299.

78   Although Wesker had completed the script of *The Journalists* by the autumn of 1972, actors from the RSC for whom it had been written refused to perform it. It received a public reading in Highgate in 1975 and was performed by an amateur group in Coventry in 1977.

79   Stoppard, Tom, *Night and Day*, p. 91.

80   Frayn, Michael, *Alphabetical Order*, p. 8.

81 Wesker, Arnold, *The Journalists*, pp. 26 & 135.

82 From *Enquirer* manuscript, reproduced with kind permission from the National Theatre of Scotland, *London Review of Books* and Andrew O'Hagan. *Enquirer* is based on verbatim interviews with forty-five practising journalists.

83 Edgar, David, *Wreckers*, pp. 30 & 37.

84 Bourdieu, *Rules of Art*, p. 124.

85 Page, Malcolm, 'The Early Years at Unity', *Theatre Quarterly* 1/IV October–December 1971, pp. 60–66.

86 Howard Brenton quoted in Kerensy, Oleg, *The New British Drama*, pp. 223–224.

87 Hare, David, 'Introduction' in *Writing Left-Handed*, p. xi.

88 Clapp, Susannah, 'Great Britain Review: A Pleasurable Sharing of Scepticism and Scorn', *Observer* 6 July 2014: http://www.theguardian.com/stage/2014/jul/06/great-britain-review-skit-a-minute (accessed 1 May 2015).

89 Page, Malcolm, The Early Years at Unity, p. 64.

90 Wesker, Arnold, 'Casual Condemnations: A Brief Study of the Critic as Censor', *Theatre Quarterly* 1/II April–June 1971, pp. 16–30.

91 Wesker, Arnold, 'A Journal of the Writing of the Journalists', *The Journalists, a Triptych*, p. 143.

92 Ibid., p. 144.

93 Hare, David, 'Sailing Downwind: On Pravda' in *Writing Left-Handed*, pp. 132–135.

94 Email conversation with Arnold Wesker, 30 April 2015.

95 Wesker gives an account of the 'legal controversy' over the play between himself and the Royal Shakespeare Company in *The Journalists: A Triptych*, pp. 7–8.

96 Wesker, Arnold, *The Journalists*, p. 60.

97 Evans, Harold, *Good Times, Bad Times*, p. 67.

98 Brenton, Howard and David Hare, *Pravda*, p. 113.

99 Billington, Michael 'Great Britain Review', Guardian, 1 July 2014: http://www.theguardian.com/stage/2014/jul/01/richard-bean-satirical-comedy-great-britain (accessed 1 May 2015).

100 Stoppard, Tom, *Night and Day*, p. 61.

101 Brenton, Howard and David Hare, *Pravda*, p. 117.

102 Bean, Richard, *Great Britain*, p. 100.

103 For example *Defence of the Realm* (1985, Chapter 5), and *State of Play* (2009, Conclusion).

104 Interview with James Meek.

105 For a detailed discussion of the relationship between the American 'new journalism' and fiction, see Underwood, Doug, *The Undeclared War between Fiction and Journalism* (2013).

106 Interview with David Edgar, *Theatre Quarterly* IX/33 Spring 1979, pp. 3–34.

107 Wesker, Arnold, *Journalists*, p. 136; Meek, James, *We Are Now Beginning*, p. 120.

Conclusion:
'People should probably have newsprint on their hands when they read it': Imagining Journalism in the Internet Age in Britain and the United States[1]

I

For more than one hundred years, writers from all genres and all brows have been closely watching and commenting on the behaviour and direction of British journalism. We have seen how narratives written by former or practising journalists can help recreate the lives and literary struggles of journalists of the past, exposing in minute detail their often agonized personal response to developments in their industry. Another finding of this book is that creative artists at times appear to apprehend, in their fictions, great seismic changes in journalism and its standing in society often years before industry executives and academics do. In the past few years, writers and directors have begun to contemplate the future of journalism in the Internet age. Can we employ their fictions, in novels, theatre and in film, as a kind of crystal ball with which to predict the future? The sheer quantity of fictions about journalism discussed here shows that the subject is one of enormous concern to writers both directly involved in the industry as well as those who have nothing to do with it save anxiously waiting for reviews of their latest work. Screenwriter Martin Stellman (*Defence of the Realm*, 1985, see Chapter 5), who has been 'struggling to write a new "State of Britain" political thriller' thinks that the twenty-four-hour availability of news and comment is both cause for optimism and pessimism. 'It may be that that the wild frontier that is still the Internet – I'm thinking of the blogosphere, Wikileaks and the like – has opened the way to a brand of fearless journalism that is perhaps completely new.' On the other hand, the information that Edward Snowden laid bare as well as several successful uses of Freedom of Information legislation since 2005 have, for Stellman at least, made it harder to write a thriller about power and the press. 'Today we are blasé about corruption, cover up and conspiracy, completely unsurprised by political and corporate dirty tricks. What can you say that is new and shocking when everyone knows it already?' he asks.[2]

That journalism is confronting profound and epochal change today is so accepted that the 'Death of the Newspaper' or the 'End of Journalism' are almost taken for granted.[3] Even sober and respected academics call it 'this moment of mind-blowing uncertainty in the evolution of journalism'.[4] One recent survey of American newspaper readership declines, extending the regression slope along its existing angle suggests newspapers will run out of readers in March 2044.[5] While many newspapers in the United Kingdom, the United States and across Europe, including the *Financial Times* and *New York Times*, are successfully employing paywalls, digital subscriptions and other online models, a stable financial model for all kinds of traditional newspapers is still an uncertain prospect.[6] Some online-only journalism sites like *BuzzFeed*, *Vice News* and *Salon.com* are building a loyal readership although the economic health and the standard of journalism of these websites are very mixed. The U.S. Center for Public Integrity (*publicintegrity.org*), an independent investigative journalism organization funded by public philanthropic subscription, won the Pulitzer Prize for Investigative Reporting in 2014. Andrew Leonard, staff writer at highbrow website *Salon.com*, suggests for readers, at least, there is now a 'golden age' of Internet journalism, with 'more content of all kinds than you can possibly consume' although he acknowledges that hundreds of talented journalists have left the industry in recent years.[7] While the *New York Times* now has more than one million digital subscribers, 166 newspapers closed in the United States 2008–2010.[8] While the *Guardian* continues to evolve into a global newspaper – opening its latest office in San Francisco in the autumn of 2015 – local newspapers in Britain continue to disappear or move to online only. A recent House of Commons Early Day Motion noted the disappearance of more than 157 local newspapers between 2008 and December 2014.[9] The consequent 'dramatic decline' in the coverage of 'Town Hall' news means that local authorities in charge of multi-million-pound budgets are increasingly unaccountable.[10] However, the rise in online journalism jobs means that while there are fewer journalists working in Britain today than in the 1990s, more people self-described as journalists in the 2011 census than they did in 2001 (just over 63,000 in 2011, just under 60,000 in 2000).[11] This rise in the numbers of journalists at a time when hundreds of jobs in local newspapers have been lost underlines the dizzying speed of the deep structural changes that are taking place in the industry. As respected journalism scholar Bob Franklin admitted recently, 'It is the *pace* of change as much as its character which is striking and which leaves publishers, industry analysts and academics struggling to make their research findings and scholarly discussions relevant and timely.'[12]

Themes relating to journalism's future have been given a variety of treatments by the narrative arts. These include the fruitful collaboration between old-style print journalists and young, keen bloggers in holding power to account; the spectre of anonymous, unaccountable virtual commentators able to ruin lives and the notion that a lean and hungry 'blogosphere' can act as watchdog over a complacent and corrupted print press. American fictions are more optimistic than British ones, continuing a trend with its roots in the First Amendment to the US Constitution guaranteeing freedom of the new nation's press and given rocket boosters by Clark Kent/Superman in the 1930s and Woodward/Bernstein in the 1970s.[13]

A favourite among nostalgic newspaper journalists is the American film *State of Play* (2009), starring Russell Crowe and directed by Kevin Macdonald.[14] Although the film follows a similar plot to the earlier BBC series of the same name, the emphasis is not so much on political corruption as the future of journalism. Kevin Macdonald, while developing the original script, realized that journalism is going through 'an interesting time. Newspapers are dying throughout the world, and what it will be like when there are no more reporters running around is interesting to contemplate.'[15] The film is set in a newsroom reminiscent of that of the *Washington Post* in *All the President's Men* (1976), only '35 years on and nobody's tidied up', a nod to the magnitude of the newspaper industry's decline since its Watergate apogee.[16] Despite the decline, however, the film proposes a future where foot-slogging newspaper reporters pass on their skills and liberal principles to the Internet-savvy new generation of journalists who, like the young blogger Della Frye, are 'hungry … cheap and she churns out copy every hour'. Della's words, after she and newspaper reporter Cal McCaffrey have exposed the corrupt relationships between Capitol Hill and the defence industry, however, even today sound hopelessly nostalgic, quite apart from being unrealistic: 'People should probably have newsprint on their hands when they read it.'

The latest retelling of *House of Cards* (Netflix, 2013), this time set in Washington DC puts faith in journalism's ability constantly to renew itself. The series' creator Beau Willimon had been a columnist on the *Columbia Spectator*, and, via Twitter, has asserted his fondness for his past involvement in journalism. Although scheming congressman Frank Underwood gets the better of the journalists on his trail, the permanence of journalism as a profession for principled, hard-working investigative reporters is not in question. While the *Washington Herald* newspaper is struggling to maintain relevance, the new website *slugline* evolves from a slapdash amateurish site to a vehicle for serious political news and comment, attracting experienced newspaper journalists as well as bean-bag surfing college graduates uploading their articles via their mobile phones. *Shattered Glass* (2004) is a 'biopic' about Stephen Glass, the twenty-five-year-old *New Republic* reporter who fabricated most of his articles and nearly destroyed the one-hundred-year-old 'in-flight magazine of Air Force One' in 1998. While *New Republic* editors and reporters are complacent about anomalies in Glass's copy, the whistle is blown by journalists on *Forbes Digital Tool*, the online site for *Forbes Magazine* (now *Forbes.com*). Director Billy Ray contrasts the well-dressed *New Republic* journalists (preppy blazers, chinos, brown leather loafers), working separately in their individual offices, to the casually dressed *Forbes* journalists collaborating in an open plan paint-peeling warehouse, phoning contacts, checking databases, reading archive material in the same way print journalists have always done. *Forbes* reporter Adam Penenberg's article appeared online on 10 May 1998, in the very early days of online journalism. At the end of the film, in black-and-white typewriter-style text, the audience is informed that Penenberg's article 'was hailed as a breakthrough for internet journalism'. Several recent American novels, many by recovering 'bloggers', however, have highlighted the difficulties of Web-based journalism: the pressure to produce 'clickbait', the regurgitation of pre-published stories rather than producing original journalism and online bloggers 'sitting in their mother's basements and ranting' rather than contributing to rational public debate.[17]

British fictions tend towards this more pessimistic view. In James Meek's novel *The Heart Broke In* (2012) 'evil tabloid editor' Val Oatman leaves the struggling world of newspapers to set up a website 'The Moral Foundation' with a brief to expose celebrity immorality: 'It's the fucking celebrity secret police online.'[18] When celebrities' lawyers try to issue writs against the website, 'They found it had melted away. Its offices had been shut down a month earlier and its staff paid off. Its servers in Chile were paid up a year in advance and no one seemed to know how the data could be accessed.'[19]

Unlike a newspaper, which at least has a physical presence, a postal address and visible reporters, this semi-anonymous, unaccountable yet deeply intrusive site represents a bleak image of the future of journalism after the death of newspapers. This idea is discussed by journalists in the National Theatre of Scotland production *Enquirer* (2012). The old-time journalist Hywel reminisces of his days on the *Neath Guardian*: when walking down the main street of the Welsh town, 'I'd get stopped and challenged on every single thing that I'd written … Journalism at it's best, I think, is connected to a community.' As opposed to the 'footslogging' tradition of newspaper journalism, Hywel has no time for the young people hired by his newspaper to write the online edition: 'Can I tell you the thing that really, really, really pisses me off about the web? They hired kids with no experience whatsoever. They won't leave the office, they just sit there like battery farm chickens, you know … I said to them "I don't want you quoting Twitter, I want you to call people."'

Similarly in Annalena McAfee's *The Spoiler*, journalism today bears as much resemblance to the journalism of a mythical newspaper 'golden age' as does 'lavatory graffiti to the Sistine Chapel'.[20] Veteran journalist Honor Tait wonders how important stories about injustice can possibly be distinguished by readers amidst the deluge information that now surrounds us: 'These timeless stories of injustice now bleated ineffectually, shouted down like Calvinist preachers at a carnival, by brash accounts of the private lives of royalty and popstars, actors and footballers. Political coverage, too – its trivial bellicosity, puffed-up personalities, old-fashioned sex scandals … was reduced to the parochial, a subset of show business.'[21]

Maybe it is in the British character to be more pessimistic than Americans. Maybe it is more fashionable in British literary circles to construct a negative image of journalism. Certainly *The Spoiler*'s several references to Evelyn Waugh's *Scoop* imply that any idea of a previous 'golden age' of journalism is erroneous. The only character in these later British narratives who has any hope in journalism's online future is Gabe in *Enquirer*, a woman journalist with a successful blog that has enabled her to reach her audience directly, bypassing the masculine newspaper structure:

> I don't mourn the end of all this shit. I'm off to do my blog. Old Fleet Street and El Vino's and all that misogynist, drunken, Oxbridge-educated crap. You know the great thing about new media: it allows a girl from Bumfuck College of Further Education to come out and raise her voice. My Twitter account already has 20,000 followers. More people read me than the *Independent*.

Her comment is an interesting addendum to the conclusions of Chapter 7 although very few journalists have been able to convert blogs and Twitter followers into hard cash unless linked to traditional media such as a newspaper column or a book. In addition, the 'trolling' of prominent and outspoken women journalists and campaigners on Twitter and other social media sites confirms that sexist views of women journalists don't stop at the doors of the traditional press.[22]

II

For all the criticism levelled at the popular press by early twentieth-century writers, it only takes a cursory comparison between popular newspapers of the first six or seven decades of the twentieth century and today, to conclude that earlier papers were of a far higher standard than modern ones, in terms of 'news' subject matter, prose-style and literary and cultural content. With today's literary classes having removed themselves from the pages of popular newspapers – where can we find today's equivalent of Rose Macaulay, J. B. Priestley, Arnold Bennett, Edith Sitwell, Storm Jameson and Evelyn Waugh writing in twenty-first-century tabloids? – Benjamin Franklin's famous quote 'our critics are our best friends, they show us our faults' comes to mind. Early twentieth-century writers may have despaired of contemporary press standards, but they regularly contributed to the popular press, providing readers with educative, thought-provoking or socially radical discussion.[23] The papers they wrote for were incomparably the better for their involvement, something their proprietors shrewdly recognized.

One could argue that writers, in the fictional depiction of the journalist and the newspaper world, have won the image battle. The established and hackneyed stereotype of the journalist in modern fiction is epitomized in characters like Rita Skeeter in J. K. Rowling's *Harry Potter* books, murderous editor Vernon Halliday in Ian McEwan's *Amsterdam* and the entire ghastly cast of unsympathetic journalist characters from Lennox Mark the proprietor to Mary Much the magazine editress in A. N. Wilson's *My Name Is Legion*. Are not the hollowed-out figures of Vernon Halliday, Mary Much and Iain Banks' Cameron Colley symptomatic of an industry in decline? After Stephen Fry called journalists covering the BAFTA awards 'media scum', John in *Enquirer* comments: 'a sort of current has entered the water system of public discourse', although hating its press has long been a British pastime.[24]

Even in their grossest portraits, novelists have complex attitudes to journalism and its practitioners. Journalist and author A. N. Wilson, from whose mind emerge the horrific Lennox Mark and Mary Much, says he did not produce these figures out of hate, but out of a deep and abiding fondness for the profession he has been involved with: 'I think some of the best writing to appear in my lifetime has been in the British press – Auberon Waugh, Paul Foot, Richard Ingrams,

Nigel Dempster in his glory days, Christopher Hitchens, some of what these people wrote is a hundred times better than much literary fiction.'[25] Although some might disagree with his argument, his words show his novel should not be seen as a hatchet job on modern journalism, but more as a cracked mirror whose image should show modern journalism how it is perceived even by those closely engaged with it. Philip Norman, now best known for his lengthy biographies of the Rolling Stones and the Beatles, still occasionally writes for the *Daily Mail*, which, he says, 'is still a writers' paper. The amount of space newspapers still have, every day, to publish the written word, is extraordinary'. Eric Clark, now a writer of non-fiction books, particularly investigations as well as thrillers, still writes for the *Saturday Telegraph* magazine, 'one of the few papers you can still write 2,500 to 3,000 word articles for'. Even though James Meek gradually realized that the limitations of daily journalism were never going to allow him to write what he wanted, 'I think journalism helped my fiction. It forced me to go out and talk to people.'[26] Even J. K. Rowling in her Leveson testimony stressed: 'I acknowledge and support the vital role that the press plays as part of a free and democratic society. As an author I strongly believe in freedom of expression.'

These writers have produced novels portraying journalists as selfish, scheming and cynical (A. N. Wilson and J. K. Rowling), wild, excessive, bacchic hypocrites (Philip Norman), shady, manipulative and adulterous traitors (Eric Clark) and jealous, insecure and hurtling towards mental breakdown (James Meek). 'With friends like these ...', as the saying goes. James Meek has acknowledged that he would find a good journalist difficult to write about, and that readers would not like a 'preachy' crusading journalist who wants to change the world. Eric Clark also says that for a writer, 'people with faults, the morally compromised, are much more interesting'. Good journalists, then, don't make for good fiction, especially not in the post-Leveson twenty-first century, which is a great shame, particularly when the answer I hear most when I ask potential students why they want to study journalism is, 'I want to make a difference.'

III

The journalist and author Julie Burchill once remarked that when she discovered writing, 'it was as if she'd found her mother tongue'.[27] The urge to write is presented as a powerful force by so many journalist-novelists studied here even if the profession they have to mould their writing into has deep structural faults.

For Eric Clark, for example, James Fenn, the hero of his novel *The Sleeper*, 'a mad keen young journalist, not yet twenty-two, determined to be where the action was when it came', is Eric Clark.[28] 'There is more of me in James than in any other character I have written. I madly wanted to be a journalist. I moved to London at 21, *I was burning for it*, to be where the action was. The writing is hard work, *but the words have got to get out*' (my emphasis).[29] This almost visceral desire is expressed by dozens of journalists in this book, from the Edwardian period to today. Novels studied here reveal that the 'voice of the siren' has to be obeyed and show that there will always be people drawn to journalism for sound, noble reasons, because they love to write, because they are burning with something to say, not because they want to hack people's phones or stalk celebrities down dark alleys.[30] The job security may not be what it was, the financial rewards may not be what they were, it may be harder to make one's voice heard above the din of information, but none of this will prevent principled and passionate writers from trying to communicate their thoroughly researched reports and genuinely held opinions.

The problem is there is such a din that it is so difficult for readers to be able to assess what is the most accurate version of events, the importance of each point being made to them. There are now more than 200 million active blogs on the Internet and 316 million active Twitter users producing 500 million tweets a day.[31] The disorientation and distortion that exposure to too much news produces, as expressed by Robert Burton in 1621 (see the epigraph at the front of this book), has intensified a thousand fold over the past 400 years. In the Internet age, computer screens, mobiles and tablets spray us with information like water canon loaded with words. How should we respond? Bourdieu suggests that, counter-intuitively perhaps, the more journalism we consume, the more politically apathetic we become: 'Journalism shows us a world ... full of incomprehensible and unsettling dangers from which we must withdraw for our own protection ... this worldview fosters fatalism and disengagement.'[32] No sensible citizen, journalist or politician should want that outcome but that particular genie is well and truly out of the bottle. But like the helpful elves of fairy tale, the image of Fourth Estate journalism conjured in Guy Thorne's *When It Was Dark* (see Chapter 1), 'good journalism has a way of being there when we need it most'.[33] It was certainly there in July 2011, like a *deus ex machina* on the eve of the attempted takeover of BSkyB by Rupert Murdoch's News Corporation. The journalist Nick Davies' revelations about the Hacking of Milly Dowler's phone by *News of the World* journalists emerged at the eleventh hour. The 'feat of skilful and determined reporting not surpassed in British journalism's post-

WWII record' forced News Corporation to withdraw its bid for the remaining 61 per cent stake in the satellite television channel.[34]

In most other periods examined in this book, writers have reluctantly accepted that for all its imperfections, journalism fulfils a vital function in a liberal democracy. In British fiction this acceptance is grudging indeed. John Le Carré perhaps sums up the attitude most succinctly when he writes in his novel about journalists and spies, *The Honourable Schoolboy*: 'It is not the English habit, as a rule, to accord distinction to journalists.'[35] However, fictions of the past – as indeed the delightful characterization of 'old' Craw and Jerry Westerby attest in Le Carré's novel – have found at least something to cheer, if faintly. During the First World War, while there was little to cheer in the reporting of hostilities, writers acknowledged journalism's role in creating a public arena for the discussion of new challenges such as mass bereavement and food rationing. In the interwar period, 'middlebrow' writers suggested in their fictions that a partial, truncated version of the truth was better than none and that journalists with courage and independent spirit were needed to warn of the rise of totalitarianism and scrutinise politicians of all political colours. In the post–Second World War years, writers argued for the preservation of liberal journalistic values in the face of rapid commercialization. However, contemporary British narratives present a wholly bleak picture. Martin Amis' *Yellow Dog*, Annalena McAfee's *The Spoiler*, Richard Bean's *Great Britain* and Ian McEwan's *Amsterdam* offer no redemptive pathway, implying there is nothing worth saving in the whole rotten edifice. Of course, a country without a free press is also a country where those writers would probably be at least censored if not imprisoned. For writers who require freedom of speech as an essential underpinning of their art, the careful nurturing of good journalism and transparent political processes should be important concerns. The closure of the print editions of the *Independent* and *Independent on Sunday* in March 2016 further diminishes media plurality in Britain. Their loss must concentrate minds on the severe problem of how journalism as a 'public good' will survive at a time when nobody seems to want to pay for it. It was an irony not lost on many commentators that the film *Spotlight*, celebrating the investigative journalism of the *Boston Globe*, was lauded at the 'BAFTAs' on the same weekend as the *Independent*'s print demise was announced. The film, although only set in the early 2000s, has an air of sepia-tinted nostalgia about it, as if already the skills and commitment of the journalists on the *Boston Globe* belong to the past. Associate director of the National Theatre of Scotland John Tiffany wrote thus as *Enquirer* opened in London in October 2012: 'most reporters I have known have never hacked a phone or raked through anybody's bin. Instead they were champions of the public interest … journalism is one of the parents of democracy and it needs looking after so it can look after us.[36]

He is of course right. Perhaps, in Britain, we take our freedoms too much for granted. With so much unchecked fabrication, misconception and inaccuracy on the Internet, we need good journalists more than ever. Who knows, maybe if modern writers created a good journalist in their fiction, rather than the easy 'media scum' stereotype, it might encourage more politically committed and expressively gifted people into the profession to save it, and us.

Notes

1   From the 2009 film *State of Play*.
2   Email interview with Martin Stellman.
3   See for example Charles, Alec and Gavin Stewart (eds) *The End of Journalism* (2011); Meyer, Philip, *The Vanishing Newspaper* (2009); Franklin, Bob, 'The Future of Journalism' (2014).
4   Domingo, David, Pere Masip and Irene Costera Meijer quoted in Franklin, 'The Future of Journalism', p. 481.
5   Meyer, *The Vanishing Newspaper*, p. 19.
6   See for example Brock, George, *Out of Print* (2013).
7   Leonard, Andrew, 'Sorry Everyone: The Future of Journalism Is Still up in the Air', August 2014 http://www.salon.com/2014/08/24/sorry_everyone_the_future_of_journalism_is_still_up_in_the_air/ accessed 23 September 2015.
8   http://newspaperdeathwatch.com/; http://www.businessinsider.com/the-us-has-lost-more-than-166-print-newspapers-since-2008-2010-7?IR=T accessed 20 September 2015.
9   http://www.parliament.uk/edm/2014-15/585 accessed 23 September 2015.
10 Morrison, James, 'Spin, Smoke-filled Rooms and the Decline of Council Reporting', p. 193.
11 Office of National Statistics, via email.
12 Franklin, 'The Future of Journalism', p. 481.
13 For a through discussion of American representations of journalists see Ehrlich, Matthew and Joe Saltzman, *Heroes and Scoundrels*.
14 The veteran newspaper journalist Bryan Appleyard, for example, admits: 'I teared up in the closing credits' in an interview with Kevin Macdonald, 'The Genuine Article' *Sunday Times* Culture, 5 April 2009, pp. 4–7.
15 Kevin Macdonald, interview with Bryan Appleyard, *Sunday Times* Culture, 5 April 2009.
16 Ibid.

17 Ehrlich, Matthew C. and Joe Saltzman, *Heroes and Scoundrels*, p. 147.

18 Meek, James, *The Heart Broke In*, pp. 111 & 359.

19 Ibid., p. 521.

20 McAfee, Annalena, *The Spoiler*, p. 408.

21 Ibid., p. 345.

22 See for example http://www.psmag.com/health-and-behavior/women-arent-welcome-internet-72170 accessed 27 September 2015.

23 J. B. Priestley would discuss the social divisions and poverty in northern towns in his popular press columns; Storm Jameson discussed feminism as well as more trivial subjects in Rothermere's popular papers; Evelyn Waugh wrote a series of features on modern manners for the *Daily Mail* in the early 1930s.

24 Stephen Fry made these comments at the 2012 BAFTA Awards.

25 Email conversation with A. N. Wilson April 2015.

26 Interviews with Philip Norman, Eric Clark and James Meek.

27 Quoted in Barber, Lynn, *Demon Barber*, p. 30.

28 Clark, Eric, *The Sleeper*, p. 11.

29 Interview with Eric Clark.

30 Courlander, Alphonse, *Mightier than the Sword*, p. 45.

31 Gaber, Ivor, 'Three Cheers for Subjectivity', p. 33; https://about.twitter.com/company accessed 27 September 2015.

32 Bourdieu, Pierre, *On Television and Journalism*, p. 8.

33 Hachten, William A., *The Troubles of Journalism*, p. 179.

34 Page, Bruce, *The Murdoch Archipelago*, p. 3.

35 Le Carré, John, *The Honourable Schoolboy* p. 40

36 Tiffany, John, 'Newspapers Are in Crisis. But Just What Have We Lost – And What Can Be Saved?' *Observer*, 7 October 2012.

Bibliography

Primary sources (1): Archives consulted

British Newspaper Archive, British Library.
Cambridge University Library: Leavis, F. R. 'The Relationship of Journalism to Literature' PhD 66.
The Journalist archive, National Union of Journalists.
Mass Observation Archive, University of Sussex.
Northcliffe Papers, British Library.
Wren Library, Trinity College Cambridge: The Papers of Dame Rose Macaulay.

Primary sources (2): Novels, plays, poetry, etc.

(Where a work is referred to in more than one chapter, it is referenced in the chapter it is first mentioned in, apart from the Introduction.)

Chapter 1

Browning, Elizabeth Barrett, *Aurora Leigh* (1853–6). London: The Women's Press, 1982.
Courlander, Alphonse, *Mightier than the Sword*. London: T. Fisher Unwin, 1912.
Davidson, John, 'Fleet Street' and 'Fleet Street: Song' in Sloan, John (ed.), *Selected Poems and Prose of John Davidson*. Oxford: Clarendon Press, 1995.
Davidson, John, *The Poems of John Davidson Volume II*. Edinburgh: Scottish Academic Press, 1973.
Doyle, Arthur Conan, *The Lost World* (1912). London: Puffin Books, 1994.
Doyle, Arthur Conan, *The Poison Belt* (1913). Ware: Wordsworth Classics, 1995.
Ford, Ford Madox (with Joseph Conrad), *The Inheritors* (1901). Milton Keynes: Lightening Source, 2012.
Gibbs, Philip, *The Street of Adventure* (1909). London: Heinemann, 1923.
Gissing, George, *New Grub Street* (1891). Oxford: Oxford World Classics, 1998.
Hodson, James Lansdale, *Grey Dawn – Red Night* (1929). London: Simkin and Marshall, 1951.
Howard, Keble, *Lord London* (1913). New York: McBride Nast and Co., 1914.
Jerome, Jerome K., *Three Men on the Bummel* (1900). Bristol: J. Arrowsmith Ltd., 1914.

Jerome, Jerome K., *Tommy and Co* (1904). Rockville, MD: Serenity, 2011.

Kipling, Rudyard, *The Man Who Would Be King* (1888). Oxford: Oxford University Press, 2008.

Kipling, Rudyard, 'A Burgher of the Free State' (1900), in *The Sussex Edition*, Vol. 30. London: Macmillan, 1938.

Kipling, Rudyard, 'The Village That Voted the Earth Was Flat' and 'The Press' (1913/14), in *A Diversity of Creatures*. London: Macmillan, 1917.

Lucas, E. V., *London Lavender* (1912). London: Methuen, 1927.

MacGill, Patrick, *Children of the Dead End* (1914). Dingle: Brandon Book Publishers, 1982.

Montague, C. E., *A Hind Let Loose* (1910). London: Penguin Books, 1936.

Sergeant, Adeline, *The Work of Oliver Byrd*. London: James Nisbet and Co., 1902.

Thorne, Guy, *When It Was Dark: The Story of a Great Conspiracy* (1903). LaVergne: Legacy Reprint, 2009.

Thurston, Katherine, Cecil, *John Chilcote MP* (1904). Edinburgh: William Blackwood, 1906.

Trollope, Anthony, *The Prime Minister* (1876). Oxford: Oxford University Press, 1973.

Wallace, Edgar, *The Four Just Men* (1905). Oxford: Oxford Popular Classics, 1995.

Wallace, Edgar, *The Council of Justice* (1908). Oxford: Oxford Popular Classics, 1995.

Wodehouse, P. G., *Psmith Journalist* (1909). London: Penguin, 1983.

Wyllarde, Dolf, *The Pathway of the Pioneer* (1906). London: Methuen, 1914.

Chapter 2

Aldington, Richard, 'The Retort Discourteous' in *Little Review*, 2/4 (June–July 1915), p. 4.

Chesterton, G. K., *The Napoleon of Notting Hill*. London: John Lane, 1904.

Graves, Robert, *Robert Graves, the Complete Poems*. Manchester: Carcanet, 1995.

Macaulay, Rose, *Non-Combatants and Others* (1916). London: Capuchin Classics, 2010.

McKenna, Stephen, *Sonia: Between Two Worlds* (1917). New York: George H. Doran, 1917.

Owen, Wilfred, *The Poems of Wilfred Owen*. London: Chatto and Windus, 2006.

Pound, Ezra, *A Draft of XVI Cantos* (1924). London: Faber and Faber, 1998.

Sassoon, Siegfried, 'Fight to a Finish' (1917), collected in *The War Poetry of Siegfried Sassoon*. London: Faber and Faber, 1983.

Sassoon, Siegfried, *The War Poems of Siegfried Sassoon*. London: William Heinemann, 1919.

Thomas, Edward, *Selected Poems of Edward Thomas* (ed.) Thomas R. S. London: Faber and Faber, 1964.

Tomlinson, H. M., *All Our Yesterdays*. London: Cassell and Co., 1930.

Wells, H. G., *Mr Britling Sees It Through*. London: Macmillan, 1916.

Chapter 3

Auden, W. H., *Look Stranger* (1936). London: Faber, 2001.

Bowen, Elizabeth, 'Recent Photograph' (1926) in *The Collected Stories of Elizabeth Bowen*. London: Penguin, 1980.

Buchan, John, 'The Last Crusade' (1928) in Daniell, David (ed.), *The Best Short Stories of John Buchan*. London: Panther Books, 1985.

Currey, Stella Martin, *Paperchase End*. London: Arrowsmith, 1934.

Doyle, Arthur Conan, *The Land of Mist* (1926). Ware: Wordsworth Classics, 1995.

Frankau, Gilbert, *Life and Erica* (1925). London: Macdonald and Co., 1947.

Gerhardie, William, *Doom* (first published as *Jazz and Jasper*, 1928). London: Macdonald and Co., 1974.

Gibbons, Stella, *Cold Comfort Farm* (1932). London: Longmans Green, 1942.

Holtby, Winifred, *South Riding* (1936). London: Virago Modern Classics, 1996.

Hunt, Cecil, *Paddy for News*. London: Hodder and Stoughton, 1933.

Hutchinson, A. S. M., *If Winter Comes* (1921). Milton Keynes: Lightening Source, 2009.

Huxley, Aldous, *Crome Yellow* (1921). London: Chatto and Windus, 1931.

Jameson, Storm, *Company Parade* (1934). London: Virago Modern Classics, 1982.

Jameson, Storm, *Love in Winter* (1935). London: Capuchin Classics, 2010.

Jameson, Storm, *None Turn Back* (1936). London: Virago Modern Classics, 1984.

Joyce, James, *Ulysses* (1922). Oxford: Oxford World Classics, 2008.

Lane, Margaret, *Faith, Hope and No Charity*. London: William Heinemann, 1935.

Langley, Noel, *There's a Porpoise Close behind Us*. London: Arthur Barker, 1936.

Lawrence, D. H., *Kangaroo* (1923). Sidney: Collins Publishers (Australia), 1989.

Macaulay, Rose, *Potterism* (1920). Milton Keynes: Tutis Digital Publishing, 2008.

Macaulay, Rose, *Crewe Train* (1926). New York: Carroll and Graf, 1986.

Macaulay, Rose, *Keeping up Appearances* (1928). London: Methuen, 1986.

Muggeridge, Malcolm, *Picture Palace* (1934). London: Weidenfeld and Nicolson, 1987.

Murry, John Middleton, *The Things We Are* (1922). Memphis: General Books, 2009.

'M. Z. 4796', 'The Pressgoat' in *Adelphi* 1/II, July 1923, pp. 115–122.

Nicolson, Harold, *Public Faces* (1932). New York: Popular Library, 1960.

Priestley, J. B., *Wonder Hero*. London: William Heinemann, 1933.

Rossetti, Christina, 'A Birthday' in Quiller-Couch (ed.), *The Oxford Book of Victorian Verse*. Oxford: Clarendon Press, 1919, p. 780.

Sayers, Dorothy L., *Murder Must Advertise* (1933). London: Hodder and Stoughton, 2003.

Sitwell, Osbert, *Before the Bombardment*. London: Duckworth, 1926.

Sullivan, J. W. N., *But for the Grace of God*. London: Jonathan Cape, 1932.

Waugh, Evelyn, *Vile Bodies* (1930). London: Penguin, 1981.

Wilkinson, Ellen, *The Division Bell Mystery*. London: Harrap and Co., 1932.

Woolf, Virginia, *Mrs Dalloway* (1925). London: Triad Grafton, 1989.

Chapter 4

Ambler, Eric, *The Dark Frontier* (1936). London: Fontana, 1984.

Ambler, Eric, *Uncommon Danger* (1937). London: Penguin Modern Classics, 2009.

Auden, W. H. and Christopher Isherwood, *The Dog beneath the Skin*. London: Faber and Faber, 1935.

Bingham, John, *Fragment of Fear* (1965). New York: Simon and Schuster, 2007.

Clark, Eric, *The Sleeper* (1979). London: Coronet, 1987.

Fleming, Ian, *Casino Royale* (1953). London: Vintage, 2012.

Greene, Graham, *Stamboul Train* (1932). London: Vintage, 2004.

Greene, Graham, *England Made Me* (1934). London: Penguin, 1976.

Greene, Graham, *Brighton Rock* (1938). London: Vintage, 2004.

Greene, Graham, *The Quiet American* (1955). London: Vintage: 2004.

Harling, Robert, *The Paper Palace* (1951). London: The Reprint Society, 1952.

Harling, Robert, *The Enormous Shadow* (1955). London: The Reprint Society, 1956.

Hilton, James, *Knight without Armour* (1933). London: Hodder Paperback, 1970.

Isherwood, Christopher, *Mister Norris Changes Trains* (1935). London: Triad Granada, 1984.

Jameson, Storm, *In the Second Year* (1936). Nottingham: Trent Editions, 2004.

Le Carré, John, *The Honourable Schoolboy* (1977). London: Sceptre, 2011.

Lehmann, John, *Evil Was Abroad*. London: Cresset Press, 1938.

Lyall, Archibald, *Envoy Extraordinary*. London: Desmond Harmsworth, 1932.

Marsh, Nagaio, *Death in a White Tie* (1938). London, Harper Collins, 1999.

Maugham, Somerset, *Ashenden* (1928). London: Vintage, 2000.

Muggeridge, Malcolm, *Winter in Moscow* (1934). Grand Rapids: Eerdmans Publishing Co., 1987.

Powell, Anthony, *Venusberg* (1932). London: Heinemann, 1955.

Priestley, J. B., *The Shapes of Sleep* (1962). London: The Book Club, 1963.

Smith, Stevie, *Novel on Yellow Paper* (1936). London: Jonathan Cape, 1969.

Von Arnim, Elizabeth, *The Enchanted April* (1922). London: Vintage Classics, 2015.

Waugh, Evelyn, *Scoop* (1938). London: Penguin, 2000.

Chapter 5

Auden, W. H., *The Orators* (1932) published in *The English Auden*. London: Faber and Faber, 1977.

Bean, Richard, *Great Britain*. London: Oberon Books, 2015.

Bennet, Arnold, *What the Public Wants* (1909). Port Chester: Elibron Classics, 2006.

Bennett, Arnold, *Lord Raingo*. London: Cassell and Co., 1926.

Brenton, Howard and Hare, David, *Pravda: A Fleet Street Comedy*. London: Methuen, 1985.

Buchan, John, *Castle Gay*. London: Hodder and Stoughton, 1930.

Day Lewis, Cecil, *The Magnetic Mountain*. London: Hogarth, 1933.

Fagan, James Bernard, *The Earth* (1909). London: T. Fisher Unwin, 1913.

Mullin, Chris, *A Very British Coup* (1982). London: Politicos (Methuen), 2006.

Sprigg, Christopher St John, *Fatality in Fleet Street*. London: Eldon Press, 1933.

Wells, H. G., *The Autocracy of Mr Parham*. London, Heinemann, 1930.

West, Rebecca, *Sunflower* (1926). London: Virago, 1990.

Wilson, A. N., *My Name Is Legion*. London: Arrow Books, 2004.

Chapter 6

Cronin, A, J., *The Northern Light* (1958). London: The Companion Book Club, 1961.

Dickens, Monica, *My Turn to Make the Tea* (1951). London: Penguin, 1962.

Forster, Peter, *The Spike* (1965). London: Penguin, 1965.

Frayn, Michael, *Towards the End of the Morning* (1967). London: Faber and Faber, 2000.

Greene, Graham, *The End of the Affair* (1951). London: Vintage, 2004.

Hodson, James Lansdale, *Morning Star*. London: Victor Gollancz Ltd., 1951.

Manning, Olivia, *The Balkan Trilogy* (1960). London: Penguin, 1981.

Mount, Ferdinand, *The Clique* (1978). London: Faber Finds, 2010.

Norman, Philip, *Everyone's Gone to the Moon*. London: Hutchinson, 1995.

Orwell, George, *1984* (1949). London: Penguin, 2013.

Osborne, John, *Look Back in Anger* (1956). London: Faber and Faber, 1986.

Powell, Anthony, *Hearing Secret Harmonies* (1975). London: Arrow Books, 2005.

Priestley, J. B., *Festival at Farbridge*. London: Heinemann, 1951.

Reid, Philip, *Harris in Wonderland*. London: Jonathan Cape, 1973.

Sayle, Murray, *A Crooked Sixpence* (1961). London: Revel Barker Publishing, 2008.

Waterhouse, Keith, *Billy Liar* (1959). London: Penguin Books, 2010.

Waugh, Evelyn, *Put Out More Flags* (1942). London: Penguin Modern Classics, 2004.

Williams, Gordon, *The Upper Pleasure Garden*. London: Secker and Warburg, 1970.

Woolf, Virginia, *Between the Acts* (1941). Oxford: Oxford University Press, 2000.

Chapter 7

Bennett, Arnold, *Hilda Lessways* (1911). Kelly Bray: House of Stratus, 2003.

Bretherton, Eva, 'The Eleventh Hour' in *The Quiver*, 52/11 (1917), pp. 885–891.

Burchill, Julie, *Ambition*. London: Corgi, 1989.

Dixon, Ella Hepworth, *The Story of a Modern Woman* (1894). Memphis: General Books, 2011.

Dobbs, Michael, *House of Cards* (1989). London: BCA, 1992.

Ferguson, Rachel, *The Brontes Went to Woolworths* (1931). London: Bloomsbury, 2009.

Finch, Tim, *The House of Journalists* (2013). London: Vintage, 2015.

Le Carré, John, *A Murder of Quality* (1962). London: Penguin, 2011.

Macaulay, Rose, *Mystery at Geneva*. London: Collins, 1922.

Macaulay, Rose, *Going Abroad*. London: Collins, 1934.

Maxwell, Betty, 'Cupid Wields a Pen' in *The Quiver*, 56/6 (1917), pp. 488–493.

McAfee, Annalena, *The Spoiler* (2011). London: Vintage, 2012.

Rowling, J. K., *Harry Potter and the Goblet of Fire* (2000). London: Bloomsbury, 2005.

Walters, Minette, *The Devil's Feather* (2005). Basingstoke: Pan Books, 2012.

Weldon, Fay, *Darcy's Utopia* (1990). London: Flamingo, 1991.

Chapter 8

Amis, Martin, *Yellow Dog* (2003). London: Vintage, 2004.

Banks, Iain, *Complicity* (1993). London: Abacus, 1995.

Bennett, Arnold, *The Pretty Lady*. London: Cassell and Co., 1918.

Burn, Gordon, *Fullalove* (1995). London: Faber and Faber, 2004.

Edgar, David, *Wreckers*. London: Methuen, 1977.

Frayn, Michael, *Alphabetical Order* (1975). London: Methuen Drama, 2009.

Lucie, Doug, *The Shallow End*. London: Methuen Drama, 1997.

McEwan, Ian, *Amsterdam* (1998). London: Vintage, 2005.

Meek, James, *We Are Now Beginning Our Descent*. London: Canongate, 2008.

Stoppard, Tom, *Night and Day*. London: Faber and Faber, 1978.

Waterhouse, Keith, *Jeffrey Bernard Is Unwell* (1989). London: Samuel French, 1991.

Wesker, Arnold, *The Journalists: A Triptych*. London: Jonathan Cape, 1979.

Conclusion

Meek, James, *The Heart Broke In*. London: Canongate, 2012.

Primary sources (3): Films and television

Defence of the Realm, dir. David Drury (1985).

Fortunes of War (BBC TV), dir. James Cellan Jones (1987).

House of Cards (BBC TV), dir. Paul Seed (1990).

House of Cards (Netflix), executive producer Beau Willimon (2013).

Shattered Glass, dir. Billy Lane (2004).

State of Play, dir. Kevin Macdonald (2009).

Primary sources (4): Contemporary non-fiction: Journals, memoirs, essays, articles and others

Aldington, Richard, 'A Solemn Dialogue' in *Egoist*, 3/7 (July 1916), pp. 105–106.

Alec-Tweedie, Mrs, *Me and Mine: A Medley of Thoughts and Memories*. London: Hutchinson, 1932.

Ambler, Eric, *Here Lies Eric Ambler* (1985). London: Penguin.

Amis, Martin, *Experience: A Memoir*. New York: Hyperion, 2000.

'An Old Oriental', 'The Woman at Work' in *Englishwoman's Review*, 35/3 (1904), pp. 151–153.

Angell, Norman, *The Press and the Organisation of Society* (1922). Cambridge: Cambridge Minority Press, 1933.

Appleyard, Bryan, 'The Genuine Article' in *Sunday Times*, Culture, 5 April 2009, pp. 4–7.

Ayres, Chris, *War Reporting for Cowards*. London: John Murray, 2005.

Barber, Lyn, *Demon Barber* (1998). London: Penguin, 1999.

Baumann, Arthur, 'The Functions and Future of the Press' in *Fortnightly Review*, 107 (April 1920), pp. 620–627.

Bell, Martin, *Through Gates of Fire* (2003). London: Phoenix, 2004.

Bennett, Arnold, *Journalism for Women: A Practical Guide* (1897). Quedgeley: Dodo Press, 2011.

Bennett, Arnold (ed.) and Newman Flower, *The Journals of Arnold Bennett, Volume I*. London: Cassell and Co., 1932.

Bennett, Arnold (ed.) and Newman Flower, *The Journals of Arnold Bennett, Volume II*. London: Cassell and Co., 1932.

Bennett, Arnold (ed.) and James Hepburn, *Letters of Arnold Bennett, Volume I*. London: Oxford University Press, 1966.

Berry, Paul and A. G. Bishop (eds), *Testament of a Generation: The Journalism of Winifred Holtby and Vera Brittain*. London: Virago, 1985.

Bertrand, Claude-Jean, *The British Press: An Historical Survey*. Paris: OCDL, 1969.

Blundern, Edward, *Undertones of War* (1928). London: Collins, 1965.

Bragg, Melvyn, 'The Present Tense', interview with Dennis Potter, in *New Left Review*, 1/205 (May–June 1994), pp. 131–140.

Briffault, Robert, 'The Wail of Grub Street' in *English Review*, 31 (June 1921), pp. 512–516.

Brittain, Vera, *Testament of Youth* (1933). London: Weidenfeld and Nicholson, 2009.

Brittain, Vera, *Testament of Friendship* (1940). London: Virago, 1992.

Burchett, Wilfred, *The Writings of Wilfred Burchett* George Burchett and Nick Shimmin (eds) (2008). Cambridge: Cambridge University Press.

Castlerosse, Viscount Valentine, *Valentine's Days*. London: Methuen, 1934.

Churchill, Randolph, 'The Daily Newspaper: Notes on the Press in Britain and America', *Encounter*, March 1956, pp. 19–25.

Clarke, Patricia and David Footman (eds), *In Memoriam Archie, 1904–1964: A Symposium on Archibald Laurence Lyall by His Friends*. Privately Printed, 1966.

Clarke, Tom, *My Northcliffe Diary*. London: Gollancz, 1931.

Cockburn, Claud, *In Time of Trouble*. London: Rupert Hart-Davis, 1957.

Cummings, A. J., *The Press and a Changing Civilisation*. London: John Lane and the Bodley Head, 1936.

Dicey, Edward, 'Journalism New and Old' in *Fortnightly Review*, 77 (May 1905), pp. 904–918.

Dixon, Ella Hepworth, *As I Knew Them – Sketches of People I Have Met on the Way*. London: Hutchinson, 1930.

Doyle, Arthur Conan, *Through the Magic Door* (1907). Cambridge: Cambridge University Press, 2012.

Doyle, Arthur Conan, *Memories and Adventures* (1924). London: Greenhill Books, 1988.

Eliot, T. S., 'Reflections on Contemporary Poetry' in *Egoist*, July 1919, p. 39.

Enright, D. J., 'The Literature of the First World War' in Ford, Boris (ed.), *The Modern Age*. London: Pelican Books, 1963.

Ervine, St John, 'The Future of the Press' *Spectator*, 29 November 1930.

Escott, T. H. S., 'Old and New in the Daily Press' in *Quarterly Review*, 227 (April 1917), pp. 353–368.

Evans, B. Ifor, 'The Rise of Modern Journalism' in *Fortnightly Review*, 127 (March 1930), pp. 233–240.

Evans, Harold, *Good Times, Bad Times*. London: Weidenfeld and Nicolson, 1983.

Falk, Bernard, *He Laughed in Fleet Street*. London: Hutchinson, 1931.

Ferguson, Rachel, *We Were Amused*. London: Jonathan Cape, 1958.

Ford, Ford Madox, *Return to Yesterday* (1931). Manchester: Carcanet, 1999.

Frayn, Michael, *Travels with a Typewriter*. London: Faber and Faber, 2009.

Fyvel, T. R., 'The Stones of Harlow: Reflections on Subtopia' in *Encounter*, June 1956, pp. 11–17.

Gellhorn, Martha, *The Face of War* (1959). London: Granta Books, 1998.

Gerhardie, William, *Memoirs of a Polyglot* (1931). London: Robin Clark, 1990.

Gibbs, Philip, *Adventures in Journalism*. London: Heinemann, 1923.

Grant Duff, Shiela, *The Parting of Ways*. London: Peter Owen, 1982.

Graves, Robert, *Goodbye to All That* (1929). London: Penguin Modern Classics, 1969.

Greene, Graham, *A Sort of Life* (1971). London: Penguin Books, 1972.

Greene, Graham, *Reflections*. London: Penguin Books, 1990.

Grigson, Geoffrey, 'Review of the Re-issue of The Press and the Organisation of Society by Norman Angell' in *Scrutiny*, 1/4 (March 1933), pp. 416–417.

Hare, David, 'Introduction' in *Writing Left Handed*. London: Faber and Faber, 1991, pp. ix–xv.

Hare, David, 'Sailing Downwind: On Pravda' in *Writing Left Handed*. London: Faber and Faber, 1991, pp. 132–135.

Harmsworth, Alfred, 'The Making of a Newspaper' in Lawrence, Arthur (ed.), *Journalism as a Profession*. London: Hodder and Stoughton, 1903, pp. 167–189.

Henderson, Philip, *The Novel Today: A Study in Contemporary Attitudes*. London: John Lane the Bodley Head, 1936.

Herd, Harold, *The Making of Modern Journalism*. London: George Allen and Unwin, 1927.

Hoggart, Richard, 'Mass Communications in Britain' in Ford, Boris (ed.), *The Modern Age* (1961), Pelican Guide to English Literature series, London: Penguin, 1963, pp. 442–457.

Holles, Robert, 'Death of a Magazine: The End of *John Bull*' in *Encounter*, August 1960, pp. 42–48.

Holtby, Winifred, 'Little Bo-Peep' in *Time and Tide*, 16 August 1930, p. 1049.

Huddleston, Sisley, 'The Human Spirit in Shadow' in *The Atlantic Monthly*, November 1920, pp. 595–607.

Hunt, Cecil, *Ink in My Veins*. London: Robert Hale Ltd., 1948.

Isherwood, Christopher, *Christopher and His Kind*. New York: Farrar, Straus Giroux, 1976.

James, Lionel, *High Pressure: Beings Some Record of Activities in the Service of the Times Newspaper* (1929). London: John Murray, 1932.

Jameson, Storm, *Journey from the North Volume I* (1969). London: Virago, 1984.

Jerome, Jerome K., *My Life and Times*. London: Hodder and Stoughton, 1926.

Jones, Kennedy, *Fleet Street and Downing Street*. London: Hutchinson, 1920.

Kipling, Rudyard, *Something of Myself* (1937). Ware: Wordsworth, 2008.

Knightley, Phillip, *A Hack's Progress*. London: Vintage, 1998.

Koestler, Arthur, *Dialogue with Death* (1937). London: Hutchinson, 1966.

Lamb, Christina, *Small Wars Permitting: Dispatches from Foreign Lands*. London: Harper Press, 2008.

Lascelles, Alan, *End of an Era: Letters and Journals of Sir Alan Lascelles*. London: Hamish Hamilton, 1986.

Leavis, F. R., 'Manifesto' in *Scrutiny*, 1/1 (May 1932), p. 2.

Leavis, Q. D., *Fiction and the Reading Public* (1932). London: Pimlico, 2000.

Leavis, Q. D., 'Fleet Street and Pierian Roses' in *Scrutiny*, II/4 (March 1934), pp. 387–393.

Levin, Bernard, 'Let Them Publish and Be Damned' in *Times*, 7 June 1973, p. 18.

Low, Frances, *Press Work for Women*. London: Upcott Gill, 1904.

Lucas, E. V. and C. L. Graves, *Signs of the Times*. London: Alston Rivers, 1907.

Lyall, Archie, *Russian Roundabout: A Non-Political Pilgrimage*. London: Harmsworth, 1933.

Lytton, Neville, *The Press and the General Staff*. London: Collins, 1920.

Macaulay, Rose, *A Casual Commentary*. London: Methuen, 1925.

Macaulay, Rose (ed.), Ferguson Smith, *Dearest Jean: Rose Macaulay's Letters to a Cousin*. Manchester: Manchester University Press, 2011.

Macdonagh, Michael, *The Reporter's Gallery*. London: Hodder and Stoughton, 1913.

Macdonald, Dwight, 'Amateur Journalism: Notes of an American in London' in *Encounter*, November 1956, pp. 13–23.

Mackenzie, Compton, *My Life and Times, Octave 3 1900–1907*. London: Chatto and Windus, 1964.

Mann, William, 'The Beatles Revive Hopes of Progress in Pop Music' in *Times*, 29 May 1967, p. 9.

Massingham, H. W., 'Journalism as a Dangerous Trade' in *Spectator*, 1 December 1923, pp. 839–840.

Masterman, C. F. G., *From the Abyss: Of Its Inhabitants, by One of Them* (1902). New York: Garland, 1980.

May, Derwent, 'Review of Towards the end of the Morning' in *The Listener*, 22 June 1967, p. 829.

McKenna, Stephen, *While I Remember*. New York: George H. Doran, 1921.

Montague, C. E., *Disenchantment* (1922). London: Chatto and Windus, 1939.

Muggeridge, Malcolm, *Chronicles of Wasted Time, Part One The Green Stick*. London: Collins, 1972.

Murdoch, Iris, 'Against Dryness: A Polemical Sketch' in *Encounter*, January 1961, pp. 16–20.

Murry, John Middleton, 'Editorial' in *Adelphi*, 1/1 (June 1923), pp. 2–3.

Nicolson, Harold, *Diaries 1931–1939*. London: Collins, 1967.

Nolan, Martin, 'Graham Greene's Unquiet Novel; On Film and in Print, *The Quiet American* Still Fascinates' in *New York Times*, 30 January 2003, p. 8.

'Notes of the Week' in *New Age*, XXV/24 (9 October 1919), p. 385.

Orwell, George, *Homage to Catalonia* (1938). London: Penguin Classics, 2000.

Orwell, George, 'London Letter to *Partisan Review*' 15 April 1941 in *Collected Essays, Journalism and Letters Volume II My Country Right or Left 1940–1943* (1968), London: Penguin, 1984, pp. 137–149.

Owen, Wilfred (ed.) and John Bell, *Selected Letters*. Oxford: Oxford University Press, 1998.

Peacocke, Emilie, *Writing for Women*. London: A and C Black, 1936.

Peel, Mrs Charles, *Life's Enchanted Cup*. London: John Lane and the Bodley Head, 1933.

Plowman, Max (ed.) and Plowman, D., *Bridge into the Future: The Letters of Max Plowman*. London: Andrew Dakers, 1944.

Political and Economic Planning (PEP), *Report on the British Press*. London: PEP, 1938.

Ponsonby, Arthur, *Falsehood in Wartime* (1928). California: Institute for Historical Review, 1991.

Pound, Ezra, 'Pastiche' in *The New Age*, 23 October 1919, p. 432.

Priestley, J. B., *English Journey*. London: Heinemann, 1934.

Priestley, J. B., 'Mass Communication' in *Thoughts in the Wilderness*, London: Heinemann, 1957, pp. 8–13.

Pryce-Jones, David, 'Towards the Cocktail Party' in Sissons, Michael and Philip French (eds), *Age of Austerity*. London: Hodder and Stoughton, 1963, pp. 211–230.

Royal Commission on the Press 1947–1949. London: His Majesty's Stationery Office, 1949.

Saintsbury, George, 'Dullness' in *Criterion*, 1/1 (October 1922), p. 5.

Sassoon, Siegfried, *Memoirs of a Foxhunting Man* (1928). London: Faber and Faber, 1999.

Sassoon, Siegfried, *Memoirs of an Infantry Officer* (1930). London: Faber and Faber, 1989.

Sassoon, Siegfried, *Siegfried's Journey*. London: Faber and Faber, 1945.

Simonis, H., *Street of Ink*. London: Cassell and Co., 1917.

Smith, Aidan, 'Interview: Author Gordon Williams on Straw Dogs and Being Scottish' in *Scotsman*, 12 October 2012. Accessed online 12 December 2014 http://www.scotsman.com/lifestyle/books/interview-author-gordon-williams-on-straw-dogs-and-being-scottish-1-2575926.

Spender, J. A., 'The Press and Public Life' in *The Public Life*, Vol. II/6. London: Cassell and Co., 1925.

Stannard, Russell, *With the Dictators of Fleet Street, the Autobiography of an Ignorant Journalist*. London: Hutchinson, 1934.

Steed, Henry Wickham, *The Press*. London: Penguin Books, 1938.

Steevens, G. W., *From Cape Town to Ladysmith*. Edinburgh: Blackwoods, 1900.

Stott, Mary, *Before I Go*. London: Virago, 1985.

Sullivan, J. W. N., 'The Contributors' Club' in *Adelphi*, 1/2 (July 1923) p. 155.

Sykes, Christopher, 'Thoughts on the Press' in *Encounter*, pp. 92–94.

Taylor, D. J., 'Gordon Who?' in *Guardian*, 22 October 2003. Accessed online 12 December 2014 http://www.theguardian.com/books/2003/oct/22/fiction.features11

Thompson, Denys, 'The Times in School' in *Scrutiny*, 3/4 (March 1935), pp. 378–382.

Thompson, Denys, 'A Hundred Years of the Higher Journalism' in *Scrutiny*, 4/1 (June 1935), pp. 24–35.

Tomlinson, H. M., *A Mingled Yarn*. London: Duckworth, 1953.

Trevelyan, G. M., 'The White Peril' in *The Nineteenth Century*, December 1901, pp. 1043–1055.

Verschoyle, Derek, 'Review' *of The Dog Beneath the Skin* in *Spectator*, 7 February 1936, p. 211.

Wallace, Edgar, *People*. London: Hodder and Stoughton, 1929.

Waterhouse, Keith, *City Lights* and *Streets Ahead* (1994, 1995). London: British Library, 2013.

Waterhouse, Keith, *How to Live to Be 22*. London: British Library, 2013.

Waugh, Evelyn, *Remote People* (1931). London: Penguin Classics, 2002.

Waugh, Evelyn, *Waugh in Abyssinia* (1936). London: Methuen, 1986.

Waugh, Evelyn, *Robbery under Law*. London: Chapman and Hall, 1939.

Waugh, Evelyn (ed.) and Michael Davie, *The Diaries of Evelyn Waugh*. London: Penguin, 1979.

Waugh, Evelyn (ed.) and Donat Gallagher, *Essays, Articles and Reviews by Evelyn Waugh*. London: Methuen, 1983.

Wells, H. G., *The Salvaging of Civilisation*. London: Cassell and Co., 1921.

West, Rebecca (ed.) and Kime Scott, *Selected Letters of Rebecca West*. New Haven: Yale University Press, 2000.

Wilkinson, Ellen, 'Thinking in Blood' in *Time and Tide*, 1 April 1933, pp. 381–384.

Wodehouse, P. G., *Over Seventy*. London: Herbert Jenkins, 1957.

Wolfe, Tom (ed.), *The New Journalism* (1975). Basingstoke: Picador, 1996.

Woolf, Virginia, 'Two Soldier-Poets' in *Times Literary Supplement*, 11 July 1918, p. 323.

Woolf, Virginia, *A Room of one's Own* (1929). London: Penguin, 2004.

Woolf, Virginia, 'Middlebrow: Unpublished letter to the editor of the *New Statesman*' in *The Death of the Moth and Other Essays* (1942). London: Hogarth Press, 1947.

Woolf, Virginia, *A Writer's Diary*. London: Triad Grafton, 1953.

Wright, Peter, *Spycatcher: The Candid Autobiography of a Senior Intelligence Officer*. New York: Viking Penguin, 1987.

Select criticism

Adamthwaite, Anthony, 'The British Government and the Media 1937–1938' in *Journal of Contemporary History*, 18/2 (April 1983), pp. 281–297.

Adkins, Lisa and Bev Skeggs (eds), *Feminism after Bourdieu*. Oxford: Blackwell, 2005.

Allen, Charles, *Kipling Sahib: India and the Making of Rudyard Kipling* (2007). London: Abacus, 2009.

Atkin, Jonathan, *A War of Individuals: Bloomsbury Attitudes to the Great War*. Manchester: Manchester University Press, 2002.

Atkins, John, *The British Spy Novel*. London: John Calder, 1984.

Ayers, David, *English Literature of the 1920s*. Edinburgh: Edinburgh University Press, 1999.

Beaumont, Jacqueline, 'The British Press during the South African War' in Connelly, Mark and David Welch (eds), *War and the Media: Reportage and Propaganda*. London: I. B. Tauris, 2005, pp. 1–18.

Beckett, Charlie, *Supermedia: Saving Journalism so It Can Save the World*. Oxford: Blackwell, 2008.

Beddoe, Deirdre, *Back to Home and Duty: Women between the Wars 1918–1939*. London: Pandora, 1989.

Bennett, Tony and Janet Woollacott, *Bond and Beyond: The Political Career of a Popular Hero*. Basingstoke: Macmillan, 1987.

Bentley, Nick (ed.), *Contemporary British Fiction*. Edinburgh: Edinburgh University Press, 2008.

Bergonzi, Bernard, *A Study in Greene: Graham Greene and the Art of the Novel*. Oxford: Oxford University Press, 2006.

Bingham, Adrian, *Gender, Modernity and the Popular Press in Inter-War Britain*. Oxford: Clarendon Press, 2004.

Bingham, Adrian, *Family Newspapers*? Oxford: Oxford University Press, 2009.

Bourdieu, Pierre, *Rules of Art: Genesis and Structure of the Literary Field*. Cambridge: Polity Press, 1996.

Bourdieu, Pierre, *On Television and Journalism* (1996). London: Pluto Press, 1998.

Bourdieu, Pierre, *On Television and Journalism*. London: Pluto Press, 1998.

Bourdieu, Pierre, 'The field of Cultural Production' in Finkelstein and McCleery (eds), *The Book History Reader* (2002). London: Routledge, 2010, pp. 77–101.

Boyce, George, 'The Fourth Estate: The Reappraisal of a Concept' in Boyce, George, James Curran and Pauline Wingate (eds), *Newspaper History: From the 17th Century to the Present Day*. London: Constable, 1978, pp. 19–40.

Bradbury, Malcolm, *The Modern British Novel* (1993). London: Penguin Books, 1994.

Braybon, Gail, *Women Workers in the First World War*. London: Croom Helm, 1981.

Brendon, Piers, *The Life and Death of the Press Barons*. London: Secker and Warburg, 1982.

Briganti, Chiara and Kathy Mezei, *Domestic Modernism, the Interwar Novel and E H Young*. Andover: Ashgate, 2006.

Briggs, Asa, *The Golden Age of Broadcasting*. Oxford: Oxford University Press, 1965.

Brock, George, *Out of Print: Newspapers, Journalism and the Business of News in the Digital Age*. London: Kogan Page, 2013.

Brown, Erica and Mary Grover (eds), *Middlebrow Literary Cultures: The Battle of the Brows 1920–1960*. Basingstoke: Palgrave Macmillan, 2012.

Buitenhuis, Peter, *The Great War of Words: Literature as Propaganda 1914–18 and After*. London: B. T. Batsford, 1989.

Burnett, Guy, 'Nobody Does It Better: Ian Fleming's James Bond turns Sixty' in *Society*, 51/2 (2014), pp. 175–179.

Carey, John, *The Intellectuals and the Masses: Pride and Prejudice amongst the Literary Intelligentsia, 1880–1939*. Chicago: Academy Chicago, 1992.

Carter, Cynthia, Gill Branston and Stuart Allan (eds), *News, Gender, Power*. London: Routledge, 1998.

Casey, Janet, 'Middlebrow Reading and Undergraduate Teaching' in Brown and Grover (eds), *Middlebrow Literary Cultures: The Battle of the Brows 1920–1960*. Basingstoke: Palgrave Macmillan, 2012, pp. 25–36.

Chalaby, Jean, *The Invention of Journalism*. Basingstoke: Macmillan, 1998.

Chalaby, Jean, 'Northcliffe as Proprietor and Journalist' in Catteral, Peter, Colin Seymour-Ure and Adrian Smith (eds), *Northcliffe's Legacy: Aspects of the British Popular Press 1896–1996*. Basingstoke: Macmillan, 2000.

Chambers, Deborah, Linda Steiner and Carole Fleming, *Women and Journalism*. London: Routledge, 2004.

Charles, Alec and Gavin Stewart (eds), *The End of Journalism: News in the Twenty-First Century*. Bern: Peter Lang, 2011.

Chippendale, Peter and Chris Horrie, *Stick It Up Your Punter*. London: Simon and Schuster, 1999.

Cockburn, Claud, *Bestseller: The Books That Everyone Read 1900–1939* (1972). London: Penguin, 1975.

Coleman, Stephen, Scott Anthony and David Morrison, *Public Trust in the News: A Constructivist Study of the Social Life of the News*. Oxford: Reuters Institute for the Study of Journalism, 2009.

Collier, Patrick, *Modernism on Fleet Street*. Aldershot: Ashgate, 2006.

Curran, James, 'The Press as an Agency of Social Control' in Boyce, George, James Curran and Pauline Wingate, *Newspaper History: From the 17th Century to the Present Day*. London: Constable, 1978, pp. 51–75.

Curran, James, 'The Industrialisation of the Press' in *Power without Responsibility*. London: Routledge, 2010.

Curran, James, Angus Douglas and Garry Whannel, 'The Political Economy of the Human-Interest Story' in Smith, Anthony (ed.), *Newspapers and Democracy*. Boston: Massachusetts Institute of Technology, 1980.

Currell, Melville, *Political Woman*. London: Croom Helm, 1974.

Davies, Dido, *William Gerhardie, a Biography*. Oxford: Oxford University Press, 1991.

Davies, Nick, *Flat Earth News*. London: Vintage, 2009.

Das, Santanu (ed.), *Cambridge Companion to the Poetry of the First World War*. Cambridge: Cambridge University Press, 2013.

Demoor, Marysa (ed.), *Marketing the Author: Authorial Personae, Narrative Selves and Self-Fashioning, 1880–1930*. Basingstoke: Palgrave Macmillan, 2004.

Dorril, Stephen, 'Russia Accuses Fleet Street: Journalists and MI6 during the Cold War' in *The International Journal of Press/Politics*, 20/2 (2014), pp. 204–227.

Dover, Robert and Michael S. Goodman, 'Spooks and Hacks: Blood Brothers' in *British Journalism Review*, 20/4 (2009), pp. 55–61.

Ehrlich, Matthew C. and Joe Saltzman, *Heroes and Scoundrels: The Image of the Journalist in Popular Culture*. Chicago: University of Illinois Press, 2015.

Elsaka, Nadia, 'New Zealand Journalists and the Appeal of "Professionalism" as a Model of Organisation: An Historical Analysis' in *Journalism Studies*, 6/1 (2005), pp. 73–86.

Farrar, Martin, *News from the Front: War Correspondents on the Western Front 1914–1918*. Stroud: Sutton Publishing, 1998.

Feather, John, *A History of British Publishing*. London: Routledge, 2005.

Franklin, Bob, 'The Future of Journalism in an Age of Digital Media and Economic Uncertainty' in *Journalism Studies*, 15/5 (September 2014), pp. 481–499.

Franks, Suzanne, *Women and Journalism*. London: I. B. Tauris, 2013.

Fraser, Nancy, 'What's Critical about Critical Theory? The Case of Habermas and Gender' in Seyla Benhabib and Drucilla Cornell (eds), *Feminism as Critique: Essays on the Politics of Gender in Late-Capitalist Society*. Cambridge: Polity Press, 1987, pp. 31–56.

Fussell, Paul, *The Great War and Modern Memory*. Oxford: Oxford University Press, 1975.

Gaber, Ivor, 'Three Cheers for Subjectivity' in Charles, Alec and Gavin Stewart (eds), *The End of Journalism: News in the Twenty-First Century*. Bern: Peter Lang, 2011, pp. 30–38.

Gannon, Franklin Reid, *The British Press and Germany 1936–1939*. Oxford: Clarendon Press, 1971.

Gardiner, Juliet, *The Thirties: An Intimate History*. London: Harper Press, 2010.

Good, Howard, *Acquainted with the Night: The Image of Journalists in American Fiction 1890–1930*. New Jersey: The Scarecrow Press, 1986.

Gopsill, Tim and Greg Neale, *Journalists: 100 Years of the NUJ*. London: Profile Books, 2007.

Greenslade, Roy, *Press Gang: How Newspapers Make a Profit from Propaganda*. London: Macmillan, 2003.

Griffiths, Dennis, *Fleet Street: Five Hundred Years of the Press*. London: British Library Publications, 2006.

Gross, John, *The Rise and Fall of the Man of Letters: English Literary Life since 1800*. London: Weidenfeld and Nicholson, 1969.

Haber, L. F., *The Poisonous Cloud: Chemical Warfare in the First World War*. Oxford: Clarendon Press, 1986.

Habermas, Jurgen, *The Structural Transformation of the Public Sphere: An Inquiry into a Category of Bourgeois Society* (1962). Cambridge, MA: MIT Press, 1989.

Hachten, William A., *The Troubles of Journalism: A Critical Look at What's Right and Wrong with the Press*. New Jersey: Lawrence Erlbaum Associates, 2005.

Hall, Stuart, Chas Critcher, Tony Jefferson, John Clarke and Brian Roberts, *Policing the Crisis: Mugging, the State and Law and Order*. Basingstoke: Macmillan, 1978.

Hall, Valerie, *Women in Journalism: A Sociological Account of the Entry of Women into the Profession of Journalism in Great Britain until 1930*. PhD diss., Essex University, 1978.

Hammill, Faye, 'Afterword' in Brown and Grover (eds), *Middlebrow Literary Cultures: The Battle of the Brows 1920–1960*. Basingstoke: Palgrave Macmillan, 2012, pp. 231–233.

Hampton, Mark, *Visions of the Press in Britain, 1850–1950*. Chicago: University of Illinois Press, 2004.

Harding, Jason, *The Criterion: Cultural Politics and Periodical Networks in Inter-war Britain*. Oxford: Oxford University Press, 2002.

Herman, Edward and Noam Chomsky, *Manufacturing Consent*. New York: Pantheon Books, 1998.

Hewison, Robert, *Too Much: Art and Society in the Sixties 1960–75*. London: Methuen, 1986.

Hiley, Nicholas, 'Lord Kitchener Resigns: The Suppression of *The Globe* in 1915' in *Journal of Newspaper and Periodical History*, 1992, pp. 28–41.

Hitchens, Christopher, 'Introduction' to Waugh, Evelyn, *Scoop*. London: Penguin, 2000, pp. v–xiv.

Holloway, Gerry, *Women and Work in Britain since 1840*. London: Routledge, 2005.

Hopkins, Chris, *English Fiction in the 1930s*. London: Continuum Publishing, 2006.

Horrie, Chris, *Tabloid Nation: From the Birth of the Daily Mirror to the Death of the Tabloid*. London: Andre Deutsch, 2003.

Hoskins, Robert, *Graham Greene: An Approach to the Novels*. New York: Garland, 1999.

Hudson, Miles and John Stanier, *War and the Media*. Stroud: Sutton Publishing, 1997.

Hynes, Samuel, *The Auden Generation: Literature and Politics in England in the 1930s*. London: The Bodley Head, 1976.

Jago, Michael, *The Man Who Was George Smiley: The Life of John Bingham*. London: Biteback Publishing, 2013.

Johnston, John, *English Poetry of the First World War: A Study in the Evolution of Lyric and Narrative Form*. Princeton: Princeton University Press, 1964.

Kaarsholm, Preben, 'Imperialism and New Journalism circa 1900' in Breitinger, E. and R. Sanders (eds), *Studies in Commonwealth Literature*. Gunter Narr Verlag: Tubingen, 1985, pp. 179–192.

Keating, Peter, *The Haunted Study: A Social History of the English Novel 1875–1914*. London: Secker and Warburg, 1989.

Kent, Sylvia, *The Woman Writer: The History of the Society of Women Writers and Journalists*. Stroud: History Press, 2009.

Kerensky, Oleg, *The New British Drama*. London: Hamilton, 1977.

Kibble, Matthew, 'The Betrayers of Language: Modernism and the *Daily Mail*' in *Literature and History*, 11/1 (2002), pp. 62–80.

Kiberd, Declan, '*Ulysses*, Newspapers and Modernism' in *Irish Classics*. London: Granta Books, 2000, pp. 463–481.

King, Cecil, *The Future of the Press*. London: MacGibbon and Kee, 1967.

Knightley, Phillip, *The First Casualty: The War Correspondent as Myth-maker from the Crimea to Kosovo* (1975). London: Prion Books, 2000.

Korte, Barbara, *Represented Reporters: Images of War Correspondents in Memoirs and Fiction*. Bielefeld: Transcript, 2009.

Koss, Stephen, *Fleet Street Radical*. London: Allen Lane, 1973.

Koss, Stephen, *The Rise and Fall of the Political Press: The Twentieth Century*. London: 1984.

Lane, Richard, Rod Mengham and Philip Tew (eds), *Contemporary British Fiction*. Cambridge: Polity Press, 2003.

Lashmar, Paul, 'Urinal or Conduit? Institutional Information Flow between the UK Intelligence Services and the News Media' in *Journalism*, 14/8 (2013), pp. 1024–1040.

Leapman, Michael, *Treacherous Estate: The Press after Fleet Street*. London: Hodder and Stoughton, 1992.

Lee, Alan, *The Origins of the Popular Press in England 1855–1914*. London: Croom Helm, 1976.

LeFanu, Sarah, *Rose Macaulay*. London: Virago, 2003.

LeMahieu, D. L., *A Culture for Democracy: Mass Communication and the Cultivated Mind in Britain between the Wars*. Oxford: Clarendon Press, 1988.

Lonsdale, Sarah, 'Roast Seagull and Other Quaint Bird Dishes: The Development of Features and Lifestyle Journalism during the First World War' in *Journalism Studies*, 16/6 (2015) pp. 800–815.

Lovelace, Colin, 'British Press Censorship during the First World War' in Boyce, George, James Curran and Pauline Wingate (eds), *Newspaper History: From the 17th Century to the Present Day*. London: Constable, 1978, pp. 305–319.

Lutes, Jean Marie, *Front-Page Girls: Women Journalists in American Culture and Fiction 1880–1930*. Ithaca: Cornell University Press, 2006.

Maisel, Richard, 'The Decline of the Mass Media' in *Public Opinion Quarterly*, 37/2 (1973) pp. 159–170.

Margach, James, *The Abuse of Power*. London: W. H. Allen and Co., 1978.

Marwick, Arthur, *Culture in Britain since 1945*. Oxford: Basil Blackwell, 1991.

Mayes, Tessa (ed.), *Disclosure: Media Freedom and the Privacy Debate after Diana*. London: London International Research Exchange Media Group, 1998.

McCall, Leslie, 'Does Gender Fit? Bourdie, Feminism and Conceptions of Social Order' in *Theory and Society*, 21 (December 1992), pp. 837–867.

McDonald, Peter, *British Literary Culture and Publishing Practice 1880–1914*. Cambridge: Cambridge University Press, 1997.

McLaughlin, Greg, *The War Correspondent*. London: Pluto Press, 2002.

McNair, Brian, *Journalists in Film: Heroes and Villains*. Edinburgh: Edinburgh University Press, 2010.

Meyer, Philip, *The Vanishing Newspaper: Saving Journalism in the Information Age*, Columbia: University of Missouri Press, 2009.

Mickalites, Carey James, 'Martin Amis's *Money*: Negotiations with Literary Celebrity' in Postmodern Culture, 24/1, September 2013, online: http://muse.jhu.edu/journals/postmodern_culture/v024/24.1.mickalites.html#f07 accessed 7 April 2015.

Montefiore, Jan, *Rudyard Kipling*. Tavistock: Northcote, 2007.

Morrison, James, 'Spin, Smoke-filled Rooms and the Decline of Council Reporting by British Local Newspapers: The Slow Demise of Town Hall Transparency' in Charles, Alec and Gavin Stewart (eds), *The End of Journalism: News in the Twenty-First Century*. Bern: Peter Lang, 2011, pp. 193–209.

Moss, Alfred, *Jerome K Jerome: His Life and Work*. London: Selwyn and Blount, 1928.

Mulhern, Francis, 'The Marxist Aesthetics of Christopher Caudwell' in *New Left Review*, 85 (December 1974), pp. 37–57.

Murdock, Graham and Peter Golding, 'The Structure, Ownership, and Control of the Press 1914–1976' in Boyce, George, James Curran and Pauline Wingate (eds), *Newspaper History: From the Seventeenth Century to the Present Day*. London: Constable, 1978, pp. 130–148.

Murphy, Catherine, *On an Equal Footing with Men? Women and Work at the BBC 1923–1939*. PhD diss., Goldsmiths University, 2011.

Oliver, Reggie, *Out of the Woodshed: The Life of Stella Gibbons*. London: Bloomsbury, 1998.

Ommundsen, Wenche, 'From Altar to the Marketplace and Back Again: Understanding Literary Celebrity' in Redmond, Sean and Sue Holmes (eds), *Stardom and Celebrity: A Reader*. London: Sage, 2007, pp. 244–255.

Onslow, Barbara, *Women of the Press in Nineteenth-Century Britain*. Basingstoke: Macmillan, 2000.

O'Sullivan, Patrick, 'Patrick MacGill: The Making of a Writer' in Sean Hutton and Paul Stewart (eds), *Ireland's Histories: Aspects of State, Society and Ideology*. London: Routledge, 1992, pp. 203–222.

Page, Bruce, *The Murdoch Archipelago* (2003). London: Simon and Schuster, 2011.

Page, Bruce, David Leitch and Phillip Knightley, *Philby: The Spy Who Betrayed a Generation* (1968). London: Sphere Books, 1977.

Paul, Pamela, *Pornifed: How Pornography Is Damaging Our Lives, Our Relationships and Our Families*. New York: Times Books, 2005.

Read, Anthony and David Fisher, *Colonel Z: The Secret Life of a Master of Spies*. London: Hodder and Stoughton, 1984.

Ross, Karen, 'Women at Work: Journalism as an En-gendered Practice' in *Journalism Studies*, 2/4 (2001), pp. 531–544.

Samuels, Stuart, 'The Left Book Club' in *Journal of Contemporary History*, 1/2 (1966), pp. 65–86.

Sandbrook, Dominic, *Never Had It So Good: A History of Britain from Suez to the Beatles* (2005). London: Abacus, 2013.

Sanders, Karen and Mark Hanna, 'British Journalists' in Weaver, David and Lars Wilnat (eds), *The Global Journalist in the Twenty First Century*. London: Routledge, 2012, pp. 220–233.

Seymour-Ure, Colin, 'Northcliffe's Legacy' in Catteral, Peter, Colin Seymour-Ure and Adrian Smith (eds), *Northcliffe's Legacy: Aspects of the British Popular Press 1896–1996*. Basingstoke: Macmillan, 2000, pp. 9–23.

Shannon, Richard, *A Press Free and Responsible: Self-Regulation and the Press Complaints Commission 1991–2001*. London: John Murray, 2001.

Shaw, Tony, *Eden, Suez and the Mass Media: Propaganda and Persuasion during the Suez Crisis*. London, New York: I. B. Tauris, 1996.

Slater, Ian, *Orwell: The Road to Airstrip One*. New York, London: Norton and Company, 1985.

Sloan, John, *John Davidson, First of the Moderns*. Oxford: Clarendon Press, 1995.

Snoddy, Raymond, *The Good, the Bad and the Unacceptable: The Hard News about the British Press*. London: Faber and Faber, 1992.

Spalding, Frances, *Stevie Smith: A Critical Biography*. London: Faber and Faber, 1999.

Starkman, Dean, *The Watchdog That Didn't Bark: The Financial Crisis and the Disappearance of American Journalism*. New York: Columbia University Press, 2014.

Stewart, Daxton, 'Harry Potter and the Exploitative Jackals: Media Framing and Credibility Attitudes in Young Readers' in *The IJPC Journal*, 2 (Fall 2010), pp. 1–33.

Sustein, Cass, *Republic.com*. Princeton: Princeton University Press, 2001.

Taylor, A. J. P., *English History 1914–1945*. Oxford: Oxford University Press, 1965.

Taylor, A. J. P., *Beaverbrook*. London: Hamish Hamilton, 1972.

Taylor, A. J. P., 'Introduction' in Read, Donald (ed.), *Edwardian England*. London: Croom Helm, 1982.

Taylor, D. J., *After the War: The Novel and England since 1945*. London: Flamingo, 1994.

Thompson, Brian Lindsay, *Graham Greene and the Politics of Popular Fiction and Film*. Basingstoke: Palgrave Macmillan, 2009.

Thorpe, Michael, *Siegfried Sassoon: A Critical Study*. Oxford: Oxford University Press, 1966.

Tunstall, Jeremy, *Journalists at Work*. London: Constable, 1971.

Tulloch, John, 'A Little Bit Salem': Rebekah Brooks of News International and the Construction of a Modern Witch' in *Ethical Space*, 10/1 (2013), pp. 4–7.

Tusan, Michelle Elizabeth, *Women Making News: Gender and Journalism in Modern Britain*. Chicago: University of Illinois Press, 2005.

Tynan, Kathleen, *The Life of Kenneth Tynan*. London: Weidenfeld and Nicolson, 1987.

Uglow, Jenny, 'Fielding, Grub Street and Canary Wharf' in Treglown and Bennett (eds) *Grub Street and the Ivory Tower: Literary Journalism and Literary Scholarship from Fielding to the Internet*. Oxford: Oxford University Press, 1998, pp. 1–21.

Underwood, Doug, *Journalism and the Novel 1700–2000*. Cambridge: Cambridge University Press, 2008.

Underwood, Doug, *The Undeclared War between Journalism and Fiction: Journalists as Genre Benders in Literary History*. Basingstoke: Palgrave Macmillan, 2013.

Vernon, Betty, *Ellen Wilkinson*. London: Croom Helm, 1982.

Waller, Philip, *Readers, Writers and Reputations: Literary Life in Britain 1870–1918*. Oxford: Oxford University Press, 2006.

West, Nigel (ed.), *The Faber Book of Espionage* (1993). London: Faber and Faber, 1994.

West, Nigel, 'Fiction, Faction and Intelligence' in Jackson, Peter (ed.), *Understanding Intelligence in the Twenty-First Century: Journeys into Shadows*. London: Routledge, 2004, pp. 122–134.

Whale, John, *The Politics of the Media*. London: Fontana, 1980.

White, Cynthia, *Women's Magazines 1693–1968*. London: Michael Joseph, 1970.

Williams, Francis, *Dangerous Estate* (1957). Cambridge: Patrick Stephens, 1984.

Wilson, Charles, *First With the News: The History of W. H. Smith, 1792–1972*. London: Jonathan Cape, 1985.

Wingate, Pauline, 'Newsprint: From Rags to Riches – and Back Again?' in Smith, Anthony (ed.), *Newspapers and Democracy*. Boston: Massachusetts Institute of Technology, 1980.

Wyk Smith, Malvern van, *Drummer Hodge: The Poetry of the Anglo-Boer War 1899–1902*. Oxford: Oxford University Press, 1978.

Index

Note: The letter 'n' following locators refers to notes.